Programming

Microsoft®

Internet Explorer 5

Scott Roberts

PUBLISHED BY
Microsoft Press
A Division of Microsoft Corporation
One Microsoft Way
Redmond, Washington 98052-6399

Library of Congress Cataloging-in-Publication Data
Roberts, Scott, 1969-
    Programming Microsoft Internet Explorer 5 / Scott Roberts.
       p. cm.
    ISBN 0-7356-0781-8
    1. Internet programming.   2. Microsoft Internet Explorer.
I. Title.
QA76.625.R63   1999
005.2'762--dc21   99-27216
                                         CIP

Printed and bound in the United States of America.

1 2 3 4 5 6 7 8 9   QMQM   4 3 2 1 0 9

Distributed in Canada by Penguin Books Canada Limited.

A CIP catalogue record for this book is available from the British Library.

Microsoft Press books are available through booksellers and distributors worldwide. For further information about international editions, contact your local Microsoft Corporation office or contact Microsoft Press International directly at fax (425) 936-7329. Visit our Web site at mspress.microsoft.com.

Acquisitions Editor: Eric Stroo
Project Editor: Victoria Thulman
Manuscript Editor: Chrisa Hotchkiss
Technical Editor: Julie Xiao

To my wife, Andrea, for her love and support through this project
and all the projects that I undertake. Thank you for always
being there for me. Ti amo da impazzire.

To my mother, for everything you went through to provide
me with the happiest childhood possible.

Contents

Contents

Contents

Contents

Preface

When I first joined Microsoft, I was lucky to be hired as a developer support engineer on the Internet Client Developer Support Team. I feel that I was lucky because I was given the opportunity to work with customers who were creating Internet applications for the greatest Web browser on the market—Microsoft Internet Explorer. During my time in support, I saw first-hand the exciting applications that customers were building using Microsoft products and technologies. Customers would often contact us for information about how to implement different features in their applications using Internet Explorer. These features included DHTML, scripting, and the WebBrowser control. As time went on, I learned a lot about writing applications for Internet Explorer and using Internet Explorer components. I used a lot of what I learned on a daily basis to help customers create the best applications possible. One aspect of my work concerned me, however—I was able to help customers only when they called Developer Support with questions or problems.

I searched long and hard for a comprehensive book on programming for Internet Explorer to which I could refer customers, but I wasn't able to find one. So I decided to write my own. This book is based on the knowledge I acquired while working as a support engineer as well as information I have learned since moving to the development side of Internet Explorer. This book constitutes years of my own experience as well as the experience of those who contributed to it by providing suggestions, samples, comments, and so on. I hope you find this book helpful as you create applications for Internet Explorer, now and in the future.

Throughout the course of writing this book, many people have contributed in one way or another—answering questions, providing samples, and so on. I'd like to start my acknowledgments by thanking the entire Microsoft Internet Explorer development team for creating by far the best browser on the market. Without this excellent product, browsing the Web wouldn't be so exciting, and this book wouldn't even exist.

More specifically I'd like to thank my friend Nick Dallett, who was previously with the Internet Client Developer Support Team and is now on the Microsoft Windows Update team. Nick spent hours upon hours helping me by providing technical reviews of my chapters and samples as well as providing a number of his own samples. Nick spent many sleepless nights and weekends creating these samples for this book: DHTML Ledger, DHTML Memo, DHTML Soup, DHTML Ledger Behavior, Ledger HTA, Memo HTA, and Page Controller. Having these samples made the writing of this book go much faster.

I would also like to thank the following people from the Internet Client Developer Support Team: Mark Harper, who reviewed the section on Code Download in Chapter 5 and whose comments provided more help than I could have possibly asked for; Jason Strayer, who answered some very tough Internet Explorer, DHTML Object Model, and Visual C++ questions; Mark Davis, who provided the AtlBehave sample in Chapter 11 and answered questions regarding the OC96 specification, the DHTML Object Model, and Visual C++; Jess Judge, who provided the ClientCaps and LinkBuilder samples in Chapter 11 and answered general questions regarding the Client Capabilities and Persistence Behaviors; Dave Templin, who debugged my WebBand sample and suggested fixes; Heidi Housten, who provided the TOC Behavior sample for Chapter 11; Rene Schuchter, who answered general Code Download questions; and Sharon Malmquist, who always pushed me to do bigger and better things. Without Sharon, I might not have been driven enough to write this book. Thanks also to the Internet Client Developer Support Team as a whole for the many long hours its staff put in to help customers understand how to develop applications for Microsoft Internet Explorer. Keep up the great work.

From the Internet Explorer SDK documentation group I would like to thank Jerry Drain and Dennis McCreery for help solving problems with the Internet Explorer headers and libraries. Also, I'd like to thank Matt Oshry for help with various documentation questions. Matt went out of his way to help me more times than I can count. I just have to say that the entire MSDN Online Web Workshop team has created the best documentation product I have ever used.

On the development side of Internet Explorer, I would like to thank Dave Massy, the Program Manager for DHTML Behaviors, who always went out of his way to help me. Dave assisted me tremendously by reviewing Chapter 11 and explaining some new additions to *IDocHostUIHandler*, and for that I am extremely grateful. I would like to thank Phil Cooper for reviewing Chapter 4 and for answering questions about HTML Applications and the DHTML Object Model. I think we all should thank Phil, as he is the person who created HTAs. Thanks, Phil, for hiring me as a developer on the Trident Extensibility team. It's been exciting so far and I hope the excitement never ends.

I would also like to thank the following people whose contributions helped enhance the quality of this book: April Hill from the Microsoft Museum for answering questions regarding Internet Explorer ship dates for Chapter 1; Eric Berman for answering questions about Web Accessories; Sundaram Ramani for contributing his HTMLSpy HTA sample; Strohm Armstrong for his help with Explorer Bars and Desk bands; and Alan Auerbach for answering questions regarding the WebBrowser Control questions and events. Alan is another one of those people who always goes out of his way to help.

From Microsoft Press, I would like to thank Eric Stroo for helping me get this project off the ground; Victoria Thulman, the project editor of this book, for helping me with structure and content; and Julie Xiao, the technical editor of this book, for checking and double-checking all technical facts and code. In addition, thanks go to Joshua Trupin and Joanne Steinhart for help with publishing portions of this book in *MIND* magazine.

Finally, I would like to thank my wife, Andrea. I know that I dedicated this book to her but I just can't thank her enough. Throughout the many months that I was writing, she never once complained. She has always been supportive of everything I have done. Her support alleviated a lot of day-to-day stresses, which enabled me to finish the writing two months ahead of schedule. Thank you for always being there for me and for being the mother of my child. I'll say it again in Italiano: Ti amo moltissimo.

Using the Companion CD

WHAT'S ON THIS CD?

The CD included with this book contains all the sample programs discussed in the book, Microsoft Internet Explorer 5, and the electronic version of this book. All the samples are located in the Samples folder.

Installing the Sample Files

You can view the samples from the CD, or you can install them on your hard disk and use them to create your own Internet Explorer applications.

Installing the sample files requires approximately 2.5 MB of disk space. To install the sample files, insert the CD into your CD-ROM drive; the CD's navigation window should appear automatically. If the window doesn't appear, run Setup.exe. If you have trouble running any of the sample files, refer to the Readme.txt file in the root directory of the CD or to the text in the book that describes the sample program.

You can uninstall the files using the navigation window or by selecting Add/Remove Programs from the Microsoft Windows Control Panel.

SUPPORT

Every effort has been made to ensure the accuracy of this book and the contents of the companion disc. Microsoft Press provides corrections for books through the World Wide Web at the following address: *http://mspress.microsoft.com/support/*.

If you have comments, questions, or ideas regarding this book or the companion disc, please send them to Microsoft Press using either of the following methods:

Postal Mail
Microsoft Press
Attn: Programming Microsoft Internet Explorer 5 Editor
One Microsoft Way
Redmond, WA 98052-6399

E-mail
MSPINPUT@MICROSOFT.COM

Please note that product support is not offered through the above mail addresses. For support information regarding Microsoft Internet Explorer 5, you can call Standard Support at (425) 635-7011 weekdays between 6 a.m. and 6 p.m. Pacific time. You can also search Microsoft Personal Support Center at *http://support.microsoft.com/support*.

Part I

Working with HTML and DHTML

Chapter 1

Evolution of Internet Explorer

Since the dawn of the computer age, people have searched for ways to make computers easier to use. Initially, text-based terminals provided the primary link between users and their computing applications. Despite developers' best attempts to simplify this interface, it took a hacker—someone in love with the technology—to find satisfaction in working with it. Users weren't able to interact with their applications in a meaningful, intuitive way until the advent of point-and-click operating systems such as Microsoft Windows. The mouse and the graphical user interface (GUI) revolutionized the way the world thought about computing and made computers accessible and enjoyable for millions of people.

The popularity of the Internet and the World Wide Web brought computer usability to a new level. Through a series of hyperlinks, users could navigate from one page of information (a Web page) to the next. The only problem with these pages was that information on them was static—users couldn't interact with the information in the same way they could in Microsoft Windows applications. To fulfill the users' need to interact, forms were introduced in HTML 2. Using HTML forms, users could send information to the owners of a Web page. With two-way traffic possible on the Web, the path was paved for Internet applications.

Over time, computers have become simpler to operate, but with this ease of use has come internal complexity. The more a computer program is designed to anticipate the user's needs, the more it requires complex logic, convoluted graphic rendering, and subroutine piled on top of subroutine—challenges for the designers and developers of such a program. Developing applications for the Internet, however, hasn't followed this trend. As tasks have become easier for the users, they have also become easier for the designers and developers.

INTERNET EXPLORER 1 AND 2

Microsoft Internet Explorer initiated many of these advances. Version 1 (shown in Figure 1-1), which was shipped as part of Windows 95 on August 24, 1995, made it easy to create Internet applications.

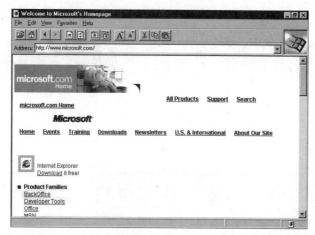

Figure 1-1. *Internet Explorer 1.*

Using Internet Explorer version 1 and version 2 (shipped November 17, 1995, and shown in Figure 1-2), you could create Web-based applications using standard HTML. Consequently, you could use Internet Explorer as a means of disseminating information all over the world with Web pages created using only HTML.

Figure 1-2. *Internet Explorer 2.*

Your Web page users could also interact with you via HTML forms. Internet Explorer provided a way to build Web-based applications that allowed your customers to perform tasks such as ordering your products online without calling your company. These applications not only save your company a ton of money, they save your customers a lot of time and hassle: no more busy signals or waiting in a queue.

INTERNET EXPLORER 3

So now you're probably thinking, "This is awesome. Internet Explorer versions 1 and 2 gave me so much; why did Microsoft need to go any further?" Well, as you might have guessed, you can do much more with a Windows application than you can with a basic HTML page. For example, when creating a Windows application, you can include any number of ActiveX controls. Internet Explorer 1 and 2 didn't even have the ability to host ActiveX controls. That's where Internet Explorer 3 stepped up to the plate. The release of version 3 (shown in Figure 1-3) on August 13, 1996, brought us closer to creating a full-blown application for the Web using Internet Explorer. Version 3 introduced new features that contributed to Internet Explorer's programmability and reusability.

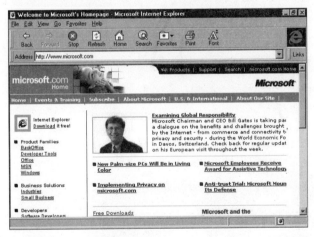

Figure 1-3. *Internet Explorer 3.*

ActiveX Controls

One of the most significant Internet Explorer 3 features was the ability to host ActiveX controls on Web pages. ActiveX controls are dynamic-link libraries (DLLs) that expose some functionality through the Component Object Model (COM). ActiveX controls allow you to do just about anything on your Web page that you can do in a normal Windows application. With these new capabilities came security risks, however, so version 3 introduced the concept of security models to prevent people from creating ActiveX controls that could trash your computer. We'll talk about how to create ActiveX controls in Chapter 5.

Scripting Support

In the past, all data had to be blindly sent to a server. A program running on the server checked the data entered by the user. If some data was incorrect or missing, the Web page was redisplayed with an explanation of the problem. This predicament caused users a lot of frustration, as they constantly had to enter data and resubmit forms to determine whether all the information was correct. It was also time-consuming, especially when users were connected to the Internet using slow modem lines.

Version 3 of Internet Explorer introduced support for scripting using Microsoft JScript and Microsoft Visual Basic Script (VBScript). Now you could call methods and access properties on the ActiveX controls that you had included on your Web page. In addition, you could validate data in a form before submitting the data to your Internet server for processing. If any of the data was incorrect, the user was alerted and prompted to enter the correct data.

Internet Explorer Object Model

As mentioned earlier, with versions 1 and 2, all information displayed on a Web page was static: you had to decide which information was going to be on the page as you were designing it, and once Internet Explorer displayed the page, you couldn't access the information on it.

With scripting support and the Internet Explorer object model (later named the DHTML Object Model), you could decide what to display on the page as the page was loaded. Also, you could access information from script on a Web page by using the DHTML objects, enabling you to validate form data before sending it to your server.

WebBrowser Control

So far, we've examined only the programmability of Internet Explorer. What if you wanted to include Internet functionality in your own Windows applications? For instance, you might want to create your own Web browser for school children. With this type of Web browser, you might want to be able to control which Web pages children could view. Or you might want to make your Web browser extremely easy for children to use. Of course, you might not want to go through the trouble of creating an entire Web browser application from scratch. If you were to do that, you'd have to be an expert in many different technologies—communications, COM, C++, Internet standards and protocols, security, and so forth.

Many Web browsers exist on the market. Wasn't there a simple way to reuse some of the functionality that's already out there? Starting with Internet Explorer 3, there was. Internet Explorer 3 was the first browser on the market to allow its technology to be reused. Microsoft shipped an ActiveX control with version 3 named the WebBrowser control. Using this control, you could build your own Web browser application by using any COM-aware development tool, such as Visual C++, Visual Basic, Microsoft Visual J++, and even Microsoft Visual FoxPro. And the WebBrowser control also let you control Internet Explorer itself.

INTERNET EXPLORER 4

All this new programmability included with Internet Explorer 3 brought us one step closer to creating full-blown Web applications that were as good as Windows applications, but they still weren't quite up to par with their Windows-based cousins. Thus, Internet Explorer 4 was developed. (See Figure 1-4.) Version 4, released on September 30, 1997, provided huge advances in programmability and reusability. This version introduced lots of new features, many of which we'll be discussing in detail in this book.

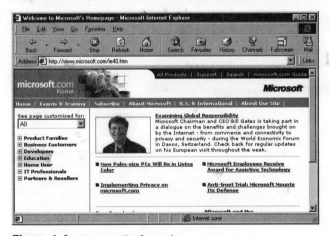

Figure 1-4. *Internet Explorer 4.*

Dynamic HTML

Internet Explorer 3 allowed you to determine what to display on a Web page as Internet Explorer was rendering it. However, once the page was finished loading, you couldn't change what was displayed without accessing the server again to obtain the updated information.

Version 4 of Internet Explorer introduced Dynamic HTML (DHTML). DHTML provided enhancements to the Internet Explorer Object Model—now called the DHTML Object Model—that enabled you to change the content of a Web page after the page finished loading. In Chapter 3, you'll see how to use DHTML in combination with script to dynamically change the contents of a Web page.

Data Binding

One of the most significant features that Internet Explorer 4 introduced as part of DHTML was data binding. If you've ever worked with Visual Basic, you can understand what this means for programmability. Data binding lets you attach, or bind, an HTML element on a Web page to data in a database. Any time data in that database is changed, the information contained in that bound HTML element is changed on the fly, without your browser having to visit the server and load another Web page. Also, data binding allows you to update the data in a database without the hassles of submitting a normal HTML form.

As an example, let's say you're working with Microsoft Excel. Excel gives you the ability to bind your spreadsheet to a database table so that changes made to the values in the database will be reflected in your spreadsheet on the fly and vice versa. Prior to Internet Explorer 4, you could actually do this from an HTML Web page. To update the database or refresh the values contained in the fields in a table, the user had to click a Submit button so that the Web page could make a round-trip to the Internet server. With data binding support in Internet Explorer 4, it was no longer necessary to visit the server and load a new Web page. The information on a Web page could be changed dynamically to reflect the current state of data in the database. Data binding brought Internet Explorer another step closer to becoming a full-fledged development platform. Data binding is one of those topics that could take up many chapters, perhaps even an entire volume. For that reason, I will not be talking about it in this book. For more information, refer to the documentation on the MSDN Online Web Workshop: *http://msdn.microsoft.com/workshop*.

WebBrowser Control Enhancements

Although the WebBrowser control was introduced in Internet Explorer 3, version 4 added several features to it. As well as providing new functionality relative to hosting the control, Internet Explorer 4 introduced features that allowed you to control some aspects of the browser that you couldn't control before. (The WebBrowser control is covered in more detail in Chapter 6 and later chapters.)

Explorer Bars

Internet Explorer 4 introduced a new user interface feature named Explorer Bars. These bars look like frames on a Web page but are linked to the browser and not to a particular Web page. Two types of Explorer Bars exist: the Explorer band and the Communication band. The Explorer band is the most common. It appears vertically inside the browser. Internet Explorer 4 offered four default Explorer bands: the Search band (Figure 1-5), the Favorites band (Figure 1-6), the History band (Figure 1-7), and the Channels band (Figure 1-8). They all appear vertically on the left-hand side of Internet Explorer's main window. Internet Explorer 5 doesn't contain the Channels band; instead, it contains the Folders band. For details about the Folders band, refer to Chapter 10.

Figure 1-5. *Internet Explorer 4 Search band.*

Figure 1-6. *Internet Explorer 4 Favorites band.*

Figure 1-7. *Internet Explorer 4 History band.*

Figure 1-8. *Internet Explorer 4 Channels band.*

The second type of Explorer Bar, the Communication band—or Comm band—is displayed horizontally at the bottom of Internet Explorer's main window. Internet Explorer 4 and later versions also install the Desk band, which is attached to the Active Desktop. See Chapter 10 for more information on this band. Unfortunately, Internet Explorer 4 didn't provide any default Comm or Desk bands, but it did give you the ability to create your own Explorer Bars and the Desk band that were attached to the browser or the desktop. You'll create your own Explorer Bars and the Desk band in Chapter 10.

Browser Helper Objects

When you create a Web application for Internet Explorer, it's often helpful to know when a user starts up the browser so that you can track Web page statistics. Or perhaps you want to use Internet Explorer on your corporate intranet, and you want to restrict navigation to certain Web sites. There were no easy solutions to this problem in Internet Explorer 1 or 2. And in version 3 of Internet Explorer, the only solution to either of these scenarios was to create your own Web browser and host the WebBrowser control. With Internet Explorer 4, you could use a new programmability and reusability feature known as Browser Helper Objects (BHOs). BHOs are COM objects that Internet Explorer automatically creates whenever a user starts a new instance of Internet Explorer. Using BHOs, you can hook into the browser to control navigation or to dynamically change the content of a Web page. Chapter 12 covers BHOs in more detail.

INTERNET EXPLORER 5

Internet Explorer 4 offered many new features to enhance its programmability and reusability, but as a development platform, it was insufficient. That's where Internet Explorer 5 comes to the rescue. (See Figure 1-9.) Finally a platform exists that lets you create fully functional Web-based Internet applications. Using Internet Explorer 5, you can create applications that run in the browser, applications that reuse browser components, or applications that run outside the browser as normal Windows applications. To provide this functionality, version 5 extends a few of the features first introduced in version 4 and also introduces some new technologies that solidify Internet Explorer as a development platform.

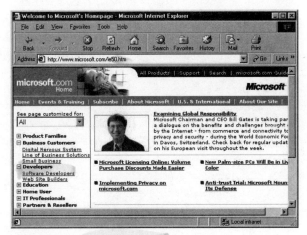

Figure 1-9. *Internet Explorer 5.*

INTERNET EXPLORER 5 AS A DEVELOPMENT PLATFORM

You might be wondering what I mean by a development platform. It's any tool, component, application programming interface (API), operating system (you get the idea) that developers can use to create their own applications. For example, Windows is a development platform. Developers who create applications for Windows reuse the Windows API so that they don't have to reinvent the wheel. They also use the Windows API so that their applications will run on top of Windows.

The same applies to the Internet Explorer development platform. Web developers use APIs and COM objects provided by Internet Explorer to create applications that use Internet Explorer components and run on top of the Internet Explorer platform. In the most general sense, these APIs and COM objects include DHTML, script, the WebBrowser control, and many other components and functionality.

DHTML Behaviors and HTML Components (HTCs)

When developing applications for a platform such as Windows or Internet Explorer, you must be able to reuse specific functionality of your application. If you've created applications using C++, for instance, you can reuse functionality such as libraries of source code. Also, with COM, you can reuse a component's entire functionality without even having to look at its source code. If you couldn't reuse functionality like this, you probably wouldn't want to write applications for Windows. You would always have to create your applications from scratch.

Well, the same goes for Internet Explorer. You have to be able to reuse functionality for Internet Explorer to be accepted as a development platform. To that end, Internet Explorer 5 introduces DHTML Behaviors. Behaviors are extremely lightweight components that you can reuse from one Web page to the next. You can enhance the default Behavior of a specific HTML element by attaching a Behavior to the element. You can implement Behaviors as binary components using C++ and COM or simply DHTML and script. Behaviors that are created using DHTML and script are referred to as HTML Components (HTCs). Chapter 11 covers DHTML Behaviors and HTCs as well as the default Internet Explorer 5 Behaviors.

Persistence

Internet Explorer 5 persistence means just what it sounds like—Internet Explorer allows you to retain Web page information, styles, variables, and state from one browser session to another. So the next time your users navigate to your Web page, they can return to the exact place where they left off. For instance, let's say you have a collapsible list of items on a menu. Your user might go three or four levels deep into the menu hierarchy. Using versions of Internet Explorer earlier than version 5, if the user navigated away from that Web page or shut down the browser, the next time he navigated to that page, he would have to start all over again. Using Internet Explorer 5 persistence, the user is able to retain the exact position in the menu hierarchy when leaving a page. The user can pick up where he left off the next time he navigates to that page. This feature is commonly used in the MSDN Online Web Workshop: *http://msdn.microsoft.com/workshop*. We'll examine persistence further in Chapter 11 when we talk about DHTML Behaviors.

Client Capabilities

As anybody who has created Windows applications will tell you, if you can't determine the capabilities of the platform on which your application is running, you won't be able to provide your users with the best experience possible. With Internet Explorer 5's new client capabilities technology, you can determine certain capabilities that the browser supports, such as the speed of the user's Internet connection. Client capabilities are covered in Chapter 11.

HTML Applications

HTML Applications (HTAs) are full-blown applications that run on their own under Windows, which means that they don't have any of the security restrictions imposed on Web pages. HTAs are Windows applications just like Microsoft Word and Microsoft Excel. And the best part is that you can create them using only DHTML and script. You don't need to learn C++, Visual Basic, and COM. If you know DHTML and script, and you've already created Web pages, you've basically already created an HTML Application. Chapter 4 covers HTAs in more detail.

Printing

One of the most common questions people ask is, "How can I print from script?" Prior to Internet Explorer 5, you had to create an ActiveX control and let the control do it for you. Well, that solution didn't exactly promote Internet Explorer as a development platform. Obviously, any development platform must have good support for printing if it's going to be used by the masses. Finally, with Internet Explorer 5, you can print from script—using the *window.print* method. Also, events tell you when a page is going to be printed and when it's finished. More on this in Chapter 3.

Dynamic Properties

Up until Internet Explorer 5, all properties of HTML tags on a Web page were determined when the page was designed. For instance, if you wanted to change the size of a block of text based on some value entered by the user, you had to jump through hoops. Using Internet Explorer 5, you can specify an expression to be used at run time to calculate the value of a property. More on this in Chapter 3.

XML

XML (Extensible Markup Language) provides a method for describing and exchanging data. Whereas HTML is used for displaying data, XML is used for working directly with data. Support for XML was first introduced in Internet Explorer 4 but wasn't really complete until Internet Explorer 5. Along with XML comes support for XSL (Extensible Stylesheet Language), which provides a language for expressing style sheets. It consists of a language for transforming XML documents into HTML documents or into other XML documents, and an XML vocabulary for specifying formatting semantics. (The topic of XML is outside the scope of this book. For more information about XML, refer to the book *XML in Action* [Microsoft Press, 1999].)

Increased Performance

All these great Internet Explorer 5 features would be meaningless without the most important new feature of all—increased performance. Internet Explorer 5 is about 25 percent faster than version 4, mainly because of some major changes in the underlying implementation of Internet Explorer. For Web pages that contain tables, you will find that Internet Explorer is a lot faster than that. I think you will be quite pleased by how fast your Internet applications run under Internet Explorer 5.

Why Program Using Internet Explorer 5?

So now I bet you're thinking, "All these new features of Internet Explorer 5 are cool, but what can I do with them?" The possibilities are endless. In the simplest case, you could add help to your application. Doing so in the past wasn't easy. You had to create an .rtf file in a specific format. Then you had to run your .rtf file through the help compiler to generate a Windows help file. What a pain.

Now, using Internet Explorer 5—and more specifically, the WebBrowser control—you can easily add help to your application. If you know how to create a Web page, you already know how to add help to your applications. You don't need to learn the correct format of the .rtf help files or know how to use the help compiler. It's as simple as adding the WebBrowser control to a dialog box or a form and navigating to the Web pages you're using for help. For a real-world example, see the

MSDN Library viewer for Visual Studio 6 in Figure 1-10. The MSDN Library viewer uses the WebBrowser control to display help via Web pages.

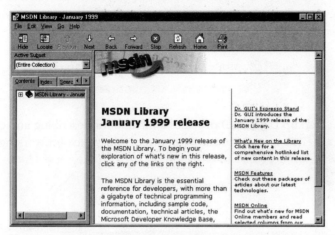

Figure 1-10. *MSDN Library viewer for Visual Studio 6.*

OK, so now you see how easy it is to *webify* your help pages. But what else can you do? I showed you the simplest case. In a more advanced case, you can create an entire browser of your own. The WebBrowser control provides you with this capability. Using the WebBrowser control, you can create your own browser application without having to implement the code to perform the actual download of the Web pages, images, and so forth. You don't have to worry about implementing support for JavaScript, VBScript, ActiveX controls, security, authentication, and so on. The WebBrowser control does this. Also, you don't have to worry about supporting the latest Internet protocols and standards. If the standards change, so will the underlying components of the WebBrowser control. You don't have to update your browser application every time a standard changes.

A real-world example that uses the WebBrowser control to integrate Web browsing functionality into the product is Microsoft Money 99. (See Figure 1-11 on the following page.) Anyone who has used the Internet will have no trouble using Money 99. Money 99 uses the WebBrowser control to display Web pages, thereby providing a familiar interface to its users. Using the WebBrowser control made developing Money 99 easy. The developers of this product didn't have to worry about implementing the code to link one page to the next, displaying images, and so on. All they had to do was use the WebBrowser control, and it took care of the rest. Then the Money 99 development team had to create only the necessary Web pages to provide their users with an appropriate interface.

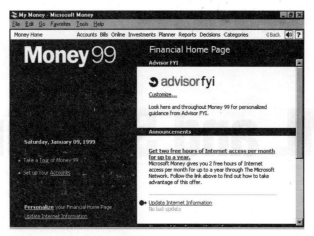

Figure 1-11. *Microsoft Money 99.*

Money 99 isn't the only Microsoft product that uses Internet Explorer components. Microsoft Outlook Express, Microsoft Expedia, and Microsoft Office 2000 also use this technology, and you'll be seeing a lot more products in the future. Using Internet Explorer components makes life a lot easier for developers, and it decreases the development time.

Reusing the WebBrowser control requires you to know Visual Basic, Visual C++, Visual J++, or some other COM-aware development tool. What if you know only DHTML and script? Can you still use the Internet Explorer development platform? *Yes!* Because reusing the WebBrowser control isn't the only way to reuse Internet Explorer. Internet Explorer 5 provides many ways for you to create Internet applications using only DHTML and script. For example, you can create an order-entry application that connects to the corporate database. Or you can create a shopping cart application that allows your customers to order your products on the Web. The possibilities are endless. You'll find countless ways to use the Internet Explorer 5 platform on the World Wide Web.

WHAT'S NEXT?

Before examining advanced Internet Explorer features such as DHTML, ActiveX controls, the WebBrowser control, and so forth, you must first understand the fundamentals. In Chapter 2, you'll create Web pages using simple HTML and script. After you've mastered the basics, you'll be ready for DHTML, ActiveX controls, and whatever Internet Explorer 5 can throw at you.

HTML and Scripting

As you learned in Chapter 1, one of the most significant features introduced in Microsoft Internet Explorer 4 and expanded in Internet Explorer 5 is Dynamic HTML (DHTML). DHTML allows you to change the contents of a Web page on the fly—perhaps in response to some action from the user—without revisiting the server. You can use simple DHTML and script to accomplish the tasks that were previously only possible using Active Server Pages (ASP) or Common Gateway Interface (CGI) programs. Because you don't have to revisit the server to obtain additional information to display, you also don't have to display a new Web page each time your user enters data that requires validation or some sort of response. This increases your users' satisfaction when they're working with your Web application. It also allows your Web application to act more like a typical Microsoft Windows application.

Before I can explain all the cool features of DHTML (in Chapter 3), you must first understand basic HTML and programming in script, including Microsoft JScript and VBScript.

WHERE TO GO FOR MORE INFORMATION

The best place for information about HTML is the MSDN Online Web Workshop: *http://msdn.microsoft.com/workshop*. Probably the best place for quick information about scripting is the Microsoft Scripting Technologies Web site: *http://msdn.microsoft.com/scripting*. If you don't find what you need there, check out the Microsoft Press Web site: *http://mspress.microsoft.com*.

INTRODUCTION TO HTML

According to the definition in the MSDN Library, "Hypertext Markup Language, or HTML, is a system of marking up or tagging a document so that it can be published on the World Wide Web. Documents prepared in HTML include reference graphics and formatting tags. You use a Web browser (such as Microsoft Internet Explorer) to view these documents." That pretty much sums it up. HTML is a way of marking text so that the text is formatted in a specific way when displayed by a Web browser. One of the great characteristics of HTML and the World Wide Web is that they follow a set of standards as dictated by the World Wide Web Consortium, or W3C. (The W3C URL is *http://www.w3.org*.) Consequently, as long as the Web browser that you're using follows the W3C standards, HTML that you write for one browser will work in other browsers, without needing to be changed, as long as those other browsers follow the standards. Internet Explorer 5 follows the HTML 4 specification as dictated by W3C, so if you create HTML for Internet Explorer, that HTML will work the same in other browsers that follow the W3C standards.

Tags

All HTML pages consist of a number of markup tags. A tag begins with a less than sign (<) and ends with a greater than sign (>). In between the less-than and greater-than signs is text that indicates the purpose of the tag and any number of attributes. An attribute describes some characteristic of the tag. Some examples of valid HTML tags follow:

```
<HTML> - Start of HTML
<HEAD> - Start of HEAD section
<BODY> - Start of BODY section
<SCRIPT LANGUAGE="VBScript">  - Script tag with LANGUAGE attribute.
</H1>  - End of H1 block
```

If an HTML tag is a block tag, it is required to have an opening tag and a corresponding closing tag. Tags that are not block tags do not require a closing tag. An opening tag opens a block of HTML code and consists of the less-than sign, followed by the name of the tag and any attributes, and finally the greater-than sign. The closing tag closes a block of HTML code and consists of the less-than sign, a forward slash (/), the name of the tag and any attributes, and finally the greater-than sign. The tag </H1>, shown in the example above, is a closing tag.

Valid HTML code must be wrapped in the opening <HTML> tag and the closing </HTML> tag, and all other HTML tags must fall within them. The following code shows you the smallest HTML page you can create, but it doesn't produce any results.

```
<HTML>
</HTML>
```

An HTML page typically has two sections, the head section and the body section. The head section is surrounded by opening and closing head tags, shown here:

```
<HEAD>
</HEAD>
```

You can include certain HTML tags within the head section that describe your HTML page. Anything you include within the head section is read and interpreted by Internet Explorer before the actual Web page is displayed. One of the most important tags that you'll want to include in the head section is the <TITLE> tag. The text that you place within the opening and closing title tags is displayed in Internet Explorer's title bar while the page is still loading, so the user will know that she has reached the correct page. The following HTML code displays the title "My Web Page" in the title bar, as shown in Figure 2-1.

```
<HTML>
<HEAD>
    <TITLE>My Web Page</TITLE>
</HEAD>
</HTML>
```

Figure 2-1. *Internet Explorer title bar.*

Another tag that is typically placed in the head section is the <SCRIPT> tag. It is usually best to place all your script functions within the head section so that Internet Explorer reads and interprets this script before the actual Web page is displayed. This way, all calls to script functions will succeed if nothing is wrong with the script functions.

NOTE For information about other tags that you can place within the head section, take a look at the HTML references section of the MSDN Online Web Workshop: *http://msdn.microsoft.com/workshop*.

The second section of an HTML page, the body section, follows the head section and is surrounded by opening and closing body tags, shown here:

```
<BODY>
</BODY>
```

The body section is where you put all the elements that you want displayed on your Web page, including any text, buttons, and text boxes. Creating a simple

HTML page is easy. If you want to display some unformatted text on your Web page, all you have to do is type that text between the opening and closing body tags, as in this example:

```
<HTML>
<HEAD>
    <TITLE>My Web Page</TITLE>
</HEAD>
<BODY>
    This is my very simple Web page that includes only unformatted text.
</BODY>
</HTML>
```

> **NOTE**   Content in an HTML document includes *tags*, such as <B> and </B>, that specify the presentation of text in a document. When the browser accesses a page, the HTML parser reads the contents of the file and creates HTML elements from the tags. It is the HTML *elements* that you can program. However, the terms "HTML tag" and "HTML element" are often used interchangeably.

See how easy it is! Now we have a real Web page that will work in any Web browser. This page is really boring, though. Without text formatting, Web pages wouldn't be any more exciting than a document that you created using Microsoft Windows Notepad. Let's take a look at some formatting options that will make your Web pages more exciting.

Headings

In HTML, you can create different heading levels in your document to help you organize the document into sections, just as you might do when writing a book. The book you are reading now uses several different levels of headings. For example, the section "Introduction to HTML" uses heading level 1 (H1). This section uses heading level 2 (H2). HTML provides you with six levels of headings: H1, H2, H3, H4, H5, and H6, with H1 being the largest and H6 being the smallest. Heading tags are block tags, and you must specify opening and closing tags. Examples of each of these headings are shown in Figure 2-2.

To create a heading, you simply include text within the opening and closing heading tags, as in this example code:

```
<BODY>
    <H1>This is heading level 1.</H1>
    <H2>This is heading level 2.</H2>
    <H3>This is heading level 3.</H3>
    <H4>This is heading level 4.</H4>
    <H5>This is heading level 5.</H5>
    <H6>This is heading level 6.</H6>
</BODY>
```

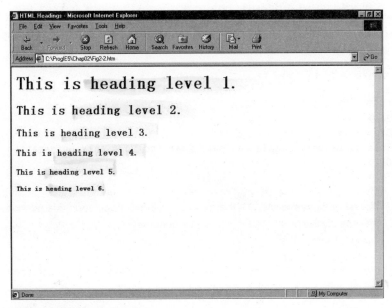

Figure 2-2. *HTML headings.*

Formatting Text

In addition to creating headings for your document, you can format normal text that you want to display. You can center the text, underline it, use a specific color, and so on. The possibilities are endless. The most important formatting tags are described next.

Paragraphs

Along with using headings to structure your Web page, you can add structure by grouping common text into paragraphs. HTML provides a paragraph tag, <P>, which groups text into paragraphs. The paragraph tag inserts a blank line on your Web page before the text that follows the paragraph tag and after the closing paragraph tag. The paragraph tag is a block tag and the only case in which closing tags aren't required. If you don't specify a closing paragraph tag, a new paragraph will start when Internet Explorer encounters another paragraph tag. So it's considered good coding practice to include the closing paragraph tag. And future versions of Internet Explorer might require it. Here's an example of using the paragraph tag:

```
<P>This is a paragraph.</P>
```

Blank lines

You might sometimes want to insert a line break into your page. You could just use a paragraph tag, but using a break tag, <BR>, is often more convenient and sometimes makes more sense. If you just want to include blank lines but aren't actually creating a new paragraph of text, using the break tag is more suitable. The break tag isn't a block tag, so it doesn't require a closing tag. You can place the break tag wherever you want to insert a line break. The following examples use the break tag:

```
Here is some text followed by a line break.<BR>
<BR><BR>
The above inserts two blank lines into the Web page.<BR>
```

Alignment

Perhaps you want to align your text a certain way on a page. HTML provides a couple of techniques to do this. Most HTML tags have an attribute named ALIGN, which you can use to center, right-justify, or left-justify the text within the element. If you don't specify this attribute, the text is left-justified by default.

> **NOTE**   Not all tags support this attribute. Check out the MSDN Online Web Workshop to determine whether a specific element supports this attribute.

Let's look at a few examples of the ALIGN attribute. The heading and paragraph tags both support the ALIGN attribute. Here are three examples of tags that show how to use the ALIGN attribute:

```
<H1 ALIGN=LEFT>This is heading level 1.</H1>
<H2 AlIGN=RIGHT>This is heading level 2.</H2>
<P ALIGN=CENTER>This is a centered paragraph.</P>
```

If you just want to center a block of text, you can use the <CENTER> tag. (Note that not all browsers support this tag.) The <CENTER> tag is a block tag, and it requires you to specify the closing tag. If you do not specify the closing tag, all the elements on your Web page that follow the opening <CENTER> tag will be centered. Using the <CENTER> tag is different from using the ALIGN=CENTER attribute—the <CENTER> tag can be used to center a block of HTML, whereas the ALIGN=CENTER attribute centers only the text contained within the tag to which the ALIGN attribute is applied. Here's an example of using the <CENTER> tag:

```
<CENTER>Here is some text that is centered.</CENTER>
```

The results of this HTML code are shown in Figure 2-3.

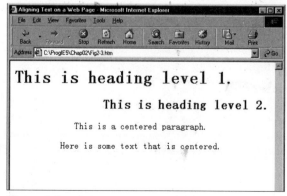

Figure 2-3. *Aligning text on a Web page.*

Bold, underline, italic, and strikethrough

HTML also provides text-highlighting tags that enable you to style your text with bold, underline, italic, and strikethrough. To make your text appear bold, use either the <B> or the <STRONG> tag. The <STRONG> tag is the preferred method of bolding text because it allows Internet Explorer to choose the correct method for applying the style according to the user's current settings. To underline text, use the <U> tag. To italicize text, use the <I> or the <EM> tag. The <EM> tag is preferred over <I> for the same reason that <STRONG> is preferred over <B>. For strikethrough type, you can use either the <S> or the <STRIKE> tag. In this case, <S> is as good as <STRIKE>. These text-formatting tags are all block tags, and the closing tag is required for each. Here are some examples of the text-formatting tags:

```
<B>Here is some text in bold type.</B><BR>
<STRONG>Here is some text in strong type,
    which is usually shown in bold.</STRONG><BR>
<U>Here is some underlined text.</U><BR>
<I>Here is some text in italic type.</I><BR>
<EM>Here is some text that is emphasized,
    which is usually shown in italic type.</EM><BR>
<S>Here is some text in strikethrough type.</S><BR>
<STRIKE>Here is some more text in strikethrough type.</STRIKE><BR>
```

The results of these tags are shown in Figure 2-4.

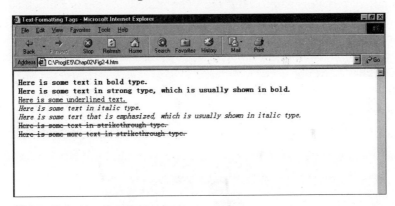

Figure 2-4. *Text-formatting tags.*

Font

Using the <FONT> tag, you can change the font face, size, and color of text. The <FONT> tag is a block tag, and the closing tag is required. To specify a font face, size, or color that's different from the default, use the <FONT> tag's FACE, SIZE, and COLOR attributes. For the FACE attribute, you specify the name of the font face you want to use. For the SIZE attribute, you specify a size from 1 through 7, where 1 is the smallest and 7 is the largest. For the COLOR attribute, you specify the name of the color or the red-green-blue (RGB) color value for the color. (The MSDN Online Web Workshop lists all the colors that Internet Explorer supports.) The following examples use the <FONT> tag and its attributes to change font face, size, and color. Figure 2-5 shows the results of using the <FONT> tag.

```
<FONT FACE="Arial" SIZE="2" COLOR="DarkViolet">
    Face=Arial, Size=2, Color=DarkViolet
</FONT>
<BR>
<FONT FACE="Times New Roman" SIZE="4" COLOR="#0000FF">
    Face=Times New Roman, Size=4, Color=Blue
</FONT>
<BR>
<FONT FACE="Courier" SIZE="5" COLOR="DarkMagenta">
    Face=Courier, Size=5, Color=DarkMagenta
</FONT>
```

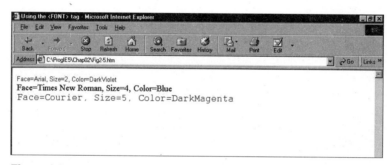

Figure 2-5. *Using the <FONT> tag can change font face, size, and color.*

Horizontal lines

Sometimes when structuring your Web pages, you'll want to draw horizontal lines of differing sizes. To draw horizontal lines, use the <HR> tag. (HR is an acronym for horizontal rule, by the way.) The <HR> tag has attributes that allow you to change the alignment, color, size, and width of the line being drawn. You've already seen the ALIGN and COLOR attributes. The SIZE and WIDTH attributes both take a value that's the size or width of the line, in pixels. Here are a few examples of different lines that you can draw using the <HR> tag:

```
A standard line
<HR>
<BR>
A right-justified line with width of 300
<HR ALIGN=RIGHT WIDTH=300>
<BR>
A centered blue line of size 10 and width of 200
<HR ALIGN=CENTER SIZE=10 COLOR="Blue" WIDTH=200>
```

The results of this HTML code are shown in Figure 2-6.

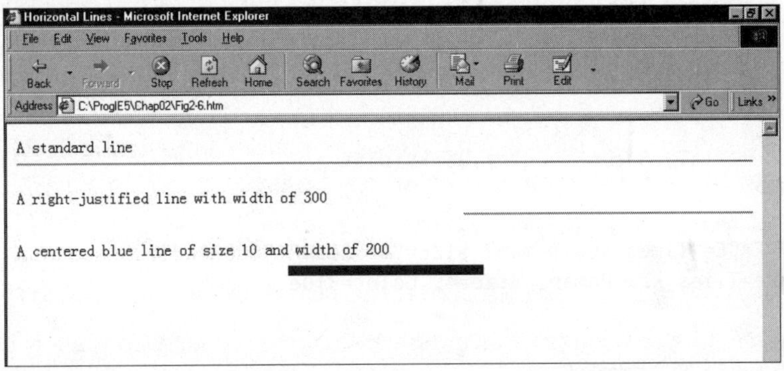

Figure 2-6. *Horizontal lines.*

Hyperlinks

What good would a Web page be if it didn't contain links to other Web pages? Inserting hyperlinks to other Web pages is easy using the anchor tag, <A>. Like many other tags, the anchor tag is a block tag, and the closing tag </A> is required. The most important attribute of the anchor tag is the HREF attribute. The value of HREF is the Uniform Resource Locator (URL), which indicates where Internet Explorer should navigate when a user clicks the hyperlink.

To create a hyperlink, you simply insert some text between the opening and closing anchor tags in your Web page. The text should describe what Internet Explorer will do when the user clicks on the hyperlink. Of course, for the hyperlink to respond when clicked, you'll have to include the HREF attribute and a URL. In addition, you can wrap any text or other HTML tag on your Web page using the anchor tags, as you'll see in the next section. Here are some examples of hyperlinks that you can create with the anchor tag:

```
<A HREF="http://www.microsoft.com">Microsoft Home Page</A>
<A HREF="file://C:\">View the Contents of your C: drive</A>
```

Images

So far, I've explained only how to insert text into your Web pages. If that were all you could do, your Web page would be pretty boring, don't you think? Luckily, Internet Explorer also allows you to insert images into your Web pages using the <IMG> tag. The <IMG> tag has many attributes, but SRC is the most important one. The SRC attribute is to the <IMG> tag what the HREF attribute is to the anchor tag. The SRC attribute is a URL that tells Internet Explorer where to get the image that you want to display. Internet Explorer can display many types of images—.bmp, .emf, .gif, .jpeg, .jpg, .png, and .wmf files, to name a few.

You can also change the size of images that you want to display by using the HEIGHT and WIDTH attributes, which take the number of pixels that you want for the height and width of the image. One other attribute of particular interest is the BORDER attribute. By default, Internet Explorer displays a border around an image. The BORDER attribute takes a number that specifies the thickness of the border drawn around the image. You can turn off the border by specifying 0 for the BORDER attribute. Here are a few examples of ways you can display images on your Web pages:

```
<IMG SRC="MyBitmap.bmp">
<IMG BORDER=0 SRC="file://c:\SomeJPG.jpg">
<IMG HEIGHT=500 WIDTH=500 SRC="http://yourserver.com/SomeGif.gif">
```

One cool advantage of including an image on your Web page is that you can turn it into a hyperlink—when a user clicks on it, Internet Explorer navigates to the URL you specify. All you have to do is wrap the <IMG> tags with anchor tags. Easy, huh? Here are a few examples:

```
<A HREF="http://yourserver.com/default.htm"><IMG SRC="MyBitmap.bmp"></A>
<A HREF="http://www.microsoft.com/ie/"><IMG SRC="IE.jpg"></A>
```

Ordered and Unordered Lists

Sometimes when providing information on a Web page, you'll want to list information either in an ordered list or in an unordered list. HTML provides the <OL> tag to enable you to create ordered lists and the <UL> tag to create unordered lists. Both of these tags are block tags, and the corresponding closing tags are required. By default, the ordered lists are numbered using decimal numbers starting at 1, and the unordered lists are bulleted lists. However, you can use the TYPE attribute with either the ordered or unordered lists to change their styles. For example, you could create an ordered list using letters or roman numerals. Table 2-1 shows the different styles that you can specify with the TYPE attribute. (Although both the <OL> and <UL> tags have a TYPE attribute, the attribute is seldom used because it doesn't make sense to specify that an unordered list be numbered. However, you *can* do it!)

TABLE 2-1
VALUES FOR THE TYPE ATTRIBUTE

Value	Description
1	List items are numbered.
a	List items are labeled with lowercase letters.
A	List items are labeled with uppercase letters.
i	List items are labeled with lowercase roman numerals.
I	List items are labeled with uppercase roman numerals.

To include items in a list, you use the list-item tag, <LI>. The <LI> tag also has a TYPE attribute that takes the same values as those listed in Table 2-1, so you can change the style anywhere in the list. Typically, however, you'll want to maintain the same style throughout the entire list. Here's code for an ordered list of items that uses uppercase roman numerals:

```
<OL TYPE="I">
    <LI>List Item 1
    <LI>List Item 2
    <LI>List Item 3
    <LI>List Item 4
</OL>
```

The results of this HTML code are shown in Figure 2-7.

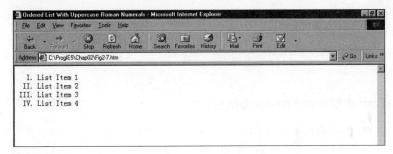

Figure 2-7. *Ordered list using uppercase roman numerals.*

The following HTML code will display an unordered list:

```
<UL>
    <LI>List Item 1
    <LI>List Item 2
    <LI>List Item 3
    <LI>List Item 4
</UL>
```

Figure 2-8 shows the results of this HTML code.

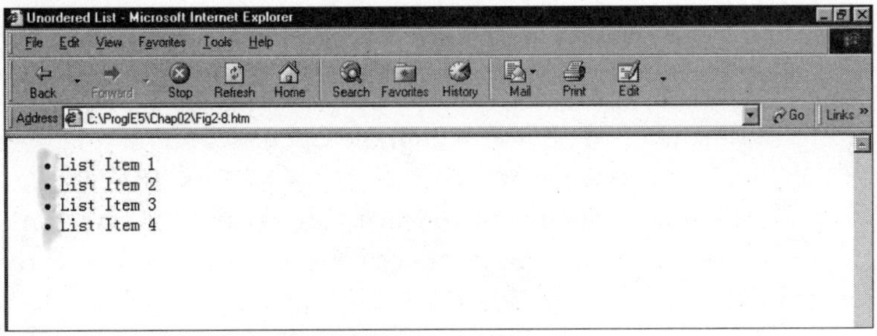

Figure 2-8. *Unordered list using bullets.*

In addition to specifying one level of items in a list, you can nest <OL> or <UL> tags so that you'll have multiple levels in your list. Here's HTML code for a multilevel, unordered list:

```
<UL>
    <LI>List Item 1
    <LI>List Item 2
    <UL>
        <LI>List Item 3
        <LI>List Item 4
    </UL>
</UL>
```

The results of this HTML code are shown in Figure 2-9. As you can see, the type of bullet used for the second level of items in the list is different to reflect the new level.

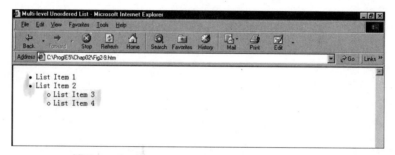

Figure 2-9. *Multilevel, unordered list using bullets.*

Select Boxes

A select box contains a list of items from which you can choose one. This list is typically in a drop-down style. Before the list is opened, the first item in the list is usually displayed. The other items can be displayed by clicking a down arrow button next to the drop-down list. Although the default is to display only the first item in the list, you can alter this behavior. You can choose to show the first item, the first two items, or all the items in the list.

To create a select box, you use the <SELECT> tag. The <SELECT> tag is a block tag, and the closing tag is required. Within the opening and closing select tags, you include <OPTION> tags that specify items in the list. (The <OPTION> tag isn't a block tag.) When including an <OPTION> tag, you'll also usually supply the VALUE attribute to associate a value with the item in the select box. This attribute is typically used for referencing the item in script in the select box. You can also specify the attribute named SELECTED for the item that you want selected by default. Here's an example of a select box that contains three items:

```
<SELECT>
   <OPTION VALUE="1" SELECTED>Item 1
   <OPTION VALUE="2">Item 2
   <OPTION VALUE="3">Item 3
</SELECT>
```

Figure 2-10 shows the results of this HTML code:

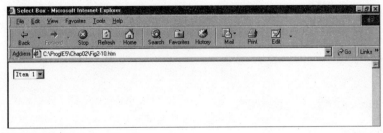

Figure 2-10. *Select box.*

Tables

Tables provide you with a way to group information into columns and rows. HTML's <TABLE> tag enables you to build tables. The <TABLE> tag is a block tag, and the closing tag is required. A discussion of tables could go on for a long time, so I'll just provide you with the basics for creating them.

To create a basic table, you first insert the opening and closing table tags in your Web page. If you want a border displayed around your rows and columns, use the BORDER attribute to specify the size of the border. You can also specify the height and width of your table using the HEIGHT and WIDTH attributes. In the case of tables, these attributes take values in either pixels or percentages.

To create rows in your table, use the <TR> tag. Use the <TH> tag to create headings in your table, and use the <TD> tag to create columns. The <TR>, <TH>, and <TD> tags are all block tags, and the corresponding closing tags are required. The following HTML code demonstrates how to create a simple table:

```
<TABLE BORDER=1 WIDTH="50%">
   <TR>
      <TH>Heading 1</TH>
      <TH>Heading 2</TH>
   </TR>
   <TR>
      <TD>Row 1 - Column 1</TD>
      <TD>Row 1 - Column 2</TD>
   </TR>
   <TR>
      <TD>Row 2 - Column 1</TD>
      <TD>Row 2 - Column 2</TD>
   </TR>
</TABLE>
```

The results of this HTML code are shown in Figure 2-11.

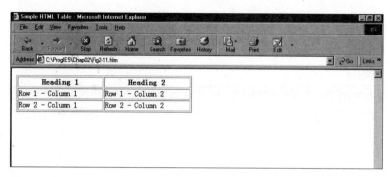

Figure 2-11. *Simple HTML table.*

Intrinsic Controls

Internet Explorer provides you with a number of intrinsic controls—buttons, text boxes, select boxes, and so forth—that are natively supported by Internet Explorer and HTML. You can insert an intrinsic control into your Web page using the <INPUT> tag. This tag has an attribute named TYPE that allows you to specify the type of control you want to insert into your Web page. Table 2-2 lists the types of intrinsic controls that you can insert. We'll discuss the controls that are used mainly with forms later in this chapter.

TABLE 2-2
TYPES OF INTRINSIC CONTROLS

Type of Control	Description
Button	Button control.
Checkbox	Check box that is either checked or unchecked.
File	File upload control. Used mainly with forms.
Hidden	Hidden control.
Image	Image control that causes the form to be uploaded.
Password	Similar to the text control except that the text entered isn't displayed.
Radio	Radio button control that is used for mutually exclusive sets of values.
Reset	Button that resets the data in a form when clicked. Used mainly with forms.
Submit	Button that submits the form when clicked. Used mainly with forms.
Text	Single-line text entry control.

Another important attribute of the <INPUT> tag is VALUE. You can use it to specify the text that is displayed for certain controls. The VALUE attribute has a different meaning depending on the type of control you're using. For instance, if you specify the type of control as Button, the text you specify for the VALUE attribute will appear inside the button. If the type of control is Text, the text you specify for the VALUE attribute will appear inside the text box. Other controls require other attributes. For example, the Radio control type requires that you specify a NAME attribute.

NOTE Refer to the documentation for the <INPUT> tag in the MSDN Online Web Workshop for more information about required attributes.

Here are some examples of intrinsic controls that you can create with the <INPUT> tag. We'll use a few of these controls in the next chapter when we examine DHTML.

```
<INPUT TYPE=BUTTON VALUE="Button">
<BR>
<INPUT TYPE=TEXT VALUE="Some Text">
<BR>
<INPUT TYPE=PASSWORD VALUE="MyPassword">
<BR>
<INPUT TYPE=CHECKBOX>Check Box
<BR>
<INPUT TYPE=RADIO NAME="Radio1">Radio Button 1
<INPUT TYPE=RADIO NAME="Radio2">Radio Button 2
```

Figure 2-12 displays the results of this HTML code.

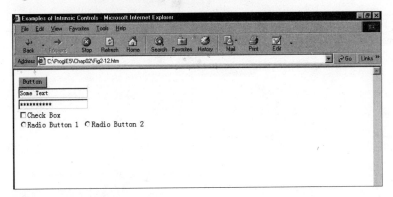

Figure 2-12. *Examples of intrinsic controls.*

Comments

Commenting involves adding information on your Web page that will help describe what you intended when you created the Web page. A user trying to navigate your Web page can't view the text that you include in a comment; the text is viewable only when a user looks at the source of your Web page.

Commenting your Web pages is extremely important. Suppose you spent hours creating a Web page with a specific goal in mind. If you didn't include comments, months down the road when you or somebody else had to make changes to the page, hours could be spent figuring out what you were originally trying to accomplish.

HTML provides you with two methods to include comments in your HTML code. The first, and more traditional, method is to use the <!-- and --> tags. As long as these tags do not appear in the Script block, Internet Explorer ignores any elements you place within the tags and the browser won't display the elements as part of your Web page. The other method for including comments is to use the <COMMENT> tag. The <COMMENT> tag is a block tag, and the closing tag is required. Again, the browser won't display anything you place within the <COMMENT> tags. Here are a couple of examples of using comment tags:

```
<!-- This is a comment using the traditional comment tags.  -->
<COMMENT> Here is a comment using the newer comment tags. </COMMENT>
```

Frames

Frames are a little bit more complicated than the other HTML elements we've been discussing. Frames provide a way to show multiple Web pages in one window. One HTML page—which contains HTML code that specifies how the frames are to appear—is the driver page. The <FRAMESET> tag is used to describe the structure of the frames. It is a block tag, and the closing tag is required. You use one of two attributes to describe how the page is to look. If you want the frames to be laid out horizontally, you use the ROWS attribute. If you want the frames to be laid out vertically, you use the COLS attribute. The values that you specify for the ROWS and COLS attributes indicate the size of each frame. You can specify these values in pixels, as a percentage of the total available space, or as a percentage of the remaining space available. Usually, you'll use a percentage to indicate the size of each frame. For example, to create a frameset that will contain three frames laid out vertically, you would code the <FRAMESET> tag like this:

```
<FRAMESET COLS="33%, 33%, *">
</FRAMESET>
```

The preceding code creates three frames. The first two are each 33 percent of the entire width of the page. The last frame takes up all the remaining space in the window.

The <FRAMESET> tag creates only the frames. To load pages into each frame, you use the <FRAME> tag. Two attributes of the <FRAME> tag are important: the SRC attribute, which indicates which URL to load into the frame; and the NAME attribute, which indicates the name of the frame. This name can be used in anchor tags to indicate which frame should load the URL. The following HTML code uses the frameset defined in the preceding code to load the three pages into the frames.

```
<FRAMESET COLS="33%, 33%, *">
   <FRAME NAME="FRAME1" SRC="http://www.microsoft.com/">
   <FRAME NAME="FRAME2" SRC="http://mspress.microsoft.com/">
   <FRAME NAME="FRAME3" SRC="http://www.microsoft.com/ie/">
</FRAMESET>
```

The results of this HTML code are shown in Figure 2-13. For the driver page, note that you should include the opening and closing HTML tags, but *not* the opening and closing body tags. You can include <HEAD> tags if you want to.

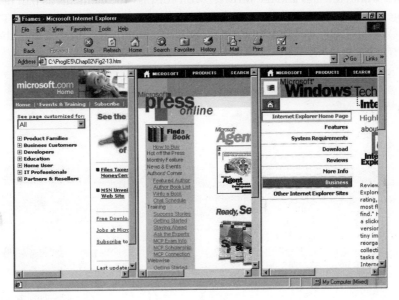

Figure 2-13. *Frames.*

HTML Forms

HTML forms enable you to create Web-based forms for your users that are just like paper-based forms. You use the <FORM> tag to create them. (The <FORM> tag is a block tag, and the closing tag is required.) The <FORM> tag allows you to group together intrinsic controls, such as text boxes, check boxes, radio buttons, and submit buttons, that will enable your users to enter information and then submit that information to a program that is running on your Web server. Typically, forms are submitted to your server when the user clicks a submit button. Remember that the submit button is created by inserting an <INPUT> tag with the TYPE attribute set to Submit.

Besides the ID attribute, which is used to identify the form and all HTML tags, the most important attribute of the <FORM> tag is the ACTION attribute. The value of the ACTION attribute indicates the URL of the application that will be executed when a user presses the submit button.

Another important attribute is the METHOD attribute, which indicates how the form data is sent to the server application. The METHOD attribute has two values: Get and Post. If you specify Get, the form data is appended to the URL specified by the ACTION attribute before opening that URL. If you specify Post, the form data is sent through an HTTP post transaction. In both cases, the form data is sent as a series of name=value pairs, where name is the name of a form element (such as "Text1" in the next example), and value is either the value entered by the user or, if nothing is entered by the user, the value specified by the VALUE attribute. These name=value pairs are separated by ampersand characters (&).

Let's take a look at a simple example. The following HTML code is for a form that contains one text box and a submit button. When the submit button is pressed, the program indicated by the METHOD attribute is executed.

```
<FORM METHOD="GET" ACTION="http://yourserver.com/DoSomething.asp"
  ID="Form1">
  <INPUT TYPE="TEXT" NAME="Text1">
  <INPUT TYPE="SUBMIT">
</FORM>
```

In this example, after I pressed the submit button, the value I entered into the text box was appended to the URL specified by the ACTION attribute before that URL was opened. For example, if I entered the text *Something* into the text box, the URL that would open is *http://yourserver.com/DoSomething.asp?Text1=Something*.

> **NOTE** Well, that concludes the introduction to HTML. For information about HTML tags not covered in this chapter, check out the MSDN Online Web Workshop *(http://msdn.microsoft.com/workshop)* or study one of the many great Microsoft Press books on the topic, such as *HTML in Action*, by Bruce Morris (1996), and *Dynamic HTML Reference and Software Development Kit: Comprehensive Reference to DHTML for Microsoft Internet Explorer 5*, by Microsoft Corporation (1999).

THE BASICS OF SCRIPTING

This section is a short tutorial on scripting in which I present the basic concepts. To help you understand these concepts, I show how they apply to both JScript and VBScript. I also let you know where to go for more information along the way.

Scripting encompasses many different programming languages that can be used within the context of a Web page. Scripting languages are usually a subset or at least distantly related to some high-level programming language that can be used to develop full-fledged Windows applications. By subset, I mean that a scripting language includes some but not all the programming constructs associated with its parent language. For example, Internet Explorer natively supports two scripting languages: JScript and VBScript. (Other scripting languages can be created for use with Internet

Explorer as well, but the discussion of how to create scripting engines for Internet Explorer is outside the scope of this book.)

JScript is Microsoft's implementation of the ECMA 262 language specification. (JScript is sometimes referred to as JavaScript or ECMAScript.) JScript is a full implementation of this specification, plus it has some enhancements that allow it to take advantage of Internet Explorer. JScript is similar to the Java programming language in its look and feel, but JScript is only distantly and indirectly related to the Java programming language. JScript contains some of the programming idioms of Java such as functions and objects, but it doesn't include them all. Unlike Java, in which you have to explicitly declare all variables, JScript is loosely typed—you don't have to explicitly declare the data types of all variables.

VBScript, however, *is* a subset of the Visual Basic programming language. You can use VBScript in many programming environments in addition to Internet Explorer, such as Microsoft Internet Information Server. VBScript is a direct subset of Visual Basic, so it contains some of the programming constructs available in Visual Basic but not all of them. If you're already familiar with Visual Basic, you'll have no trouble learning VBScript. If you don't happen to know Visual Basic, take the time to learn VBScript. Once you do, you'll be well on your way to understanding the entire family of Visual Basic programming languages. Although other browsers support the ECMA 262 specification (ECMAScript), only Internet Explorer natively supports VBScript.

NOTE For more information about the Visual Basic family of programming languages, please consult MSDN Online Web Workshop: *http://msdn.microsoft.com.*

The most important point to remember about scripting is that it's the backbone of DHTML, so you must have a basic understanding of scripting before you can go on to DHTML. By using script, you can manipulate a Web page to retrieve and change its contents. If you're already a fluent script programmer, feel free to skip the rest of this chapter. If you already know one of the scripting languages natively supported by Internet Explorer, you might want to read through the rest of this chapter anyway because it covers both JScript and VBScript.

Adding Script to a Web Page

The first skill you have to learn when writing script for Internet Explorer is how to add script to a Web page. To add script to a Web page, you use an HTML tag named <SCRIPT>. As with many other HTML tags, the <SCRIPT> tag is the one that opens a block of HTML code. Therefore, you must use the corresponding </SCRIPT> tag to delineate the closing of the block of HTML code. Script contained within the <SCRIPT> and </SCRIPT> tags is typically referred to as a script block. You can place the script block anywhere in the head or body section of a document, although it's usually best to place it in the head section so that it's parsed before the document is actually displayed. Remember, though, that script blocks must be in either the head or the body section and cannot sit alone as independent sections in the document. Also, a Web page can contain any number of script blocks, but combining adjacent script blocks into one is more efficient.

As with most HTML tags, the <SCRIPT> tag has a set of attributes that describe the script block. The most important of these attributes is the LANGUAGE attribute, which tells Internet Explorer which script engine to load to parse the code contained within the script block. For example, the following script block uses the LANGUAGE attribute to tell Internet Explorer to load the JScript scripting engine to parse and interpret the script code within the script block.

```
<SCRIPT LANGUAGE="JScript">
<!--
-->
</SCRIPT>
```

In addition to specifying the "JScript" value for the LANGUAGE attribute, you can also specify "JavaScript" or "ECMAScript" to tell Internet Explorer that the script block contains JScript code. JScript, JavaScript, and ECMAScript can all be used interchangeably.

To tell Internet Explorer that a script block contains VBScript, you can specify "VBScript" or "VBS" for the value of the LANGUAGE attribute, as in the following example:

```
<SCRIPT LANGUAGE="VBScript">
<!--
-->
</SCRIPT>
```

You're probably wondering why I included HTML comment tags (<!-- and -->) within each of the script block examples. Not all browsers support scripting, and not all browsers that do support scripting support both JScript and VBScript. To maintain compatibility with other browsers, use HTML comment tags to tell the browsers that don't support scripting to ignore the script code contained within the HTML comment tags. If you don't surround your script code with HTML comment tags, browsers that don't support scripting will display the script code as normal HTML text. You don't have to worry about the <SCRIPT> and </SCRIPT> tags. Any HTML tags that aren't recognized by a browser are effectively ignored.

Statements

A statement is a grouping of one or more items and symbols that perform some action. In all scripting languages, a specific character terminates a statement. In JScript, a semicolon terminates a statement. (Although you can have more than one statement on a single line, doing so is considered bad programming practice and should be avoided.) In VBScript, the end-of-line character terminates a statement. Let's look at some examples of statements that you might use in JScript and VBScript. Assume that these script statements and all the following script examples are contained within the appropriate script blocks, as discussed earlier. These are JScript statements:

```
c = a + b;
var wnd;
wnd = window.open();
```

These are VBScript statements:

```
c = a + b
Dim wnd
wnd = window.open()
```

As you can see, each line contains one statement. (Don't worry if you don't understand what these statements accomplish. The rest of this chapter will explain it.) Notice that a semicolon terminates the JScript statements, and the end-of-line character terminates the VBScript statements.

Statements can be grouped together in what's referred to as a block. This block concept is similar to a script block in that a block always groups together a number of statements. As mentioned earlier, all the script contained within the <SCRIPT> and </SCRIPT> tags is known as the script block. Within the script block, script code can be grouped further into code blocks. You can group code statements into blocks in several ways. Typically, statements are grouped together in blocks using functions, subroutines, or conditional statements.

Comments

As with HTML code, using comments to indicate what your script code is doing is extremely important. The comments you enter into your script code are ignored by the script interpreter, so the performance of your script code isn't affected by them.

Different script developers have different standards for comments. Some developers enter one comment for each line of script. Others enter a block of comments before a block of script. Some developers place comments at the end of a line of script code, while others enter a comment on a line of its own. I like to use a mixture of all these techniques. When appropriate, I use a block of comments to explain my intentions for a block of script code. This block of comments might be only one line or many lines. My preference is to start the block of comments on the line immediately preceding the line or block of script code that the comments are describing. If the purpose of a line of script code isn't evident, I enter a comment immediately following the line of script on the same line as that line of code. These are just my preferences. You'll decide on your own techniques for comments as you get more into scripting.

To enter a comment in JScript, you use the double slash (//) characters. All text following these characters and on the same line as these characters is considered commented out and is ignored by the JScript engine. As an example, I've added comments to the script that I introduced in the "Statements" section to make the script more understandable:

```
// Determine the total number of items
// in the inventory, and then open a new
// browser window to allow the customer
// to add items to his/her shopping cart.
c = a + b;
var wnd;   // wnd contains a handle to the open window.
wnd = window.open();
```

Comments in VBScript are entered by using the single-quote character ('). As in JScript, all text after the comment character and on the same line is considered commented out and will be ignored by the VBScript scripting engine. (If you must use the single quote as a character and not as a comment delimiter—perhaps in a string, for example—you must enclose the single quote in double quotes ("'").) Here's the previous example using VBScript:

```
' Determine the total number of items
' in the inventory, and then open a new
' browser window to allow the customer
' to add items to his/her shopping cart.
c = a + b
Dim wnd    ' wnd contains a handle to the open window.
wnd = window.open()
```

Variables

A variable is a kind of placeholder for data that you can reuse within your script code. For example, you might want to create a variable named *TotalItems* that keeps track of the total number of items that a user has chosen to purchase. To perform some action on the variable, such as adding or subtracting from it, you just refer to it by name. Later in this chapter, the "Operators" section explains different operations that you can perform on a variable.

You don't have to explicitly declare variables in JScript and VBScript. However, it is good programming practice to declare all variables before you use them. To declare a variable in JScript, you use the *var* keyword. You aren't required to declare all variables before using them except in one case. In a JScript function, you must declare all variables that are local to that function. (Functions are covered later in this chapter.) JScript variables can be of any length but must follow these rules:

■ The first character must be a letter (either uppercase or lowercase), an underscore (_), or a dollar sign ($).

■ Characters following the first character can be letters, numbers, underscores, or dollar signs.

■ Variable names can't contain spaces or periods (that is, a full stop).

■ Variables should not have names that conflict with intrinsic objects or functions.

■ A variable name can't be one of the following JScript reserved words:

❏	break	❏	if	❏	true
❏	continue	❏	in	❏	typeof
❏	delete	❏	new	❏	var
❏	else	❏	null	❏	void
❏	false	❏	return	❏	while
❏	for	❏	this	❏	with
❏	function				

■ A variable name can't be one of the future JScript reserved words shown here:

❏	case	❏	do	❏	import
❏	class	❏	enum	❏	super
❏	catch	❏	export	❏	switch
❏	const	❏	extends	❏	throw
❏	debugger	❏	finally	❏	try
❏	default				

Also, keep in mind that JScript variables are case sensitive. For example, a variable named *TotalItems* isn't the same as one named *totalItems*.

When declaring a variable in JScript, you can also initialize that variable to some value. The type of the value that you use to initialize the variable implicitly indicates the type of the variable itself. If you declare a variable without initializing it, it exists, but its value is undefined. If you want to initialize a variable but don't want to give it any particular value, you can initialize it to *null*. Also, before you can actually use a variable, you must declare it either explicitly, using the *var* keyword, or implicitly, by setting the variable equal to some value. The following are examples of ways to declare variables in JScript:

```
var TotalItems;
var totalCost = 0.0;
var selectedItem = null;

price_per_widget = 2.50;
var totalWidgets = 10;
var totalWidgetCost = totalWidgets * price_per_widget;
```

Most of the rules that apply to declaring JScript variables apply to VBScript as well, with a few exceptions:

- Variables in VBScript aren't case sensitive. Therefore, a variable named *TotalItems* is exactly the same as one named *totalItems*.

- VBScript variables must not exceed 255 characters.

- The VBScript reserved words are different from the JScript reserved words, as shown in the following list:

❑ Call	❑ For	❑ Public
❑ Case	❑ Function	❑ ReDim
❑ Dim	❑ If	❑ Rem
❑ Do	❑ Loop	❑ Select
❑ Each	❑ Next	❑ Set
❑ Exit	❑ Option	❑ Sub
❑ Explicit	❑ Private	

As in JScript, you can declare a VBScript variable in two ways: implicitly and explicitly. Implicitly declaring a variable in VBScript is the same as in JScript—just set the variable equal to some value. To explicitly declare a variable in VBScript, you use either the *Dim*, *Private*, or *Public* keyword. (VBScript keywords aren't case sensitive. When declaring a variable, you can use *Dim*, *dim*, or any combination of uppercase and lowercase.)

Determining whether to use *Dim*, *Private*, or *Public* depends on what scope or lifetime you want to impose on the variable. Scope is an advanced scripting topic and is therefore outside the scope (pun intended!) of this book. Typically, you'll use *Dim* and won't have to worry about *Private* or *Public*.

Here's the same example that I used for JScript, revised to work in VBScript. Also, note that I didn't initialize any variables when declaring them. This is a restriction of VBScript that does not exist in JScript.

```
Dim TotalItems
Dim totalCost
totalCost = 0.0
Dim selectedItem
selectedItem = null

price_per_widget = 2.50
Dim totalWidgets
totalWidgets = 10
Dim totalWidgetCost
totalWidgetCost = totalWidgets * price_per_widget
```

Remember that I mentioned that declaring your variables before you use them is good programming practice? To see why this is a good idea, consider a variable named *TotalItems* that's used to keep track of the total number of items selected by a user. Let's just say that you've been keeping track of the total number of items selected by adding 1 to *TotalItems* each time the user selects an item. When the user is finished selecting items, she clicks a button to display the total number of items selected. When coding the script that displays the total number of items, you accidentally typed *TotalItem* instead of *TotalItems* making the total number of items displayed 0. Bewildered, your user selects all the items again and clicks the button that displays the total number of items, only to find that 0 is displayed again. Had you been required to declare all variables before you used them, this problem wouldn't have occurred.

Fortunately, VBScript's Option Explicit statement provides a way to require that all variables be declared before they're used. This statement should be the first statement in your script. As an example, take a look at the following VBScript code. Can you find the error that would *not* exist if I did not include the Option Explicit statement?

```
Option Explicit
Dim TotalItems
TotalItem = 10
```

That's right, I misspelled *TotalItems* as *TotalItem* when I was trying to set the variable equal to 10. If I hadn't specified the *Option Explicit* statement, using *TotalItem* would not have generated an error, and my total number of items as represented by *TotalItems* would have been 0.

Data Types

When defining variables in the previous section, we didn't have to worry about the type of data contained within a variable. The type of data contained in the variable is implicitly set the first time you initialize the variable, but you still need to understand the types of data supported by both JScript and VBScript.

JScript supports six types of data: numbers, strings, objects, Booleans, null, and undefined. I'll explain all of these except objects, which are covered in the next chapter. VBScript supports only one type of data: variant.

Numbers

JScript variables can contain both integer and floating-point numbers. A variable that contains an integer can contain negative or positive whole numbers, including 0. A variable that contains a floating-point number can contain a positive or negative number that includes either a decimal point, an exponent that's represented by either a lowercase or an uppercase "e", or both. This exponent represents 10 to the power of the number that follows the lowercase or uppercase "e" in scientific notation. For example, the number 1,250,000 can be represented in scientific notation in the following ways, although typically, 1,250,000 would be represented as 1.25e6:

```
1.25e6
12.5e5
125e4
1250e3
```

The exponent can also be a negative number. For example, you can represent .0025 in scientific notation as 2.5e–3. As you can see, there's a pattern to scientific notation. Usually, one number is to the left of the decimal place followed by the rest of the digits on the right, plus the exponent.

Integer numbers can be represented using different bases. In your day-to-day life, you typically encounter only decimal numbers, which are base 10 and easy to deal with. However, integers can also be represented as octal (base 8) and hexadecimal (base 16) numbers.

You can specify that a number is octal by placing a 0 in front of it. Octal numbers can contain only the digits 0 through 7. If a number contains a leading 0 but is followed by the digit 8 or 9, the number is interpreted as a decimal number. Some examples of octal numbers follow. I listed the decimal equivalent next to each number so that you can more easily understand them.

Octal	Decimal
01	1
010	8
021	17

You can specify that a number is hexadecimal (or hex, for short) by placing a 0x in front of it. Hex numbers can contain only the digits 0 through 9 and letters A through F. The letter A represents 10 in decimal, the letter B represents 11, and so forth. The letters A through F can be in either uppercase or lowercase. Following are some examples of hex numbers. Again, I listed decimal equivalents next to the numbers to make them easy to understand.

NOTE The formulas for converting between bases are outside the scope of this book. If you need to convert between number bases, using the Calculator program that comes with Windows or a good scientific calculator is the easiest way.

Hex	Decimal
0x1	1
0x10	16
0xA	10
0x21	33
0xFF	255

Strings

A string is a series of characters enclosed in single or double quotation marks. A string is special because it is also an object. Here are some examples of strings:

```
var str1 = "Hello, World!";
var str2 = '"Hello, Tom", said Mary.';
var str3 = "";
```

The variable *str1* should be pretty obvious. It just contains a string of characters that say "Hello, World!". However, *str2* deserves further consideration. If a string will contain double quotation marks, as in the case of quoting something said, the entire string must be enclosed in single quotes. Notice that *str3* contains no characters—a string can contain zero or more characters. When it contains no characters, it's referred to as a zero-length string.

Booleans

Boolean variables can contain only one of two different values—*true* or *false*. Boolean values are most often used in conditional expressions, which we'll look at later in this chapter. One important point to remember about the values *true* and *false* is that, unlike in any other programming language, they can't be interchanged with the numbers 1 and 0, respectively.

Null and undefined

The null data type is used when a variable contains nothing and has no value. The undefined data type is merely a value that is given to a variable after it's declared and before it's set to any other value. You can't tell what type of data is contained in the variable; you know only that the data is undefined.

Variants

Unlike JScript variables, VBScript variables can contain only one type of data—a variant. A variant holds many other types of data depending on how the variant is being used. The setup of a variant isn't important here—what is important is the type of data that can be held in a variant. The easiest way to understand this data type is to ignore the fact that the actual data type is a variant. When you're dealing with the data, it will appear to you as if you're dealing directly with the data type stored in the variant. Table 2-3 lists all the data types that can be held in a variant and briefly describes them.

TABLE 2-3
ALLOWABLE DATA TYPES IN A VARIANT

Data Type	Description
Empty	Empty or uninitialized. Value is *0* for numeric variables and a zero-length string for string variables.
Null	No valid data.
Integer	Integer value in the range −32,768 through 32,767.
Long	Long integer value in the range −2,147,483,648 through 2,147,483,647.
Single	Single-precision floating-point number.
Double	Double-precision floating-point number.
Currency	Currency value representing money.
Date	Data from January 1, 100, through December 31, 9999.
String	Variable-length string of characters.
Object	Objects that can be assigned to refer to an actual object of an application.
Error	Error number.
Boolean	Boolean value containing either True or False.
Byte	Single-character value from 0 through 255.
Array	Array of data.

To determine the type of data contained in a variant in VBScript, you can use the *VarType* function. This function returns a constant that represents the type of data contained in the variant. For example, if the variant contains a Boolean data value, the *VarType* function will return the *vbBoolean* constant. Also, it's possible to convert between data types stored in a variant using any of the VBScript conversion functions.

Arrays

Arrays are provided in both JScript and VBScript. Arrays provide you with a way to group together a number of different items of the same type in one data structure. For example, let's say you were writing script to keep track of the total cost of all items that a particular customer ordered. You can build an array that contains the cost of each item that was ordered by the customer. In JScript, you would define the array using the *new* operator, which allows you to create a new object, and the *Array()* constructor.

```
var charges = new Array(100);
```

In VBScript, you'd define the array like this:

```
Dim charges(100)
```

In both JScript and VBScript, even though these arrays are defined as having a size of 100, the first element in the array is 0 and the last is 99 because arrays in JScript and VBScript are zero-based. Remember this fact when you're accessing elements in an array. If you wanted to access the 54th element in the array, you'd reference element 53. In JScript, you reference an item in an array using the array name and an array index enclosed in square brackets. In VBScript, you reference items in an array using the array name and an array index enclosed in parentheses.

This example shows you how to set and get values in JScript arrays:

```
charges[0] = 10.50;  // Set item number 0, the first item, to 10.50.
var itemPrice = charges[0];  // Get the value of the first item.
charges[3] = 1.25;  // Set the value of the fourth item to 1.25.
```

This example shows you how to set and get values in VBScript arrays:

```
charges(0) = 10.50   ' Set item number 0, the first item, to 10.50.
Dim itemPrice
itemPrice = charges(0)   ' Get the value of the first item.
charges(3) = 1.25   ' Set the value of the fourth item to 1.25.
```

Operators

Operators do just what their name suggests—they perform some sort of operation on a variable or on literal data. Literal data consists of numbers (0 through 9), single characters (a through z and A through Z), and strings of characters. When an operation is performed on a variable or a literal data item, the variable or literal data item is referred to as an operand. You can perform operations such as assignment, addition, subtraction, multiplication, division, modulo, equality, inequality, and so forth. For example, to add two variables and assign the value of the addition to a third variable, you might write VBScript code like this:

```
Dim a, b, c
a = b + c
```

In this case, the operators are the assignment operator (=) and the addition operator (+). The operands are a, b, and c.

Table 2-4 lists the basic JScript operators, and Table 2-5 lists the basic VBScript operators. I purposely omitted the more advanced ones such as the bitwise operators. They're better left to a more advanced discussion of scripting.

TABLE 2-4
BASIC JSCRIPT OPERATORS

Arithmetic		*Logical/Comparison*	
Description	*Symbol (Prec.)*	*Description*	*Symbol (Prec.)*
Unary Negation—returns a negative number if the value it is applied to is positive, and vice versa.	– (1)	Logical Not—logically negates a value. For instance, returns *false* if the value is *true*, and vice versa.	! (1)
Increment—increases the value of a variable by 1.	++ (1)	Less than—determines whether the value on the left-hand side (lhs) of this operator is less than the value on the right-hand side (rhs).	< (4)
Decrement—decreases the value of a variable by 1.	—— (1)	Greater than—determines whether the lhs is greater than the rhs.	> (4)
Multiplication—multiplies two numbers.	* (2)	Less than or equal to—determines whether the lhs is less than or equal to the rhs.	<= (4)
Division—divides two numbers.	/ (2)	Greater than or equal to—determines whether the lhs is greater than or equal to the rhs.	>= (4)
Modulo—returns the remainder of the division of two numbers.	% (2)	Equality—determines whether the lhs is equal to the rhs.	== (5)
Addition—adds two numbers. Also used for string concatenation.	+ (3)	Inequality—determines whether the lhs is not equal to the rhs.	!= (5)
Subtraction—subtracts one number from another.	– (3)	Logical AND— returns *true* if the expressions on the lhs and the rhs are both true. Otherwise, returns *false*.	&& (6)
		Logical OR— returns *true* if either of the expressions on the lhs and the rhs is true. Returns *false* only if they're both false.	|| (6)

TABLE 2-5
BASIC VBSCRIPT OPERATORS

Arithmetic			*Logical/Comparison*	
Description	*Symbol (Prec.)*		*Description*	*Symbol*
Exponentiation—raises the left-hand side (lhs) value to the power of the right-hand side (rhs) value.	^ (1)		Equality—determines whether the lhs is equal to the rhs.	=
Unary Negation—returns a negative number if the value it's applied to is positive, and vice versa.	– (1)		Inequality—determines whether the lhs is not equal to the rhs.	<>
Multiplication—multiplies two numbers.	* (1)		Less than—determines whether the value on the left-hand side (lhs) of this operator is less than the value on the right-hand side (rhs).	<
Division—divides two numbers and returns a floating-point number.	/ (1)		Greater than—determines whether the lhs is greater than the rhs.	>
Integer division—divides two numbers and returns an integer.	\ (1)		Less than or equal to—determines whether the lhs is less than or equal to the rhs.	<=
Modulo—returns the remainder of the division of two numbers.	Mod (1)		Greater than or equal to—determines whether the lhs is greater than or equal to the rhs.	>=
Addition—adds two numbers. Also can be used for string concatenation.	+ (2)		Object equivalence—determines whether the object on the lhs is equivalent to the object on the rhs.	Is
Subtraction—subtracts one number from another.	– (2)		Logical Not—logically negates a value. For instance, if the value is *true*, it returns *false*, and vice versa.	Not
String concatenation— concatenates two strings.	& (2)		Logical AND—returns *true* if the expressions on the lhs and the rhs are both true. Otherwise, returns *false*.	And
			Logical OR—returns *true* if either of the expressions on the lhs and the rhs is true. Returns *false* only if they're both false.	Or

Note that I've listed the operators in order of their precedence. The precedence of an operator determines the order in which it's evaluated in an expression. For example, consider the following equation:

```
result = 2 + 10 * 5
```

If you read this equation left to right, the value of *result* would be *60*. However, according to the rules of precedence, the value of *result* is actually *52* because the multiplication operator has a higher precedence than the addition operator.

When two operators have the same precedence, they're evaluated left to right. For example, consider this equation:

```
result = 2 + 10 - 4
```

After evaluating, the value of *result* is 8. The addition and subtraction operators have the same precedence, so the equation is evaluated left to right. If you look again at the operator table for JScript, you'll see that a number in parentheses appears below each operator. You can use this number to determine whether one operator has the same precedence as another. These numbers appear only in the first column of the VBScript table because precedence is straightforward in VBScript. The comparison operators all have the same precedence and are evaluated in left-to-right order. The arithmetic operators are ordered by their precedence, and the numbers below the operators indicate which operators have the same precedence.

You can override the precedence of an operator by using parentheses. However, inside the parentheses, normal precedence rules apply. For example, let's look again at the original expression (2 + 10 * 5) that resulted in the value *52*. This time, however, we'll use parentheses:

```
result = (2 + 10) * 5
```

Because of the parentheses, the expression 2 + 10 is evaluated first. The result is 12, which is then multiplied by 5. That means the value of *result* is *60* in this case. (As you're referring to these tables, remember that I haven't included the more advanced operators.) For information about these operators and their precedence, see one of the references listed in the "Where to Go for More Information" section.

It should be pretty easy to understand how most of the operators in Tables 2-4 and 2-5 work. String concatenation, however, deserves some explanation. String concatenation involves joining multiple strings together end to end. In both JScript and VBScript, you can use the addition operator to concatenate strings, as in the following examples. The first example is in JScript:

```
var str;
str = "Hello " + "World!";
```

This example is in VBScript:

```
Dim str
str = "Hello " + "World!"
```

Although using the addition operator for concatenation does work in VBScript, using the string concatenation operator (&) is considered better coding style. Using the & operator in VBScript makes your code easier to read. Say, for example, that you have two variables that contain strings, and you concatenate them using the addition operator. By looking only at the addition of the two variables, nobody can tell whether the variables hold numeric or string data. The individual maintaining your VBScript code would have to look for the initialization of the two variables to determine your intentions. On the other hand, if you used the string concatenation operator, it would be clearly evident that you're concatenating two strings and not adding numeric data.

Here's the same example using the string concatenation operator instead. Note, however, that the string concatenation operator is specific to VBScript. This operator has a totally different meaning in JScript.

```
Dim str
str = "Hello " & "World!"
```

Expressions

An expression in scripting is any combination of variables, operators, constant values, and other expressions that form some result. In the discussion of variables and operators, you've already encountered expressions. A simple expression consists of one operator and two operands. Here's an example of a simple JScript expression:

```
var a = b + c;
```

In this expression, *a* is set to equal the value of *b* added to the value of *c*. More complex expressions can contain multiple operators and operands, as in this VBScript example:

```
Dim a
a = b + c * 10
```

This example actually contains two expressions. Because of the rules of precedence, we can use parentheses to clarify the example:

```
Dim a
a = b + (c * 10)
```

Now it's easy to see that *c * 10* is the first expression to be evaluated. The second expression that is evaluated is *b + the result of c * 10*. Let's say that *c* is 5 and *b* is 4. The result of the first expression, *c * 10*, is 50. The second expression, then, is *4 + 50*. Therefore, after both expressions are evaluated, *a* is equal to 54.

Arithmetic operators aren't the only ones that you can use in expressions. You can also use any of the operators in Tables 2-4 and 2-5. For example, you can use the logical operators in expressions:

```
Dim c
c = a <> b
```

In this VBScript example, *c* is set to the result of the expression *a <> b*. If you look at Table 2-5, you'll see that <> is the inequality operator. Therefore, the expression *a <> b* means "is *a* not equal to *b*?" If *a* is not equal to *b*, then *c* will be set to *true*. If *a* is equal to *b*, then *c* will be set to *false*.

Expressions don't always have to include the assignment operator as they have in all the examples so far. In some situations, expressions don't include assignments at all, as you'll see in the next section about program flow. Just remember that, at the very least, an expression contains one operator and at least one operand. Wait a minute! Didn't I say earlier that a simple expression consists of one operator and two operands? Yes, I did. However, in some cases, an operator requires only one operand. Take, for instance, the case of the JScript increment operator, ++. This operator requires only one operand. Take a look at the following example:

```
var count = 0;
count++;
```

Here I defined a variable named *count* and gave it an initial value of 0. Then I applied the increment operator to the *count* variable. The increment operator increases the value of *count* by 1. Therefore, the value of *count* after applying the increment operator is 1. So, as you can see, an expression requires at least one operator and one operand.

Controlling Program Flow with Conditional Statements

What good would any programming language be if it didn't provide a way to execute code based on the result of some condition? Both JScript and VBScript provide conditional statements that allow you to choose which block of script to execute based on some condition. The types of conditional statements in JScript and VBScript are basically the same. The way these concepts are implemented is different based on the language. I'll cover each of the types of conditional statements and how to use them in both JScript and VBScript.

If blocks

An *If* block is a series of statements that tests whether the result of an expression is true or false and executes a block of code based on the result. In JScript, you use the *if* statement followed by an expression in parentheses, as in the following example:

```
if (a == 10)
    b = a;
```

In this block of code, the value of *a* is tested to see whether it's equal to 10. If the value of *a* is equal to 10, *b* is set to the value of *a*. This simple example contains only one line of code to be executed if the result of the expression is true. If you want to execute multiple lines of code, you surround the block of code with braces ({}). Here's the same example with some additional code:

```
if (a == 10)
{
    b = a;
    str = "a is equal to 10";
}
```

As you can see, this is much easier to read. Therefore, it's often smart to use braces even if the code block contains only one line of code.

To use *If* blocks in VBScript, you use the *If* keyword, followed by an expression that evaluates to True or False, and the *Then* keyword. In addition, you must use the *End If* keyword clause to designate the end of the code block. Unlike JScript, the *End If* keyword clause must be used even if the code to be executed consists of only one line. Here's the previous example written in VBScript:

```
If a = 10 Then
    b = a
    str = "a is equal to 10"
End If
```

The only situation in which the *End If* clause isn't required occurs when the entire statement is on a single line, like this:

```
If a = 10 Then b = a
```

You can also specify alternative blocks of code that will be executed if the expression in the initial *If* block is evaluated to False. In JScript, you can use the *else if* and *else* clauses to execute alternative blocks of code. The best way to illustrate how to use these is with another example:

```
if (a == 10)
{
    str = "a is equal to 10";
}
else if (a == 11 || a == 12)
{
    str = "a is equal to 11 or 12";
}
else
{
    str = "a is not equal to 10, 11, or 12";
}
```

In this example, *a* is first tested to see whether it's equal to 10. If so, *str* is set to the string "a is equal to 10" and none of the additional *else if* or *else* clauses are evaluated. If *a* isn't equal to 10, the *else if* clause is evaluated. In this case, *a* is evaluated to see whether it's equal to 11 or 12. If it is, *str* is set equal to the string "a is equal to 11 or 12" and the final *else* clause isn't evaluated. If *a* isn't equal to 10, 11, or 12, the code in the final *else* block is executed, in which case *str* is set equal to the string "a is not equal to 10, 11, or 12".

You can also specify alternative blocks of code to be executed in VBScript using *ElseIf* and *Else* clauses. These clauses work exactly the same as *else if* and *else* in JScript. Here's the example that I just showed you but written in VBScript syntax:

```
If a = 10 Then
    str = "a is equal to 10"
ElseIf a = 11 Or a = 12 Then
    str = "a is equal to 11 or 12"
Else
    str = "a is not equal to 10, 11 or 12"
End If
```

When creating *If* blocks in either JScript or VBScript, you can have as many *else if* (JScript) or *ElseIf* (VBScript) statements as you want. However, the *if/If* statement must always be first, and the *else/Else* statement must always be last in the series.

Selection blocks

Another form of conditional statement is *selection*. In *selection*, an expression is evaluated once. The result of the expression is then compared against a number of cases in the *selection* block. If any of the values of the cases match the value of the expression, the code below the *case* statement is executed. In addition, it's possible to include a default case that's executed if none of the other cases matches the value of the expression. *selection* blocks differ from *if* blocks in that the expression in a *selection* block is evaluated only once. In an *if* block, many expressions can be evaluated depending on whether you have *else if* statements. *selection* blocks tend to be speedier than *if* blocks.

In JScript, *selection* blocks are often referred to as *switch* statements or *case* blocks because to implement a *selection* block in JScript, you use a *switch* statement in conjunction with a number of *case* statements. They work exactly as I just described. First the expression in the *switch* statement is evaluated. Then the value returned from the expression is tested against each *case* statement, in order. If the value of the expression matches a value in a *case* statement, the code below the *case* statement is executed. If the value of the expression doesn't match any of the values of the *case* statements, the code below the default label is executed if it's present. Here's the example that I used for JScript *if* blocks, using *selection* instead:

```
switch(a)
{
    case 10:
        str = "a is equal to 10";
        break;
    case 11:
        str = "a is equal to 11";
        break;
    case 12:
        str = "a is equal to 12";
        break;
    default:
        str = "a is not equal to 10, 11, or 12";
        break;
}
```

You might be wondering what the deal is with the *break* statements that I included. In JScript *switch* statements, if you don't include the *break* statement, program execution continues through the rest of the case statements. In other words, if I didn't include the *break* statements and the value of *a* were 10, all lines of code below the case statement for 10 would be executed. This means that at the end of this *switch* statement, *str* would contain the string "a is not equal to 10, 11, or 12"—not at all what we intended. So be careful.

However, this fact makes it easy for you to execute the same block of code for multiple values of the expression. In the example for JScript *if* blocks, I used the same line of code to execute the following: if *a* is equal to 11 or equal to 12. The *switch* statement had two *case* statements—one for 11 and one for 12. You can use the knowledge of program flow that I just mentioned to condense the code a bit.

```
switch(a)
{
    case 10:
        str = "a is equal to 10";
        break;
    case 11:
    case 12:
        str = "a is equal to 11 or 12";
        break;
    default:
        str = "a is not equal to 10, 11, or 12";
        break;
}
```

As you can see in the *selection* block, if the value of *a* is 11 or 12, *str* is set to the string "a is equal to 11 or 12". This is much more efficient and much easier to read.

In VBScript, the concept of selection is almost exactly the same as in JScript. The only difference is the statements you use. To evaluate the expression, you use the *Select Case* clause. To test the value of the expression, you use *Case* statements. To specify a default case, you use the *Case Else* clause. Also, whereas JScript uses braces to denote the beginning and ending of the *selection* block, VBScript uses the *Select Case* and *End Select* clauses to denote the beginning and ending of the *selection* block, respectively. Let's take a look at the JScript selection example written in VBScript:

```
Select Case a
    Case 10:
        str = "a is equal to 10"
    Case 11:
        str = "a is equal to 11"
    Case 12:
        str = "a is equal to 12"
    Case Else:
        str = "a is not equal to 10, 11, or 12"
End Select
```

In this VBScript *selection* block, I didn't use the *break* statement as I did in JScript because program execution in VBScript is different from program execution in JScript. Execution in a VBScript *selection* block doesn't fall through if you don't specify a *break* statement. Only the code associated with the correct *Case* statement is executed. Although this means that problems won't occur if you forget a *break* statement, it also means that you can't group *Case* statements together as I did in the previous JScript example.

Loops

Looping gives you the ability to run the same block of code as many times as you want. This allows you to perform such tasks as adding up all the values in an array or requesting user input and displaying a message while the user is entering incorrect data. The various ways to execute loops are similar in JScript and VBScript; therefore, I'll cover each method in turn and explain how it applies to both JScript and VBScript.

While loops

A *while* loop is used to specify that a block of code should be executed while some condition is true. In JScript, *while* loops are coded using the *while* keyword. In VBScript, you use a combination of the *While* and *Wend* keywords. For instance, remember the array earlier in this chapter that keeps track of the total cost of all the orders that a customer made? We can use a *while* loop in JScript to tally up the total charges for that customer, like this:

```
var total = 0.0;
var chargeNum = 0;
var charges = new Array(100);

while (chargeNum < 100)
{
    total += charges[chargeNum];
    chargeNum++;
}
```

This example first defines a counter named *chargeNum* that keeps track of the current position in the *charges* array. This counter is initially set to 0. The *while* loop is executed while the expression "chargeNum < 100" is true. In other words, the *while* loop executes while *chargeNum* is less than 100, which is the total number of items in the array. Each time through the *while* loop, the current charge in the array is added to the current total. Next, *chargeNum* is incremented by 1. This is an important step because if we didn't increment *chargeNum* by 1, we would create what's known as an infinite loop—a loop that never ends.

Two JScript keywords are worth mentioning at this point—*break* and *continue*. When you want to exit a JScript loop, you can specify the *break* statement. For example, you can stop the tallying of items in the array when you reach an item equal to 0.0. This way, if only three charges are in the array, you don't have to tally up all the items in the array. You can tally up just the first three:

```
while (chargeNum < 100)
{
    if (charges[chargeNum] == 0)
        break;
    total += charges[chargeNum];
    chargeNum++;
}
```

The *continue* statement allows you to skip the rest of the code in the code block and continue executing the next iteration of the loop. For example, what if a charge in the array is negative? In reality, this would probably be a credit in our bills, but in our example we don't allow negative numbers. You can use the *continue* statement to skip negative values:

```
while (chargeNum < 100)
{
    if (charges[chargeNum] < 0)
        continue;
    total += charges[chargeNum];
    chargeNum++;
}
```

Coding this looping example in VBScript is easy. All you have to do is use the *While* and *Wend* keywords:

```
Dim total
Dim chargeNum
Dim charges(100)

total = 0.0
chargeNum = 0

While chargeNum < 100
    total = total + charges(chargeNum)
    chargeNum = chargeNum + 1
Wend
```

Do loops

The *do* loops are quite flexible. They allow you to execute a block of code at least once while a condition is true, until a condition is false, or until a condition is true (VBScript only). The way *do* loops function is somewhat different in JScript and VBScript. In JScript, a *do* loop has a specific syntax and works in a particular manner. *Do* loops in VBScript have many different variations. The basic concept is that a *do* loop executes a block of code at least once. This concept is different from *while* loops in that a *while* loop might never execute a block of code, depending on the expression being evaluated.

To implement *do* loops in JScript, you use the *do* and *while* keywords in conjunction. Let's take the example we've been working with in this section and convert it to a *do* loop:

```
do
{
    total += charges[chargeNum];
    chargeNum++;
} while (chargeNum < 100);
```

In this case, the block of code is first executed, and then the condition is checked. The outcome is basically the same. In this example, using a *do* loop didn't buy us anything. However, if you run into a situation in which you want to execute a block of code one or more times, a *do* loop is the answer.

In VBScript, the *Do* loop has many variations, but each variation uses the *Do* and *Loop* keywords in some fashion. For instance, you might want to execute a block of code one or more times while some condition is true, as we did in the earlier JScript example. In VBScript, you can accomplish this using the *Do* keyword in combination with the *Loop While* clause. Here's the VBScript code that executes a block of code one or more times while some condition is true:

```
Do
    total = total + charges(chargeNum)
    chargeNum = chargeNum + 1
Loop While chargeNum < 100
```

You can also execute a block of code 0 or more times, in the same way you can with a *While* loop. Actually, many people prefer using a *Do* loop in this manner rather than using the *While* loop in VBScript. To do this in VBScript, you use the *Do While* clause in combination with the *Loop* keyword, as in this example:

```
Do While chargeNum < 100
    total = total + charges(chargeNum)
    chargeNum = chargeNum + 1
Loop
```

Sometimes you might want to execute a block of code one or more times until some condition is true. For instance, using the example we've been working with so far, you might want to loop until *chargeNum* is equal to 100 instead of while it's less than 100. To do this, you can use the *Do* keyword in combination with the *Loop Until* clause, as in this example:

```
Do
    total = total + charges(chargeNum)
    chargeNum = chargeNum + 1
Loop Until chargeNum = 100
```

You can also execute this block of code 0 or more times using the *Do Until* clause in combination with the *Loop* keyword, like so:

```
Do Until chargeNum = 100
    total = total + charges(chargeNum)
    chargeNum = chargeNum + 1
Loop
```

For loops

In the *while* and *do* loops, I had to keep a counter variable to tell me the current position of the array. Then, in each case, I had to manually increment the counter variable. What a pain. "Isn't there an easier way?" you ask. Fortunately for you and me, there is. Both JScript and VBScript have what are known as *for* loops, which allow you to execute a block of code while some condition is true. "Big deal," you say. "Isn't that what *while* and *do* loops are for?" The major advantage of *for* loops is that they automatically increment a counter variable for you. Let's convert our JScript example from a *while/do* loop to a *for* loop:

```
var total = 0.0;
var charges = new Array(100);
```

(continued)

```
for (var chargeNum = 0; chargeNum < 100; chargeNum++)
{
    total += charges[chargeNum];
}
```

This code provides the same result as the code using the *while* and *do* loops, but it's easier to read. Let's analyze this a bit, shall we? The *for* loop consists of three parts, each separated by a semicolon. The first part—*var chargeNum = 0*—is the initialization section. This is where you define and initialize your counter variables. The next section is the conditional expression. This expression is evaluated each time through the loop. When this expression returns *false*, the loop is exited. The third section in the *for* loop is the increment section. This is where you specify how you want the counter variables to be incremented. In this case, I had the *for* loop increment *chargeNum* by 1 each time through the loop. The incrementing of the counter variable occurs after each time the code block is executed and before the conditional expression is tested.

Coding a *For* loop in VBScript is simple. You just use the *For*, *To*, *Step*, and *Next* keywords. Let's convert this example to VBScript:

```
Dim total
Dim chargeNum
Dim charges(100)
total = 0.0

For chargeNum = 0 To 99 Step 1
    total = total + charges(chargeNum)
Next
```

Using the *Step* keyword, you can specify how much to increment the counter variable. You can step by 1, 2, or the value of some variable.

For each /For...in

Another form of the *for* loop makes life even easier. If you're dealing with arrays, you can use a special form of the *for* loop to iterate through an entire array. This version of the *for* loop iterates only through the actual number of items in the array. In other words, if you define the array as having a size of 100, but it contains only three items, this version of the *for* loop will stop after three items. In JScript, you can use the *for...in* keywords to loop through an entire array. Let's convert our JScript sample once again to use this construct:

```
var total = 0.0;
var charges = new Array(100);
for (var chargeNum in charges)
{
    total += charges[chargeNum];
}
```

In VBScript, you use the *For Each* and *Next* keywords in conjunction to perform the same function. Let's convert our JScript example to VBScript:

```
Dim total
Dim chargeNum
Dim charges(100)

total = 0.0

For Each chargeNum in charges
    total = total + charges(chargeNum)
Next
```

As you can see, loops give you tremendous control over the flow of your programs. And remember, you can combine conditional statements with loops to give you the ultimate control.

Subroutines and Functions

Often when writing script, you find yourself typing the same bit of code over and over again. Perhaps you're writing code to check the value of a variable and perform some action depending on the value of that variable. Wouldn't it be great if you could write the code just once and reuse it whenever you needed to? Guess what? You can.

By using subroutines and functions, you can group blocks of code together and execute them whenever you want just by calling the subroutine or the function by name. But what's the difference between subroutines and functions? Subroutines are blocks of code that perform some action when called but don't return anything to the caller. Functions are the same as subroutines, but they do return results to the caller. VBScript has both subroutines and functions; JScript has only functions, so you can choose whether or not to return results to the caller. The best aspect of subroutines and functions in JScript and VBScript is that tons of them are available for you to use from third-party developers as well as from the two scripting languages themselves. So you can reuse code that was written by somebody else, and you don't have to reinvent the wheel. For example, you'll use two functions provided in both JScript and VBScript most often: *alert* and *prompt*. (The *alert* and *prompt* functions are actually members of the *window* object. More on that in the next chapter.) The *alert* function displays a message box that contains some text that you want to display to the user. To call the *alert* function (or any other function, for that matter) from JScript, simply specify the name of the function and its parameters in parentheses. The *alert* function takes one input parameter that's the string you want to display to the user. Here's how you can display the string "Hello, World!" to the user in JScript:

```
alert("Hello, World!");
```

To call the *alert* function from VBScript, simply specify the name of the function and its parameters. When calling a subroutine or a function in VBScript, you don't have to include the parentheses unless you're going to use the return value from a function. (More on that later in this chapter.) Here's how you can display the string "Hello, World!" to the user in VBScript:

```
alert "Hello, World!"
```

Figure 2-14 shows the dialog box displayed by a call to the *alert* function in JScript or VBScript.

Figure 2-14. *Dialog box displayed by a call to the* alert *function.*

VBScript also includes another function that's similar to the *alert* function named *MsgBox*, and it can be used to display a message to the user. The difference between the *alert* and *MsgBox* functions is that the *MsgBox* function is much more versatile. You can specify a number of different arguments to tell it how the message box should be displayed. For example, you might want to ask the user a question and provide him or her with buttons to select Yes or No. Also, you'll want to know which button the user pressed. Fortunately, *MsgBox* returns the value of the button that was pressed. For example, to ask the user whether you should proceed, you would call the *MsgBox* function, like this:

```
<SCRIPT LANGUAGE="VBScript">
    Option Explicit
    Dim Ans

    Ans = MsgBox("Should I proceed?", vbYesNo)
```

```
    If Ans = vbYes Then
        ' Do something cool
    End If
</SCRIPT>
```

Note that I used parentheses when calling the *MsgBox* function in this case. That's because I needed to set the *ans* variable to the return value of the *MsgBox* function. The dialog box displayed by this call to the *MsgBox* function is shown in Figure 2-15.

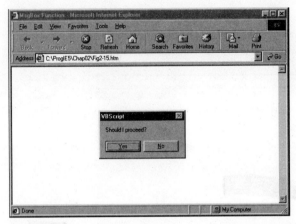

Figure 2-15. *Dialog box displayed by a call to the* MsgBox *function.*

Another important function is the *prompt* function. It allows you to display a message box to ask the user to input some data. This message box contains an input field for the user to input data. You can also specify a default value for the input field when displaying the message box. If you don't specify a default value, the string "undefined" is displayed in the input field. The *prompt* function returns the value that the user typed in the input field. For example, if you want to ask the user to enter the price of an item, you can call the *prompt* function from JScript, like this:

```
var price = 0.0;
price = prompt("Please enter the price of the item", price);
```

This example displays a message box containing the specified string and the default value *0* in the input field. You can perform the same action from VBScript, like this:

```
Dim price
price = 0.0
price = prompt("Please enter the cost of the item", price)
```

Figure 2-16 shows the dialog box displayed by a call to the *prompt* function in JScript or VBScript.

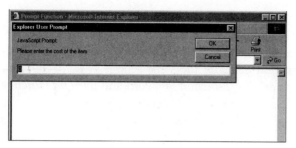

Figure 2-16. *Dialog box displayed by a call to the* prompt *function.*

Now that you have learned how to call functions and subroutines, you're probably wondering how you can create your own. In JScript, you use the *function* keyword to create a function. For instance, if you wanted to create a function that asks the user for the current price of an item, validates the entered price, and displays a message box to tell the user whether the price is valid, you could create the following function:

```
function getPrice(defaultPrice)
{
    var price = defaultPrice;
    price = prompt("Please enter the price of the item", price);

    if (price != null)
    {
        if (price < 0)
            alert("The price of an item cannot be negative.");
        else
            alert("The price you entered is correct.");
    }

    return price;
}
```

The *getPrice* function takes one argument that specifies the default price to be displayed in the message box when prompting the user. The *price* variable is set equal to *defaultPrice*, and then the *prompt* function is called. If the user clicks the Cancel button, the *prompt* function returns *null*. That's why I check *price* to see whether it's *null*. If *price* isn't equal to *null*, I then check to see whether it's negative. If it's negative, I display a message box to tell the user that the price of an item can't be negative. If the item is positive, I display a message box to tell the user that everything is okay. Finally, I return the price entered by the user using the JScript *return* operator. You can call the *getPrice* function in the same way you call the *alert* and *prompt* functions. Here's one way you might call the *getPrice* function:

```
var cost = 0;
cost = getPrice(10.50);
```

Coding this function in VBScript is pretty easy, so let's go ahead and do it. The following VBScript function performs the same actions as the JScript function I just described. However, it uses the *Function* keyword and the *End Function* clause to specify the beginning and ending of the function:

```
Function getPrice(defaultPrice)
    Dim price
    price = defaultPrice
    price = prompt("Please enter the price of the item", price)

    If VarType(Price) <> vbNull Then
        If price < 0 Then
            MsgBox "The price of an item cannot be negative."
        Else
            MsgBox "The price you entered is correct."
        End If
    End If

    getPrice = price
End Function
```

As I mentioned, this VBScript code performs the same actions as the JScript code. The main difference is in the way the actions are executed. To return a value from a VBScript function, in the statement, the name of the function is set equal to the value you want to return, like the last statement in the function before the *End Function* clause in the previous example. The other major difference is how the code checks for a null return value from the *prompt* function. Remember that the only VBScript data type is variant. Most of the time, you shouldn't have to worry about this fact. But in this case, you do. To check for null values, you have to use the *VarType* function, which tells you the type of data that's being represented by the variant data type. In this case, if the user presses Cancel, the return value of the *prompt* function is a variant with the *vbNull* data type. The following is one way that you might want to call this function:

```
Dim cost
cost = getPrice(10.50)
```

As I mentioned at the beginning of this section, one other type of function exists in VBScript—a subroutine. Recall that a subroutine is a function that doesn't return a value; therefore, it's much easier to code. In the preceding example, a bit of code checks to see whether the price entered by the user is valid. This bit of code could be used in a lot of different places. Therefore, you'd better put it in a subroutine. To create a subroutine in VBScript, you use the *Sub* keyword with the *End Sub* clause. Here's a VBScript subroutine that validates the price of an item:

```
Sub checkPrice(price)
    If VarType(Price) <> vbNull Then
        If price < 0 Then
            MsgBox "The price of an item cannot be negative."
        Else
            MsgBox "The price you entered is correct."
        End If
    End If
End Sub
```

You can then call the *checkPrice* subroutine from within the *getPrice* function.

```
Function getPrice(defaultPrice)
    Dim price
    price = defaultPrice
    price = prompt("Please enter the price of the item", price)

    checkPrice price

    getPrice = price
End Function
```

You can easily see how using functions and subroutines can condense your code and reduce the amount of typing that you have to do.

CREATING A SIMPLE SCRIPT APPLICATION

Now that you know the basics of writing script code using JScript and VBScript, you can create Web pages that contain script. Let's create a simple script application. After you learn about objects and DHTML in the next chapter, you'll be able to create more complex scripting applications. The following sample application simply displays a message box to ask for the user's name. Then it displays another message box that says hello to the user. I'll demonstrate how to do this in both JScript and VBScript. The JScript code appears in Listing 2-1. The VBScript code appears in Listing 2-2. This code is also available on this book's companion CD.

The code in Listings 2-1 and 2-2 is pretty self-explanatory. A function is created named *getName* that prompts the user for a name using the *prompt* function. The *getName* function takes a parameter that will be used for the default value displayed by the *prompt* function. The *getName* function returns the name entered by the user or *null* if the user clicks the Cancel button. If the name returned from *getName* isn't *null*, a message box is displayed that says "Hello" to the user. The script in the body section of the HTML calls the *getName* function in a *do* loop until the user presses Cancel in the prompt dialog box.

SayHelloJS.htm

```
<HTML>
<HEAD>
    <TITLE>SayHelloJS - Say Hello JScript</TITLE>

    <SCRIPT LANGUAGE="JScript">
        function getName(name)
        {
            return prompt("What is your name?", name);
        }
    </SCRIPT>
</HEAD>
<BODY>
    <H2>Press Refresh to Start Again</H2>

    <SCRIPT LANGUAGE="JScript">
        var name = "you";

        do
        {
            name = getName(name);

            if (name != null)
                alert("Hello " + name);
        } while (name != null);
    </SCRIPT>
</BODY>
</HTML>
```

Listing 2-1.

SayHelloVB.htm

```
SayHelloVB.htm<HTML><HEAD>
    <TITLE>SayHelloVB - Say Hello VBScript</TITLE>

    <SCRIPT LANGUAGE="VBScript">
        Function getName(name)
            getName = prompt("What is your name?", name)
        End Function
    </SCRIPT>
</HEAD>
```

Listing 2-2.

(continued)

Listing 2-2. *continued*

```
<BODY>
    <H2>Press Refresh to Start Again</H2>


    <SCRIPT LANGUAGE="VBScript">
        Dim name
        name = "you"

        Do
            name = getName(name)

            If VarType(name) <> vbNull Then
                MsgBox "Hello " & name
            End If
        Loop Until VarType(name) = vbNull
    </SCRIPT>
</BODY>
</HTML>
```

Figure 2-17 shows the dialog box that asks for the user's name, and Figure 2-18 shows the dialog box that displays the hello message. The dialog box that displays the hello message looks a little different in the JScript example than in the VBScript example—in the JScript example I used the *alert* function and in the VBScript example I used the *MsgBox* function. Figure 2-18 shows the dialog box displayed by the VBScript example.

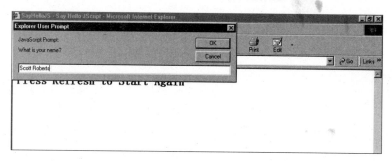

Figure 2-17. *Dialog box that asks for the user's name.*

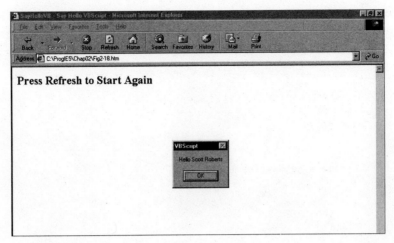

Figure 2-18. *Dialog box that displays the hello message.*

WHAT'S NEXT?

This chapter laid the groundwork for building DHTML applications by teaching you how to create Web pages using basic HTML and script. Now that you have the basics under your belt, it's time to learn how to use DHTML. In the next chapter, I'll tell you all about DHTML, including the DHTML Object Model.

Chapter 3

Programming with DHTML

After reading Chapter 2, you should be able to program for Microsoft Internet Explorer using basic HTML and script. Now we'll move on to the really cool aspects of Internet Explorer programming. This chapter covers most of the Dynamic HTML (DHTML) features that were introduced in Internet Explorer 4 as well as those that were added to version 5. (I'll explain some of the other exciting DHTML features as the book progresses.) First we'll look at DHTML and the DHTML Object Model, which enables you to access every HTML element on a Web page. Then we'll check out all the interesting features of DHTML—cascading style sheets (CSS) and positioning, dynamic properties, printing support, mouse capture, and context menus. DHTML is the basis for most of the material we're going to cover in the rest of the book.

So you're probably wondering what Dynamic HTML means. Well, it means exactly what it sounds like—DHTML is HTML that is dynamic. As you'll recall from Chapter 1, prior to Internet Explorer 4, HTML was static. Whatever you placed on a Web page stayed the same throughout the life of that Web page. The only way you could change the contents of a page was to somehow invite the user to refresh the page so that Internet Explorer could go to your Web server and get a new version of the page. If your Web page was accepting data from a user, you couldn't validate that information on the fly. You had to make another trip to the server to validate it, usually by having the user click a button on a form, click on a hyperlink, or use a refresh <META> tag to force Internet Explorer to refresh the page after a certain amount of time.

Not only are these techniques clumsy, they're inefficient. Why should Internet Explorer have to make another trip to your Web server to update your Web page or validate data entered by the user? In a typical Microsoft Windows application, you don't have to revisit a server to update information or validate data in a dialog box or other window. Usually, your program performs this kind of action dynamically. This makes the entire user experience much more pleasant.

Using DHTML, you can build Web-based applications that act just like typical Windows applications. You can dynamically update your Web page or perform data validation without having to revisit your server, and all this can be done on the client side. Let's take a look at the DHTML Object Model.

WHERE TO GO FOR MORE INFORMATION

This chapter provides a good general introduction to Dynamic HTML. If you want more advanced information, take a look at the MSDN Online Web Workshop or the book *Dynamic HTML Reference and Software Development Kit: Comprehensive Reference to DHTML for Microsoft Internet Explorer 5* (Microsoft Press, 1999) by Microsoft Corporation.

DHTML OBJECT MODEL

As you learned in Chapter 1, starting with version 3, Internet Explorer provided an object model: a hierarchy of interconnected and interrelated objects, such as the window, the document, and the different elements on a Web page that are represented by HTML tags. This hierarchy of objects enables you to traverse the Web page document to interrogate it. In other words, the object model enables you to determine which information on the Web page has been entered by the user.

In the Internet Explorer 3 object model, the data on a Web page was static—you could read what was on the page, but you couldn't actually change it after the Web page had loaded. Additions to the Internet Explorer 4 and 5 object models allowed you to change the information displayed on a Web page, so now your pages are dynamic! You can access and change almost every item on your page, thereby providing a much richer experience for your users. The capability to make pages dynamic resulted in a name change for the object model, from Internet Explorer Object Model to DHTML Object Model. Figure 3-1 shows a diagram of the DHTML Object Model.

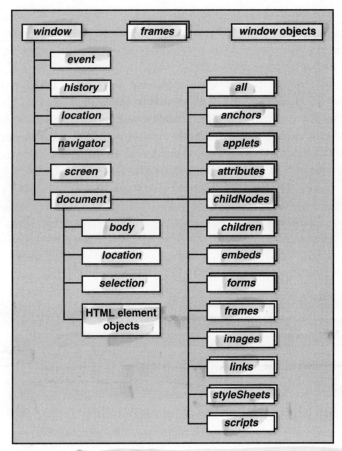

Figure 3-1. *DHTML Object Model, previously known as Internet Explorer Object Model.*

Objects

Before learning about the objects in the DHTML Object Model, you need to understand what an object is and what it can do. In real life, an object is anything from a coffee cup to a car. In Internet Explorer terms, an object is anything from the window in which a Web page is displayed to an HTML element on that page. Every object is made up of methods, properties, events, and collections. An Internet Explorer Web page contains many objects. Each HTML element is itself an object that has methods, properties, and events, and might contain collections. And some objects on a Web page aren't necessarily represented by an HTML element, such as the window in which the Web page is displayed.

Methods

Methods are the actions performed by an object. For example, the methods of your car would be drive, stop, turn, and so on. Methods accept input parameters and return values, but not always. Calling a method of an object is just as easy as accessing a property of the object. (Properties, which define the object, are described in the next section.) Let's look at an example of an object by using a car analogy. Suppose we have the *MyCar* object. We can call the *drive* method to force the car to move. The *drive* method takes one input parameter that equals the speed, in miles per hour, at which we want to move. After calling the *drive* method, we can call the *stop* method to stop the car. Obviously, this example is simple. In reality, we might have a distance property that tells us how far we've gone, and we might stop only after we've traveled a certain distance. Moving and stopping the car by using methods in Microsoft JScript is simple, as shown here:

```
MyCar.drive(65);
MyCar.stop();
```

Properties

Properties are all the characteristics that define the object. For instance, your car has a specific color, such as white, red, or blue. Also, your car might be compact, medium-sized, or large. The color and size of your car are both properties of the car. Some properties of a Web page object might be its height, width, or color. Properties can be read-only, write-only, or read/write. A read-only property is a property whose value you can read but not change. A write-only property is one whose value you can change but never read. And a read/write property is one that you can read and change.

Scripting a property of an object is simple. Let's consider again our car object named *MyCar*. *MyCar* has the properties of color and size. The color property is read/write, and the size property is read-only. Using Microsoft VBScript, here's how we would script the properties of *MyCar* to change its color and read its size:

```
Dim sizeOfCar
MyCar.color = "red"
SizeOfCar = MyCar.size
```

Events

Events are notifications that are triggered by an object. Just like methods, events can have input parameters. Sometimes information about an event is stored in another object known as an event object. An *event* object provides a way for the object that is sending a notification to specify pertinent information about the notification. The object that triggers the notification sets the properties of the *event* object that pertain to the current event. *Event* objects are maintained by Internet Explorer.

The process of triggering a notification is called firing an event. Clients of an object handle the events they are interested in. To handle an event, you have to create an event handler function for it.

You can handle events for Internet Explorer in three ways. The first way is by creating an event handler that is named by combining the name of the object with the name of the event. Suppose the *MyCar* object causes two events named *OnCrash* and *OnStalled*. In our car example, an event handler in VBScript for the *OnCrash* event is created by combining the name of the object, *MyCar*, with the event to be handled, *OnCrash*, as shown in the code that follows. In VBScript, you join the name of the object and the name of the event with the underscore (_) character. You don't have to worry about capitalization because VBScript isn't case sensitive.

```
<SCRIPT LANGUAGE="VBScript">
Sub MyCar_OnCrash
    MsgBox "Aaaahhhh!!!"
End Sub
</SCRIPT>
```

The way you create event handlers in JScript is similar to the way you create them in VBScript—you simply combine the name of the object with the name of the event. In JScript, however, you join the object and the name of the event with a period, or as my British friends like to call it, a full stop. Remember that JScript is case sensitive, so you must use the correct case for the object and event name when you create event handlers by joining the name and the object. Handling the *OnStalled* event in JScript is as easy as this:

```
<SCRIPT LANGUAGE="JScript">
MyCar.OnStalled()
{
    alert("Time to buy a new car.");
}
</SCRIPT>
```

Most Internet Explorer Web page developers that I know prefer the second way to handle events: using the FOR and EVENT attributes of the <SCRIPT> tag to bind a block of script to a particular event of a particular object. Here's how you can use this approach to handle the *OnStalled* event in VBScript:

```
<SCRIPT LANGUAGE="VBScript" FOR=MyCar EVENT=OnStalled>
    MsgBox "Can somebody give me a lift?"
</SCRIPT>
```

Although this approach is convenient if you have only one or two event handlers on your Web page, if you have many it can quickly become cumbersome. I prefer the first method for handling events. It's easier to have one script block on a Web page with as many event handlers inside the script block as you want.

The third way to handle events for objects applies only to HTML elements (or HTML tags). When inserting an HTML element on a Web page, you specify events that you want to handle as attributes of the HTML element. You can specify inline script for the event handler or specify a function that will be called when the event occurs. JScript is the default language used for this type of event handler, but you can change the language by using the LANGUAGE attribute. For example, the element <BUTTON>, which is also an object, fires an event named *onclick*. Here are a few examples of how you can use this approach to handle events for the *onclick* event of the *button* object:

```
<BUTTON onclick="alert('Clicked')">Click Me</BUTTON>
<BUTTON LANGUAGE="VBScript" onclick="MsgBox 'Clicked'">Click Me</BUTTON>
<BUTTON onclick="btnClicked()">Click Me</BUTTON>
```

The first line of code calls a JScript function named *alert* when the button is clicked. The second line calls a VBScript function named *MsgBox* when the button is clicked; in this line, I had to specify the LANGUAGE attribute with a value of *VBScript* to change the default language for scripting events. The third line of code calls a JScript function named *btnClicked* when the button is clicked.

Collections

A collection is an object that is also a group of objects. Because a collection is an object, it has properties and methods just like any other object. Collections are usually contained within another object and are typically accessed through a property of another object. For example, your car has a collection of wheels, a collection of turn signals, and another collection of headlights. Likewise, the *MyCar* object has *wheels*, *signals*, and *headlights* collections, and it would most likely have *wheels*, *signals*, and *headlights* properties to provide us with access to its collections.

Collections usually have a *length* property that tells you how many objects are in the collection, and an *item* method that allows you to gain access to a specific object within the collection. Other collections might have other properties, methods, or both, as you'll see when I talk about collections in the DHTML Object Model. Writing script for collections is just as easy as writing script for methods and properties. For example, to determine how many wheels are on our car in VBScript, we'd write this code:

```
Dim numWheels
numWheels = MyCar.wheels.length
```

You might think this code looks a little strange. But remember that *wheels* is a property of the *MyCar* object that returns a collection of wheels, and that a collection is just an object that has its own properties and methods. The *length* property is just a member of the *wheels* collection object. By using what's known as object chaining in VBScript and JScript, you can join together properties or methods that return objects. The preceding code is the same as the next bit of code, but object chaining makes the it much easier to read and to write:

```
Dim numWheels
Dim wheelsColl

Set wheelsColl = MyCar.wheels
numWheels = wheelsColl.length
```

Collection objects typically have a method named *item* that allows you to access a specific item within the collection. The *item* method usually takes two parameters. The first parameter can be either a number or a string that specifies the item you want. If you specify a number for this parameter, *item* returns the element in the collection at the position you specified. The first element in the collection has a value of *0*, the second element has a value of *1*, and so on. If you specify a number for the first parameter, you don't have to worry about specifying the second parameter.

If you specify a string for the first parameter, the *item* method returns a collection of elements. All HTML elements on a Web page can have a NAME attribute, an ID attribute, or both associated with them. The collection returned from the *item* method when you specify a string for the first parameter is a group of all the elements on the Web page that have a name or an ID that matches the string you specify. In this case, you can specify a number for the second parameter that indicates the position of the element in the collection created by *item*.

To better understand this concept, let's look again at the *wheels* collection of the *MyCar* object. The front tire on the left side of the car is the first tire in the collection. Using VBScript, you can access the front tire like this:

```
Dim frontTire1
Set frontTire1 = MyCar.wheels.item(0)
```

The *item* method returns a tire object that is stored in a variable named *frontTire1*.

There's another way to access the *frontTire* object. You'll often see script like this for accessing an object in a collection:

```
Dim frontTire1
Set frontTire1 = MyCar.wheels(0)
```

This looks kind of strange, doesn't it? The *item* method is the default method for a collection object. The default method is called when no method of an object is selected. In the case of the *wheels* collection, because we didn't specify a method to call, Internet Explorer passes the parameter in parentheses to the default method, which is the *item* method.

In addition to accessing an object in a collection using a numeric index, you can access an object by name. Let's say that the *frontTire* object has a NAME attribute or an ID attribute of *FrontTire*. Using this name, we can call the *item* method and pass it the name of the front tire. Remember, though, that when we pass a string to the *item* method, the method returns a collection of objects that match the name we supply, even if only one object has that name. Therefore, we must supply a numeric index for the second parameter.

For this example, let's assume that only one tire has the name *FrontTire*. With that in mind, we'll pass an index of *0* for the second parameter, because the object we want will be the first object in the collection returned by the *item* method. Here's how we would access the *frontTire* object from JScript using the name of the tire:

```
var frontTire;
frontTire = MyCar.wheels.item("FrontTire", 0);
```

Also, because the *item* method is the default method of the collection, we can access the *frontTire* object without actually typing the name of the *item* method into our script. Here's how we can access the *frontTire* object by forcing Internet Explorer to call the default method in JScript:

```
var frontTire;
frontTire = MyCar.wheels("FrontTire", 0);
```

DHTML OBJECTS

Now that you understand the concept of an object and its methods, properties, events, and collections, let's examine the most important objects in the DHTML Object Model. These objects are the ones you'll encounter frequently when writing script for your Web pages or when creating full-blown Web applications, which I'll show you how to do in Chapter 4. We'll start off with the objects you'll use the most and progress to some of the lesser-used objects.

Each HTML tag on a Web page is represented by an object in the DHTML Object Model, so there are far too many objects to discuss in this book. After I explain the most common objects that you'll use, I'll cover methods, properties, and events that are common to most HTML elements on a Web page. Knowing these will make creating Web-based applications for Internet Explorer 5 easier.

window Object

The *window* object is the mother of all objects. It's the topmost object in the DHTML Object Model. The *window* object represents an open window in Internet Explorer. When you open a new instance of Internet Explorer, the *window* object is created first. It gives you access to an HTML document and all the HTML elements in the document. The *window* object also allows you to retrieve information about the state of the window.

When you open a new window, typically only one *window* object is created. However, if the Web page being displayed inside the window contains frames, one *window* object will be created for the topmost, or parent, window, and one *window* object will be created for each of the frame windows. In that case, the *window* objects within the frame windows are child windows of the topmost *window* object.

You've already seen and used one of the methods of the *window* object—the *alert* method. You can call the *alert* method whenever you want to display a dialog box to alert the user of something important. You might have noticed previously that when I called the *alert* method, I didn't specify the *window* object. You can call any of the methods, properties, events, or collections of the *window* object without having to specify it. If you don't specify an object name, Internet Explorer assumes that you mean the topmost *window* object. But if you want to call a method or property of a *window* object in a frame, you must specify the name of the *window* object in the frame. I'll show you how to do this shortly.

Methods

The *window* object for Internet Explorer 5 contains 26 methods—far too many to explain in detail. So I've listed all the methods and a short description of each in Table 3-1 on the following pages. I'll cover a few of the most common methods that you'll use—*open, close, navigate, showModalDialog,* and *showModelessDialog*—in a little more detail. We've already looked at *alert* and *prompt*.

TABLE 3-1
METHODS OF THE *WINDOW* OBJECT

Method	Description
alert	Displays a dialog box containing a message and an OK button.
attachEvent	Attaches the specified function to an event so that the function gets called whenever the event is fired on the *window* object.
blur	Causes the window to lose focus and fires the *onblur* event.
clearInterval	Clears the interval previously set by the *setInterval* method.
clearTimeout	Clears the timeout previously set by the *setTimeout* method.
close	Closes the window associated with the *window* object specified.
confirm	Displays a confirm dialog box that contains a message and the OK and Cancel buttons.
detachEvent	Detaches the specified function from an event so that the function is no longer called when the event is fired by the *window* object.
execScript	Enables you to dynamically execute script.
focus	Sets the focus to the specified *window* object and causes the *onfocus* event to fire.
moveBy	Moves the screen position of the window by the x and y offsets specified.
moveTo	Moves the screen position of the upper left corner of the window to the specified x and y coordinates.
navigate	Causes the window to navigate to the specified URL.
open	Opens a new window and causes it to navigate to the specified URL.
print	Prints the document that's loaded in the window.
prompt	Displays a dialog box with a message and an input field.
resizeBy	Changes the current size of the window by the specified x and y offsets.
resizeTo	Sets the current size of the window to the specified values.
scroll	Scrolls the window to the specified x and y offsets at the upper left corner of the window.
scrollBy	Scrolls the window by the specified x and y offsets relative to the current scroll position.
scrollTo	Causes the window to scroll to the specified x and y coordinates at the upper left corner of the window.
setInterval	Causes an expression to be evaluated each time the specified interval elapses.
setTimeout	Causes an expression to be evaluated after the specified timeout has occurred.

Method	Description
showHelp	Displays the specified help file.
showModalDialog	Displays a modal dialog box that shows the HTML document given by the specified URL. This dialog box is application modal, meaning that the Web page that called this method can't be accessed until this dialog box is closed.
showModelessDialog	Displays a modeless dialog box that shows the HTML document given by the specified URL. In contrast to a modal dialog box, the Web page that called *showModelessDialog* can be accessed while this dialog box is displayed.

The *open* method is probably the *window* object method that you'll use most often. This method enables you to open a new Internet Explorer window from your Web page. When opening the window, you can specify the URL that Internet Explorer should navigate to. In addition, you can specify other options that determine how the new window will appear. For instance, you can specify whether you want the new window to have a toolbar, a status bar, or an address bar.

Let's check out a few examples to learn how to use the *open* method. The first example, which is in JScript, simply opens a new Internet Explorer window with all the default options to navigate to Microsoft's home page. We'll specify a name of the window as the second parameter. We can use this name as the TARGET attribute for the <FORM> tag or anchor (<A>) tag.

```
var wnd;
wnd = window.open("http://www.microsoft.com", "MSHOME");
```

As the example shows, the *open* method returns a *window* object for the new window so that you can access the different methods, properties, and so on, of the new window. Another method of the *window* object that you'll probably want to call is the *close* method. You'll invariably want to close the new window at some point, unless you expect the user to close it. To close the new window, just call the *close* method, like this:

```
wnd.close();
```

For a more advanced example, let's open a new Internet Explorer window with a height of 200 pixels and a width of 100 pixels. This new window won't have a menu bar, toolbar, status bar, or address bar. We'd want this type of window to display if we wanted to provide a help screen in response to the user clicking a Help button on our page. We'll use VBScript to implement the Help button and the Help window, as shown in Listing 3-1 on the next page. The results of the HTML code are shown in Figure 3-2.

HelpWnd.htm

```
<HTML>
<HEAD>
    <TITLE>Help Window</TITLE>
    <SCRIPT LANGUAGE="VBScript">
    Sub ShowHelpWindow
        window.open "HelpPage1.htm", "HelpWnd", _
          "height=200,width=500,toolbar=no,status=no,menubar=no,location=no"
    End Sub
    </SCRIPT>
</HEAD>
<BODY>
    <BUTTON onclick="ShowHelpWindow()">Help</BUTTON>
</BODY>
</HTML>
```

Listing 3-1.

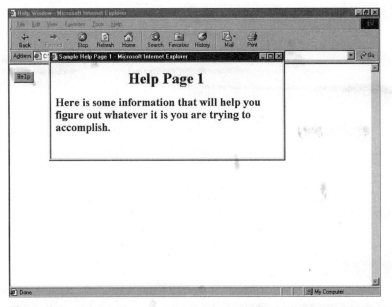

Figure 3-2. *Help window.*

Another reason you might want to use the *open* method is to allow your users to navigate through multiple pages of help using the same Help window. This basically provides context-sensitive help for our application. To accomplish this in our simple example, we'll place multiple buttons on the main Web page. Each button will display different help pages using the same window. This time, we'll use Jscript, as shown in Listing 3-2. Figure 3-3 (on page 82) shows the results of the code.

MPgWnd.htm

```
<HTML>
<HEAD>
    <TITLE>Figure 3-3: Displaying Multiple Help Pages
           in the Same Window
    </TITLE>

    <SCRIPT LANGUAGE="JScript">
    function ShowHelpWindow(helpPage)
    {
        var sFeatures = "height=200,width=500,";
        sFeatures += "toolbar=no,status=no,";
        sFeatures += "menubar=no,location=no";

        window.open(helpPage, "HelpWnd", sFeatures);
    }
    </SCRIPT>
</HEAD>
<BODY>
    <BUTTON onclick="ShowHelpWindow('HelpPage1.htm')">
        Help (Page 1)
    </BUTTON>
    <BUTTON onclick="ShowHelpWindow('HelpPage2.htm')">
        Help (Page 2)
    </BUTTON>
</BODY>
</HTML>
```

Listing 3-2.

Listing 3-2 deserves a little closer inspection. In the script section of the page, we first created a function named *ShowHelpWindow* that is called when either the button for Page 1 or the button for Page 2 is clicked. Next we called the *open* method of the *window* object to open a new window using the height and width that we specified along with other features of the window. Now that wasn't too painful, was it? Using the *window.open* method enables you to provide content to your users for help or anything else you can think of.

Two other important methods of the *window* object are *showModalDialog* and *showModelessDialog*. The *showModalDialog* method allows you to create a modal dialog box that retains the focus until the dialog box is closed. In other words, as long as this dialog box is open, the user can't work inside the parent window that opened it. The *showModelessDialog* method allows you to create a modeless dialog box. Unlike *showModalDialog*, the *showModelessDialog* method allows your user to continue working in the parent window.

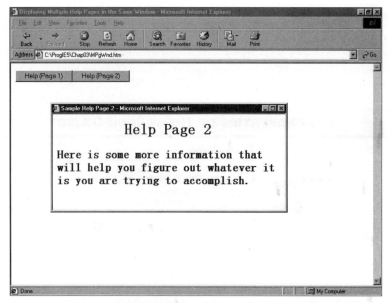

Figure 3-3. *Displaying multiple help pages in the same window.*

The *showModelessDialog* and *showModalDialog* methods are similar to the *open* method. The windows that open with *showModelessDialog* and *showModalDialog* act like normal Microsoft Windows dialog boxes in that they always remain on top of the parent window. To talk about the position of these windows more technically, we say that they have a higher Z-order than the parent window. (The Z-order of a window shows the window's position in a stack of overlapping windows.) Also, the windows created with *showModelessDialog* and *showModalDialog* have a default size that makes them appear more like normal Windows dialog boxes, whereas the window opened by a call to the *open* method has the default height and width of a normal Internet Explorer window.

Calling *showModelessDialog* and *showModalDialog* is easy. All we need is the URL of the Web page that we want to show in the newly opened dialog box. As with the *open* method, we can pass different parameter values to specify how the new dialog box should appear. However, *showModelessDialog* and *showModalDialog* don't return a *window* object. To see how easily we can call them, take a look at this JScript code:

```
showModalDialog("http://www.microsoft.com");
showModelessDialog("http://www.microsoft.com");
```

Properties

In Internet Explorer 5, the *window* object has 28 properties—far too many to discuss in detail. Table 3-2 provides a short description of all the properties of the *window* object, and we'll look briefly at those most widely used: *document, navigator, event, history,* and *location.*

TABLE 3-2
PROPERTIES OF THE *WINDOW* OBJECT

Property	Description
clientInformation	Returns the *navigator* object
closed	Returns a Boolean value to signify whether the specified window is closed
complete	Returns a Boolean value to indicate whether the specified window is fully loaded
dataTransfer	Provides access to different predefined clipboard formats that can be used in transferring data
defaultStatus	Sets or retrieves the message that will be displayed in the status bar at the bottom of the window by default
dialogArguments	Sets or retrieves the arguments passed into a dialog window that was created by a call to either *showModalDialog* or *showModelessDialog*
dialogHeight	Sets or retrieves the height of a dialog window that was created by a call to either *showModalDialog* or *showModelessDialog*
dialogLeft	Sets or retrieves the left coordinate of a dialog window
dialogTop	Sets or retrieves the top coordinate of a dialog window
dialogWidth	Sets or retrieves the width of a dialog window
document	Returns the object that represents an HTML document loaded into a window
event	Returns the *event* object that provides information about an event that's been fired
external	Returns an object that represents the host of the Web page (This property is discussed further in Chapter 9.)
history	Returns an object that provides information regarding previously visited URLs
length	Returns the number of frames contained in a particular window

(continued)

PROPERTIES OF THE *WINDOW* OBJECT *continued*

Property	Description
location	Returns an object that provides information about the current URL
name	Sets or retrieves the name of the window
navigator	Returns an object that provides information about Internet Explorer, such as the major and minor version numbers
offscreenBuffering	Sets or retrieves whether objects are rendered offscreen before being displayed to the user
opener	Sets or retrieves the object that opened the current window
parent	Returns the parent object of the current window
returnValue	Sets or retrieves the return value from a dialog window
screen	Returns an object that provides information regarding the client's screen
screenLeft	Returns the coordinates of the left edge of the client's screen
screenTop	Returns the coordinates of the top edge of the client's screen
self	Returns the current *window* object
status	Sets or retrieves the text that's displayed in the status bar of the window
top	Returns the topmost *window* object that is its own parent

The *document* property is probably the most important of the window properties that you'll use. The *document* property gives you access to the Web page document and allows you to retrieve and change the data on a page. The *document* property of the *window* object returns an object—the *document* object. I'll cover the *document* object in more detail following the discussion of the *window* object.

The *navigator* property is another important property, especially if you want to provide support for different versions of Internet Explorer or even other browsers. The *navigator* property returns the *navigator* object, as you might have guessed. This object gives you access to version information for the browser. I'll talk more about this object in the "*navigator* Object" section of this chapter.

The *window* object's event property returns an *event* object that provides information about an event that was fired somewhere in the window. This object contains information for any event that was fired for any object on the Web page because of what's known as event bubbling. Most events that are fired for objects on a Web page "bubble up" the object model hierarchy. Eventually, all events that bubble up reach the *window* object, so it makes sense to keep information about events in an object that can be retrieved from a property of the *window* object. I'll talk more about the *event* object in the "*event* Object" section of this chapter.

The *history* property returns a *history* object that provides information about URLs that Internet Explorer has navigated to previously. The methods of this object won't give you the actual URLs of the previously navigated sites, but they will allow you to cause Internet Explorer to navigate backward or forward one or more pages in the history. I won't discuss this object further, but I encourage you to read the documentation for it in the MSDN Online Web Workshop *(http://msdn.microsoft.com/workshop)*.

The *location* property returns a *location* object that provides information about the current URL that Internet Explorer has navigated to in the window. This object has a property named *href* that gives you the full current URL. Also, this object has other properties that give you different sections of the URL, such as the path name, port number, and text that follows a hash symbol (#) or a question mark (?) in the URL. I won't discuss the *location* object further, but I encourage you to visit—you guessed it—MSDN Online Web Workshop.

Events

In Internet Explorer 5, the *window* object fires 10 events. Remember, though, that you can handle any event that bubbles from below the *window* object as if it were fired by the *window* object. Table 3-3 briefly describes all the events that are fired directly by the *window* object. The only event that I'll cover now is *onload*. I'll discuss the *onafterprint* and *onbeforeprint* events later in this chapter in the "Printing Support" section.

TABLE 3-3
EVENTS OF THE *WINDOW* OBJECT

Event	Description
onafterprint	Fires immediately after printing the HTML document in the window.
onbeforeprint	Fires immediately before printing the HTML document in the window.
onbeforeunload	Fires before a page is unloaded.
onblur	Fires when the window loses the focus.
onerror	Fires when there's an error loading the window.
onfocus	Fires when the window receives the focus.
onhelp	Fires when the user presses the F1 key to invoke the help function. This event fires only if the window has the focus.
onload	Fires when the document in the window is completely finished loading.
onresize	Fires when the size of the window is about to change.
onunload	Fires right before the window is unloaded.

The *onload* event is fired when the Web page document is completely finished loading. Only after *onload* is fired can you safely call methods of objects on the Web page, because *onload* indicates that every object on the Web page has finished loading and is ready to be used.

> **WARNING**   In the time that I spent as a developer support engineer for Microsoft, I saw many problems occur when users tried to access methods or properties of a document or HTML elements on a page before the *onload* event was fired. Wait until the *onload* event fires before you try to change or retrieve information about the Web page. I can't stress this enough. Handling the *onload* event is just as easy as handling any other event from an object, as I showed you earlier.

Here is one way to handle the *onload* event from VBScript:

```
<SCRIPT LANGUAGE="VBScript">
Sub Window_onLoad
    ' Now you can safely access the document.
End Sub
</SCRIPT>
```

Remember the third approach to handling the *onload* event? (If you don't remember the other approaches to handling the *onload* event, I encourage you to re-read the "Events" section on page 85. The third approach was to handle the event by specifying it as an attribute of an HTML tag. You might be wondering how to handle window events without a <WINDOW> tag. Certain window events—*onblur, onfocus, onload,* and *onunload*—can be handled without a <WINDOW> tag by specifying each as an attribute of the <BODY> tag. In the following example, which shows how to do this in JScript, the *WindowLoaded* JScript function is called when the window is completely finished loading:

```
<BODY onload="WindowLoaded()">
```

Collections

The *window* object has only one collection—*frames*—which is a collection of all the frames on a Web page; in other words, it contains all the *window* objects that are in frames on the current page. If you need access to the actual *frame* object, you should use the *document.all* collection, which I'll explain when discussing the *document* object in the next section. Like other collections, the *frames* collection has an *item* method that you can use to access a specific frame in the collection by numeric index or name. The *item* method for the *frames* collection doesn't return a collection if you specify a string for the first parameter. It always returns the first *window* object that has the given name.

The *frames* collection also has a *length* property that you can use to retrieve the number of *window* objects in the collection. If the Web page has no frames, the *length* property returns the value *0*.

If we write script for a Web page that will be displayed in a frame, we can easily access methods, properties, and so forth, of the other frames by using the parent property of the *window* object. For example, let's say we're writing VBScript for a page that will be displayed in the second frame. (Remember that because the items in a collection are zero-based, the first frame is frame 0, and the second frame is frame 1.) The script we write will cause frame 0 to navigate to a new URL. Here's the VBScript that displays a page in the second frame:

```
Sub btn_onclick
    parent.frames(1).navigate "http://www.microsoft.com"
End Sub
```

> **NOTE** Internet Explorer doesn't allow you to access properties or methods of a frame's objects that are in a different domain from the one in which the script is written. In other words, if frame 0 has navigated to the microsoft.com domain, and frame 1 is in a different domain, script on the page in frame 1 can't access the properties and methods of the objects in frame 0. This security restriction was implemented to keep hidden frames from monitoring where you navigate to or obtaining password information from you.

document Object

The *document* object represents the HTML document and is one of the most important objects in the object model. The *document* object allows you to obtain access to the elements on a Web page and leverage the power of DHTML. As with the *window* object, I'll cover the most important methods, properties, events, and collections of the *document* object.

Methods

The *document* object has 33 methods. Table 3-4 gives a short description of all of them. The methods that you'll probably use most often are *open, write, writeln,* and *close*. I'll talk a little more about these and show you how to use them. I'll also talk about two really exciting methods—*createElement* and *insertAdjacentElement*.

TABLE 3-4
METHODS OF THE *DOCUMENT* OBJECT

Method	Description
appendChild	Appends an element to the document as a child.
applyElement	Applies one element to another element.
attachEvent	Attaches a function to an event so that the function will be called whenever the event fires.
clear	Clears the document.
cloneNode	Makes a copy of the document.
close	Closes and flushes the *document object*.
createDocumentFragment	Creates a new instance of the *document object*.
createElement	Creates an instance of an element for the specified tag.
createStyleSheet	Creates a style sheet for the document.
createTextNode	Creates a text string from the given value.
detachEvent	Detaches the specified function from an event so that the function will no longer be called when the event fires.
elementFromPoint	Returns the element at the specified x and y coordinates.
execCommand	Executes a command.
getAdjacentText	Returns the adjacent text character.
hasChildNodes	Returns whether or not the given node has children.
insertAdjacentElement	Inserts an element at the specified location.
insertBefore	Inserts an element into the document hierarchy.
open	Opens the document. This is typically used in conjunction with *write* or *writeln*.
queryCommandEnabled	Returns whether the command can be successfully executed using *execCommand*.
queryCommandIndeterm	Returns whether the state of the specified command is indeterminate.
queryCommandState	Returns the current state of the command.
queryCommandSupported	Returns whether the current command is supported on the current range.
queryCommandValue	Returns the current value of the given command.
recalc	Recalculates all dynamic properties in the current document. (I cover this method later in this chapter in the section "Dynamic Properties" on page 108.)

Method	Description
releaseCapture	Removes mouse capture from the document. (I cover this method later in this chapter in the section "Dynamic Properties" on page 108.)
removeChild	Removes a child node from an element.
removeNode	Removes the document from the document hierarchy.
replaceAdjacentText	Replaces the adjacent text with the specified text.
replaceChild	Replaces an existing child element with a new child element.
replaceNode	Replaces the document with a new element.
swapNode	Switches the location of two objects in the document hierarchy.
write	Writes HTML code to the document.
writeln	Writes HTML code to the document, followed by a new-line character.

To write HTML in the document, we can use the *open, write, writeln,* and *close* methods in conjunction. You might be wondering why we'd want to do this when we could just type in the HTML code when we create the page. Well, let's say we're creating a Web-based database application. In this application, we want the contents of our Web page to differ depending on the values stored in the database, so we use a little script code in combination with calls to the *open, write, writeln,* and *close* methods. Here's an example of how to use the method calls:

```
<SCRIPT LANGUAGE="VBScript">
    document.open

    ' val is a Boolean data value that was previously
    ' retrieved from the database
    If val = True Then
        document.write "<H1>Heading 1</H1>"
    Else
        document.write "<H1>Heading 2</H1>"
    End If

    document.close    ' You must have matching open and close calls
</SCRIPT>
```

Obviously, this example doesn't accomplish anything. Notice that this script code isn't inside a subroutine, which means that it's inline script code that will be executed as the document is being loaded. In this script code, we first called the *open* method to open the document, which is just like opening a file. Then, based on a Boolean value we previously retrieved from the database, we wrote out either Heading 1 or Heading 2. Finally, we closed the document.

> **TIP** To be safe, always have matching calls to *open* and *close*. If you don't, you might not run into problems immediately, but trust me—you will eventually. I've seen it happen many times.

The other two methods I want to introduce you to are *createElement* and *insertAdjacentElement*. These two methods really show the power of DHTML. By using them, you can dynamically add HTML elements to your page, perhaps in response to user input. The *createElement* method is used to create a new *element object*, and the *insertAdjacentElement* method is used to insert the element at some position adjacent to another element on the page.

For example, here's a Web page that contains a text box and a button. After the user enters his name into the text box and presses the button, an <H2> element is inserted into the page with a nice hello message. Listing 3-3 shows the JScript code to perform this action. The results of Listing 3-3 are shown in Figure 3-4.

InsElmt.htm

```
<HTML>
<HEAD>
    <TITLE>Inserting Elements into a Document</TITLE>
    <SCRIPT LANGUAGE="JScript">
        function btnClicked()
        {
            var newElement = document.createElement("H2");

            document.body.insertAdjacentElement("BeforeEnd", newElement);
            newElement.innerText = "Hello there " + txtName.value;
        }
    </SCRIPT>
</HEAD>
<BODY>
    <INPUT TYPE="TEXT" ID="txtName">
    <BUTTON onclick="btnClicked()">SayHello</BUTTON>
</BODY>
</HTML>
```

Listing 3-3.

Listing 3-3 deserves closer inspection. The Web page first displayed to the user contains only an input text box and a button. When the user enters his name into the text box and presses the button, the *btnClicked* function is called, because we hooked this function into the *onclick* event of the <BUTTON> tag as an attribute. The *btnClicked* function firsts created a new element object for the <H2> element using the *createElement* method.

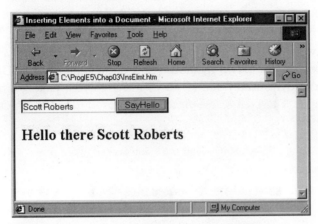

Figure 3-4. *Inserting elements into a document.*

Next, we called the *insertAdjacentElement* method by using the *body* object. (We also could have chosen the *button* or *input* object.) The first parameter of the *insertAdjacentElement* is important. It tells Internet Explorer where to place the new element adjacent to another. We can specify four values: *BeforeBegin*, *AfterBegin*, *BeforeEnd*, and *AfterEnd*. In the case of the *body* object, the only allowable values are *AfterBegin* and *BeforeEnd*. All values are valid for other objects.

After inserting the new element, we set its associated text to the hello message by calling the *innerText* method of the newly created object. I will talk more about *innerText* later in this chapter in the section "Other HTML Elements Important To DHTML."

Properties

The *document* object contains 35 properties. A short description of each is shown in Table 3-5 on the next page. I'll discuss only one of these properties, the *body* property, at some length. (You were already introduced to the *body* property in the example provided in the section titled "Methods," which starts on page 87.) The *body* property gives you access to the object that is represented in the document by the <BODY> tag. This object allows you to obtain and change the contents of the elements displayed to the user. A few methods enable you to change the document dynamically, and these are discussed later in this section.

TABLE 3-5
PROPERTIES OF THE *DOCUMENT* OBJECT

Property	Description
activeElement	Returns the object that has the keyboard focus.
aLinkColor	Sets or retrieves the color for all active links in the document.
bgColor	Sets or retrieves the background color of the document.
body	Returns the *body* object that's represented by the <BODY> tag.
charset	Returns the character set for the document.
cookie	Sets or retrieves the string value of a cookie, which is a small piece of information stored by the browser.
defaultCharset	Sets or retrieves the default character set.
designMode	Switches between browsing and editing mode.
documentElement	Returns the *document* object.
domain	Sets or retrieves the security domain for the document.
expando	Sets or retrieves whether or not arbitrary variables can be created within the document.
fgColor	Sets or retrieves the foreground text color.
fileCreatedDate	Returns the date a file was created.
fileModifiedDate	Returns the date a file was last modified.
fileSize	Returns the size of a file.
firstChild	Returns a reference to the first child in the *childNodes* collection.
lastChild	Returns a reference to the last child in the *childNodes* collection.
lastModified	Returns the date the Web page was last modified.
linkColor	Sets or retrieves the color of the hyperlinks in a document.
location	Returns an object that contains information about the current URL.
nextSibling	Returns a reference to the next sibling of an object.
nodeName	Returns the name of an element.
nodeType	Returns the type of the node requested.
nodeValue	Sets or retrieves a node's value.
parentNode	Returns the parent node of an object in the document.
parentWindow	Returns the parent window for the document.
previousSibling	Returns a reference to the sibling immediately preceding the specified object.
protocol	Returns the protocol (access method) of a particular URL.
readyState	Returns the current state of the document (in other words, whether or not the document is finished loading).
referrer	Returns the URL of the previous Web page.

Property	Description
selection	Returns an object that represented the currently selected block of text, object, or objects.
title	Returns an object that contains the title of the document.
uniqueID	Returns a unique identifier for the document. This unique identifier is generated when you access the *uniqueID* property.
URL	Sets or retrieves the URL of the current document.
vlinkColor	Sets or retrieves the color of hyperlinks that have already been visited.

Events

The *document* object has 21 events, which are listed in Table 3-6. Because you've already seen some of the most important events and the rest are pretty self-explanatory, I won't discuss them further.

TABLE 3-6
EVENTS OF THE *DOCUMENT* OBJECT

Event	Description
onclick	Fires when the user clicks the left mouse button in the document
oncontextmenu	Fires when the user clicks the right mouse button in the client area of the document
ondblclick	Fires when the user double-clicks inside the document
ondrag	Fires continuously on the *source* object during a drag operation
ondragend	Fires on the *source* object at the close of a drag operation when the mouse is released
ondragenter	Fires on the target element when the document being dragged enters a drop target that is valid
ondragleave	Fires on the target element object during a drag operation when the mouse moves out of a valid drop target
ondragover	Fires on the target element while the document being dragged is over a valid drop target
ondragstart	Fires on the *source* object when the user first starts to drag a selection of text or an object
ondrop	Fires on the target object during drag-and-drop when the mouse button is released
onhelp	Fires when the user presses the F1 key
onkeydown	Fires on the down stroke when the user presses a key

(continued)

EVENTS OF THE *DOCUMENT* OBJECT *continued*

Event	*Description*
onkeypress	Fires after the user presses a key
onkeyup	Fires when the user releases a key
onmousedown	Fires when the user clicks on the document with the right or left mouse button
onmousemove	Fires when the user moves the mouse pointer anywhere over the document
onmouseout	Fires when the user moves the mouse pointer outside the document
onmouseover	Fires when the user moves the mouse pointer into the document
onmouseup	Fires when the user releases a mouse button while over the document
onpropertychange	Fires when a property of the document changes
onreadystatechange	Fires whenever the ready state for document has changed

Collections

The *document* object contains 14 collections, described in Table 3-7. Once you know how to work with one collection, you can work with them all, so I'm only going to discuss the *all* collection. The *all* collection comprises all elements contained in a document.

The *all* collection contains three methods and one property. I've already discussed the property (*length*) and one of the methods (*item*). Another method is *tags*. The *tags* method will retrieve a collection of all the objects in the *all* collection that have the specified HTML tag name. The final method is *urns*. It returns a collection of all the objects to which the specified behavior is attached. (Chapter 11 covers behaviors in more detail.)

TABLE 3-7
COLLECTIONS OF THE *DOCUMENT* OBJECT

Collection	*Description*
all	Returns a collection of all elements contained in the document.
anchors	Returns a collection of all the *anchor* objects in the document.
applets	Returns a collection of all the *applet* objects in the document. These objects are represented by the <APPLET> and <OBJECT> tags.
attributes	Returns a collection of attributes of an object.
childNodes	Returns a collection of the child nodes for the specified object.
children	Returns a collection of the direct descendants of an object.

Collection	Description
embeds	Returns a collection of all the *embed* objects in the document. The *embed* object is represented in the document by the <EMBED> tag.
forms	Returns a collection of all the *form* objects in the document.
frames	Returns a collection of all the *window* objects that exist on a Web page.
images	Returns a collection of all the *img* objects in the document. The *img* object is represented by the <IMG> tag.
links	Returns a collection of all the *anchor* objects that specify the *href* property and all the *area* objects in the document. The *area* object is represented by the <AREA> tag.
scripts	Returns a collection of all the *script* objects in the document. The *script* object is represented in the document by the <SCRIPT> tag.
styleSheets	Returns a collection of all the *styleSheet* objects in the document.

To learn how to use the *all* collection, look at this simple JScript example:

```
<SCRIPT LANGUAGE="JScript">
function listAllElements()
{
    for (var i = 0; i < document.all.length; i++)
    {
        alert(document.all(i).tagName);
    }
}
</SCRIPT>
```

This JScript function loops through all the objects in the *all* collection. The *length* property specifies how many objects are in the collection. For each iteration through the loop, an alert dialog box is displayed to list the name of the tag at the current position in the collection. See how easy it is to use collections?

navigator Object

The *navigator* object provides information about the browser in which your Web application is running, including the type of browser and its version. The most important component of the *navigator* object is its properties. I won't cover the methods and collections of the *navigator* object for a couple of reasons. First, it has only two methods, which aren't used that often. Second, the two collections are provided only for compatibility with other browsers and are therefore not implemented. No events exist for the *navigator* object.

Properties

The properties of the *navigator* object are listed in Table 3-8.

TABLE 3-8
PROPERTIES OF THE *NAVIGATOR* OBJECT

Property	Description
appCodeName	Returns the code name of the browser. (*Mozilla* is the code name returned by Internet Explorer.)
appMinorVersion	Returns the minor version of the browser.
appName	Returns the name of the browser.
appVersion	Returns the platform and version of the browser.
browserLanguage	Returns the current browser language.
cookieEnabled	Returns whether or not client-side cookies are enabled.
cpuClass	Returns a string that indicates the CPU class of the system on which the browser is running—for example, x86 and Alpha.
online	Returns whether or not the system is running in offline mode. This property is true when the user has chosen Work Offline from the Internet Explorer File menu.
platform	Returns the platform on which the browser is running.
systemLanguage	Returns the default language for the system.
userAgent	Returns the HTTP user-agent request header as a string.
userLanguage	Returns the current user language.

One of the most important reasons you'll use the *navigator* object is to determine the type and version of the browser in which your Web page is running. You can determine the name and version of the browser from the *appVersion* property. The string returned by the property contains the browser version, type, and the platform on which the browser is installed. For example, the string returned by the *appVersion* property for Internet Explorer 5 running on Windows NT is "4.0 (compatible; MSIE 5.0; Windows NT)". We can use JScript or VBScript string indexing functions to retrieve the information we want. For example, here's how we can extract the type and version of the browser in JScript:

```
var navVersion = navigator.appVersion;
var strArray = navVersion.split(";");
alert("The type and version of the browser are " + strArray[1]);
```

We created a variable named *navVersion* that holds the string that is returned from the *appVersion* property. This variable is a JScript *string* object, so we then call the *split* method to split the string into an array of strings. The string is split based on the semicolon. The string returned from *appVersion* gives us an array of three strings. The string at position 1 in the array is the string that indicates the type and version of the browser.

If we merely want to retrieve the name of the browser, the *navigator* object provides us with a property named *appName* that returns the name of the browser. This string is typically more descriptive than the name of the browser in the *appVersion* string. Here's the VBScript code to display the name of the browser:

```
MsgBox navigator.appName
```

event Object

The *event* object is extremely important when handling events on a Web page. It provides you with information about the event that occurred. This information could be the object that fired the event, the type of event, or other pertinent information such as the *x*-coordinate and *y*-coordinate of the mouse pointer when the event was fired.

Just like the *navigator* object, the most important component of the *event* object is its properties. In fact, the *event* object doesn't have any methods or events, and it has only two collections, which are of minor importance. So I'll concentrate on the properties and only briefly mention the collections of the *event* object.

Properties

The *event* object contains 26 properties, short descriptions of which are shown in Table 3-9 on the next page. Each of the properties of the *event* object is pretty easy to understand. To get you started, we'll look at a couple of them: *srcElement* and *cancelBubble*. The *srcElement* property returns a reference to the object that fired the event. Using this reference, you can obtain information about the object, such as its ID, name, and type. For example, we can create event handlers that handle all *onmouseover* events for the document. Each time the mouse is moved over an element on the Web page, the *onmouseover* event fires for that element. Because of the event bubbling mechanism we talked about earlier, the *onmouseover* event will bubble up the object hierarchy. If *onmouseover* had no handlers to cancel the bubbling, it would eventually reach the *document* object.

TABLE 3-9
PROPERTIES OF THE *EVENT* OBJECT

Property	Description
altKey	Returns whether the Alt key is pressed or not.
button	Returns which mouse button, if any, is pressed.
cancelBubble	Sets or retrieves whether or not the current event should bubble up the hierarchy of event handlers.
clientX	Returns the *x*-coordinate of the mouse pointer's position when the mouse button is clicked. This coordinate is relative to the size of the client area of the window.
clientY	Returns the *y*-coordinate of the mouse pointer's position when the mouse button is clicked. This coordinate is relative to the size of the client area of the window.
ctrlKey	Returns whether or not the Ctrl key is pressed.
dataFld	Returns the data column that is affected by the *oncellchange* event.
fromElement	Returns the object that the mouse pointer is exiting. This property applies only during the *onmouseover* and *onmouseout* events.
keyCode	Sets or retrieves the Unicode key code of the key that caused the event.
offsetX	Returns the horizontal coordinate of the mouse pointer's position. This coordinate is relative to the object that fired the event.
offsetY	Returns the vertical coordinate of the mouse pointer's position. This coordinate is relative to the object that fired the event.
propertyName	Returns the name of the property that has changed. This *event* object property should be used with the *onpropertychange* event.
reason	Returns the reason for completion for a data source object.
recordset	Returns a recordset if the object is a data provider.
repeat	Returns whether or not an event is being repeated.
returnValue	Sets or retrieves the value that will be returned from the event.
screenX	Returns the *x*-coordinate of the mouse pointer's position, in pixels. This position is relative to the screen.
screenY	Returns the *y*-coordinate of the mouse pointer's position, in pixels. This position is relative to the screen.
shiftKey	Returns whether or not the Shift key is pressed.
srcElement	Returns the object that fired the event.
srcFilter	Returns the *filter* object that fired the *onfilterchange* event.
srcUrn	Returns the universal resource name (URN) of the behavior that fired the event.

Property	Description
toElement	Returns the object being moved to. This property applies only to the *onmouseover* and *onmouseout* events.
type	Returns the name of the event.
x	Returns the *x*-coordinate of the mouse pointer's position when the event fired.
y	Returns the *y*-coordinate of the mouse pointer's position when the event fired.

To show in VBScript how to create event handlers that handle all *onmouseover* events for the document, we can use the following code and write the name of the tag that fired the event in the status area of the browser:

```
Sub document_onmouseover
    window.status = window.event.srcElement.tagName
End Sub
```

In this example, we set the *status* property of the *window* object to the name of the tag that fired the *onmouseover* event. We get this tag name by first getting the *event* object from the *window* object.

> **NOTE**   The previous example is one case in which you must specify the *window* object when accessing one of the properties of the *window* object. The *window* object must be specified when retrieving the *event* object via the *event* property. In VBScript, the code can't read *event.srcElement.tagName*. Trying to read this string results in a syntax error. You don't have to specify the *window* object if you're using JScript.

Next we get the *srcElement* property from the *event* object. Finally, we get the name of the tag from the *tagName* property of the object returned by the *srcElement* property.

In the previous example, we were able to handle all *onmouseover* events that were fired by elements on the page just by creating an event handler for the document's *onmouseover* event. We can do this because of Internet Explorer's event bubbling mechanism. (Not all events bubble up. See the MSDN Online Web Workshop documentation for the event in question to see whether it bubbles up.) If for some reason we want to cancel event bubbling somewhere along the way, we can set the *cancelBubble* property of the *event* object to *true*.

For example, let's say that on a page we have a button that has an ID of *btnClick*, and we want to handle the *onmouseover* event for the button to change the text of the button. In this case, we don't want the *onmouseover* event to bubble up to the document. We'll also handle the *onmouseout* event to change the text of the button back to its original state. In Listing 3-4 is the VBScript code that shows how to do this.

```
CaBubble.htm

<HTML>
<HEAD>
   <TITLE>Canceling Event Bubbling</TITLE>

   <SCRIPT LANGUAGE="VBScript">
   Sub document_onmouseover
      window.status = window.event.srcElement.tagName
   End Sub

   Sub btnClick_onmouseover
      btnClick.value = "Mouse Over"
      window.event.cancelBubble = True
   End Sub

   Sub btnClick_onmouseout
      btnClick.value = "Click Me"
   End Sub
   </SCRIPT>
</HEAD>
<BODY>
   <H1>Event Object Example</H1>
   <BUTTON ID="btnClick">Click Me</BUTTON>
</BODY>
</HTML>
```

Listing 3-4.

In Listing 3-4, we have a button on the page with an ID of *btnClick*. When the *onmouseover* event for the button fires, we change the text inside the button by setting the button's *value* property to *"Mouse Over"*. Then we set the *cancelBubble* property of the *event* object to *true* so that the event isn't bubbled up to the document—the document event handler for *onmouseover* isn't called. When we move the mouse away from the button, the *onmouseout* event fires and we set the value of the button back to its original value, *"Click Me"*.

Collections

The *event* object has only two collections, as shown in Table 3-10.

TABLE 3-10
COLLECTIONS OF THE *EVENT* OBJECT

Collection	Description
bookmarks	Returns a collection of Microsoft Active Data Objects (ADO) bookmarks that are connected to the rows effected by the event
boundElements	Returns a collection of all elements on the page that are bound to a data set

form Object

One final object worth mentioning is the *form* object. It represents the <FORM> tag on a Web page. Using the *form* object, you can obtain information that your users entered into the form. You can validate that information before it's sent to your Web server. The *onsubmit* event and the *elements* collection are the most important components of the *form* object that help you perform the validation.

The *onsubmit* event fires after the user presses the Submit button but before the data is actually sent to the server. To validate the data in your form, you can create an event handler for the *onsubmit* event. In your event handler, you'll use the *elements* collection to obtain references to all the *input*, *select*, and *textarea* objects in your form. Using these objects, you can obtain the data that the user entered and validate it. You can also use the *elements* collection to obtain a reference to a specific object in the form by specifying the object's ID. After you're finished validating the data, if everything is OK, you return *true* from the event handler. If the data is incorrect, you can return *false* to prevent the submission of the form.

Listing 3-5 (FrmValid.htm), which is on the companion CD, creates a form that contains an Input box and a Submit button. When a user presses the Submit button, the *onsubmit* event fires. In the event handler for this method, we make sure that the user has entered only numeric characters into the Input text box. If alphabetic characters were entered, we display an error message that asks the user to reenter the data. If everything is OK, we allow the form to be submitted to the server for processing.

FrmValid.htm

```
<HTML>
<HEAD>
    <TITLE>Validating Form Data</TITLE>
```

Listing 3-5.

(continued)

Listing 3-5 *continued*

```
<SCRIPT LANGUAGE="JScript">
  function Validate()
  {
    var txtVal =
        document.forms("Form1").elements("txtNumData").value;

    if (txtVal == "" || isNaN(txtVal))
    {
      alert("Please enter only numeric values");
      return false;
    }

    return true;
  }
</SCRIPT>
</HEAD>
<BODY>
  <FORM ID="Form1" METHOD="GET"
    ACTION="http://yourserver.com/SomeApp.asp"
    onsubmit="return(Validate())">

    Please enter a numeric value:
    <INPUT TYPE="TEXT" ID="txtNumData">
    <INPUT TYPE="SUBMIT" VALUE="SUBMIT">
  </FORM>
</BODY>
</HTML>
```

In this code, we first check to see whether the user entered a value into the text box. If a value was entered, we use the JScript *isNaN* function to determine whether it was numeric. If the value is not numeric, we display an error message and return *false* so that the form will not be submitted.

You can see how we can get access to the values the user entered. First we must get access to the *form* object. We can access this object by using the *forms* collection of the *document* object. Then we can get access to individual elements in the form using the *elements* collection. The value property of the INPUT element returns the text entered by the user—that is, if the type of this element is "TEXT".

Other HTML Elements Important to DHTML

So far, we've covered in detail only the major objects of the DHTML Object Model, but remember that every HTML element on a Web page is represented as an object in the object model—too many exist to discuss in detail here. Some important methods and properties, however, are common to all elements on a page, and a few of these are important to DHTML. I'll explain these methods in the context of three objects: *body*, *div*, and *span*.

You already know that the *body* object represents the <BODY> tag on a Web page, but you don't know about the *div* and *span* objects yet. The *div* object represents a <DIV> tag on a Web page. A <DIV> tag is basically a container for HTML. It is a block tag, so the closing tag is required. This tag allows you to wrap lines of HTML so that you can perform operations on them as if they were one object. Here's an example of HTML code using a <DIV> tag:

```
<DIV ID="div1" onclick="DivClicked()">
    <H2 ID="Heading2">Heading 2</H2>
    <H3 ID="Heading3">Heading 3</H3>
</DIV>
```

The <DIV> tag has an ID attribute that is used to identify the *div* object. After assigning a value to this attribute, you can access the *div* object by name in script. (As always, you can use the *all* collection to get to this object as well.) This ID attribute allows you to handle events for all elements within the *div* block. For example, to handle the *onclick* event for either the <H2> or <H3> tags in the *div* block, you can simply create an event handler for *div1*. Because of event bubbling, when you click on either the text surrounded by <H2></H2> tags or the text surrounded by <H3></H3> tags, the *onclick* event is bubbled up to the *div* object. Here's the VBScript code for an event handler for the *div* block's *onclick* event:

```
Sub DivClicked()
    MsgBox window.event.srcElement.id
End Sub
```

This code displays a message box that shows the ID of the element that was clicked. In this case, the ID will either be "Heading2" or "Heading3" because the source element will either be the <H2> tag or the <H3> tag.

The *span* object represents a <SPAN> tag on a Web page. The <SPAN> tag is similar to the <DIV> tag. However, whereas the <DIV> tag is a container for HTML, the <SPAN> tag is a container for text. Using the <SPAN> tag and the *span* object is exactly the same as using the <DIV> tag and the *div* object.

The *insertAdjacentHTML* method is one of the few common methods of HTML elements that are important to DHTML because it enables you to insert HTML directly into a Web page adjacent to other HTML. The *insertAdjacentHTML* method is similar to the *insertAdjacentElement* method in that it allows you to insert an HTML element adjacent to another element, but whereas you can insert only an HTML element object using *insertAdjacentElement*, you can insert an entire string of HTML using *insertAdjacentHTML*. The input parameters for *insertAdjacentHTML* are similar to those for *insertAdjacentElement*. The first parameter specifies where to insert the new text relative to the object on which you are calling this method. The allowable values are *BeforeBegin, AfterBegin, BeforeEnd,* and *AfterEnd*. The *BeforeBegin* value specifies to place the text before the beginning of the object; the rest of the values should be self-explanatory. If you're calling *insertAdjacentHTML* off the *body* object, the only allowable values are *AfterBegin* and *BeforeEnd*. Here's the JScript code to show you how to use the *insertAdjacentHTML* method:

```
function DivClicked()
{
    document.body.insertAdjacentHTML("AfterBegin",
       "<H1>Heading 1</H1>");
    document.all("div1").insertAdjacentHTML("AfterEnd",
       "<I>Some Text in italics</I>");
}
```

DivClicked is called in response to the user clicking a <DIV> tag named *div1*. In this code, we first insert some Heading Level 1 text after the beginning of the body. Next we insert some text in italics after the end of the *div* block. Notice how we use the *all* collection to get a reference to the *div* object that has the ID *div1*. In this case, because only one *div* object on the Web page has the ID *div1*, we don't need to specify the second parameter of the *all* collection. (You learned about the *all* collection earlier in this chapter, in the section titled "Collections" on page 94.) Another way to access the *div1* object is by name, which is more efficient than using the *all* collection. Here's the code from the preceding example, but this time referencing the *div1* object by name:

```
function DivClicked()
{
    document.body.insertAdjacentHTML("AfterBegin",
      "<H1>Heading 1</H1>");
    div1.insertAdjacentHTML("AfterEnd", "<I>Some Text in italics</I>");
}
```

Notice that JScript is case sensitive, so we must be sure to use the correct case when referencing the name of the object. Also in JScript, we must define the object somewhere in the document before the object can be used. For instance, the script code in the previous example must exist in the Web page after the <DIV> tag that has an ID of *div1*. VBScript doesn't have either of these requirements.

Four common properties are important to DHTML: *innerHTML, innerText, outerHTML,* and *outerText*. They all work in basically the same way. The properties with names beginning with *inner* set or retrieve HTML or text between the start and end tags of the current object. The *outerHTML* property sets or retrieves the current object and its content in HTML. The *outerText* property sets or retrieves the text of the current object.

So you can see how important these properties are to making HTML dynamic. They allow you to change the text or HTML inside HTML tags or to change the tags to something completely different. Let's look back at our example that used <DIV> tags. Here's the HTML code again to refresh your memory:

```
<DIV ID="div1" onclick="DivClicked()">
   <H2 ID="Heading2">Heading 2</H2>
   <H3 ID="Heading3">Heading 3</H3>
</DIV>
```

What if we want to change the text of the <H2> tag named *Heading2*? We can do so using the *innerText* property in VBScript, like this:

```
Sub DivClicked()
   Heading2.innerText = "New Heading"
End Sub
```

If we want to change the tag for *Heading3* from an <H3> tag to an <H4> tag, we could use the *outerHTML* property, like this:

```
Sub DivClicked()
   Heading3.outerHTML = "<H4 ID='Heading4'>Heading 4</H4>"
End Sub
```

Notice that in the preceding code, we're changing the ID of the tag. The next time we click on the *div* block, the script will result in a syntax error because *Heading3* will no longer exist. Therefore we might want to consider leaving the ID as it is.

Let's say that instead of changing each HTML element within the *div* block, we want to change all the HTML within the *div* block. We can do so using the *innerHTML* property of the *div* object named *div1*. Here's the VBScript code that changes the entire contents of the *div* block:

```
Sub DivClicked()
   div1.innerHTML = "<H1 ID='Heading1'>Heading 1</H1>" _
                  & "<I>Some Text in Italics</I>"
End Sub
```

Now that you know how easily you can make your Web pages dynamic, I bet you're ready to change them all today!

OTHER COOL DHTML FEATURES

In addition to the DHTML objects I have showed you so far, Internet Explorer offers a lot of other exciting features. Some of these features, such as cascading style sheets and positioning, dynamic properties, printing support, mouse capture, and context menus, are discussed in the following sections.

Cascading Style Sheets

If you've used Internet Explorer since version 3, cascading style sheets (CSS) are nothing new to you, although they weren't dynamic until Internet Explorer 4 and 5. If you've never used them, a little overview is in order. Basically, style sheets are design templates that give you control over the layout and presentation aspects of your Web page. They allow you to separate the design of your Web page from the actual content of the page. A discussion of CSS could fill an entire chapter, perhaps even a small book. We'll just focus on what you can do with CSS in Dynamic HTML.

To add CSS to a Web page, you typically use the <STYLE> tag, which is a block tag and requires a closing tag. You should specify the *style* block only in the <HEAD> section of the document. Using the <STYLE> tag, you can specify colors, fonts, and so on for elements on a Web page, like this:

```
<STYLE>
   BODY { background-color: green; }
   A    { text-decoration: none; color: blue;  }
</STYLE>
```

In this example, the background color for the document will be green, and all links on the page will be blue with no text decoration (for example, no underline). Any styles we set in the *style* block apply to all elements on the page of that type. If we want to set the style only for a particular element, we can specify the style as an attribute of the element. For example, to specify a style for one anchor tag, we'd use the STYLE attribute, like this:

```
<A ID="A1" HREF="http://yourserver.com/"
   STYLE="text-decoration: none; color: blue">Some Link</A>
```

As I discussed earlier, each tag on a Web page is represented in the DHTML Object Model by an object of a similar name. In this case, the *style* object represents the <STYLE> tag. Therefore, we can dynamically change the style of an element from within the script. We can change the color of an anchor tag from blue to red when the mouse pointer moves over it, like this:

```
<SCRIPT LANGUAGE="VBScript">
   Sub A1_onmouseover
      A1.style.color = "red"
   End Sub

   Sub A1_onmouseout
      A1.style.color = "blue"
   End Sub
</SCRIPT>
```

Here we're handling the *onmouseover* and *onmouseout* events for the anchor tag that has an ID of *A1*. We set the *color* property of the *style* object to *red* in the *onmouseover* event handler and *blue* in the *onmouseout* event handler. (In VBScript, we can access an HTML object by name. So we can access the *style* object by referring to the *anchor* object by name: *A1*. We can also do this in JScript, but we must make sure the object is defined before we try to access it, so this script block would have to be placed after the anchor tag in the document in JScript.)

Positioning

One aspect of CSS that really shows off the power of DHTML is positioning. CSS positioning gives you the ability to move HTML elements around on your Web page after the page is loaded. Positioning is accomplished by using a combination of script and different properties of the *style* object. The most important property for positioning is the *position* property. It has three possible values: *Static*, *Absolute*, and *Relative*. *Static* indicates that no special positioning exists. *Absolute* indicates that the object is positioned regardless of the layout of the surrounding objects. In other words, once you place the object, it doesn't move unless you manually move it. *Relative* indicates that the object is positioned relative to other objects on the page. The object moves automatically when the object or objects to which it is relative moves.

Along with the position property, you can use many other properties to set or change the actual position of the element on the page, such as *left, right, posLeft, posRight,* and *posTop*. (There are too many properties to list! As you probably guessed, you can refer to the MSDN Online Web Workshop for more information about them.)

One other point to note about style sheets is that if an inline style isn't set for an HTML element, a default style is applied. In Internet Explorer 4, you couldn't access the default style applied to an element, but in Internet Explorer 5, you can by using the *currentStyle* property of the element.

The easiest way to show you the power of CSS positioning is with a funny DHTML example named DHTML Soup. When you click the Begin message, the letters that spell *Dynamic HTML* rise out of a pot and line up at the top. When all the letters have lined up, they start to jiggle. This sample uses CSS positioning to create these effects. Also, when you move your mouse pointer over the letters, they change color. This sample uses CSS to create this effect as well. DHTML Soup is shown in Figure 3-5 on the next page and is also included on the companion CD.

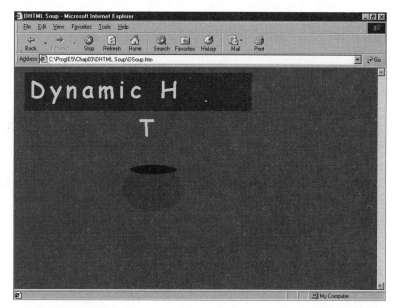

Figure 3-5. *DHTML Soup.*

Dynamic Properties

Prior to Internet Explorer 5, the properties of objects were static. For example, if a value of one property depended on the value of another property, you had to manually calculate the value of the dependent property every time the other property was changed. In version 5, properties are dynamic. You can specify an expression, or a formula, for a property, which can reference other property values. Each time the referenced property value changes, the expression is reevaluated for the property in question.

Using dynamic properties, you can create a DHTML spreadsheet that is similar to a Microsoft Excel spreadsheet. This spreadsheet is basically an HTML table that allows users to enter a value or an expression in a cell. For example, an expression can specify that the cell's value be the sum of the values of other cells. To implement dynamic properties, you use four methods: *getExpression*, *recalc*, *removeExpression*, and *setExpression*.

The *setExpression* method allows you to set an expression for a property by using script. You can also set expressions inline by using the STYLE attribute. For example, let's say we set up a <SPAN> tag:

```
<SPAN ID="SP1" STYLE="top:20">Text Block 1</SPAN>
```

We could create another span block whose size is based on the size of the first span block—*SP1*:

```
<SPAN ID="SP2" STYLE="top:expression(SP1.offsetTop)">Text Block 2</SPAN>
```

Whenever the top position of *SP1* changes, the top position of *SP2* will automatically change as well. Here's how we can set an expression in script using the *setExpression* method:

```
SP2.style.setExpression("top", "SP1.offsetTop", "jscript");
```

The first parameter is the name of the property to which the expression will be added. The second parameter is the expression using either JScript or VBScript syntax. The third parameter is the language to be used when evaluating the expression.

The *getExpression* method returns the expression for the current object. It will also recalculate the expression for the property in question.

The *recalc* method recalculates dynamic properties. Calling *recalc* with a value of *false* (the default) will recalculate all expressions in the document for properties that have changed since the last *recalc* was performed. Calling *recalc* with a value of *true* will force recalculation of all expressions in the document, whether they've changed or not. Finally, the *removeExpression* method deletes an expression that's connected to a property.

Printing Support

In Internet Explorer versions earlier than 5, you couldn't print the contents of a Web page using only script without an ActiveX control. (You'll learn how to build an ActiveX control in Chapter 5.) With version 5, you can print using script. Also, you can receive notifications in the form of events when the user chooses to print the document, which allows you to change the contents of the document before the document is printed—for example, to add headers and footers. After the document is printed, you receive another event, which you can handle to change the document back to the way it was before printing. And your users never see these changes!

To print the document from script in Internet Explorer 5, you use a new method of the *window* object named *print*. This method has no input parameters and is therefore easy to use. Calling *print* from within script has the same effect as the user choosing Print from the Internet Explorer File menu. Here's how to call *print* to print the document in JScript:

```
window.print();
```

Printing can't get any simpler than that. When we call *print* or when the user chooses Print from the File menu, two events fire. Before the document is actually printed, the *onbeforeprint* event fires. We can handle *onbeforeprint* to make changes to the document before it is printed, perhaps to add multiline headers and footers. Currently, we can't add multiline headers and footers using the Internet Explorer Print dialog box, so using the *print* method is pretty handy. The following code shows how to use VBScript to add multiline headers and footers to the document before it is printed.

```
Sub window_onbeforeprint
    document.body.insertAdjacentHTML "AfterBegin", _
            "<DIV ID='Header'>" _
        & "    <FONT SIZE=2><B>Company Information</B>" _
        & "    </FONT>" _
        & "    <BR>" _
        & "    <FONT SIZE=1><I>Page Number 1</I>" _
        & "    </FONT><BR><BR>" _
        & "</DIV>"

    document.body.insertAdjacentHTML "BeforeEnd", _
            "<BR><BR>" _
        & "<DIV ID='Footer' " _
        & "    STYLE='position:absolute;" _
        & "            top:expression(document.body.offsetHeight)'" _
        & "    <FONT SIZE=2><B>Document1.htm</B>" _
        & "    </FONT>" _
        & "    <BR>" _
        & "    <FONT SIZE=1><I>(C) Copyright 1999, My Company</I>" _
        & "    </FONT>" _
        & "</DIV>"
End Sub
```

In this code example, we're just using the *insertAdjacentHTML* method to insert text before the document prints. Notice that we wrapped the HTML we're inserting into the page with the <DIV> tags. You'll see why in a moment. When setting the footer, we used a combination of CSS and dynamic expressions to print the footer at the bottom of the document. We set the top of the footer block using the *top* property of the *style* object. We set this property equal to the *offsetHeight* of the body, which is calculated dynamically using the *expression* property of the *style* object.

Next we'll want to change the page back to normal after the printing job finishes. Here's how to do that using VBScript:

```
Sub window_onafterprint
    Header.outerHTML = ""
    Footer.outerHTML = ""
End Sub
```

Now you can see why we wrapped the HTML code that we inserted with the <DIV> tags. We needed an object that we could reference. In the previous code, we simply set the *outerHTML* property of the objects referenced by the names *Header* and *Footer* to an empty string, thus removing the HTML that we had previously inserted into the *onbeforeprint* event handler.

Mouse Capture

Mouse capture enables you to specify one particular object to handle all mouse events; in other words, you create one event handler for a specific mouse event instead of writing event handlers for every object for which you want to handle mouse events. (The mouse events you can handle are listed in Table 3-11.) Mouse capture is important because it tells Windows applications that you want mouse messages even when the mouse pointer goes outside your window. (By default, mouse messages will be sent to the window below the pointer.) Mouse capture's most obvious use is for drag-and-drop operations where you need to know that the mouse button is released in another window.

TABLE 3-11
MOUSE EVENTS

Mouse Event	Description
onmousedown	Fires when an object is clicked with either mouse button
onmouseup	Fires when a mouse button is released while over an object
onmousemove	Fires when the mouse is moved over an object
onclick	Fires when the left mouse button is clicked on an object
ondblclick	Fires when an object is double-clicked with the left mouse button
onmouseover	Fires when the mouse pointer is moved into an object
onmouseout	Fires when the mouse pointer is moved outside of an object

To implement mouse capture, we use the *setCapture* and *releaseCapture* methods, which accomplish exactly what you'd expect given their names. The *setCapture* method sets the object that will handle all the mouse events for the Web page. Calling *setCapture* is easy. Here's how to call it in JScript:

```
object1.setCapture();
```

In this code, *object1* is an arbitrary name of some HTML element on the Web page. The *object1* object will handle all the mouse events. Once we've set the mouse capture by using *setCapture*, we can handle mouse events just as we normally would, but all these events will be handled by just one object. In our mouse event handlers, we can use the *srcElement* property of the *event* object to determine which element fired the mouse event.

The *releaseCapture* method removes mouse capture from the object. Calling *releaseCapture* is as easy as calling the *setCapture* method. Here's how to call it in VBScript:

```
object1.releaseCapture()
```

We can call the *releaseCapture* method off the *document* object as well as the object to which we originally set mouse capture. Calling *releaseCapture* off the document makes determining which object has the mouse capture unnecessary, which is helpful when we're setting and releasing mouse capture programmatically. In addition to losing the mouse capture by calling *releaseCapture*, you'll also lose it in these three cases:

- When displaying a modal dialog box, such as the modal dialog box displayed by a call to the *alert* or *MsgBox* functions, or when displaying a context menu

- When switching focus to another application or browser window

- When scrolling through the Web document (This doesn't seem to be true if you use the scroll wheel to scroll through the document.)

Also note that when mouse capture is lost, the *onlosecapture* event is fired. An example of using mouse capture is included on the companion CD and is shown in Figure 3-6.

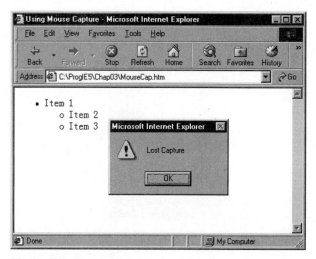

Figure 3-6. *Mouse capture.*

Context Menus

One of the most common questions people ask is: "How can I disable the Internet Explorer context menus using script?" Prior to Internet Explorer 5, you couldn't. But now the *oncontextmenu* event, which is a member of the *document* object, allows you to disable the Internet Explorer context menu simply by setting the *event* object's *returnValue* property to *false*. Here's how to do this using VBScript:

```
Sub document_oncontextmenu
    window.event.returnValue = False
End Sub
```

When the user clicks the right mouse button on the document, your event handler will be called. Because you're setting *returnValue* to *false*, the context menu is never displayed. Disabling context menus is as easy as that.

EXAMPLES: DHTML MEMO AND DHTML LEDGER

Now that you're an expert DHTML programmer, let's look at some examples that demonstrate the kind of web-based applications you can create using only DHTML and script. These are real-world examples—not like the simple examples I've shown you so far. The first is a DHTML Memo example, which acts almost exactly like Microsoft Notepad but runs in the context of a Web page. When you open DHTML Memo, you'll see a Web page that contains an editing window in which you can type in a document. Take a look at Figure 3-7.

Figure 3-7. *DHTML Memo.*

In Figure 3-7, the DHTML Memo window has a title bar with Minimize/Restore, Maximize/Restore, and Exit buttons like a typical Windows application window. You can even move the editing window around on the page by clicking the title bar and then dragging it. Unlike Windows Notepad, DHTML Memo has a toolbar that you can use to change the font face, size, and color, and to change the text to bold, italic, or underline. All changes made using this toolbar effect the entire document. However, you can modify the code so that changes made using the toolbar affect only the selected text or the text that's typed after a change is made. I'll leave these modifications as exercises for you.

DHTML Memo's best part is that it's all written in DHTML and script! No C, C++, Microsoft Visual Basic, or Java code is used at all. Give this sample a try by loading the DMemo.htm file from the companion CD. I think you'll be impressed.

The second example application is DHTML Ledger, which is shown in Figure 3-8. The window of this ledger looks similar to the window in a normal Windows spreadsheet application such as Microsoft Excel.

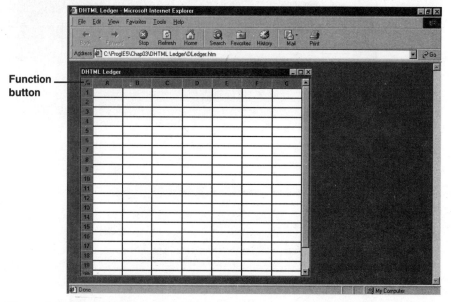

Figure 3-8. *DHTML Ledger.*

The DHTML Ledger window offers some of the same functionality as the DHTML Memo window: it has a title bar and Minimize/Restore, Maximize/Restore, and Exit buttons, and you can drag the window around inside Internet Explorer. This spreadsheet allows you to enter each value into a cell. Also, you can enter a formula into a cell by using the Expression Builder. To use the Expression Builder, enter some values in a few cells, click on an empty cell, and then click the *fx* button in the top left corner of the ledger window.

The *fx* button invokes the DHTML Expression Builder-Web Page Dialog dialog box by calling the *showModalDialog* method, as shown in Figure 3-9. Follow the instructions in the dialog box to specify one or more cells in the text box.

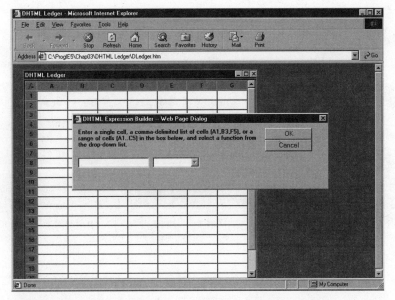

Figure 3-9. *DHTML Expression Builder-Web Page Dialog dialog box.*

If you specify only one cell, you can take its inverse or square it by selecting a function from the drop-down list. If you specify two cells, you can add, multiply, or average the values in the cells. (Subtraction and division are left as exercises for you.) If you specify a range of cells, you can sum or average the values of the cells. After you click the OK button, a *dynamic* property is inserted into the cell that you clicked on before invoking the Expression Builder. The *dynamic* property is inserted using the *setExpression* method. Because a *dynamic* property is used, updating any of the source cells updates the value in the destination cell.

Try out the DHTML Ledger example, and I'm sure you'll be even more impressed than you were with DHTML Memo. The best part is, just like DHTML Memo, this DHTML spreadsheet was written entirely using DHTML and script. You can find the sample (named DLedger.htm) on the companion CD. Because of Internet Explorer's security limitations, the only task you can't perform with these applications is saving files to your hard drive. In Chapter 11, I'll show you how to write real-world applications like these that also allow you to save files to disk.

WHAT'S NEXT?

Now that you see how easily you can create applications using DHTML and script, I bet you're ready to start converting all the applications you've written to applications using DHTML and script, or to start writing new applications using the techniques discussed in this chapter. You're probably wondering whether creating applications using DHTML and script can get any better than this. Guess what? It can, and it will. Just as the discussion of HTML and script in Chapter 2 laid the groundwork for this chapter, the overview of DHTML in this chapter lays the groundwork for what we're going to discuss in the rest of this book, including creating ActiveX controls, hosting the WebBrowser control, accessing the DHTML object model from your Visual Basic and Microsoft Visual C++ applications, and developing HTML applications. Get ready, because here we go!

Chapter 4

Writing HTML Applications

Writing applications for Microsoft Windows usually requires that you know at least one and sometimes several programming languages and development tools. Depending on the type of application you are creating and your particular preference, you might decide to use C++, Basic, or Java. You might also be required to know Microsoft Visual C++, Microsoft Visual Basic, or Microsoft Visual J++. But what you need to know doesn't end there! Creating an application for Microsoft Windows 95 and later versions or for Microsoft Windows NT often involves using the Microsoft Windows 32-bit Application Programming Interface (Win32 API). Using the Win32 API requires you to learn possibly hundreds of functions. And if you're programming with Visual C++, you might have to learn to program by using the Microsoft Foundation Classes (MFC) or the Active Template Library (ATL). If your application needs to use the Component Object Model (COM), as most Internet applications do, you have to know COM architecture, and you must be able to use a lot of COM interfaces as well.

Learning all of these technologies can be quite overwhelming and time consuming. What if you could apply your knowledge of DHTML and script to writing Windows applications? Fortunately, with Internet Explorer 5, you can. Introduced by Internet Explorer 5 is a new technology known as HTML Applications. An HTML Application (HTA) is a full-fledged Windows application that you can create by using only DHTML and script—basically, an HTML document that runs as a Windows application. You can even create an HTA in its simplest form by using only HTML, but it would be static—just as a Web page that contains only HTML is static. So using DHTML and script in your HTA is the best way to provide a dynamic experience for your users.

When you create HTAs, the possibilities are endless. Any task you can perform with a normal Web page by using DHTML and script (and ActiveX controls, as you'll see in Chapter 5), you can perform in your HTA. And an HTML Application even provides many advantages over a normal Web page. First of all, an HTA runs in its own window and not in the Internet Explorer window, where Web pages are displayed, so it appears to your users to be a normal Windows application, and for good reason—it is.

Second, unlike a Web page, an HTA is trusted. So if your HTA contains frames, you can write script in one frame to access elements in the other frame, even if the other frame exists in another domain. You can't do this with a normal Web page that is running in Internet Explorer. Also, because an HTML Application contains only the menus, toolbars, icons, and other elements that you create, it is considered trusted.

Basically, an HTML Application provides all the advantages that a normal Web page offers—the DHTML Object Model, scripting, the ability to download ActiveX controls (discussed in Chapter 5), and so forth—without the user interface or strict security restriction of the browser.

CREATING HTAS

An HTA is the simplest type of Windows application that you'll ever create. The easiest way to create an HTA is to take an existing Web page that has the extension .htm or .html and change the extension to .hta. That's it! Now you have an HTML Application. Try changing the extension of a Web page that you've already created to .hta, and then double-click the file in Windows Explorer. Now your HTML Application will run in a separate window of its own and not in the Internet Explorer window.

As an alternative, if you want to allow users to access your HTA on the Internet, you can provide a link to it on a Web page just as you would for any other Web page or application. When a user clicks this link, before the HTA is opened, Internet Explorer will display the File Download dialog box (shown in Figure 4-1), which is a security measure to alert the user that an executable application is about to open. Then the user can determine what to do next—open the application or save it to disk to run later.

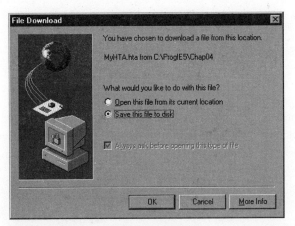

Figure 4-1. *File Download dialog box.*

You'll notice one oddity about this new HTML Application: if the Web page you converted contains a hyperlink and you click on it in the HTA, a new Internet Explorer window will be created to navigate to the hyperlink's URL. The first time you see this happen, you might be a little surprised. Normally when you click on a hyperlink, the navigation occurs in the current window. Remember, though, that HTAs are applications: they aren't Web browsers. In normal Windows applications, you don't usually change the contents of the entire application window in response to the user interaction. You might change the contents of the client area, but not the application window. (You'll create a client area in your HTA later in this chapter in the section "Creating an HTA with a Client Area.")

<HTA:APPLICATION> Tag

Although creating an HTA can be as simple as renaming an .htm or .html file to an .hta file, without using the new <HTA:APPLICATION> tag the window that you create is just a basic HTA window that contains default settings for the user interface features, as shown in Figure 4-2 on the following page. You can place the <HTA:APPLICATION> tag in any section of the HTML document, but it is recommended that you place it in the head section of the Web page for performance reasons. Also, because the <HTA:APPLICATION> tag isn't a block tag, no closing tag is needed. Listing 4-1 on the following page shows an example of a basic Web page that contains the <HTA:APPLICATION> tag. You can also find the code on the companion CD in the folder \Samples\Chap04.

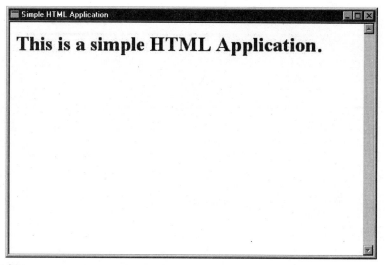

Figure 4-2. *Basic HTA window.*

Simple.hta

```
<HTML>
<HEAD>
    <TITLE>Simple HTML Application</TITLE>
    <HTA:APPLICATION>
</HEAD>
<BODY>
    <H1>This is a simple HTML Application.</H1>
</BODY>
</HTML>
```

Listing 4-1.

<HTA:APPLICATION> tag attributes

Of course, using the <HTA:APPLICATION> tag without supplying any attributes is the same as excluding it. The <HTA:APPLICATION> tag provides several attributes that allow you to control the user interface features of your HTML Application. These attributes are shown in Table 4-1.

TABLE 4-1
<HTA:APPLICATION> ATTRIBUTES

Attribute	Description	Values
APPLICATIONNAME	Sets the name of the HTA.	String value.
BORDER	Sets the type of window border for the HTA.	**thick** Thick border with a size grip and sizing border. Default for the BORDER attribute. To resize your window, you must specify this value. The other values for this attribute disable resizing. **dialog** Dialog window border. **none** No border. **thin** Thin border with a caption.
BORDERSTYLE	Sets the style of the content border in the HTA window. Maps to the Windows extended style values.	**normal** Normal border style. Default for the BORDERSTYLE attribute. **complex** Combination of the raised and sunken styles. **raised** Raised 3-D border. **static** 3-D border. Normally used for windows that don't allow user input. **sunken** Sunken 3-D border.
CAPTION	Boolean value that specifies whether the HTA displays a caption or a title bar.	**yes** Default value of this attribute. All HTA attributes that take Boolean values accept the value *yes*, *1*, or *true* for True and *no*, *0*, or *false* for False. The application title for an HTA won't display unless this attribute is set to *yes*.
ICON	Sets the path name of the icon that is used for the HTA. The icon appears in the upper left corner of the HTA window. The icon for an HTA can be either an .ico or a .bmp file.	The path name of the icon.
ID	Sets the identifier for the <HTA:APPLICATION> tag. The identifier is needed to write script to access the attributes of the HTA.	String value.
MAXIMIZEBUTTON	Boolean value that determines whether a Maximize button is displayed in the title bar.	**yes** Default value. The CAPTION attribute must be set to *yes* for the Maximize button to appear.

(continued)

\<HTA:APPLICATION\> ATTRIBUTES *continued*

Attribute	Description	Values
MINIMIZEBUTTON	Boolean value that determines whether a Minimize button is displayed in the title bar.	*yes* Default value. The CAPTION attribute must be set to *yes* for the Minimize button to appear.
SHOWINTASKBAR	Boolean value that determines whether the HTA will appear in the Windows task bar. This property does not affect whether the application appears in the list of applications that are accessible when pressing the ALT-TAB key combination.	*yes* Default value.
SINGLEINSTANCE	Boolean value that determines whether only one instance of the HTA can be run at a time. For SINGLEINSTANCE to work, the APPLICATIONNAME attribute must also be specified.	*no* Default value. The value means that multiple instances of this particular HTA can be run concurrently.
SYSMENU	Boolean value that determines whether a system menu is displayed in the HTA title bar. The system menu is displayed when you click the icon in the upper left-hand corner of the HTA. This menu contains all the commands that appear in a normal Windows system menu for an application.	*yes* Default value.
VERSION	Sets the version of the HTA. This version is for internal use only and is not interpreted in any way by the script engine or the document-rendering engine.	Default value is an empty string.
WINDOWSTATE	Sets the initial size of the HTA window.	*normal* The HTA window will be the default size for an Internet Explorer window. Default value of this attribute. *minimize* HTA window will be minimized when started. *maximize* HTA window will be maximized when it's launched.

The HTML for an HTA in Listing 4-2 uses all of the attributes listed in Table 4-1.

Complex.hta

```
<HTML>
<HEAD>
    <TITLE>Complex HTML Application</TITLE>
    <HTA:APPLICATION
        ID="oHTA"
        APPLICATIONNAME="ComplexHTA"
        BORDER="thick"
        BORDERSTYLE="sunken"
        CAPTION="yes"
        ICON="ComplexHTA.ico"
        MAXIMIZEBUTTON="no"
        MINIMIZEBUTTON="yes"
        SHOWINTASKBAR="yes"
        SINGLEINSTANCE="no"
        SYSMENU="yes"
        VERSION="1.0"
        WINDOWSTATE="normal"
    >
</HEAD>
<BODY>
    <H1>This is a complex HTML Application.</H1>
</BODY>
</HTML>
```

Listing 4-2.

Figure 4-3 on the following page shows the results of the HTA in Listing 4-2. You can find the code on the companion CD in the folder \Samples\Chap04.

Not surprisingly, you can access all the attributes in Table 4-1 using script on a Web page. You can retrieve the values of the properties corresponding to these attributes in script, but setting them has no effect.

The following example shows how to retrieve the values of all the attributes that were set in the HTA shown in Figure 4-3. It is a VBScript event handler for the *onclick* event of a button on the page loaded in this HTA. You can find the entire code for this example on the companion CD in the folder \Samples\Chap04\Scripting.hta.

```
<SCRIPT LANGUAGE="VBScript">
    Option Explicit

    Sub btnShowAtts_onclick
        Dim str

        str = "ID: " & oHTA.ID & vbCrLf _
            & "Application Name: " & oHTA.APPLICATIONNAME & vbCrLf _
            & "Border: " & oHTA.BORDER & vbCrLf _
            & "Border Style: " & oHTA.BORDERSTYLE & vbCrLf _
            & "Caption: " & oHTA.CAPTION & vbCrLf _
            & "Icon: " & oHTA.ICON & vbCrLf _
            & "Maximize Button: " & oHTA.MAXIMIZEBUTTON & vbCrLf _
            & "Minimize Button: " & oHTA.MINIMIZEBUTTON & vbCrLf _
            & "Show in task bar: " & oHTA.SHOWINTASKBAR & vbCrLf _
            & "Single Instance: " & oHTA.SINGLEINSTANCE & vbCrLf _
            & "System Menu: " & oHTA.SYSMENU & vbCrLf _
            & "Version: " & oHTA.VERSION & vbCrLf _
            & "Window State: " & oHTA.WINDOWSTATE

        MsgBox str
    End Sub
</SCRIPT>
```

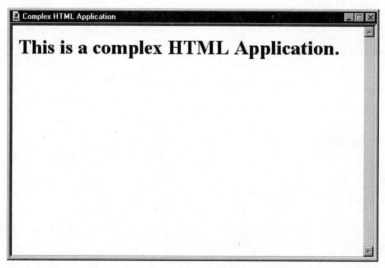

Figure 4-3. *HTA using all attributes of the <HTA:APPLICATION> tag.*

commandLine **property**

You can set most properties of the <HTA:APPLICATION> tag with their corresponding attributes. One property of the <HTA:APPLICATION> tag that isn't accessible as an attribute, however, is the *commandLine* property. Because an HTA is a full-fledged Windows application (just like any other Windows application), you can pass data to it when running it from a command line. By using the *commandLine* property of the <HTA:APPLICATION> tag, you can retrieve command line parameters that are sent to the HTML Application.

The *commandLine* property returns a string that contains the full path to the HTA and any additional parameters that are specified when running the HTA. The string that is returned is a space-delimited list of all the command line parameters. For example, you can create a simple HTML Application named Hello.hta. If the user enters his name, the application displays a hello message. You can run Hello.hta from the command line in Windows NT and specify your name like so:

```
C:\ProgIE5\Chap04>Hello.hta Scott
```

To run an HTA from the command line in Windows 95 and later versions, you must create a shortcut to the HTA that contains the path to the HTA and contains any arguments as the target of the shortcut. (The companion CD includes a sample shortcut named ShrtHello.hta, which you can find in the folder \Samples\Chap04. You'll have to change the target of this shortcut to point to the Hello.hta in your CD-ROM drive.)

When you retrieve the value of the *commandLine* property, the string that is returned contains the full pathname of the HTA and any input parameters delimited by spaces. If you retrieve the value of the *commandLine* property at this point, the string returned will look similar to this:

```
"C:\ProgIE5\Chap04\Hello.hta Scott"
```

To complete the Hello.hta example so that a hello message is displayed when you start the application, parse the command line for the first parameter that follows the path to the Hello.hta file. (This first parameter should be the user's name.) VBScript is used in this example, which is shown in Listing 4-3. You can also find the code on the companion CD in the folder \Samples\Chap04.

Hello.hta

```
<HTML>
<HEAD>
    <TITLE>Scripting the HTA:APPLICATION Tag</TITLE>
```

Listing 4-3. *(continued)*

Listing 4-3 *continued*

```
<HTA:APPLICATION
    ID="oHTA"
>

<SCRIPT LANGUAGE="VBScript">
    Option Explicit

    Dim cmdLineArray
    Dim strHello

    ' This code assumes that you have no spaces in
    ' the path to Hello.hta.  (In other words, this code
    ' splits the command line by spaces and assumes
    ' that your name is the second word.)
    '
    cmdLineArray = Split(oHTA.commandLine)
    strHello = "Hello " & cmdLineArray(1) & ", " _
            & "How are you?"

    MsgBox strHello
</SCRIPT>
</HEAD>
<BODY>
</BODY>
</HTML>
```

CREATING AN HTA WITH A CLIENT AREA

In a Windows application, you don't typically redraw the entire application window. You usually redraw only the client area of an application window. Redrawing the entire window means redrawing the menus, toolbars, and the status bar for the application. I mentioned earlier in this chapter that if you click on a hyperlink in an HTA, a new instance of Internet Explorer is created to navigate to the hyperlink. If you want the navigation to occur in your HTML Application, you can create a client area by using frames. (If you don't recall how to implement frames, refer to the discussion of the *frames* collection on pages 32–33 in Chapter 2.) When you use frames, the client area can take up the entire HTA window or just a portion of it.

Because HTML Applications are considered trusted, they aren't subject to the same security restrictions as Web pages. For instance, when a Web page that is loaded into Internet Explorer contains frames, one frame can't access the DHTML Object Model of other frames if the frames aren't in the same domain. In other words, in Internet Explorer, frames that are in different domains aren't considered trusted. In HTML

Applications, frames can be considered trusted, whether they are in the same or in different domains.

To specify that a frame is trusted, use the TRUSTED attribute of the <FRAME> or <IFRAME> tags. The value of the TRUSTED attribute is a Boolean and is *no* by default. If you set the value of TRUSTED to *yes*, Internet Explorer's normal security rules will not be applied to the frame. For a frame to be trusted, all parent frames must also be trusted.

> **NOTE**   An <IFRAME> element creates a sort of inline frame that can be inserted in a web page. By default the frame looks like a window within your Web page. For more information about <IFRAME> tags, refer to the MSDN Online Web Workshop.

To see how to create a client area in the HTA, let's develop a Web browser application named MyBrowser that allows you to navigate to Web pages in an IFRAME window. This HTA can have Back, Forward, and Go buttons just as Internet Explorer does. Figure 4-4 shows a running instance of MyBrowser.

Figure 4-4. *MyBrowser.*

The code for MyBrowser is shown in Listing 4-4. You can also find the code on the companion CD in the folder \Samples\Chap04.

MyBrowsr.hta

```
<HTML>
<HEAD>
   <TITLE>MyBrowser</TITLE>
```

Listing 4-4.   *(continued)*

Listing 4-4 *continued*

```
    <HTA:APPLICATION
      ID="oHTA"
      ICON="MyBrowser.ico"
    >

    <SCRIPT LANGUAGE="VBScript">
      Option Explicit

      Sub btnGo_onclick
        Dim strAddr

        strAddr = txtAddress.value

        If InStr(1, strAddr, "://") = 0 Then
          strAddr = "http://" & strAddr
        End If

        frmClient.document.location.href = strAddr
      End Sub

      Sub btnBack_onclick
        frmClient.history.back
      End Sub

      Sub btnFwd_onclick
        frmClient.history.forward
      End Sub
    </SCRIPT>
</HEAD>
<BODY scroll="no">
    <B>Address:</B>
    <INPUT TYPE="Text" ID="txtAddress"> 
    <INPUT TYPE="Submit" ID="btnGo" VALUE="Go">
    <BUTTON ID="btnBack" STYLE="position:relative;left:50px">
        &lt; Back</BUTTON> 
    <BUTTON ID="btnFwd" STYLE="position:relative;left:50px">
        Forward &gt;</BUTTON>
    <P>
    <IFRAME ID="frmClient"
        TRUSTED="yes"
        SRC="http://www.microsoft.com"
        WIDTH="100%"
        HEIGHT="90%"
    >
    </IFRAME>
</BODY>
</HTML>
```

In the MyBrowser example, you can type a URL in the text box and navigate to the URL by pressing the Enter key or by clicking the Go button. (The Go button is a Submit button.) When the Enter key is pressed or the Go button is clicked, the *btnGo_onclick* event handler is called. In this event handler, if the user didn't supply the Internet protocol type (in other words, HTTP, FILE, and so on), the MyBrowser application assumes that the user wanted the HTTP protocol and prepends the string "http://" to the value that was entered in the text box. Then the MyBrowser application navigates to the new Web page by changing the *href* property of the *location* object for the frame.

To obtain the *location* object, you use the *location* property of the *document* object. You can obtain the *document* object by referencing the *document* property of *frmClient*. Remember that if you supply an ID for an HTML element, you can reference that element by name in script. Because frame objects are really *window* objects, you can access the *document* object of the frame by using the window's *document* property.

You can also navigate backward and forward in the navigation history just as you can with Internet Explorer. When you click either the Back button or the Forward button, a corresponding event handler is called. In either event handler, the *history* object is obtained from the frame window. Then either the *back* or the *forward* method of the *history* object is called to navigate backward or forward in the history list.

MORE HTA EXAMPLES

Now that you can create your own HTML Applications by using only DHTML and script, let's look at two more HTA examples. These examples really show off the power of HTA. You've already seen some versions of these examples in Chapter 3: a text editor named DHTML Memo and a spreadsheet named DHTML Ledger. For this chapter, I converted these examples to HTML Applications and named them Memo and Ledger. The Memo application is shown in Figure 4-5 on the following page, and the Ledger application is shown in Figure 4-6.

The code for Memo and Ledger is basically the same as the code for their DHTML counterparts in Chapter 3, so I won't show it here. But unlike their DHTML counterparts, the HTA versions of these applications allow you to open and save files.

To start and then run the applications, simply double-click the Memo.hta file or double-click the Ledger.hta file. You can open new Memo files or Ledger files by clicking the Open button on the toolbar. I've included a few sample files on the companion CD for Memo in the folder \Samples\Chap04\Memo and sample files for Ledger in the folder \Samples\Chap04\Ledger. The Memo sample files have the extension .mem, and the Ledger sample files have the extension .lgr.

NOTE   An ActiveX control is used to display the open and save dialog boxes and to perform the actual opening and saving of the files. (In Chapter 5, you'll create your own ActiveX controls.) Therefore, before you can use one of these applications, you must register the OpenSave.dll file in the OpenSave directory by using the Regsvr32 application, like this:

```
regsvr32 OpenSave.dll
```

The Regsvr32 application resides in the \Windows\System directory on Windows 95 and later versions and in the \WinNT\System32 directory on Windows NT systems.

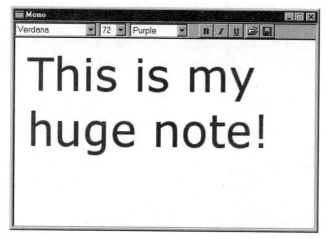

Figure 4-5. *Memo application.*

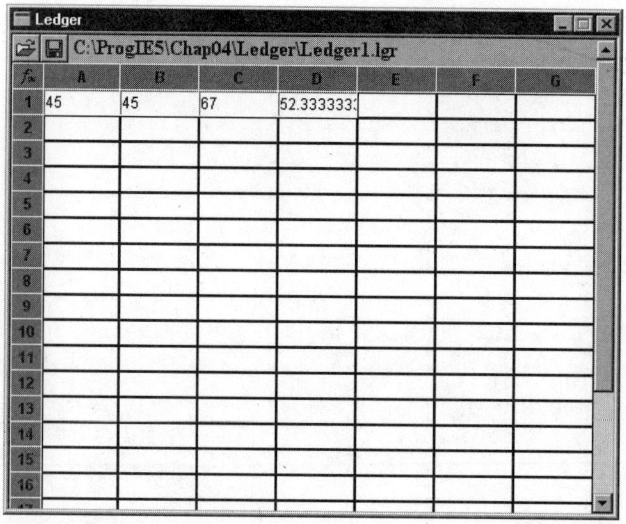

Figure 4-6. *Ledger application.*

When you're ready to save a file, just click the Save button on the toolbar. When you click the Open button or the Save button, each application will display the Open dialog box or the Save dialog box, respectively. Pretty easy, huh? But you already knew that it would be.

WHAT'S NEXT?

In this chapter, you learned how to create full-fledged Windows applications by using only DHTML and script. How much simpler can development get? In the next chapter, you'll create and use ActiveX controls on your Web pages. The concepts we'll discuss also apply to HTML Applications.

I encourage you to start using HTAs when you need to create Windows applications. You'll probably find them much easier to create than their Visual C++ and Visual Basic counterparts.

Part II

Building Internet Applications

Chapter 5

Creating ActiveX Controls

Writing Web-based applications sometimes requires you to perform actions that you can't perform on a basic Web page created by using DHTML and script. Suppose you want to include complicated functionality in your Web page. For example, you might want to access information that is on a user's client system, such as a file you want to open or to which you want to save data. Or you might want to restrict users to certain Web pages on the Internet. Perhaps you want to prevent users from visiting certain game sites on the Web.

To accomplish these objectives, you could create your own application that hosts the WebBrowser control or automates Microsoft Internet Explorer (discussed in the next chapter). Although creating an application with a WebBrowser control would give you total control and allow you to provide a lot of functionality that you couldn't otherwise provide, maybe you don't want to devote the time or resources to building a browser application just to restrict users' navigation. Using a Microsoft ActiveX control, you can hook into the Internet Explorer container and control almost any aspect of it, handle events, and access the DHTML Object Model. (I'll discuss how to hook into the Internet Explorer container in Chapter 6 in conjunction with the discussion of the WebBrowser control and Internet Explorer automation.)

This chapter explains how to create an ActiveX control first by using Microsoft Visual Basic and then by using the Active Template Library (ATL) that ships with Microsoft Visual C++. (We'll use ATL instead of Microsoft Foundation Classes, or MFC, because ATL was designed to help build ActiveX controls for the Web.) You aren't required to know COM for this chapter, but it certainly helps.

If you don't understand COM, you won't have any trouble in the section "Creating Visual Basic ActiveX Controls." You might run into snags in the section "Creating ATL ActiveX Controls," but if you follow the examples, you'll still be able to create ActiveX controls for Internet Explorer.

WHERE TO GO FOR MORE INFORMATION

If you'd like to know more about COM, check out one of the many Microsoft Press books such as *Understanding ActiveX and OLE* by David Chappell, *Inside COM* by Dale Rogerson, or *ActiveX Controls Inside Out* by Adam Denning.

If you would like more information about the other topics in this chapter, refer to the MSDN Online Web Workshop at *http://msdn.microsoft.com/ workshop*.

WHAT IS AN ACTIVEX CONTROL?

ActiveX controls are programmable elements that provide some functionality that can be reused by other applications such as Internet Explorer and applications built with such development tools as Visual Basic and Visual C++. ActiveX controls are COM objects that are stored in dynamic-link library (DLL) files and have the extension .ocx or .dll.

> **NOTE**   When the client application needs to use the ActiveX control, DLL files are loaded into the client application's address space. Because the DLL file is loaded into the same process as the client's, ActiveX controls are typically referred to as In Process (InProc for short) COM objects.

ActiveX controls are similar to the intrinsic controls discussed in Chapter 2: they typically provide a graphical interface, such as a button or a text box, through which the user can interact with the control. Also, like intrinsic controls, ActiveX controls can have methods, properties, and collections, and they can fire events. However, to be considered a control, an object isn't required to have a graphical user interface or to expose methods, properties, events, and collections. If an ActiveX control doesn't have any of these features—for example, no user interface or methods—the control is pretty boring and probably useless. Therefore, each ActiveX control example in this chapter includes a user interface and some methods, properties, and events.

Objects do exist that don't have a user interface but do expose at least one method, property, event, or collection (and sometimes all of these). This type of object is referred to as a COM object. Even without the user interface, COM objects are quite useful. COM objects are usually created to expose some functionality that doesn't require a user interface or for which a user interface just doesn't make sense—for example, you wouldn't need a user interface to have the system read data from a database and insert this data into a Web page. In the same way that ActiveX controls can be reused by client applications, COM objects can be reused by client applications. In this chapter, we'll concentrate on building ActiveX controls, but keep in mind that COM objects are just as simple (if not simpler) to create as ActiveX controls.

Inserting an ActiveX Control into a Web Page

Before you learn how to create an ActiveX control, you need to know how to insert the control into a Web page that will be loaded into Internet Explorer. We'll use Internet Explorer to test all the controls we create in this chapter. Inserting an ActiveX control into a Web page is fairly easy. You simply use the HTML <OBJECT> tag. This tag is an HTML element just like <H1>, <P>, or any of the other HTML tags covered in Chapter 2. Because all HTML elements are represented as objects in the DHTML Object Model, you can write script for <OBJECT> tags in the same way you can for any other HTML element. You'll see how to write script for ActiveX controls later in this chapter in the sections titled "Writing Script for Your Visual Basic Control" and "Writing Script for Your ATL Control."

The <OBJECT> tag has attributes like any other HTML tag. CLASSID is the most important of these attributes. It tells Internet Explorer which ActiveX control to load into the page. The CLASSID attribute points to the class ID (CLSID for short) of the ActiveX control. A CLSID is a 128-bit globally unique identifier (GUID) that identifies an ActiveX control or some other type of COM object.

GUIDs are guaranteed to be unique across time and space. For example, if somebody creates a CLSID in Antarctica (it could happen) at the same exact time that you create one in the United States, the CLSIDs will be different. (If somebody on the Klingon home world creates a GUID, the GUID will be unique there as well!) The algorithm used to create a GUID, or CLSID, is quite complex, so I won't go into it in this book. Trust me though—it does work.

You might be wondering why you can't just give an ActiveX control a name you can relate to, like "Bob," instead of a GUID, which can be difficult to read. Just imagine if you named your ActiveX control "Bob" and somebody in Zimbabwe used the same name. If a user installs your control on her machine and then installs the control from Zimbabwe, client applications that want to use the "Bob" control will always use the control from Zimbabwe. Why? Installing the "Bob" control from Zimbabwe will make your control unavailable because both controls have the same name.

In most cases, this scenario would cause major problems because the client application probably would have been built to access methods and properties that existed in your control but not in the control named "Bob" from Zimbabwe. If you use GUIDs to identify your control, client applications that reference the control by its CLSID are guaranteed to access *your* ActiveX control and not the one from Zimbabwe.

CLSIDs are stored in the Registry under the following key:

```
HKEY_CLASSES_ROOT\CLSID
```

Under this key in the Registry are possibly hundreds of CLSIDs that identify ActiveX controls and other COM objects on your system. Figure 5-1 shows the following CLSID for the Calendar control in the Registry:

```
{8E27C92B-1264-101C-8A2F-040224009C02}
```

If you look in the right-hand pane of the Registry Editor, you'll see one value for this key—(*Default*). This value specifies the "friendly" name of this control as "*Calendar Control 8.0*". All CLSIDs have the same format in the Registry: they're represented by a 128-bit number enclosed in curly braces.

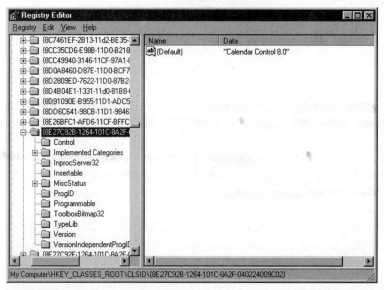

Figure 5-1. *CLSID of the Calendar control in the Registry. This figure shows the Regedit utility application that you can use to view the contents of the Registry.*

Now that you know a little more about the CLSID, let's look again at the CLASSID attribute in context. The CLASSID attribute tells Internet Explorer the CLSID of the ActiveX control that you want loaded into the Web page. When specifying the CLASSID attribute for the <OBJECT> tag, you must first prefix the CLSID value with the string "*clsid*:". Don't include the curly braces that you see displayed when viewing the CLSID in the Registry. For example, consider the case of inserting the Calendar control into a Web page. To do so, you would add the following HTML code to the Web page. The results of this code are shown in Figure 5-2.

```
<OBJECT CLASSID="clsid:8E27C92B-1264-101C-8A2F-040224009C02">
</OBJECT>
```

Internet Explorer finds the <OBJECT> tag and immediately searches for the CLASSID attribute. Internet Explorer then reads the value of the CLASSID attribute, which is the CLSID of an ActiveX control that you want inserted into the Web page, and looks up this CLSID in the Registry. If Internet Explorer finds this CLSID in the Registry, it reads a subkey named *InprocServer32*, which specifies the path and name of the DLL (.ocx or .dll file) that Internet Explorer should load to enable it to display the desired control on the Web page. Figure 5-3 on the following page shows the *InprocServer32* key for the Calendar control.

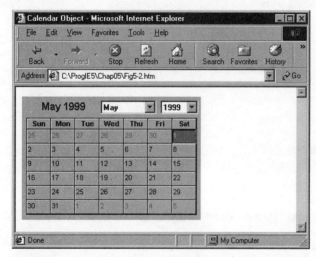

Figure 5-2. *The Calendar control inserted into a Web page.*

When you look at the right pane of Figure 5-3, which shows the *InprocServer32* key in the Registry Editor, you see that two values exist. The first value is the (*Default*) value, which specifies the path and name of the DLL to load for the ActiveX control. For the Calendar control, the (*Default*) value specifies the file mscal.ocx in the path C:\WinNT\System32. The second value is *ThreadingModel*.

NOTE I won't cover the advanced COM topic of threading models in this book. Just note that the threading model we're talking about is the Apartment model. Only controls that support at least the Apartment-threading model can safely be used on a Web page in Internet Explorer. I'll show you how to mark controls as Apartment threaded when we create ActiveX controls.

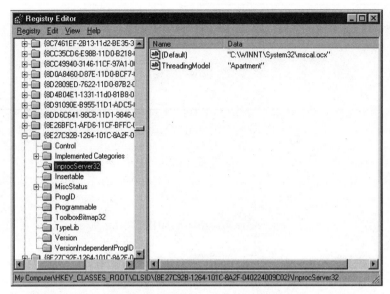

Figure 5-3. InprocServer32 *key for the Calendar control.*

Besides CLASSID, you might want to specify a couple of other important attributes for the <OBJECT> tag. To write script for an ActiveX control, you would include the ID attribute and specify any name you want for it, just as you would for any other HTML tag that you want to script. Sometimes, specifying the HEIGHT and WIDTH attributes for the <OBJECT> tag is also important. If you don't, the control might not show its user interface because Internet Explorer hasn't activated the control. We'll explore this issue further in the section "Creating Visual Basic ActiveX Controls."

Downloading an ActiveX Control to a Client's Machine

Now you know how to insert an ActiveX control into a Web page using the <OBJECT> tag in conjunction with the CLASSID attribute. This insertion technique works great as long as the ActiveX control has already been installed on the user's machine. What if the ActiveX control isn't installed on the user's machine? Do you have to send a copy of it to every user or, worse yet, go to the user's machine and install it yourself? Of course not! That's what the <OBJECT> tag is for.

The <OBJECT> tag exposes an attribute named CODEBASE. The value of this attribute specifies the URL of the ActiveX control. Hence, the ActiveX control can be located on your own machine, on your corporate intranet, or even on the other side of the world. By using the CODEBASE attribute, you can also specify the version of the control that you want installed on the user's machine. If the current version on the user's machine is the same as or later than the version you specify for the CODEBASE attribute, Internet Explorer won't download and install the version you specified—it will download and install only more recent versions of the control. The process of downloading ActiveX controls to the client machine is known as Internet Component Download.

You can specify several types of files for the CODEBASE attribute: DLL, OCX, INF, CAB, and so forth. In the simplest of cases, you can specify the name of the DLL or OCX file that contains the ActiveX control. For example, to specify that Internet Explorer should download version 8.0.0.5007 of the Calendar control from your local intranet server, you would insert an <OBJECT> tag that looks like this:

```
<OBJECT ID="CalObj"
        CLASSID="clsid:8E27C92B-1264-101C-8A2F-040224009C02"
        CODEBASE="http://someserver.com/mscal.ocx#version=8,0,0,5007">
</OBJECT>
```

When Internet Explorer finds this <OBJECT> tag, it determines whether the Calendar control is already installed on the client machine. If not, Internet Explorer downloads and installs the mscal.ocx file from the server. (In our example, let's call the server *someserver*.com.) If the Calendar control is already registered on the client machine, Internet Explorer compares the version of mscal.ocx on the client machine to the version that you specify as part of the CODEBASE attribute—*8,0,0,5007*.

NOTE When listing the version number in the CODEBASE attribute, be sure to use commas instead of periods to separate the different parts of the version.

If the version of mscal.ocx on the client machine and the version in the CODEBASE attribute are the same, Internet Explorer doesn't download mscal.ocx from *someserver*.com. If the version you specify in the CODEBASE attribute is later than the version on the client machine, Internet Explorer downloads and registers mscal.ocx from *someserver*.com. If you want to force the download of the DLL no matter what version is on the client machine, you can specify *–1,–1,–1,–1* for the version number. This version number is usually used only for testing purposes.

TIP Internet Explorer calls the *DllRegisterServer* function of a DLL to register it on the client machine. You can register a DLL yourself by using the Regsvr32 application that Microsoft Windows provides. This application will call the *DllRegisterServer* function of the DLL for you. If you want to unregister a DLL, you can specify the */u* argument to Regsvr32. In this case, Regsvr32 will call the *DllUnregisterServer* function that is exported by the DLL.

Specifying a DLL for the CODEBASE attribute is fine and dandy unless the ActiveX control needs other files to be able to work correctly. For instance, an ActiveX control built by using Visual Basic needs the Visual Basic run-time to work correctly. (The Visual Basic run-time for version 6 is in the msvbvm60.dll file.) An ActiveX control built by using MFC needs the C run-time (msvcrt40.dll) and the MFC libraries (mfc42.dll) to work correctly. (This is another reason you are better off building an ActiveX control by using ATL instead of MFC.)

In addition, the ActiveX control might depend on other files. How do you make sure that all these files are installed on the users' machines? Could you include several different <OBJECT> tags on the Web page—one for every DLL you need to download? Well, unfortunately, that won't work because of the asynchronous nature of Internet Explorer downloads. Even if it did work, having many different <OBJECT> tags on the Web page is inefficient and makes the page hard to read and understand. There's got to be a better way.

CAB files

Fortunately, there is a better way to ensure that the proper files are installed on the users' machines. You can package an ActiveX control and its dependent files into one compressed file known as a cabinet (CAB) file. A CAB file is similar to a zip file in that it compresses and combines files into a single file. Therefore you have to include only one <OBJECT> tag for your ActiveX control.

To create a CAB file, you can use either the Cabarc utility or the Makecab utility, both of which are included with the Cabinet SDK. (You can download the Cabinet SDK from MSDN Online Web Workshop at *http://msdn.microsoft.com/workshop/management/cab/cabdl.asp.*) But how do you know which files to include in the CAB file? You must include all files on which the ActiveX control depends plus another important file, which I'll talk about in the next section. The primary reason most ActiveX control downloads fail is that one or more files on which the control depends aren't installed on the client machine.

To determine which files the ActiveX control depends on, use the Microsoft Dependency Walker utility (also referred to as Depends) that ships with Visual C++ 6. To use the Microsoft Visual Studio version of Depends, from the Start/Programs menu, click Microsoft Visual Studio 6/Micosoft Visual Studio 6 Tools, and then Depends. Open any program file that you want to examine by using the File/Open menu or the Open button. Depends displays all the files that the ActiveX control depends on, as shown in Figure 5-4.

In the Depends view window, notice that all of the Calendar control's dependencies are system files. You won't have to include any other .dll or .ocx files in the CAB file. Then why create the CAB file? Because CAB files are compressed files, the time it takes users to download the ActiveX control will be much shorter. Also, CAB files allow you to distribute multiple files at once, and they can be signed, as we will talk about shortly. Get into the habit of creating CAB files any time you want to download an ActiveX control from the Web to a client machine.

> **NOTE** Although OCXs and DLLs can be signed, they allow you to distribute only one file. You can also specify an INF file for the CODEBASE attribute which will allow you to distribute multiple files. However, INF files can't be signed.

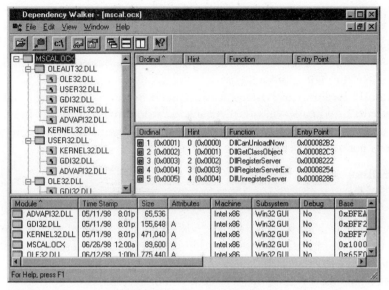

Figure 5-4. *Microsoft Dependency Walker for the mscal.ocx file.*

INF files Even though you know which dependencies the Calendar control has, before you can create the CAB file, you need an INF file—perhaps the most important file in the CAB file. An INF file is an information file with the .inf extension that provides installation instructions that Internet Explorer uses to install and register the ActiveX control and its dependencies. If you're familiar with normal Windows INF files, INF files used for downloading ActiveX controls will be familiar to you. But they're not exactly the same.

An INF file is basically a Windows INI file for downloading code in Internet Explorer. An INF file consists of a series of named sections that describe the .dll files or .ocx files that are to be downloaded and registered on the client machine. Each section contains a number of *key=value* pairs that provide needed information.

NOTE Internet Explorer uses the *GetPrivateProfileString* function to read the sections of an INF file just like Windows programs use it to read the sections of an INI file.

Although the order of the sections doesn't matter, the [Version] section usually appears first in an INF file. It specifies the version of Internet Component Download to use to download the ActiveX control. This section is required for compatibility in Microsoft Windows 95 and later versions as well as in Microsoft Windows NT. Here's how the [Version] section typically looks:

```
[Version]
signature="$CHICAGO$"
AdvancedINF=2.0
```

The next—and probably most important—section is [Add.Code], which lists all the files to be installed on the client machine. The keys in this section take the form of *filename=section-name*, where *filename* is the name of the file you want down-loaded to the client machine, and *section-name* is the name of another section in the same INF file. For example, let's say you created a Visual Basic ActiveX control. Obviously, because your control was created using Visual Basic, the Visual Basic run time must be installed on the client machine. You must include a reference to the Visual Basic run time in the INF file by using a conditional hook. The [Add.Code] section for the INF file would look like this:

```
[Add.Code]
SimpleCtrl.dll=SimpleCtrl.dll
MSVBVM60.DLL=MSVBVM60.DLL
```

Note that in the preceding [Add.Code] section, the name of the file is SimpleCtrl.dll and the name of the section is also SimpleCtrl.dll. By convention, the name of the file you want to download and the name of the section are the same, but the section could be named anything that you choose. For example, we could specify the name of the section as FooSection. The [Add.Code] section would look like this:

```
[Add.Code]
SimpleCtrl.dll=FooSection
MSVBVM60.DLL=MSVBVM60.DLL
```

Note that the files in the [Add.Code] section must be listed in order of their dependency. For example, consider this [Add.Code] section:

```
[Add.Code]
Control1.dll=Section1
Control2.dll=Section2
Control3.dll=Section3
```

In this section, Control1.dll is the main DLL. Control2.dll is listed after Control1.dll because Control1.dll depends on Control2.dll. Control3.dll is listed last because Control1.dll, Control2.dll, or both depend on Control3.dll. With this [Add.Code] section, the downloads happen in this order: Control1.dll, Control2.dll, Control3.dll.

The installations of these files occur in reverse order from the download be-cause of the dependencies of one file on the next. Control1.dll and/or Control2.dll depend on Control3.dll, so Control3.dll must be installed first so that when the in-stallations of the other two occur, registration will succeed. (Installing a DLL involves registering the control.) The same is true for Control2.dll. Because Control1.dll de-pends on Control2.dll, Control2.dll must be installed first.

NOTE Registration of a DLL will fail if a dependent file isn't available (in other words, not registered) on the system.

Let's go back to our original [Add.Code] section. Somewhere in the INF file following the [Add.Code] section, you'll include two sections—[SimpleCtrl.dll] and [MSVBVM60.DLL]. Each of these sections describes their associated files in detail. Let's start with the [SimpleCtrl.dll] section. Here's the code that would appear in the INF file for [SimpleCtrl.dll]:

```
[SimpleCtrl.dll]
file-win32-x86=thiscab
RegisterServer=yes
clsid={AEBCD9D8-ADA2-11d2-B94F-00C04FA3471C}
DestDir=
FileVersion=1,0,0,0
```

The first key in the [SimpleCtrl.dll] section is the *file* key. This key provides Internet Explorer with information about the client machine and instructions regarding where to retrieve the DLL from. To inform Internet Explorer about the client machine, use the key that indicates which type of platform you're targeting. The *file* key consists of three parts: file, which never changes; the operating system; and the CPU. For instance, the key specified in the previous example indicates that we're targeting Microsoft Windows running on a machine that uses the Intel x86 CPU chip. The possible values for the operating system are currently only *win32* for Microsoft Windows and *mac* for Apple Macintosh. The current values for the CPU are *x86*, *ppc* (Power PC), *mips*, and *alpha*.

The value of the *file* key tells Internet Explorer where to look for and then retrieve the DLL. You can specify one of three values: a URL, *ignore*, or *thiscab*. A URL can be any URL that you are already used to, such as *http://activex.microsoft.com*. The value *ignore* specifies that this file isn't required for the platform you specified. The value *thiscab* tells Internet Explorer that the DLL is in the current CAB file. For SimpleCtrl.dll, we specified *thiscab* because we intend to include the DLL in this CAB file.

The next key listed is *RegisterServer*. This key simply tells Internet Explorer whether it should register the file after the file is downloaded. The allowable values are *yes* and *no*.

Next is a familiar key, *clsid*. The value of this key is the string representation of the CLSID for the ActiveX control. With the CLSID used here, you must include the curly braces, whereas you don't include them when specifying the CLSID for the CLASSID attribute of the <OBJECT> tag. (You already know how to use the CLASSID attribute of the <OBJECT> tag.)

Next is the *DestDir* key. The value of this key tells Internet Explorer to which directory to download the DLL. If you specify a value of *10*, the DLL is downloaded to the \Windows or \WinNT directory. If you specify a value of *11*, the DLL is downloaded to the \Windows\System or \WinNT\System32 directory. If no value is specified, the DLL is downloaded to the Downloaded Program Files directory in either

\Windows or \WinNT. In the case of SimpleCtrl.dll, we didn't specify a value for *DestDir*, so the DLL will be downloaded to the Downloaded Program Files directory.

The last key included in the [SimpleCtrl.dll] section is *FileVersion*. The value of this key specifies the minimum required version of the file we specified for the *file* key. If no value is specified, any version is acceptable. For SimpleCtrl.dll, we specify that we want version 1.0.0.0 or later.

Now let's move on to the [MSVBVM60.DLL] section, which is a little different from the [SimpleCtrl.dll] section. Here's the code for [MSVBVM60.DLL]:

```
[MSVBVM60.DLL]
hook=MSVBVM60.cab_Installer
FileVersion=6,0,81,76
```

The [MSVBVM60.DLL] section contains a lot fewer keys than the [SimpleCtrl.dll] section. You'll recognize the *FileVersion* key, but what is this *hook* key? The value of the *hook* key specifies a section in the INF file that will be executed when installing the DLL. Basically, a hook is a way to override or customize the installation process for a DLL or other component that you're installing. Two types of hooks exist: unconditional and conditional. Unconditional hooks are always executed when downloading a component. Unconditional hooks are specified by using the [Setup Hooks] section, which looks like this:

```
[Setup Hooks]
hookname=section-name
```

Unconditional hooks are generally used when creating an INF file to run a setup program. If you specify an unconditional hook by using the [Setup Hooks] section, you don't specify the [Add.Code] section. Here's an example of an INF file that runs a setup program:

```
[Setup Hooks]
hookname=section-name

[section-name]
run=%EXTRACT_DIR%\setup.exe

[Version]
Signature="$Chicago$"
AdvancedInf=2.0
```

When Internet Explorer downloads a CAB file, it reads the INF file. When it doesn't find an [Add.Code] section, Internet Explorer processes the [Setup Hooks] section and executes the programs specified for the *run* key.

Conditional hooks are executed only when certain conditions are true. The type of hook used for MSVBVM60.DLL is a conditional hook. If the CLSID or version of the file specified in the [MSVBVM60.DLL] section isn't sufficient and no *file* key is specified, Internet Explorer executes the hook section that is specified as the value of the *hook* key. So a conditional hook is run only if MSVBVM60.DLL isn't registered on the system.

The hook section specified by the *hook* key for the [MSVBVM60.DLL] section is formatted in the INF file, like this:

```
[MSVBVM60.cab_Installer]
file-win32-x86=http://activex.microsoft.com/controls/vb6/VBRun60.cab
run=%EXTRACT_DIR%\VBRun60.exe
```

> **TIP** Redistributable Microsoft DLLs can be downloaded from a Web page by setting the CODEBASE attribute to the name of the CAB file located at *http:// activex.microsoft.com/controls*. You don't have to include these files in your own CAB file. Remember, though, that only those files that are listed in an associated redist.txt file on your system can be legally redistributed.

The hook section contains the *file* key again, which tells Internet Explorer where to retrieve the needed file. Here, the *file* key is pointing to another CAB file that contains all the needed files. Once again this section includes a new key named *run*. This key tells Internet Explorer to run a specific file in a specific place. In this case, Internet Explorer will—after extracting all the files from the VBRun60.cab file— execute the VBRun60.exe file in the *%EXTRACT_DIR%*. This *%EXTRACT_DIR%* might look foreign to you, but it is just simple variable substitution like you might use in an MS-DOS batch file. Wherever Internet Explorer sees *%EXTRACT_DIR%*, it substitutes the path of the directory that is used to extract the files in a CAB file. (The other variable you can specify is *%OBJECT_DIR%*. It expands to the default destination directory for ActiveX controls, which is usually the Downloaded Program Files directory under the \Windows or \WinNT directories.)

In the *hook* section for MSVBVM60.DLL, note that Internet Explorer first extracts all the files in the VBRun60.cab file. Then it executes the VBRun60.exe file, which installs the Visual Basic run time on the client machine.

You don't need to manually create INF and CAB files when packaging Visual Basic ActiveX controls for downloading over the Internet, but you do need to manually create them when packaging ActiveX controls built with other tools, so understanding the internals of INF files is useful. (You will manually create INF and CAB files in the section titled "Compiling" later in this chapter.)

To tie everything together, let's create an INF file for the Calendar control and then package the INF file and mscal.ocx files into a CAB file. As you saw from analyzing mscal.ocx using the Depends tools, all of mscal.ocx's dependencies are system files. You don't need to include any other DLLs in the CAB file. So creating the INF file for the Calendar control is quite easy. Listing 5-1 on the next page shows the code for the Calendar control's INF file. To create this file, type the code by using Microsoft Windows Notepad, save it, and name it mscal.inf.

mscal.inf

```
[Version]
signature="$CHICAGO$"
AdvancedINF=2.0

[Add.Code]
mscal.ocx=mscal.ocx

[mscal.ocx]
file-win32-x86=thiscab
RegisterServer=yes
clsid={8E27C92B-1264-101C-8A2F-040224009C02}
DestDir=11
FileVersion=8,0,0,5007
```

Listing 5-1.

The code in Listing 5-1 specifies that one file be downloaded—mscal.ocx. This file resides in the current CAB file as specified by the *file* key. We want file version 8.0.0.5007, and we want Internet Explorer to register the file after placing it in the Windows system directory (*DestDir = 11*). Notice, however, that the preferred destination directory is Downloaded Program Files. This is because on Windows NT systems, if the user isn't the administrator of the machine, the user won't have write access to the System32 directory. So the download will fail in this case.

Creating a CAB file

Now we need to create a CAB file that packages together the INF file and any files we want to download to the client machine. Use the Cabarc or Makecab utilities that are included with the Cabinet SDK to create CAB files. Both of them use a command-line interface, which means we have to run them from an MS-DOS prompt. The Cabarc utility is for viewing and extracting files in cabinet files, whereas Makecab is just for creating cabinet files. (You can also view CAB files as folders by using the Cabview shell-extension utility that is available on the Microsoft Windows Power Toys Web site: *http://www.microsoft.com/windows95/downloads/contents/wutoys/w95pwrtoysset/.*)

Let's use the Cabarc utility to create the CAB file for the Calendar control. Using Cabarc to create CAB files is easy. When calling Cabarc, we just specify the *N* argument to indicate that we want to create a new CAB file. Then we specify the name of the CAB file we want to create followed by the names of the files we want to add to the CAB file. We can use wildcards when specifying filenames. For example, to create a new CAB file named mscal.cab and add the INF and OCX files for the Calendar control to the CAB file, we can type the following in the command line:

```
cabarc N mscal.cab mscal.inf mscal.ocx
```

Alternatively, we could have used wildcards because both the files that we want to add to the CAB file begin with *mscal*. This code shows how to use wildcards to create a CAB file:

```
cabarc N mscal.cab mscal.*
```

Next we need to copy the CAB file to some location on the server and add the name of the CAB file to the CODEBASE attribute of the <OBJECT> tag on a Web page, like this:

```
<OBJECT ID="CalObj"
        CLASSID="clsid:8E27C92B-1264-101C-8A2F-040224009C02"
        CODEBASE="http://someserver.com/mscal.cab#version=8,0,0,5007">
</OBJECT>
```

We left the version alone because the version used here represents the version of the Calendar control and not the version of the CAB file.

> **NOTE** In the previous sections, I described how to package ActiveX controls for download over the Internet. In these sections, I used the Calendar control as an example for simplicity. Whenever packaging Microsoft controls for download over the Internet, you should very carefully review the End–User License Agreement (EULA), REDISTRIBUTABLES directory, and/or README.TXT files accompanying the product with which a control is installed to determine the redistribution rights of the control. If you cannot find explicit permission to reuse the control in question, visit Microsoft's Permission Web site, which is located at *http://www.microsoft.com/permission.*

Gaining Security on the Web

ActiveX controls provide reusable functionality on Web pages that fills the gaps left by DHTML and script. For example, you might write an ActiveX control that opens or saves files to your user's hard drive. This is fine if you're the only one using the control. But how can someone who doesn't know you be sure that an ActiveX control isn't going to wipe out all the files on her system? How can she protect herself? Internet Explorer provides security for Web pages so that you can prevent ActiveX controls from running or allow only trusted controls to run on your system. More on this topic in a moment.

Internet Explorer has security zones that allow you to set security levels for intranet and Internet sites and set security levels for trusted or restricted sites that you choose. To set security levels for different types of Web sites, select Internet Options from the Internet Explorer Tools menu, and click the Security tab to display the dialog box shown in Figure 5-5 on the following page.

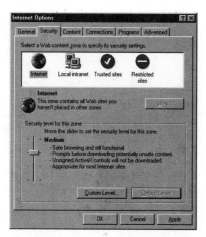

Figure 5-5. *Internet Options Security tab.*

Using this dialog box, you can set five different security levels:

■ *High.* This level is the safest way to browse the Web, but it's also the least functional. Most of the less secure features of Internet Explorer are disabled, such as the downloading of ActiveX controls. Using this level, you're completely safe from harm. At this level, unsigned ActiveX controls aren't downloaded at all. Also, you will most likely get code signing errors. (How to sign ActiveX controls will be explained shortly.)

■ *Medium.* This level provides safe browsing but includes more functionality than High. It will prompt you with a dialog box before downloading potentially unsafe content. At that point, you can decide whether to allow the download. At this level, unsigned ActiveX controls aren't downloaded at all. You're not even prompted.

■ *Medium-low.* This level is the same as Medium except that most content will be downloaded without prompts. However, Internet Explorer will prompt you before downloading signed ActiveX controls, and unsigned controls won't be downloaded at all.

■ *Low.* This level is the most functional but also the most unsafe. At this level, most content will be downloaded without prompts. Signed ActiveX controls will be downloaded without prompts, and you'll be prompted before unsigned ActiveX controls are downloaded. This level is most appropriate for the local intranet zone, not the Internet zone.

■ *Custom.* Using this level, you can determine security restrictions for individual items that can be downloaded and run, such as ActiveX controls and script. To set the Custom level, click the Custom Level button (shown in Figure 5-5) to display the dialog box in Figure 5-6. Use this dialog box to set the security restrictions for specific items that Internet Explorer might download.

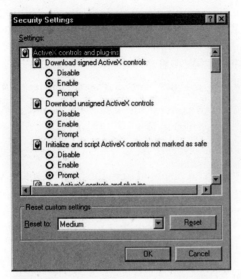

Figure 5-6. *Custom Level Security Settings dialog box.*

All levels except Low (and potentially Custom) disable the download of un-signed ActiveX controls. Signing an ActiveX control (also known as digital code sign-ing) is a way of telling users that they can trust the control because it won't do anything malicious such as wiping out all their files. Digital code signing uses Microsoft Authenticode technology to verify the contents of the CAB file by adding a digital certificate that indicates the name of the control's creator and a digital ID. This cer-tificate is obtained from a certificate authority such as VeriSign. Certificate authori-ties check on applicants, depending on the class of certificate requested, to make sure that they can be trusted. Certificate authorities usually have rigid restrictions so that not just anybody can obtain a certificate. This procedure protects users from hackers.

To digitally sign the CAB file, follow these steps.

1. Obtain the code signing tools for Internet Explorer 5 from the MSDN Online Web Workshop at *(http://msdn.microsoft.com/workshop /gallery/ tools/authenticode/authcode.asp)*.

    Before getting your file signed, be sure to use the most current code-signing tools when signing code built for Internet Explorer 5. If you sign the CAB file with an earlier version of the tools, the ActiveX control won't be downloaded and installed correctly on the client machine.

2. Obtain a certificate from a certificate authority such as VeriSign or from a server on your intranet that is running Microsoft Certificate Server. A private key is created during the certificate enrollment process. If you have not yet obtained your own certificate from a certificate authority, you can create a test certificate by using the MakeCert.exe and Cert2Spc.exe code signing utilities. First, you use the MakeCert utility to create your test X.509 certificate (.cer file) and private key (.pvk file):

    ```
    MakeCert -sv MyKey.pvk n "CN=My Software Company" MyCert.cer
    ```

    Next, use Cert2Spc to convert the .cer file to a PKCS #7 Software Publishing Certificate (.spc file)

    ```
    Cert2Spc MyCert.cer MyCert.spc
    ```

3. Using the SignCode utility you obtained from the MSDN Online Web Workshop, sign your CAB file with the certificate (.spc file) and private key (.pvk file) you either received from the certificate authority or created using the MakeCert and Cert2Spc utilities. (Note that the URL *timstamp.dll* isn't a typo. The *e* is supposed to be missing.)

    ```
    SignCode -spc MyCert.spc -v MyKey.pvk -t http://
    timestamp.verisign.com/scripts/timstamp.dll mscal.cab
    ```

Other parameters are available for SignCode, such as a parameter for identifying the Web site of the publisher and the descriptive name for the signed file. These parameters are documented in the MSDN Online Web Workshop at *http://msdn.microsoft.com/workshop/security/authcode/signing.asp*. You can also find relevant Knowledge Base articles at *http://msdn.microsoft.com/workshop/delivery/support/KB.asp*.

Safety

After signing the CAB file, users of your ActiveX control will know that the control is trustworthy, which is different from knowing that it's *safe*. Most ActiveX controls are initialized with data and scripted by using VBScript or JScript. The data used to initialize a control could come from an untrustworthy source, so you might want to block this sort of activity. Also, script can be written to access the methods and properties of an ActiveX control. Regarding those controls that access a user's files, you wouldn't want a hacker to write script that uses these controls to delete all the files on a user's system.

You can use one of two strategies to tell users that the control is safe for initialization and safe for scripting: change the Registry or implement a COM interface—

IObjectSafety. The first strategy is used for Visual Basic controls. The Registry is automatically changed for you by the Package And Deployment Wizard, or PDW, which is discussed in the section "Using PDW to Package Your Visual Basic Control." The second strategy, implementing *IObjectSafety*, is the recommended technique, although it's not natively supported by Visual Basic. We'll discuss how to implement *IObjectSafety* in the section titled "Marking ATL Controls as Safe." (To implement *IObjectSafety* in Visual Basic, consult Knowledge Base article Q182598 at *http://support.microsoft.com/support/kb/articles/Q182/5/98.asp*.)

Licensing

So far we've been discussing security for the users of the control. What about security for you, the creator of the control? You're probably thinking that security for you doesn't make sense. But suppose you create an ActiveX control that you want to sell. You need a way to ensure that only authorized developers who have proper permission can use the control. How do you ensure security like that? The answer is licensing. The subject of creating a license for a control is outside the scope of this book, but to illustrate how licensing works, we'll talk about how to use third-party licensed controls on a Web page. (For more information about creating licensed controls, see the Component Development section of the MSDN Online Web Workshop.)

To use licensed ActiveX controls, you must use the License Pack Manager, a COM object that reads a special license file known as an LPK (License PacKage) file for the control. The License Pack Manager can determine whether you're allowed to use the licensed control.

> **NOTE** The License Pack Manager reads a GUID that is stored in an LPK file and passes it to Internet Explorer. (This GUID is actually an interface ID, or IID.) Internet Explorer uses this IID when creating the control by passing it to the *IClassFactory2::CreateInstanceLic* method.

Before adding the License Pack Manager to a Web page, you must first create an LPK file for the licensed control you want to use by running Lpk_Tool.exe, a special tool that is available for download from the MSDN Online Web Workshop. Follow these easy steps to use Lpk_Tool.exe:

1. Start Lpk_Tool.exe. This tool displays the dialog box shown in Figure 5-7 on the next page. This dialog box lists all the ActiveX controls currently installed on your system.

2. Check the Show Only Controls That Support Licensing check box to display only those controls that implement *IClassFactory2*.

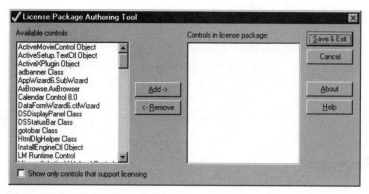

Figure 5-7. *Lpk_Tool.exe.*

3. To add controls to the license package, click the control you want in the left combo box, and then click the Add button to add it to the right combo box. Once you have included all the licensed controls that you want to use on the Web page, save the license package to a LPK file by clicking the Save & Exit button. Clicking this button displays the standard Windows File Save dialog box, in which you can specify the path and filename.

4. After creating the LPK file, add an <OBJECT> tag to the Web page that references the License Pack Manager and passes the path and name of the LPK file. Here's the code for an LPK file named SimpleCtrl.lpk:

```
<OBJECT CLASSID="clsid:5220CB21-C88D-11cf-B347-
00AA00A28331">
        <PARAM NAME="LPKPath" VALUE="SimpleCtrl.lpk">
</OBJECT>
```

The CLASSID attribute specifies the CLSID of the License Pack Manager. This CLSID should always be the one listed in the preceding code. You can include only one LPK file in a Web page. If you include more than one LPK file, Internet Explorer will ignore all but the first one. In between the opening and closing <OBJECT> tags is a <PARAM> tag. It allows you to send initialization data to the ActiveX control or COM object indicated by the <OBJECT> tag. The <PARAM> tag requires two attributes: NAME and VALUE. The NAME attribute used in the <PARAM> tag for the LPK file should always have a value of *LPKPath*. The value of the VALUE attribute specifies the path and name of the LPK file we created earlier. The path and name that you specify must be relative to the current location of the Web page being viewed. The path has to be relative; otherwise, someone could copy an LPK file from a server and reuse it, even without permission.

CREATING VISUAL BASIC ACTIVEX CONTROLS

Now that you understand how to use ActiveX controls on your Web pages, it's time to learn how to create your own. It is often more rewarding and sometimes necessary to create your own controls, as there aren't third-party controls available for everything you could possibly want to do. This section demonstrates how to create a simple Visual Basic ActiveX control that you can place on a Web page. This discussion isn't meant to be an all-inclusive tutorial. Let's just get started so you will understand the concepts discussed later in this book.

> **NOTE**   Visual Basic ActiveX controls are sometimes referred to as UserControls, so don't be confused if you hear this term. Controls created using other development tools are still referred to as ActiveX controls.

First, start Visual Basic. The New Project dialog box, shown in Figure 5-8, appears.

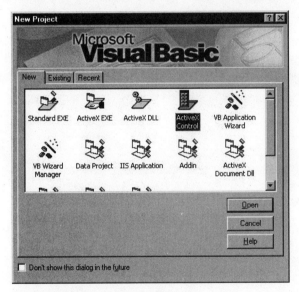

Figure 5-8. *New Project dialog box.*

In this dialog box, double-click the ActiveX Control icon. After you open the new project, the form for the Visual Basic ActiveX control is displayed (Figure 5-9 on the following page). You can design a control in this form. This window is named the Object window.

Add any of the intrinsic controls from the Control Toolbox on the left-hand side of the Visual Basic integrated development environment (IDE). For this simple example, add a PictureBox, a TextBox, and a CommandButton control to the form, as shown in Figure 5-10 on the following page.

NOTE You don't necessarily need an ActiveX control to handle what this example does because similar controls are available as HTML elements in Internet Explorer. This simple example is just meant to teach you how to create ActiveX controls.

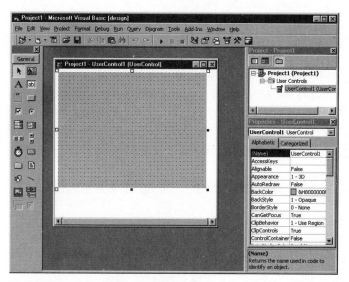

Figure 5-9. *Visual Basic ActiveX form.*

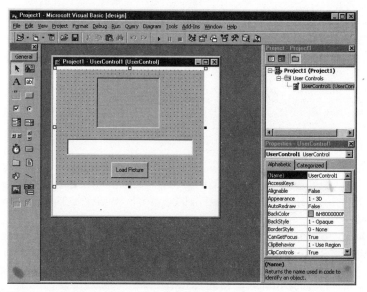

Figure 5-10. *Adding controls to a form.*

We'll design an ActiveX control with the following functionality: the PictureBox control will display a bitmap image when you enter the path to that image in the TextBox and then press the CommandButton. First just accept all the default names for all the controls. Remove the default text in the TextBox by clicking the TextBox control and then deleting the text for the *Text* property in the Properties box on the right-hand side of the IDE. (You'll have to scroll down to bring it into view.)

Next, change the text in the CommandButton control by clicking the button and changing the Caption property in the Properties box on the right-hand side of the IDE to the value *Load Picture*. Now you must add some Visual Basic code to the ActiveX control so it will actually do something. To enter code for the control, switch to Code view in the Visual Basic IDE by double-clicking somewhere on the form (or on one of the controls on the form), or by choosing Code from the View menu. If you double-click the CommandButton control on the form, the Code view window in Figure 5-11 is displayed.

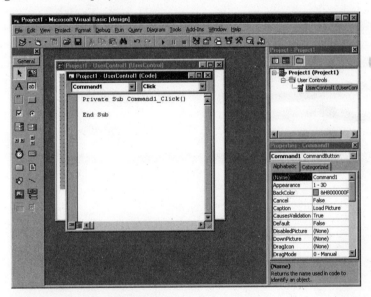

Figure 5-11. *Visual Basic Code window.*

Visual Basic tries to determine what you're going to do next. Because you clicked the CommandButton control, Visual Basic assumes that you want to write an event handler for the *Click* event of the CommandButton. This event handler looks identical to the event handlers we wrote for VBScript. It consists of the name of the object, the underscore character (_), and the name of the event. *Command1* is the default name for the first CommandButton control that you place on a form. *Command2* is the default name for the second, and so forth.

You'll want the ActiveX control to achieve this: when the Command1 button is clicked, the associated ActiveX control will load a picture from a file on the client's hard disk or from a URL. To read a graphics file from a URL, you need to use the *AsyncRead* method that is part of the *UserControl* object that represents the control. You'll want to load the file that was entered by the user. You can retrieve the filename from the *Text* property of the Text1 control, which represents the text box on the form. The code for the *Click* event handler should look like this:

```
Private Sub Command1_Click()
    AsyncRead Text1.Text, vbAsyncTypeFile
End Sub
```

When calling the *AsyncRead* method, you have to specify the type of data that you're downloading. In this case, you're downloading a file, so you should specify *vbAsyncTypeFile*, as listed in the preceding code. The *AsyncRead* method starts an asynchronous download of the file that you specify. When the download is complete, the *AsyncReadComplete* event of the control is fired. It is in your event handler for this event that you load the picture specified by the user.

To load the picture into the picture box, set the *Picture* property of the *PictureBox* object by using the text entered by the user. Open the Object drop-down list in the Code window and select *UserControl1*, then open the Procedure drop-down list in the Code window and select *AsyncReadComplete*. You'll be in the *AsyncReadComplete* event handler block. In this event handler block, type in the name of the PictureBox, *Picture1*, and then press the period character (.) in it. Visual Basic uses IntelliSense technology to display a list of all the methods and properties of the *PictureBox* object, as shown in Figure 5-12. Pretty convenient, wouldn't you say?

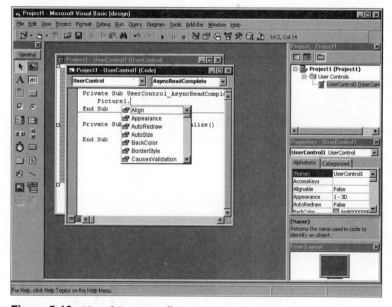

Figure 5-12. *Visual Basic IntelliSense.*

Choose the *Picture* property by scrolling to it and clicking it or by typing in the name of the property and pressing the Tab or Enter key. (You'll notice that Visual Basic will force the drop-down list to scroll as you're typing. Once the property you're looking for is highlighted, you can press Tab or Enter to select it.)

Because *Picture* is a property, we're going to set it equal to some value. You will want to set it equal to the picture that the *AsyncRead* method loaded. However, the *Picture* property of *Picture1* is a *Picture* object, which means you can't just set this property equal to the name of the file entered by the user. To set the *Picture* property, you have to use a special helper function named *LoadPicture*, which takes a string as its first parameter. This string indicates the path and name of the picture file you want to load. *LoadPicture* creates a *Picture* object by loading the picture from the path and filename that you specify.

This *Picture* object is then returned so that you can use it to set the *Picture* property of *Picture1*. When calling *LoadPicture*, use the value that was returned from the asynchronous download operation. This value is stored in the *Value* property of the *AsyncProp* object that is passed to the *AsyncReadComplete* event handler. Here's how the Visual Basic code will look for the *AsyncReadComplete* event handler:

```
Private Sub UserControl_AsyncReadComplete(AsyncProp As AsyncProperty)
    Picture1.Picture = LoadPicture(AsyncProp.Value)
End Sub
```

In addition to loading the picture that the user has specified, you might want to load a picture when the ActiveX control is first created. Creation of an ActiveX control or other object is often referred to as instantiation. When the control is first instantiated, its *Initialize* event is fired. To handle this event, you could enter the name of the event handler manually, or you could switch back to Object view and double-click on an empty area of the form. If you follow the second option, Visual Basic will create an event handler named *UserControl_Initialize*. You can enter code in this event handler to call the *AsyncRead* method to load a picture from your Web server.

You can copy the file tv.bmp included on the companion CD in the folder \Samples\Chap05\VBCtrl. This file was obtained from the samples that are available on the Visual Studio 6 CD. If you load tv.bmp from your Web server, the code for the *Initialize* event of the control should look like this. (Obviously, you should change *yourserver*.com to the name of your Web server.)

```
Private Sub UserControl_Initialize()
    AsyncRead "http://yourserver.com/tv.bmp", vbAsyncTypeFile
End Sub
```

Adding Methods

Before you package a control for use on a Web page, you'll probably want to add some methods, properties, and events to the control so that you can use it programmatically. Adding methods to a Visual Basic ActiveX control is extremely easy. All you have to do is declare a public function, which can take any number of input arguments that you specify. In addition, you can specify the *Optional* keyword to indicate that a parameter is optional. You can add a method to the control to allow the picture being displayed to be changed by using script at run time.

Create a public function named *ChangePicture* that takes one input argument. This input argument is a string that specifies the path and the name of the picture to load. Here's the code for this function:

```
Public Sub ChangePicture(ByVal txtPictureName As String)
    AsyncRead txtPictureName, vbAsyncTypeFile
End Sub
```

This function accepts the name of the picture to load. Again, the name of the picture can point to the location of the file on your local system, or it can be a URL that points to the file on your Web server or some other server on the Internet. Then you load the picture using the *AsyncRead* method. We'll discuss how to write script to call this method after we package the control for distribution on the Web.

Adding Properties

Adding properties to a control is even easier than adding methods. All you have to do is declare a property as you would declare any other global variable in Visual Basic. But instead of using *Dim*, you use the *Public* keyword to declare a property, like you did when declaring the *ChangePicture* function earlier. In our example, you can add a property to the control that can be used to determine the path and name of the current picture loaded into the PictureBox. You can name this property *CurrentPicture* and declare it:

```
Public CurrentPicture As String
```

Firing Events

Firing events from a Visual Basic ActiveX control is also easy. Simply declare the event using the *Event* keyword together with the keyword *Public*, and then use the *RaiseEvent* function to fire the event. You can even pass parameters with the event when it fires. You do this by specifying the parameters that you're going to pass when you declare the event. For the control we are creating, you can declare an event named *OnPictureChanged* that will fire each time the *Picture* object is changed. Here's the code for declaring *OnPictureChanged*:

```
Public Event OnPictureChanged()
```

The event will fire each time the picture changes. For example, *OnPictureChanged* can be fired from any of the methods in our example control, like this:

```
RaiseEvent OnPictureChanged
```

After you add the method, property, and event to the control, the code should look similar to Listing 5-2. You can find the code listing on the companion CD in the folder \Samples\Chap05\VBCtrl. Notice that I combined all the code to load the picture into the *ChangePicture* method so that I don't have to maintain multiple copies of the same code.

VBCtrl.ctl

```
Option Explicit
Public CurrentPicture As String
Public Event OnPictureChanged()

Public Sub ChangePicture(ByVal txtPictureName As String)
    CurrentPicture = txtPictureName
    AsyncRead CurrentPicture, vbAsyncTypeFile
End Sub

Private Sub Command1_Click()
    ChangePicture (Text1.Text)
End Sub

Private Sub UserControl_AsyncReadComplete(AsyncProp As AsyncProperty)
    Picture1.Picture = LoadPicture(AsyncProp.Value)
    RaiseEvent OnPictureChanged
End Sub

Private Sub UserControl_Initialize()
    ' Change the "yourserver.com" to the name of your Web server.
    ' Otherwise, the control will not work at all.
    '
    AsyncRead "http://yourserver.com/tv.bmp", vbAsyncTypeFile
End Sub
```

Listing 5-2.

Now save the project and the control. Choose a descriptive name other than the default of Project1.vbp and UserControl1.ctl. Otherwise, you'll eventually have hundreds of projects and controls on your system with the same name. Choose names such as VBCtrl.vbp and VBCtrl.ctl. (Notice how I left the file extensions alone.)

Setting the Threading Model

Before you are ready to compile your control, you must perform one more task. As you'll recall, only Apartment-threaded controls will work correctly in Internet Explorer. For Visual Basic 6, Apartment threading is the default threading model setting. If you create an ActiveX control in an earlier version of Visual Basic, you'll want to ensure that the threading model is set to Apartment.

To ensure that the threading model is set to Apartment in Visual Basic 6, invoke the Project Properties dialog box by choosing the Project Properties menu item from the Project menu. The dialog box that appears is shown in Figure 5-13. A drop-down list of the available threading models is displayed in the lower right-hand corner. Make sure the list box displays Apartment Threaded. If that option is already set correctly, click Cancel to close the dialog box. Otherwise, change the Threading Model option to Apartment Threaded, and click OK.

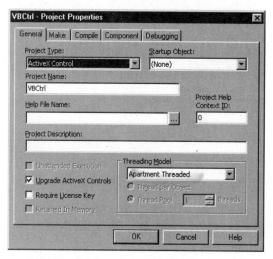

Figure 5-13. *Visual Basic Project Properties dialog box.*

Compiling

Now you're ready to compile the control. Choose Make from the File menu. (If you named the project VBCtrl like I did, the Make menu item will display as Make VBCtrl.ocx.) Visual Basic will ask you to enter a location for the OCX file. Put this OCX file in the same directory as your project files. After you package the control using the Package And Deployment Wizard, you'll be ready to test the control with Internet Explorer and write script for the control. PDW will be discussed in detail in the next section.

Immediately after you compile the control, return to the Project Properties dialog box and click the Component tab. (See Figure 5-14.) Select the Binary Compatibility option, and below it, enter the path to VBCtrl.ocx in the text box. Specifying this setting ensures that Visual Basic will use the same CLSID for the control every time the control is compiled. This step is important because if the CLSID changes, clients of the control won't be able to use it.

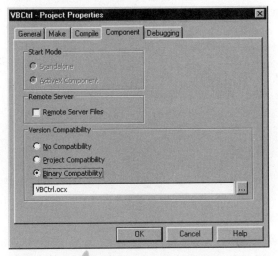

Figure 5-14. *Setting binary compatibility.*

Using PDW to Package Your Visual Basic Control

Now that you've compiled the control, let's package it so that it can be used on a Web page. We could take the time to create the INF and CAB files manually, but why do that when Visual Basic 6 provides a wizard that creates the files for you? An application known as the Package And Deployment Wizard (PDW) ships with Visual Basic 6. This application enables you to easily create packages—which are the files required to use the ActiveX control on the Web—such as the CAB, INF, and HTML files. "HTML files?" you might ask. That's right, PDW even creates a default Web page for you that includes an <OBJECT> tag with all the correct attribute settings.

Creating a package for use in Internet Explorer is relatively easy. First you need to start PDW from the Start/Programs menu, choose Microsoft Visual Studio 6/Microsoft Visual Studio 6 Tools, and then choose Package And Deployment Wizard. (The Microsoft Visual Studio 6 menu was created when you installed Visual Studio.) If you've installed only Visual Basic 6, PDW will be under the Visual Basic 6 Tools directory. After you select PDW, the dialog box shown in Figure 5-15 on the next page is displayed.

Select the project you want PDW to use to create the Internet package. Click the Browse button, locate the VBCtrl.vbp file that you created earlier, select it, and click Open. If any of the files in the project are out of date, PDW will ask whether you want to recompile the project.

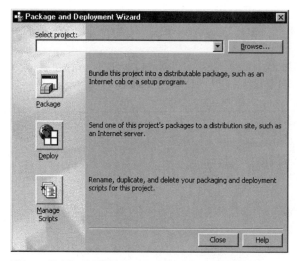

Figure 5-15. *Package And Deployment Wizard.*

Click the Package button on the left-hand side of the PDW dialog box. After PDW finishes checking your project, the Package Type dialog box in Figure 5-16 will be displayed, and you'll be asked to choose the type of package that you want to create. Choose Internet Package, and click the Next button to display the Package Folder dialog box, shown in Figure 5-17.

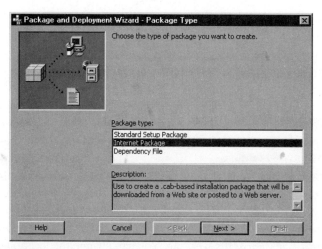

Figure 5-16. *Package Type dialog box.*

The Package Folder dialog box asks you to select a location for the package files that PDW will create. By default, PDW creates a Package directory under the directory in which the project is located. Most of the time you'll want to accept the default location and click the Next button. If the Package directory doesn't exist, PDW will ask you whether you want to create it. If you're asked, click Yes. You'll also be asked if you want to distribute the property page DLL for our example control. Property pages allow developers who are creating applications using your control to set the properties of your control at design time. You don't need property pages for this control, so click No.

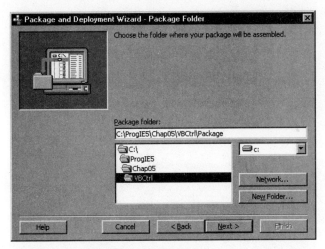

Figure 5-17. *Package Folder dialog box.*

PDW gives you a summary of the files that will be included in this package. This list should be similar to what is displayed in Figure 5-18 on the following page. Notice that the Microsoft Stock Property Page DLL (MSSTKPRP.DLL) isn't selected. That's because you chose No when asked whether you wanted to distribute the property page DLL with the package. Also notice that the VB6 Runtime and OLE Automation DLLs are somehow going to be included in this package: PDW has determined that the control needs these DLLs. You didn't have to go through the trouble of determining the dependencies yourself.

Click the Next button to display the File Source dialog box, which is shown in Figure 5-19 on the next page. Using this dialog box, you can choose where the needed files should be located. For example, you'll want VBCtrl.ocx to be included in this CAB file. However, you probably want the VB6 Runtime and OLE Automation DLLs to be downloaded from Microsoft's Web site. You can change the location values, but you'll usually want to accept the defaults.

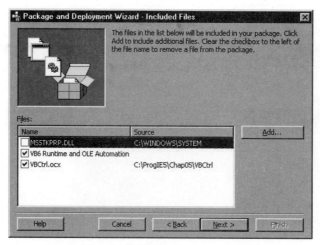

Figure 5-18. *Included Files dialog box.*

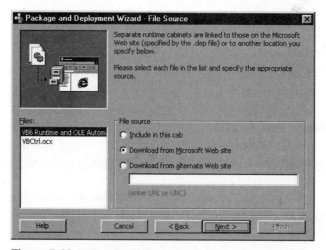

Figure 5-19. *File Source dialog box.*

Click the Next button to display the Safety Settings dialog box, shown in Figure 5-20. In this dialog box, you specify whether the control is safe for scripting, safe for initialization, or both. Some developers don't ever consider a control that accesses the user's hard disk to be safe, but you need to decide for yourself which values to specify in the Safety Settings dialog box. Although the control we created does access files on the user's hard disk, it can't do anything malicious to those files, so you're probably safe if you specify Yes for both scripting and initialization. One good rule of thumb to follow is that if something malicious could possibly be done with the control, the control is not safe.

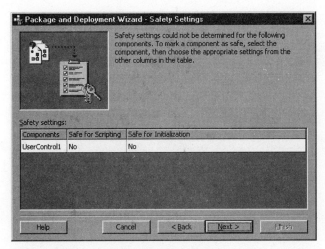

Figure 5-20. *Safety Settings dialog box.*

Remember that if you don't mark the control safe for scripting and initialization and you try to script or initialize it using <PARAM> tags, users with certain security levels for Internet Explorer will, at the very least, be warned about the control. Also, if the user's security level is high enough, the script you write for the ActiveX control won't run, and the control won't be initialized. When you're finished deciding what to do, click the Next button.

You're finally finished providing all the values that PDW needs to create the Internet Package. At this point the Finished! dialog box is displayed, as shown in Figure 5-21. Click the Finish button to have PDW create the package for you.

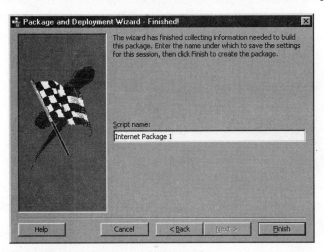

Figure 5-21. *Finished! dialog box.*

Testing

Notice that PDW created a Package directory in the Project directory after it finished creating the package. In the Package directory, PDW placed a CAB file named VBCtrl.cab, which contains an INF file and the control. PDW also created a simple HTML page that contains an <OBJECT> tag with all the necessary attributes so that the control will be displayed on the Web page. The following code lists this <OBJECT> tag:

```
<OBJECT ID="UserControl1"
    CLASSID="CLSID:412FF29B-AE0B-11D2-A9BA-444553540001"
    CODEBASE="VBCtrl.CAB#version=1.0.0.0">
</OBJECT>
```

Notice that PDW gave the control an ID of *UserControl1*. You'll use this ID when you write script for the ActiveX control. Also notice that PDW adds the necessary HTML code for using the License Pack Manager. This code, which is commented out, can make life easier for you if you need to use the License Pack Manager.

Open the HTML file that PDW created for you in Internet Explorer to test out the control. When loaded, the control should display the tv.bmp file, as is shown in Figure 5-22. Try entering a path and a filename of another picture file and then clicking the Load Picture button. If the picture isn't loaded, check the path and filename you entered. If it's correct, review the code and make sure you've typed everything correctly. If you're still having trouble, try copying and running the VBCtrl project from the companion CD, which can be found in the folder \Samples\Chap05\VBCtrl. PDW adds a comment to the HTML for the License Pack Manager that refers you to the ActiveX SDK to download the latest Lpk_Tool.exe. The ActiveX SDK existed only for Internet Explorer 3. You can download Lpk_Tool.exe from the MSDN Online Web Workshop.

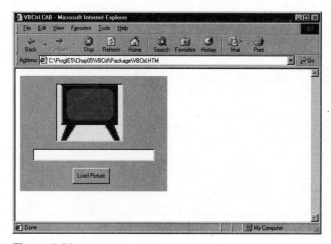

Figure 5-22. *VBCtrl in action.*

Writing Script for Your Visual Basic Control

Now that you have a working Visual Basic ActiveX control, you can write some script to access the method and property of the control and to handle its event. Writing script for an ActiveX control is the same as writing script for any object in the DHTML Object Model. You can call methods and properties and handle events using the object's ID. For example, to access the *ChangePicture* method using VBScript, insert this code into the HTML file for the Web page:

```
UserControl1.ChangePicture(Text1.value)
```

To display the value of the *CurrentPicture* property using JScript, insert this code into the HTML file:

```
alert(UserControl1.CurrentPicture);
```

To handle the *OnPictureChanged* event in VBScript, enter this code into the page:

```
Sub UserControl1_OnPictureChanged
    MsgBox "Picture Changed"
End Sub
```

To show you how easy it is to write script for ActiveX controls, the companion CD includes an enhanced version of the VBCtrl.htm file, which you can find in the folder \Samples\Chap05\VBCtrl. (See Figure 5-23.) I've added a text box and a button that allow you to change the current picture, as well as a button that displays the value of the *CurrentPicture* property when clicked.

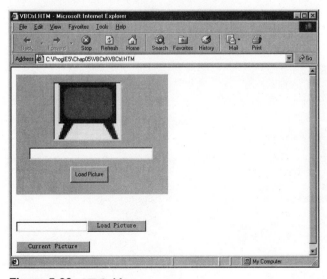

Figure 5-23. *VBCtrl.htm.*

At first you might think we have two ways to perform the same operation: one through the ActiveX control, and the other through the HTML intrinsic controls. Actually, you don't need to include a control in the user interface of an ActiveX control if sufficient replacements are available in standard HTML. In other words, you can use HTML to provide the user interface and call the methods and properties of an ActiveX control using script to provide functionality that just isn't possible using only HTML and script.

Listing 5-3 shows the source code (minus the License Pack Manager code) for the enhanced version of VBCtrl.htm. You can find the code on the companion CD in the folder \Samples\Chap05\VBCtrl.

VBCtrl.htm

```
<HTML>
<HEAD>
<TITLE>VBCtrl.HTM</TITLE>

    <SCRIPT LANGUAGE="VBS">
    Sub Btn1_onclick
        UserControl1.ChangePicture(Text1.value)
    End Sub

    Sub UserControl1_OnPictureChanged
        MsgBox "Picture Changed"
    End Sub
    </SCRIPT>

</HEAD>
<BODY>
    <OBJECT ID="UserControl1"
        CLASSID="CLSID:412FF29B-AE0B-11D2-A9BA-444553540001"
        CODEBASE="VBCtrl.CAB#version=1,0,0,0">
    </OBJECT>

    <P>
    <BR><BR>
    <INPUT TYPE="TEXT" ID="Text1">
    <BUTTON ID="Btn1">Load Picture</BUTTON>
    <P>
    <BUTTON onclick="alert(UserControl1.CurrentPicture)">
        Current Picture
    </BUTTON>
</BODY>
</HTML>
```

Listing 5-3.

Initializing from HTML

Even if you're not writing script for the ActiveX control, you can send initialization data to the control using the <PARAM> tag. The <PARAM> tag is placed between the opening and closing object tags in this example. The <PARAM> tag has two attributes: NAME and VALUE. The NAME attribute specifies the name of the property in the ActiveX control that you want to initialize. The VALUE attribute specifies the value to which the property should be set.

When Internet Explorer sees the <PARAM> tag, it passes the name and value that you specify to the ActiveX control via a property bag object. The ActiveX control then reads the properties that you specified from this object and sets them accordingly. These properties don't necessarily have the same names as the corresponding properties of the ActiveX control we covered earlier. Potentially these properties can have any arbitrary names the developer of the control chooses. In the interest of consistency, however, it's best to give these properties the same name as their counterparts in the ActiveX control. Here's how you can set the *CurrentPicture* property using the <PARAM> tag:

```
<OBJECT ID="UserControl1" WIDTH=325 HEIGHT=250
    CLASSID="CLSID:1A9B2B56-AE27-11D2-A9BA-444553540001"
    CODEBASE="VBCtrl.CAB#version=1,0,0,0">
  <PARAM NAME="CurrentPicture" VALUE="http://yourserver.com/tv.bmp">
</OBJECT>
```

Notice that I included the WIDTH and HEIGHT attributes for the <OBJECT> tag. If you don't specify the width and height of the control when using <PARAM> tags, Visual Basic assumes that these should be set to *0*. As a result, you won't see the control's user interface.

If you specify the <PARAM> tags for a Visual Basic ActiveX control, when the control is first instantiated, the *ReadProperties* event of the *UserControl* is fired. To read the properties that the <PARAM> tags are initializing, you must handle the *ReadProperties* event in the control. In the event handler, use the *PropertyBag* object that was sent to the event handler to read the properties that are being initialized. You can set the properties for the control as needed. Add the following code to the VBCtrl.ctl to read and set the *CurrentPicture* property using the Visual Basic *PropertyBag* object:

```
Private Sub UserControl_ReadProperties(PropBag As PropertyBag)
    ChangePicture PropBag.ReadProperty("CurrentPicture")
End Sub
```

Notice that we're calling the *ReadProperty* method to read the *CurrentPicture* property. The *ReadProperty* method will return the value of the *CurrentPicture* property if it finds the property in the property bag. Then we call the *ChangePicture* method to set the *CurrentPicture* property accordingly.

Printing

When the ActiveX control is on a Web page and the user chooses Print from the File menu, you typically want the control to be printed in its current state. When printing, Internet Explorer performs background printing by creating a hidden version of the current page. This hidden version contains a second instance of everything on the page. When creating this hidden page, Internet Explorer loads and initializes the ActiveX control. Before initializing the control on this hidden Web page, Internet Explorer uses the property bag object to tell the control that it should save any properties that have changed to the Internet Explorer property bag. Then, when initializing the control, Internet Explorer instructs the control to initialize itself using the values of the properties stored in Internet Explorer's property bag. That's how you can ensure that the control is printed in the current state.

You've already seen *ReadProperties*—the event of the control that is fired when the control is initialized. Before Internet Explorer creates the hidden Web page for printing, the control's *WriteProperties* event is fired to tell the control that it should save its properties to Internet Explorer's property bag. Implementing this in Visual Basic is easy. Create an event handler for the *WriteProperties* event, and use the *WriteProperty* method of the given *PropertyBag* object to save the properties. Here's how the event handler should appear in the Visual Basic code:

```
Private Sub UserControl_WriteProperties(PropBag As PropertyBag)
    PropBag.WriteProperty "CurrentPicture", CurrentPicture
End Sub
```

Now that you see how cool ActiveX controls are and how easily you can create them by using Visual Basic, you probably want to stop reading and start programming. Hold the train! There's still more to learn. Creating an ActiveX control by using Visual Basic is simple, but there's a reason: ActiveX controls created using Visual Basic can't perform some of the tasks that ActiveX controls built with C++ and ATL can. You'll see a more specific discussion about the differences in the next chapter. For now, let's talk about how to create an ActiveX control using the Active Template Library (ATL).

CREATING ATL ACTIVEX CONTROLS

Creating ActiveX controls by using C++ and ATL isn't as easy as creating them using Visual Basic, but ATL provides a lot of wizards that simplify the job. If you're a C++ programmer and are familiar with templates, you'll find ATL easy to use and understand. ATL takes a lot of the hassle out of creating ActiveX controls and other

COM objects using C++. By providing default implementations for many COM inter-faces such as *IUnknown* and *IDispatch,* ATL takes care of much of the boilerplate COM code that you probably copied from one project to the next in the past. Also, ATL provides several wizards that generate most of the code for ActiveX controls. So you can create the controls a lot faster than if you had to enter all the code manually.

Because most of the C++ type code I'll use in the rest of this book is based on ATL, this section provides a short introduction to creating ActiveX controls using ATL. Like the introduction to creating ActiveX controls using Visual Basic earlier in this chapter, this discussion isn't meant to be an all-inclusive reference to the Active Tem-plate Library. It's merely intended to get you started creating ActiveX controls by using ATL and to help you understand much of the code in later chapters. Also, just as the previous discussion about creating ActiveX controls by using Visual Basic didn't require you to have a good understanding of COM, you don't necessarily have to know COM to follow this section. But you will deal more directly with COM in this section than in the Visual Basic section, so understanding the basics of COM before you continue reading would certainly help.

To create ATL ActiveX controls, you first need to understand the internals of an ActiveX control from a COM standpoint: what's required by the COM specification for a COM object to be considered an ActiveX control. According to the OC96 (OLE Controls) standard, to be considered an ActiveX control, a COM object must be able to implement *IUnknown* and support self-registration. Self-registration means that the ActiveX control knows how to register itself. In other words, the DLL that contains the ActiveX control exports the *DllRegisterServer* function, which can be called to force the ActiveX control to register itself in the Registry. The control isn't required to be self-unregistering; however, a control is often considered rude if it is not!

The requirements are lax so that an ActiveX control can be as small as possible. You're not required to implement a large number of interfaces that you'll never need. You can implement only the smallest bit of required functionality needed by an ActiveX control. Although an ActiveX control is required to implement only *IUnknown* and self-registration, if that's all it did, the control wouldn't be especially useful. In fact, it would be downright boring. So you do need to implement enough interfaces to make the ActiveX control useful. These interfaces, listed in order of importance, are described in Table 5-1 on the next page. If you're going to use the control on a Web page, you should implement at least the first four interfaces to ensure the con-trol will work correctly in Internet Explorer.

TABLE 5-1
ACTIVEX CONTROL-RELATED INTERFACES

Interface	Description
IUnknown	Manages object lifetime (*AddRef* and *Release*) and object recognition (*QueryInterface*). Base interface for all other interfaces.
IClassFactory	Contains two methods (*CreateInstance* and *LockServer*) to deal with the creation of objects.
IOleObject	Provides the basic means for a control to communicate with its container.
IDispatch	Supports automation of COM objects.
IOleControl	Provides container support for ambient properties, keyboard mnemonics, and events.
IOleInPlaceActiveObject	Provides a direct channel between an in-place object and the container's outermost frame window and document window.
IViewObject	Enables an object to display itself directly without having to pass a data object to the caller.
IOleInPlaceObjectWindowless	Enables a windowless control to process Windows messages.
IPersistStreamInit	Supports persistence via a stream.

Some of the interfaces in Table 5-1 are more important than others. In particular, the first four are extremely important—an ActiveX control might not work on a Web page at all without them. In addition to implementing these interfaces, you'll probably want the control to have some kind of user interface or other form of visual representation. Next we'll discuss how to use ATL to create an ActiveX control that can be seen on a Web page, exposes methods and properties, and fires events.

To create an ATL ActiveX control, first start Visual C++ 6. After you get past that difficult step, choose New from the File menu, which displays the dialog box in Figure 5-24. Make sure that the ATL COM AppWizard is selected. Then enter a name in the Project Name text box on the upper right-hand side of the dialog box. For this example, name the project AtlControl. You might want to change the default location for your project to a different directory.

When you click OK, the dialog box in Figure 5-25 is displayed. Notice that the title bar states that you're performing step 1 of 1. See how easy this is going to be?!

You're creating an ActiveX control, so leave the default selection of Dynamic Link Library (DLL) alone, and click the Finish button. Click OK in the confirmation dialog box that appears. Now Visual C++ will create a number of files for you that contain the boilerplate code necessary for Internet Explorer to interact with the DLL of your ActiveX control. For example, if you look in the file AtlControl.cpp, you'll see several exported DLL functions that containers can use to communicate with the ActiveX control.

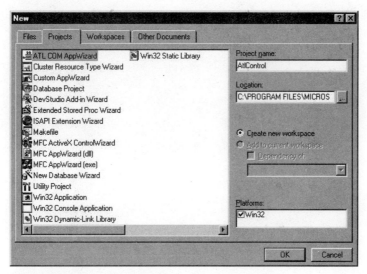

Figure 5-24. *New dialog box.*

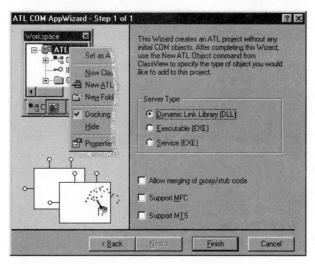

Figure 5-25. *Step 1 of the ATL COM AppWizard.*

Before this DLL can do anything exciting, you must add an ActiveX control. Right-click AtlControl Classes in the ClassView pane of Visual C++, which will bring up the context menu displayed in Figure 5-26.

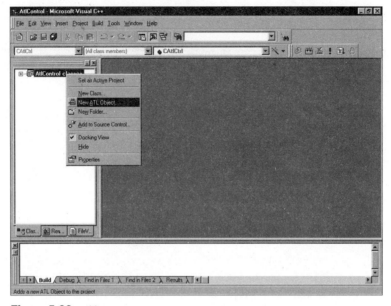

Figure 5-26. *ATL context menu.*

From this context menu, choose New ATL Object. The ATL Object Wizard dialog box shown in Figure 5-27 is displayed. It allows you to choose the type of ATL object that you want. Four categories of objects are listed on the left-hand side of the dialog box. Because you're creating an ActiveX control, select the Controls category. You can choose from seven types of controls. They are listed in Table 5-2.

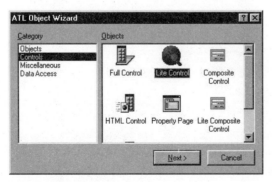

Figure 5-27. *ATL Object Wizard.*

TABLE 5-2
CONTROL TYPES AVAILABLE
IN THE ATL OBJECT WIZARD DIALOG BOX

ATL Control Type	*Description*
Full Control	Supports all the interfaces for an ActiveX control.
Lite Control	Meant to be used in Internet Explorer. Has a smaller number of interface implementations than the Full Control.
Composite Control	Can contain other controls.
HTML Control	Can display HTML Web pages.
Property Page	Used to create property pages.
Lite Composite Control	Same as the Composite Control but with fewer interface implementations.
Lite HTML Control	Same as the HTML Control but with fewer interface implementations.

Because you're creating an ActiveX control for use in Internet Explorer, choose the Lite Control, and then click the Next button. The ATL Object Wizard Properties dialog box, shown in Figure 5-28, is displayed. Using this dialog box, specify the name of the ActiveX control. Enter the name *AtlCtrl* in the Short Name field. You'll notice that the other fields are filled in automatically.

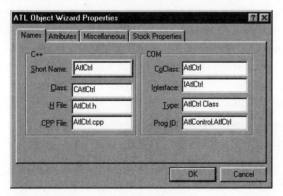

Figure 5-28. *ATL Object Wizard Properties dialog box.*

Click the Attributes tab to display the dialog box shown in Figure 5-29 on the following page. Using this tab, you can set certain attributes such as the control's threading model. Notice that Apartment threading is the default. You can leave this setting alone because the control will be used on a Web page inside Internet Explorer. Remember, ActiveX controls must be Apartment-threaded to work correctly in Internet Explorer.

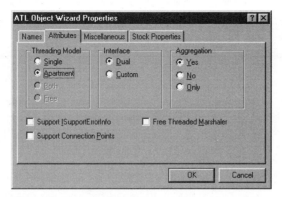

Figure 5-29. *Attributes tab.*

One other item on the Attributes tab is of great importance for this example—the Support Connection Points check box. Check this box, because events will be fired from your ActiveX control. (More discussion on connection points is in Chapter 7.) The other two tabs aren't important to this example, so you do not need to look at them. Click the OK button.

Notice that Visual C++ created a new class named *CAtlCtrl*. The *CAtlCtrl* class is the C++ implementation of the control. Before you add any methods, properties, or events, build the ActiveX control by pressing F7 or by choosing Build AtlControl.dll from the Build menu. Because you're building a control that will be downloaded across the Internet, you should set the active configuration to Win32 Release MinDependency. This setting will ensure that the control has the minimal amount of dependencies possible so that you won't have to include any other files besides AtlControl.dll in the CAB file. This is one advantage that ATL has over MFC. If you build ActiveX controls using MFC, the C run-time and MFC library files have to be downloaded to the client machine in addition to the control DLL.

> **NOTE** Setting the active configuration to Win32 Release MinDependency statically links the DLL with the run-time code needed for the control to operate correctly. If you'll be debugging the control using the Visual C++ debugger, set the configuration to Win32 Debug. If you receive a compile error indicating that the *_main* function is missing, remove the _ATL_MIN_CRT definition from the Preprocessor Definitions box on the C/C++ tab of the Project settings dialog box.

After building the control, test it using the sample HTML file that Visual C++ created in the Project directory when you created the control using the ATL Object Wizard. This HTML file contains <OBJECT> tags and the necessary CLASSID attribute to display the control on the Web page. If you load this Web page into Internet Explorer, you'll see the page shown in Figure 5-30.

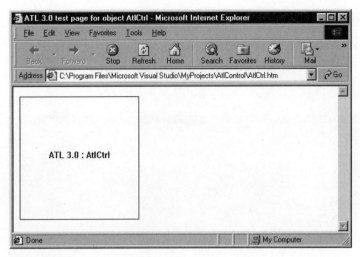

Figure 5-30. *ATL Control test page.*

Notice that ATL creates some default drawing code that displays on the Web page. At this point, close Internet Explorer and go back to your project. In the ClassView pane, expand the *CAtlCtrl* class, and then double-click the *OnDraw* method. This method is called by the ATL framework in response to the container calling the control's *IViewObject::Draw* method. (This shows the reason why the *IViewObject* interface is required if you want to provide any useful user interface for the control.) As Figure 5-30 shows, by default, ATL just prints a message that includes the version number of ATL. The default code that the ATL Object Wizard generated follows:

```
HRESULT OnDraw(ATL_DRAWINFO& di)
{
    RECT& rc = *(RECT*)di.prcBounds;
    Rectangle(di.hdcDraw, rc.left, rc.top, rc.right, rc.bottom);

    SetTextAlign(di.hdcDraw, TA_CENTER|TA_BASELINE);
    LPCTSTR pszText = _T("ATL 3.0 : AtlCtrl");
    TextOut(di.hdcDraw,
        (rc.left + rc.right) / 2,
        (rc.top + rc.bottom) / 2,
        pszText,
        lstrlen(pszText));

    return S_OK;
}
```

In the next few sections of this chapter, I'll show you how to add methods and properties to change the default message.

Adding Methods

Adding methods to the ATL control is fairly easy. For this example, let's add a method named *ChangeMessage* that will change the message displayed by the control. To add a method, right-click the *IAtlCtrl* interface in the ClassView pane of your project. The context menu shown in Figure 5-31 is displayed.

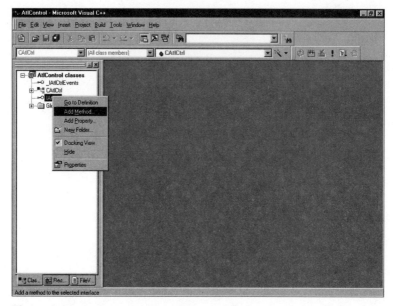

Figure 5-31. IAtlCtrl *interface context menu.*

From the context menu, choose the Add Method menu item. The Add Method To Interface dialog box, as shown in Figure 5-32, is then displayed. In this dialog box, enter the name of the method and any parameters it will accept. Enter the name *ChangeMessage* in the Method Name text box. Then add one parameter named *bstrMsg* to the Parameters text box. The string you enter to specify the input parameter should look like this:

```
[in] BSTR bstrMsg
```

The [in] specifier indicates that the *bstrMsg* parameter is an input parameter. The *bstrMsg* parameter has a type of *BSTR*. On a 32-bit Windows platform, a *BSTR* is a COM-compatible, wide-character string that has four bytes for the size of the string followed by the string itself. (For more detailed information about *BSTRs*, consult MSDN or one of the many COM books offered by Microsoft Press.) After entering the parameter string, click OK to complete the creation of the *ChangeMessage* method. Now add some code to this method so that it actually changes the message displayed on the Web page.

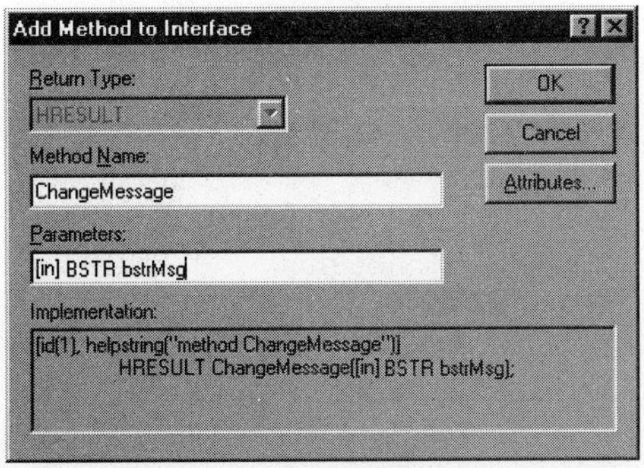

Figure 5-32. *Add Method To Interface dialog box.*

Open the AtlCtrl.h header file that contains the class definition for the *CAtlCtrl* class. Add a protected data member of type *CComBSTR* named *m_bstrMessage* to the end of the *CAtlCtrl* class definition. (A *CComBSTR* is an ATL utility class that encapsulates *BSTR* strings and provides functions that make these strings easier to use.) Add the following code to the *CAtlCtrl* class:

```
protected:
    CComBSTR m_bstrMessage;
```

Initialize the data member to a message that will be printed the first time the control is displayed. You can change the constructor to initialize *m_bstrMessage*, like this:

```
CAtlCtrl() : m_bstrMessage(bstrDefaultMsg)
{
}
```

The *m_bstrMessage* data member is set to *bstrDefaultMsg*. The *bstrDefaultMsg* variable is a global constant that stores the default message. The *bstrDefaultMsg* variable is defined at the top of the AtlCtrl.h header file, like this:

```
const CComBSTR bstrDefaultMsg = _T("Hello, Internet Explorer!");
```

Locate the *OnDraw* method, the last method in the AtlCtrl.h header file. A local variable exists in this method named *pszText* that is displayed on the Web page. Set this variable equal to the *m_bstrMessage* data member. You'll first have to convert this data member from a *BSTR* type to a *LPCTSTR* type, because *pszText* is a *LPCTSTR* variable, and *m_bstrMessage* is a *BSTR* type variable. To perform this conversion, use the OLE2T macro provided by ATL in conjunction with the USES_CONVERSION macro. Change the line containing the *pszText* variable to these two lines of code:

```
USES_CONVERSION;
LPCTSTR pszText = OLE2T(m_bstrMessage);
```

Open the AtlCtrl.cpp file. This file should contain only skeleton code for the *ChangeMessage* method. Change the code in this method so that it sets the *m_bstrMessage* data member equal to the *bstrMsg* parameter that was sent to this method. You also need to alert Internet Explorer that the ActiveX control's view has changed by calling the *FireViewChange* method, which is a member of *CComControl* class. The code for the *ChangeMessage* method should look like this:

```
STDMETHODIMP CAtlCtrl::ChangeMessage(BSTR bstrMsg)
{
    m_bstrMessage = bstrMsg;
    FireViewChange();

    return S_OK;
}
```

The entire code for this example can be found on the companion CD in the folder \Samples\Chap05\AtlControl.

Adding Properties

Now you'll add a property to the ActiveX control that allows you to retrieve the current value of the message that's displayed on the Web page. Adding a property is as simple as adding a method. Start by right-clicking *IAtlCtrl* in the ClassView pane, like you did when creating the *ChangeMessage* method. But this time, choose Add Property from the context menu. The Add Property To Interface dialog box is displayed, as shown in Figure 5-33.

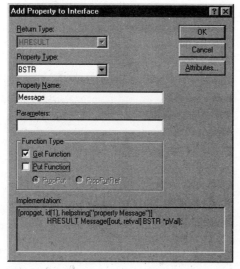

Figure 5-33. *Add Property To Interface dialog box.*

The Property Type drop-down list box allows you to choose the type of property that you want to create. Choose BSTR. Type *Message* into the Property Name text box. Although properties can accept parameters, because you'll be accessing this property using script, you won't want to specify any parameters.

The next section of the dialog box specifies the function type for the property. You'll see two types listed: Get Function and Put Function. Internet Explorer uses the Get Function type when you're retrieving the value of a property using script, and it uses the Put Function type when you're setting the value of a property using script. For this example, you want to allow only script code to retrieve the value of the property. The *ChangeMessage* method will be used to set the value of the message that's displayed. Therefore uncheck the Put Function check box. Then click OK to allow Visual C++ to create the property.

Take a look at the AtlCtrl.cpp file again. Notice that one method has been added to this file: *get_Message*. This method is the implementation of the Get Function type for the property of your ActiveX control. If you had chosen to include the Put Function type in the Add Property To Interface dialog box, Visual C++ would have created a *put_Message* method for you.

Change the *get_Message* method so that it sets the *pVal* parameter to the *m_bstrMessage* data member. That's how you'll return the current message being displayed on the Web page to script code. Now the *get_Message* method should look like this:

```
STDMETHODIMP CAtlCtrl::get_Message(BSTR *pVal)
{
    *pVal = m_bstrMessage;
    return S_OK;
}
```

Firing Events

Firing events from an ATL control is about as easy as adding methods and properties. As you've probably guessed, Visual C++ provides wizards that enable you to fire events from the control. You can add an event to the ATL control that will fire when the message in the display window changes.

Earlier, when you created the Lite Control and checked the Support Connection Points check box, Visual C++ created the *_IAtlCtrlEvents* interface. This interface is referred to as a source interface because it will be used as the source of events. Whereas methods and properties are called by clients, events are functions that are implemented in the clients and called by the controls. This topic is explained in greater detail in Chapter 7.

To add an event that will be fired by the control, right-click the _*IAtlCtrlEvents*
interface in the ClassView pane of Visual C++. The same context menu is shown that
was displayed when you created the method and property for the control. From the
context menu, choose Add Method. The Add Method To Interface dialog box that was
shown in Figure 5-32 (on page 181) is displayed. Select a return type of *void* from
the Return Type drop-down list. Enter *OnMessageChanged* for the name of the event.
You don't need to enter any parameters, as they aren't required for this event. When
you're finished, click the OK button. Visual C++ adds the *OnMessageChanged* method
to the .idl file for the control.

Next you must compile the .idl file to create a type library. Right-click AtlControl.idl
in the FileView pane of the Visual C++ IDE, and choose Compile AtlControl.idl. If
everything goes well, Visual C++ will create a type library file (.tlb) for the control.

Now you must implement a connection point for the control. Right-click *CAtlCtrl*
in the ClassView pane, and choose Implement Connection Point from the context
menu. The dialog box shown in Figure 5-34 will be displayed. Select _*IAtlCtrlEvents*
from the list of interfaces, and then click OK. Visual C++ will then create an ATL-based
proxy class that will be used for firing the *OnMessageChanged* event. This class is
named *CProxy_IAtlCtrlEvents*. In addition to creating this class, Visual C++ adds the
class to the inheritance list for *CAtlCtrl*. Adding the class is necessary so that the event
OnMessageChanged can be fired by using the *Fire_OnMessageChanged* function of
the *CProxy_IAtlCtrlEvents* class.

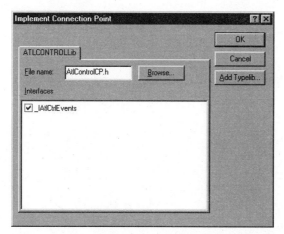

Figure 5-34. *Implement Connection Point dialog box.*

Internet Explorer has a requirement that is usually overlooked when trying
to fire events from an ActiveX control: a control must implement the interface
IProvideClassInfo2. Using *IProvideClassInfo2*, Internet Explorer retrieves the interface ID of the control's event source—*DIID__IAtlCtrlEvents*. If you don't implement
IProvideClassInfo2, the event handlers you create in script will never be called.

Fortunately, ATL provides a default implementation of *IProvideClassInfo2* named *IProvideClassInfo2Impl*.

There are two steps to implementing the *IProvideClassInfo2* interface in ATL. First, place *IProvideClassInfo2Impl* in the inheritance list for the implementation class, *CAtlCtrl*. The code should look like this:

```
class ATL_NO_VTABLE CAtlCtrl :


    public IProvideClassInfo2Impl<&CLSID_AtlCtrl,
                            &DIID__IAtlCtrlEvents,
                            &LIBID_ATLCONTROLLib>
{


};
```

Because *IProvideClassInfo2Impl* is a template class, you must specify a number of parameters. The required parameters are the CLSID of the ActiveX control (*CLSID_AtlCtrl*), the interface ID of the event source interface (*DIID__IAtlCtrlEvents*), and the GUID for the type library (*LIBID_ATLCONTROLLib*).

The second step is to add the *IProvideClassInfo* and *IProvideClassInfo2* interfaces to the COM map for the *CAtlCtrl* class. You must add both of these interfaces because *IProvideClassInfo2* is derived from *IProvideClassInfo*. Now your code should look like this:

```
BEGIN_COM_MAP(CAtlCtrl)


   COM_INTERFACE_ENTRY(IProvideClassInfo)
   COM_INTERFACE_ENTRY(IProvideClassInfo2)
END_COM_MAP()
```

You must perform one last task before the *OnMessageChanged* event can be fired—correct the name of the interface that will be referenced by the proxy class. Recall that when you were creating the control and chose to support connection points, the wizard created not only the *_IAtlCtrlEvents* interface but also a CLSID for it named *DIID__IAtlCtrlEvents*. However, the wizard that created the proxy class that you will use to fire events references this *_IAtlCtrlEvents* interface using the incorrect name *IID__IAtlCtrlEvents*. To correct this error, open the AtlCtrl.h file, and locate the connection point map for the control. The connection point map should look like this:

```
BEGIN_CONNECTION_POINT_MAP(CAtlCtrl)
CONNECTION_POINT_ENTRY(IID__IAtlCtrlEvents)
END_CONNECTION_POINT_MAP()
```

Change the interface ID for *_IAtlCtrlEvents* to *DIID__IAtlCtrlEvents*. The new code should look like this:

```
BEGIN_CONNECTION_POINT_MAP(CAtlCtrl)
CONNECTION_POINT_ENTRY(DIID__IAtlCtrlEvents)
END_CONNECTION_POINT_MAP()
```

Now all you have to do is call the *Fire_OnMessageChanged* function whenever you want to fire the event. You should call *Fire_OnMessageChanged* whenever the *Message* property has been changed. For this example, you need to call it only from within the *ChangeMessage* method. Here's the updated code for *ChangeMessage* to fire the *OnMessageChanged* event:

```
STDMETHODIMP CAtlCtrl::ChangeMessage(BSTR bstrMsg)
{
    m_bstrMessage = bstrMsg;
    FireViewChange();

    Fire_OnMessageChanged();

    return S_OK;
}
```

Marking ATL Controls as Safe

Earlier you marked Visual Basic ActiveX controls as safe for scripting and initialization by using the Package And Deployment Wizard. Unfortunately, no such ATL tool exists that creates packages like PDW does for Visual Basic. Consequently, besides having to create your own CAB and INF files, you'll also have to manually mark the control as safe for scripting and initialization. If you don't, the users will either receive a warning dialog box from Internet Explorer (as shown in Figure 5-35), or, if their security levels are set high enough, the control won't be able to be scripted or initialized at all!

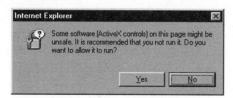

Figure 5-35. *Warning dialog box.*

For this reason, the *IObjectSafety* interface exists. An ATL ActiveX control can implement *IObjectSafety* to tell Internet Explorer that the control is safe. When loading the control, Internet Explorer queries the ActiveX control for *IObjectSafety*. If this interface is returned, Internet Explorer calls the *GetInterfaceSafetyOptions* method of

IObjectSafety to see whether the control is safe for scripting, safe for initialization, or both.

Implementing *IObjectSafety* is the preferred technique for telling Internet Explorer that your control is safe, and doing so in ATL is straightforward. The procedure is similar to the steps you follow to implement *IProvideClassInfo2*: add ATL's implementation class for the interface to the inheritance list, and then add the interface to the COM map. Regarding the first step of the process, in the same way that ATL provides the *IProvideClassInfo2Impl* class to implement *IProvideClassInfo2*, ATL also provides the *IObjectSafetyImpl* class to implement *IObjectSafety*. After adding *IObjectSafetyImpl* to the inheritance list, the code for the *CAtlCtrl* class declaration should look like this:

```
class ATL_NO_VTABLE CAtlCtrl :


    public IObjectSafetyImpl<CAtlCtrl,
                    INTERFACESAFE_FOR_UNTRUSTED_CALLER
                  | INTERFACESAFE_FOR_UNTRUSTED_DATA>
{


};
```

Like any other template class, you must specify certain parameters when inheriting from *IObjectSafetyImpl*. The first parameter is the name of the class—*CAtlCtrl*. The second parameter specifies the supported safety options for the control. Two options are currently available: *INTERFACESAFE_FOR_UNTRUSTED_CALLER* and *INTERFACESAFE_FOR_UNTRUSTED_DATA*. The first of the two indicates that the control is safe for scripting. The second indicates that the control is safe for initialization. You can specify one of the two, or specify them both by OR'ing them together.

The second step to completing the implementation of *IObjectSafety* is to add the *IObjectSafety* interface to the COM map. After adding this interface, the COM map should look like this:

```
BEGIN_COM_MAP(CAtlCtrl)


    COM_INTERFACE_ENTRY(IObjectSafety)
END_COM_MAP()
```

Initializing from HTML

In the same way that you can initialize a Visual Basic ActiveX control, you can initialize an ATL control using the <PARAM> tags. When you include the <PARAM> tags as children of the <OBJECT> tags, Internet Explorer sends the data that you specify to the control when the control is first instantiated. For example, to specify an initial value for the *Message* property, you can insert a <PARAM> tag between the opening and closing object tags for the control. This HTML code looks like this:

```
<OBJECT ID="AtlCtrl"
        CLASSID="CLSID:638B718E-AEF1-11D2-A9BA-444553540001">
        <PARAM NAME="Message" VALUE="Hello, There!">
</OBJECT>
```

This data is stored in a property bag object maintained by Internet Explorer. Internet Explorer will query the control for the *IPersistPropertyBag* interface. If the control returns a pointer to this interface, Internet Explorer calls the *Load* method of *IPersistPropertyBag* to instruct the control to load initialization data. When calling the *Load* method, Internet Explorer passes a pointer to *IPropertyBag* interface of its property bag object. The control then calls the *Read* method of the passed in *IPropertyBag* interface to retrieve the initialization data.

To make this work correctly in the AtlCtrl control, you need to follow a few steps. As usual, ATL provides a default implementation of *IPersistPropertyBag* named *IPersistPropertyBagImpl*. Add this template class to the end of the inheritance list. After adding the template class, the declaration of *CAtlCtrl* should look like this:

```
class ATL_NO_VTABLE CAtlCtrl :


    public IPersistPropertyBagImpl<CAtlCtrl>
{


};
```

Add the *IPersistPropertyBag* interface to the COM map. After adding this interface, the COM map should look like this:

```
BEGIN_COM_MAP(CAtlCtrl)


    COM_INTERFACE_ENTRY(IPersistPropertyBag)
END_COM_MAP()
```

Implement the *Load* method, as shown in the next code fragment. You can add this method to the bottom of the class declaration. With *Load*, you can retrieve the initialization data that you specified on the Web page by using <PARAM> tags.

```
STDMETHOD(Load)(LPPROPERTYBAG pPropBag, LPERRORLOG pErrorLog)
{
    CComVariant vtVal;
```

```
HRESULT hr = pPropBag->Read(L"Message", &vtVal, pErrorLog);

if (SUCCEEDED(hr) && VT_BSTR == vtVal.vt)
{
    m_bstrMessage = vtVal.bstrVal;
    m_fDirty = TRUE;
}

return hr;
}
```

In the *Load* method, we first have to declare a variable of *CComVariant*. The *CComVariant* variable is similar to *CComBSTR* in that it's a wrapper class that provides greater functionality than the data type it contains. In this case, a *CComVariant* wraps a *VARIANT* type. This variable is needed to retrieve the values of the parameters specified using <PARAM> tags. (If you need more information about *CComVariant*, refer to MSDN.)

Next we call the *Read* method of the *IPropertyBag* interface that was passed into the *Load* method. The first parameter specifies the name of the property that we want to retrieve. This parameter tacks on the 'L' specifier that converts the ANSI string to an OLE string. Here we're reading the *Message* property from the property bag. The second parameter is a *VARIANT* that will contain the value of the *Message* property when this method returns. The third parameter is a pointer to *IErrorLog* interface that the *Read* method uses to report errors. This parameter can be *NULL* if we're not interested in error information. In this case, we simply pass the pointer to *IErrorLog* interface that we received from the argument of the *Load* method.

Then we check the return value of the *Read* method. If the call to *Read* succeeded and the type of the *VARIANT* that was returned is a *BSTR* (as indicated by *vtVal.vt* being equal to *VT_BSTR*), we set the *m_bstrMessage* data member to the *BSTR* value that is contained in the *vtVal* variable. Now, when the *OnDraw* method is initially called, the value that we specified for the *Message* property will be displayed on the Web page. In addition to setting the *m_bstrMessage* data member, we also set the *m_fDirty* data member to *TRUE*. The *m_fDirty* data member indicates that the property has been changed. Here's how *m_fDirty* is defined in the *CAtlCtrl* class:

```
BOOL m_fDirty;
```

We should also initialize *m_fDirty* in the *CAtlCtrl* constructor. The constructor will look like this:

```
CAtlCtrl() : m_bstrMessage(bstrDefaultMsg),
             m_fDirty(FALSE)
{
}
```

Printing

Earlier in the discussion about creating Visual Basic ActiveX controls, you learned that Internet Explorer creates a hidden Web page used for background printing. Also, you have to handle the *WriteProperties* event and call the *WriteProperty* method of the property bag object so that the control will be printed in its current state.

> **NOTE** ActiveX controls built using Visual C++ can use *IPersistStreamInit* instead of *IPersistPropertyBag* for printing. Internet Explorer will query the control first for *IPersistPropertyBag*. If *IPersistPropertyBag* isn't found, Internet Explorer will query for *IPersistStreamInit* and, if it's found, use that interface for printing.

Ensuring that the ATL control prints in its current state is similar to the process of ensuring proper printing of Visual Basic ActiveX controls. However, you don't have an event to handle. In an ATL control, you simply have to implement the *Save* method of *IPersistPropertyBag*. The *Save* method takes three input parameters:

- ■ *pPropBag*. A property bag object as represented by *IPropertyBag*.

- ■ *fClearDirty*. A Boolean value that indicates whether you should clear the dirty flag. The *m_fDirty* data member is the dirty flag for the *CAtlCtrl* class. A value of *TRUE* indicates that the dirty flag should be cleared. A value of *FALSE* indicates that it should not.

- ■ *fSaveAllProperties*. A Boolean value that indicates whether you should save all the properties to the property bag object (*TRUE*) or only those that have changed since the control was last saved or initialized (*FALSE*).

Implementing the code for the *Save* method in the *CAtlCtrl* class is straightforward, as shown here:

```
STDMETHOD(Save)(IPropertyBag* pPropBag, BOOL fClearDirty,
                BOOL fSaveAllProperties)
{
    HRESULT hr = E_FAIL;

    if (fSaveAllProperties)
    {
        // Save all properties whether they have changed or not.
        //
        hr = pPropBag->Write(L"Message", &CComVariant(m_bstrMessage));
    }
    else if (m_fDirty)
    {
        // Save only the properties that have changed. This
```

```
        // control has only one property, so check its current
        // value against its default value. If the value has changed,
        // save it.
        //
        if (wcscmp(m_bstrMessage, bstrDefaultMsg))
            hr = pPropBag->Write(L"Message", &CComVariant(m_bstrMessage));
    }

    if (SUCCEEDED(hr) && fClearDirty)
        m_fDirty = FALSE;

    return hr;
}
```

In this code, we first define an *HRESULT* variable, *hr*, and initialize it to *E_FAIL*. *E_FAIL* is the value that will be returned from the *Save* method as the result of an error. Next, we check the *fSaveAllProperties* flag to see whether Internet Explorer wants us to save all the properties. If so, we save all the properties to the property bag by calling the *Write* method of the *IPropertyBag* interface. The *Write* method takes two input parameters—the name of the property, which is an OLE string, and the value of the property.

In this code, we have only one property to save—*Message*. So we pass the string "*Message*" for the first parameter, tacking on the 'L' specifier that converts the ANSI string to an OLE string. For the second parameter, we pass the value stored in *m_bstrMessage*. However, the *Write* method takes the address of a *VARIANT*, so we convert *m_bstrMessage* to a *VARIANT* using the *CComVariant* utility class and pass in a pointer to the object that's created.

If the *fSaveAllProperties* input parameter is *FALSE*, Internet Explorer is telling us that we don't need to save all the properties—just the ones that have changed. If this parameter is *TRUE*, we're going to save all the properties, no matter whether they have changed or not. So we check the value of the *m_fDirty* flag that indicates whether any of the properties have changed. If the value of *m_fDirty* is *TRUE*, we save only those properties that have changed. Because we have only one property, potentially we have only one property to save.

We then determine whether the property has changed by using the *wcscmp* API function, which compares the values of two wide-character strings and returns *0* if they're the same or nonzero if they're different. We determine whether *m_bstrMessage* has changed by comparing it to the default message stored in *bstrDefaultMsg*. If *m_bstrMessage* has changed, we call the *Write* method of *IPropertyBag*.

Finally, before returning from this method, we check the *fClearDirty* input parameter and check whether one of the previous calls to the *Write* method has succeeded. If *fClearDirty* is *TRUE* and one of the calls to the *Write* method has succeeded, we clear the dirty flag by setting *m_fDirty* to *FALSE*. Then we return from this method and pass the value of the *hr* local variable back to Internet Explorer.

Writing Script for Your ATL Control

Now it's time for the fun part—compiling and testing the ATL control. If you haven't already, go ahead and compile the control and fix any errors that might occur due to typos or whatnot.

To test the control, use the sample HTML page that Visual C++ created for you when you first created the control. Add some script to the page to call the *ChangeMessage* method, access the *Message* property, and handle events. The finished HTML page should look similar to the page shown in Figure 5-36. Also try changing the control and then printing it to ensure that the code you implemented to save the properties is functioning correctly.

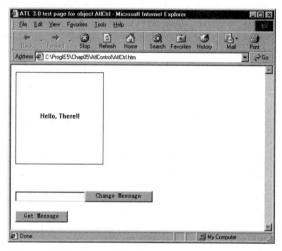

Figure 5-36. *Final ATL test page.*

The HTML code for this page is shown in Listing 5-4. You can find the code listing on the companion CD in the folder \Samples\Chap05\AtlControl.

```
AtlCtrl.htm

<HTML>
<HEAD>
    <TITLE>ATL 3.0 test page for object AtlCtrl</TITLE>

    <SCRIPT LANGUAGE="VBScript">
    Sub btnChange_onclick
        AtlCtrl.ChangeMessage Text1.Value
    End Sub
```

Listing 5-4.

```
    Sub AtlCtrl_OnMessageChanged
        MsgBox "Message Changed"
    End Sub
    </SCRIPT>
</HEAD>
<BODY>
    <OBJECT ID="AtlCtrl"
        CLASSID="CLSID:638B718E-AEF1-11D2-A9BA-444553540001">
        <PARAM NAME="Message" VALUE="Hello, There!!">
    </OBJECT>

    <P>
    <BR><BR>

    <INPUT TYPE=TEXT ID="Text1">
    <BUTTON ID="btnChange">Change Message</BUTTON>
    <P>
    <BUTTON onclick="alert(AtlCtrl.Message)">Get Message</BUTTON>
</BODY>
</HTML>
```

WHAT'S NEXT?

Now that you know how to create Visual Basic ActiveX controls and ATL ActiveX controls, we can move on to one of the greatest controls of all time: WebBrowser. This control and its interfaces allow you to access Internet Explorer and the DHTML Object Model from ActiveX controls on a Web page. So you can read or change the data from the Web page on which the control is residing. Also, the WebBrowser control allows you to add Web browsing to the Windows applications that you create in Visual Basic, Visual C++, or any COM-aware development tool. You can add rich content to the user interface or to the help system. You can even create your own Web browser application. In the next chapter, we'll talk about how to do this and much more by using the WebBrowser control and Internet Explorer automation.

Chapter 6

Hosting the WebBrowser Control and Automating Internet Explorer

I have no doubt that you'll agree the World Wide Web has revolutionized application development. Prior to the Web, developing applications that were rich in content and easy to use was sometimes a long and tedious process. Now, with just a little knowledge of DHTML and script, almost anybody can create Web applications that rival their Microsoft Windows counterparts.

Microsoft Internet Explorer 5 enables you to build almost any kind of application by using only DHTML and script (including Windows applications known as HTAs, which we talked about in Chapter 4), but suppose you wanted to create just a typical Windows application in Microsoft Visual Basic or Microsoft Visual C++? For example, you might want to create a point-of-sale system that requires access to scanners, cash registers, and credit card terminals. For such a system, using only DHTML and script might be a bit too limiting. You could create it by using a combination of ActiveX controls, DHTML, and script, but the system might be somewhat slow.

To create a point-of-sale system like the one I just described, lengthy and some-times arduous design and development phases are required—not to mention the testing phase. During the design phase, you undoubtedly create many designs of the user interface. Then when it comes time for development, you have to implement the user interface from scratch even though somebody already used a design tool to create the interface designs. Why not combine the design and development phases so that you can easily reuse the original designs in your finished application?

What if I told you that you could use Web pages to create the designs for a user interface and then just plug these pages into your application? Believe it or not, you can. Internet Explorer includes a component known as the WebBrowser control that allows you to easily integrate Web browsing into new or existing applications. With this control, you can design the user interface by using simple Web pages, which you can view and then use to navigate to new pages. To the user, this functionality appears to be part of your application. By using the WebBrowser control in combination with the DHTML Object Model, you can retrieve data that users entered into a Web page and dynamically manipulate that Web page just like you did using script in Chapter 3.

You can also use the WebBrowser control in a number of other scenarios—for example, when creating Windows help files. You probably know how much of a hassle creating Windows help files can be. You have to create Rich Text Format (RTF) files that contain special help codes. Then you have to compile your RTF files into a special format that can be read and displayed by the Microsoft Windows help sys-tem. Why should you have to compile these files just to provide help for your users? By using the WebBrowser control, you can display simple Web pages to provide help to your users. And because creating Web pages is so easy (I think my grandmother even has a home page), you'll be able to shave hours off your development cycle.

Many Microsoft products such as Microsoft Money 99, the entire Microsoft Encarta suite, and Microsoft Office 2000 are already starting to use the WebBrowser control in the ways I've described. And America Online (AOL) and CompuServe use the WebBrowser control and other Internet Explorer components to create their browser applications—they simply host the WebBrowser control, which I'm sure saved them a lot of development time and money.

In addition to creating applications that reuse the WebBrowser control, you can control the Internet Explorer browser (known as automating Internet Explorer). Perhaps you want to provide Internet functionality from your application by using the browser, or you want to enhance the browsing experience for users but still let them use their favorite browsers. The possibilities are endless.

In this chapter, I'll start with an architectural overview of the WebBrowser control in the context of hosting the control. Then I'll discuss the different interfaces, including their methods and properties, that are available when hosting the WebBrowser control and automating Internet Explorer. (Chapter 7 covers the different Internet Explorer events.) As you'll see, the interfaces of the WebBrowser control and Internet Explorer have a lot in common.

I'll also show you how to host the WebBrowser control in Visual Basic and Visual C++ applications and teach you how to automate Internet Explorer by using both of these development tools. Finally, I'll show you how to add some advanced functionality to your application, such as accessing the Internet Explorer *IWebBrowser2* interface from an ActiveX control, accessing frames on a Web page from the host application, and invoking some hard-to-reach browser functionality.

> **NOTE** Having a thorough understanding of COM is more important now than it was in previous chapters. If your knowledge of COM is only minimal, you won't have trouble with the sections involving Visual Basic, but you might struggle with the sections involving Visual C++. If you follow along closely, though, I think you'll do OK.

INTERNET EXPLORER ARCHITECTURE

The WebBrowser control consists of many different components. A lot of them are COM objects, which means that you can reuse them in your applications. If you are hosting the WebBrowser control or automating Internet Explorer, you need to know only a couple of components. Figure 6-1 on the following page shows the architecture of a WebBrowser host application such as one you might create using Visual Basic or Visual C++. As the figure shows, an application that is hosting the WebBrowser control consists of many components. The next several sections cover each of the components in turn, starting with the top component in the architecture.

> **NOTE** Many of the components involved in hosting the WebBrowser control aren't shown in Figure 6-1. These components provide functionality such as downloading Web pages and ActiveX controls (URLMON) and supporting low-level communications (WININET). I won't cover these components in this chapter because you don't need to know about them to be able to host the WebBrowser control or automate Internet Explorer. The WebBrowser control handles control of and interaction with these components for you for free. If you were to create all this functionality from scratch, it could take years of effort and lots of pain.

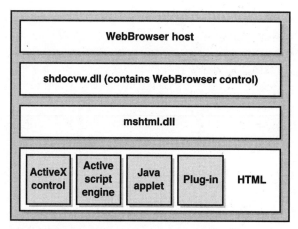

Figure 6-1. *WebBrowser host architecture. Only the most critical components needed for hosting the WebBrowser control are shown.*

WebBrowser Control Host

The first component in Figure 6-1 is the WebBrowser host, or container, which is any application that you develop to reuse the WebBrowser control. You can create applications by using Visual Basic, Visual C++, or any COM-aware development tool. The container must be able to host ActiveX controls; the WebBrowser control takes care of the rest.

The WebBrowser control is both an ActiveX control and an Active Document host. (For more information about Active Documents, refer to the MSDN documentation.) Because it's an ActiveX control, the WebBrowser can be hosted in any ActiveX control container. In other words, it can be reused just like the ActiveX controls you encountered in Chapter 5. As an Active Document host, to view a file of a particular type, the WebBrowser control loads the Active Document server that is registered for that file type. If you want to load a .doc file, the WebBrowser control loads Microsoft Word; if you want to load an .xls file, the WebBrowser loads Microsoft Excel. With HTML files, the WebBrowser control loads a component named MSHTML, which is implemented in mshtml.dll, installed by Internet Explorer, and used to read and display Web pages. You no longer have to manually build an application that can load many different file types. You just have to host the WebBrowser control in your application, and—voila!

SHDOCVW

The second component shown in Figure 6-1 is SHDOCVW (pronounced sh-doc-view), which is implemented in shdocvw.dll. It holds the WebBrowser control (as well as other controls and COM objects) and provides browsing capability for your host. In Figure 6-1, notice that the WebBrowser control sits at the second level of the host architecture—Internet Explorer uses SHDOCVW even though Internet Explorer doesn't host the WebBrowser control directly. Although the SHDOCVW component provides Internet browsing, it doesn't provide all the functionality that the Internet Explorer window offers. Even so, SHDOCVW does simplify the process of creating a Web-enabled application. At the end of this chapter in the section titled "Adding Advanced Functionality" as well as in later chapters, I'll show you how to include some functionality of the Internet Explorer window in your own applications.

MSHTML

As mentioned earlier, the MSHTML component (the third component in Figure 6-1) can read and display HTML pages. MSHTML is an Active Document server, so you can load it into the applications that are Active Document hosts. MSHTML is also an ActiveX control host. Just like the applications mentioned previously that host the WebBrowser control, MSHTML can host ActiveX controls. Remember that you can place ActiveX controls on a Web page—MSHTML is the control that hosts the ActiveX controls. And MSHTML can host other components such as Active scripting engines (like Microsoft VBScript and Microsoft JScript), Java applets, and plug-ins—not too surprising, because these components are implemented as ActiveX controls in Internet Explorer.

> **NOTE** Developers typically refer to the process of reading and displaying a Web page as parsing and rendering the page, respectively.

THE WEBBROWSER CONTROL AND INTERNET EXPLORER

The WebBrowser control and Internet Explorer have a lot in common. You access the functionality of both by using the same COM interfaces. The objects that you use to host the control or automate the browser, however, are different. For example, when hosting the control, you'll work with the *WebBrowser* object. In Visual Basic, this object is simply named *WebBrowser*. In Visual C++ applications, you'll access the WebBrowser control by using the class ID *CLSID_WebBrowser*. Of course, if you're hosting the WebBrowser control in Visual Basic or in Visual C++ using the Microsoft Foundation Classes (MFC), you won't have to create the *WebBrowser* object manually. I'll show you how to host the WebBrowser control in Visual Basic and Visual C++ later in this chapter in the section "Hosting the WebBrowser Control."

When automating Internet Explorer, you'll have to manually create the *InternetExplorer* object. In Visual Basic, this object is named *InternetExplorer*. In Visual C++, whether you're using MFC, ATL, or plain vanilla C++, you'll access the *InternetExplorer* object by using the class ID *CLSID_InternetExplorer*.

NOTE The class IDs *CLSID_WebBrowser* and *CLSID_InternetExplorer* are installed on your machine when you install Internet Explorer, but you can't use these names to reference the class IDs from a Visual C++ application unless you install the Internet Explorer headers and libraries from the MSDN Online Web Workshop. I'll show you how to use these headers and libraries later in this chapter in the section "Using Visual C++."

Before I demonstrate how to host the WebBrowser control and automate Internet Explorer in both Visual Basic and MFC, I'll explain the different interfaces included with the WebBrowser control and Internet Explorer, and I'll cover the methods and properties that belong to each. Because most of their functionality is shared in a single interface—*IWebBrowser2*—I'll refer to the WebBrowser control and Internet Explorer simply as the WebBrowser.

COMPATIBILITY WITH EARLIER VERSIONS

The Internet Explorer 5 version of the WebBrowser control is 100 percent compatible with earlier versions. So if you develop an application by using an earlier version of the WebBrowser control, the application will work correctly in Internet Explorer 5. But if you develop an application by using Internet Explorer 5, the application might not work in earlier versions. The application should work OK in Internet Explorer 4, but it probably won't work well in versions 3 and earlier.

For compatibility with the Internet Explorer version 3 of the WebBrowser control, an object named *WebBrowser_V1* is included with the WebBrowser control. (For C++ developers, this object is instantiated with *CLSID_WebBrowser_V1*.) Using the *WebBrowser_V1* object is complicated. If you need to support version 3 of Internet Explorer, develop for the lowest common denominator; in other words, develop your application on a machine with Internet Explorer 3.*x* installed. This is the best way to ensure that your application is compatible with the version you need to support.

Interfaces

The WebBrowser consists of four interfaces, three of which provide all its functionality. (The fourth interface, *DWebBrowserEvents2*, exists for events. I'll cover this interface in Chapter 7.) Prior to Internet Explorer 4, only two interfaces existed—one for the WebBrowser control (*IWebBrowser*) and the other for the Internet Explorer object (*IWebBrowserApp*). *IWebBrowser* and *IWebBrowserApp* share a lot of the same functionality, so when expanding the functionality of the WebBrowser for Internet Explorer 4, the developers decided to create a third interface—*IWebBrowser2*—that derives from the other two. Combining the functionality of the *IWebBrowser* and *IWebBrowserApp* interfaces into a new interface with more functionality just made perfect sense. (The name of the resulting interface is different because COM specification requires you to create a new interface name and GUID if functionality is added or removed.) The hierarchy in Figure 6-2 illustrates the relationship among three of the four interfaces.

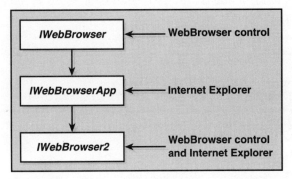

Figure 6-2.   *Hierarchy of WebBrowser interfaces.* IWebBrowser *supplies the minimum functionality. A fourth interface,* DWebBrowserEvents2, *is not shown.*

The following sections explain each interface in detail, including their methods and properties. I'll also discuss some differences between the WebBrowser control and Internet Explorer that commonly cause confusion among developers who reuse the control or automate the browser.

IWebBrowser

IWebBrowser is the interface that originally represented only the WebBrowser control. This interface provides basic browsing functionality such as navigating to a Web page or moving backward and forward in the navigation history. As you can see from Figure 6-2, *IWebBrowser* is the base interface from which all the other WebBrowser interfaces are derived. *IWebBrowser* is implemented by the WebBrowser control, so all you have to do to add Web browsing to an application is use *IWebBrowser*'s methods and properties. It has eight methods and thirteen properties.

> **NOTE**   In COM, the interface doesn't actually provide the implementation of the methods, properties, and so forth. An interface just defines the binary representation of an object. The interface must be implemented by an object such as the *WebBrowser* object or *InternetExplorer* object. For more details, refer to MSDN or any of the Microsoft Press COM books such as *Inside COM* by Dale Rogerson and *Inside OLE2* by Kraig Brockschmidt.

Methods   Table 6-1 on the next page describes the eight *IWebBrowser* interface methods, which are listed in the order in which they are defined in the vtable of *IWebBrowser*. All eight methods are related to browsing the Web. Using these methods in your applications is easy, as I'll show you later in this section. For now, I'll discuss only those methods that you'll use most often or that require explanation.

WHAT IS VTABLE ORDER?

In COM, the order in which methods appear in an interface definition is referred to as vtable order. A vtable is a virtual function table that stores pointers to the actual implementations of the methods and properties defined by an interface.

Methods and properties of base class interfaces appear before the derived class interface's methods and properties in a vtable.

TABLE 6-1
IWEBBROWSER METHODS IN VTABLE ORDER

Method	Description
GoBack	Navigates to the previous item in the history list.
GoForward	Navigates to the next item in the history list.
GoHome	Navigates to the user's default home page. This home page is a URL that is set by the user in the Internet Explorer Options dialog box and is stored in the Registry.
GoSearch	Navigates to the user's default search page.
Navigate	Navigates to a URL or to a file.
Refresh	Refreshes the current Web page.
Refresh2	Works the same way as the *Refresh* method but allows you to choose the refresh level. The value of the refresh level that you specify comes from the *RefreshConstants* enumeration, which is defined in the ExDisp.h header file. (This header file is part of the Internet Explorer 5 header files that are available for download from the MSDN Online Web Workshop.) The different values you can specify are as follows:
	REFRESH_NORMAL Performs a lightweight refresh that doesn't send the HTTP *pragma:nocache* header to the server.
	REFRESH_IFEXPIRED Performs a lightweight refresh only if the page has expired.
	REFRESH_CONTINUE For internal use only. Don't use this value.
	REFRESH_COMPLETELY Performs a full refresh that includes sending the HTTP *pragma:nocache* header to the server for HTTP protocol URLs.
Stop	Stops the current navigation.

Whenever a user employs Internet Explorer or the WebBrowser control to navigate to Web pages, the WebBrowser keeps track of where that user has been so that the user can easily return to previously viewed pages. The *GoBack* and *GoForward* methods allow you to navigate backward and forward, respectively, in this navigation history. The *GoBack* and *GoForward* methods won't work in the following situations, however:

- If you've loaded only one Web page into the WebBrowser control or Internet Explorer, the *GoBack* and *GoForward* methods have no effect because the history list doesn't currently contain any items before or after the current URL.

- If you've navigated to multiple pages but have never gone back to them, the *GoBack* method will work but the *GoForward* method will have no effect because you are at the end of the history list.

- If you've navigated to multiple pages and then gone back to where you started, the *GoForward* method will work but the *GoBack* method will have no effect because you are currently at the beginning of the history list.

Although the WebBrowser control provides the methods you need to navigate backward and forward in the history list, it doesn't give you direct access to URLs in the history list that are before or after the current item. Consequently, you can't find out where the user has been without actually navigating backward or forward in the history list using *GoBack* or *GoForward*. Once you've navigated backward or forward to the page in question, you can easily retrieve the URL of the current page by using a property that I'll discuss shortly—*LocationURL*.

Calling the *GoBack* and *GoForward* methods in Visual Basic or Visual C++ is easy. You use either the object that represents the WebBrowser control or Internet Explorer. For example, in Visual Basic you can call the methods like this:

```
WebBrowser1.GoBack            ' Hosting WebBrowser control
InternetExplorer1.GoForward   ' Automating Internet Explorer object
```

Calling the same methods in Visual C++ is similar:

```
m_webBrowser.GoBack();             // Hosting WebBrowser control
m_pInternetExplorer->GoForward();  // Automating Internet Explorer object
```

Although the *GoBack* and *GoForward* methods are quite important, *Navigate* is the most important method you'll ever use when hosting the WebBrowser control or automating Internet Explorer. *Navigate* allows you to navigate precisely to the Web page or file that you want. *Navigate* takes five parameters, or arguments, that allow you to specify the URL to navigate to and other information that defines how the navigation will occur. I'll explain these parameters in the order in which they appear in the parameter list.

The first parameter is the URL, which identifies the location and name of a Web page or file that you want to load. (The type of this parameter is *BSTR*.) The URL can be one of the standard URL protocol types you're used to, such as HTTP and FILE, or it can be the full path and name of a file on your system, such as C:\MyFile.htm.

> **NOTE**   If you specify the full path and name of a file on your system, the WebBrowser will convert this path to a standard URL by prepending the string that you specify like this: *file:///.* Notice the three forward slashes (*///*). Although only two forward slashes are used when specifying a URL, the WebBrowser will prepend the file protocol specifier and add three forward slashes to the file path that you specify. Knowing that the WebBrowser uses three forward slashes is important if you need to parse the URL string of the current Web page.

By using the second parameter, *Flags*, you can dictate how or even where to load the specified URL. (The type of this parameter is a pointer to *VARIANT*.) The values for *Flags* come from an enumeration named *BrowserNavConstants*, which is defined in the ExDisp.h header file and contains six values, described in the following list. You can specify one or more of these values for the *Flags* parameter (some of which aren't currently implemented, mind you).

- *navOpenInNewWindow*. Causes a new window to open to display the URL. By default, this value will cause a new Internet Explorer browser window to open even if you are hosting the WebBrowser control in your application. I'll show you how to change this behavior in Chapter 7.

- *navNoHistory*. Specifies that the URL parameter shouldn't be added to the history list.

- *navNoReadFromCache*. Not currently implemented.

- *navNoWriteToCache*. Not currently implemented.

- *navAllowAutoSearch*. If the URL you specify cannot be found, the AutoSearch facility of the WebBrowser will attempt to find the correct URL by navigating to common domains such as .com, .edu, and .org. If the AutoSearch fails, the URL will be passed to a search engine.

- *navBrowserBar*. Loads the URL into the Explorer Bar, if possible. (You'll learn more about Explorer bars in Chapter 10.)

The third parameter is *TargetFrameName*. It allows you to specify in which frame of the Web page the navigation should occur. (This parameter type is a pointer to a *VARIANT*.) This string can be a name that exists on the current Web page or a special value such as *_top* or *_search*. The *_top* value specifies that the URL should be loaded over the top of the current Web page and not in one of the frames that might exist on the current Web page. The *_search* value specifies that the Search band should be opened. (This value has effect only if you're automating Internet Explorer.) If the frame name you specify doesn't exist, a new Internet Explorer window will be opened.

You can use the *PostData* parameter (the fourth parameter) to specify data to send to the server with an HTTP Post transaction. (The type of this parameter is a pointer to *VARIANT*.) The Post transaction is used to send data that has been gathered by an HTML form. If you don't specify any data for this parameter, the *Navigate* method will use the HTTP Get transaction. Also, if you don't specify an HTTP protocol URL (in other words, if you specify a FILE protocol URL), the *PostData* parameter will be ignored.

You can use the fifth parameter, *Headers*, to send HTTP header information to the server. (The type of this parameter is a pointer to *VARIANT*.) These headers are added to those that the WebBrowser control will normally send. As with the *PostData* parameter, if you don't specify an HTTP protocol URL for the first parameter, *Headers* will be ignored.

Calling the *Navigate* method is a little more difficult than calling *GoBack* or *GoForward*, but if you're navigating only to a URL and not passing any of the additional parameters, it's easy. For example, to navigate to Microsoft's home page by using Visual Basic, you can call *Navigate* like this:

```
WebBrowser1.Navigate "http://www.microsoft.com"
```

The Visual Basic code to call *Navigate* is so easy because all parameters except the first one are optional. In contrast, in Visual C++ you can't exclude any of the parameters. If you want to navigate to Microsoft's home page by using Visual C++ without specifying values for one or more of the parameters other than the first one, you must pass in empty *VARIANT* structures. In an MFC application, you would call *Navigate* like this:

```
COleVariant vtEmpty;
m_webBrowser.Navigate(_T("http://www.microsoft.com"), &vtEmpty, &vtEmpty,
                &vtEmpty, &vtEmpty);
```

This example demonstrates how to call *Navigate* when hosting the WebBrowser control in an MFC application. I passed the first parameter as a normal string instead of a *BSTR* because MFC provides a wrapper class for the WebBrowser control, and the first parameter for the *Navigate* method of this wrapper class is a *LPCTSTR*, which is a normal string. The other parameters of *Navigate* take pointers to *VARIANT* structures. If you don't want to specify any values for these parameters, don't just pass *NULL* to them—if you do, your application could crash. You must pass the address of an empty *VARIANT* structure. The preceding code used the *COleVariant* class, which is similar to the *CComVariant* class that you encountered in Chapter 5. *COleVariant* simply wraps a *VARIANT* to make the *VARIANT* structure easier to use.

Properties   Now that you've seen all the methods of *IWebBrowser*, you probably want to see the properties. (Demanding, aren't we?) The *IWebBrowser* interface has thirteen properties, described in Table 6-2 on the next page. I've listed these properties in the order in which they appear in the vtable of *IWebBrowser*. The properties in Table 6-2 appear in the vtable after all the methods of *IWebBrowser*, so if you want to know the entire vtable layout for the *IWebBrowser* interface, just combine Tables 6-1 and 6-2, adding the properties after the methods. (Of course, *IWebBrowser* inherits from *IDispatch* and *IUnknown*, and their methods appear first in the vtable.)

TABLE 6-2
IWEBBROWSER PROPERTIES IN VTABLE ORDER

Property	Description
Application	Returns the automation object (*IDispatch*) implemented in the application that is hosting the WebBrowser control, if the object is available. If an automation object isn't available in the host application, this property returns the automation object of the WebBrowser control.
Parent	Returns the automation object (*IDispatch*) of the parent of the WebBrowser control, which is usually the container—for example, your host or the Internet Explorer window.
Container	Returns the automation object (*IDispatch*) of the container of the WebBrowser control. Usually, this value is the same one that is returned by the *Parent* property.
Document	Returns the automation object (*IDispatch*) for the active document. If HTML is currently being displayed in the WebBrowser, the *Document* property gives you access to the DHTML Object Model.
TopLevelContainer	Returns a Boolean value that indicates whether Internet Explorer is the top-level container of the WebBrowser control. In other words, returns *true* if Internet Explorer is the host application.
Type	Returns the type of the object that has been loaded by the WebBrowser control. For example, if the document loaded is an HTML document, *Type* returns *Microsoft HTML Document 5.0*. If the document is a Word document, *Type* returns *Microsoft Word Document*.
Left	Returns or sets the distance between the internal left edge of the WebBrowser control's window and the left edge of its container's window.
Top	Returns or sets the distance between the internal top edge of the WebBrowser control's window and the top edge of its container's window.
Width	Returns or sets the width (horizontal dimension), in pixels, of the WebBrowser's window.

Property	Description
Height	Returns or sets the height (vertical dimension), in pixels, of the WebBrowser's window.
LocationName	Returns a string that contains the name of the resource (in other words, the HTML page, the Word document, the folder, and so on) that the WebBrowser is currently displaying. If the resource is an HTML page, this string is the title of the page. If the resource is a file or folder, this string is the name of that file or a folder— for example, foo.doc for a Word document or Temp for the temp directory.
LocationURL	Returns the URL of the resource that the WebBrowser is currently displaying.
Busy	Returns a Boolean value that indicates whether the WebBrowser is currently loading a URL. If this property returns *true*, you can use the *Stop* method to cancel the navigation that is occurring.

After reviewing Table 6-2, it should be pretty clear to you when to use the properties. A few of them, however, warrant more explanation. One property of *IWebBrowser* that you'll probably use quite a bit is *LocationURL*, which gives you the URL of the document that is currently loaded into the WebBrowser window. Obtaining the value of *LocationURL* from Visual Basic is easy:

```
Dim strLocation
strLocation = WebBrowser1.LocationURL
```

When you're hosting the WebBrowser control in Visual C++ with MFC, the MFC wrapper class makes accessing *LocationURL* just as easy. You simply call the *GetLocationURL* method, which returns a *CString* object. If you want to access *LocationURL* when automating Internet Explorer or when hosting the WebBrowser control in a C++ application that's not built by using MFC, you must call a method that represents *LocationURL* and pass to this method a pointer to a *BSTR*. The *BSTR* that you pass will contain the value of the property upon returning from this method. Here's how to access the *LocationURL* property in C++:

```
BSTR bstrURL;
m_pInternetExplorer->get_LocationURL(&bstrURL);
```

> **NOTE** When accessing the *LocationURL* property from C++ (other than by using the MFC wrapper class), you call a method named *get_LocationURL*. In COM, properties are typically accessed via functions that prepend either *put_* or *get_* to their names, depending on whether you're setting or retrieving the property. When setting a property, you call the *put_* method. When reading a property, you call the *get_* method.

The most important property of *IWebBrowser* is the *Document* property, which lets you access the document that is being displayed in the WebBrowser window. If the document is an HTML document, once you get access to the document using the *Document* property, you can retrieve or change the document's contents by using the DHTML Object Model.

> **NOTE**   The *Document* property returns an automation object (*IDispatch)* that represents the document being displayed. If the document being displayed is an HTML document, you can query the automation object for an interface of the *HTMLDocument* object and use it to access the DHTML Object Model. I'll show you how this is done in Visual Basic and Visual C++ in Chapter 8.

Accessing the *Document* property in Visual Basic is quite easy. After declaring a variable (for example, *HtmlDoc*), just set the variable to the value returned by the *Document* property:

```
Set HtmlDoc = WebBrowser1.Document
```

Accessing the *Document* property in an MFC application hosting the WebBrowser control is just as easy. Call the *GetDocument* method of the MFC wrapper class:

```
IDispatch* pDisp;
pDisp = m_webBrowser.GetDocument();
```

GetDocument returns a pointer to the *IDispatch* interface that represents the document. If *GetDocument* fails, the object returned will be equal to *NULL*.

In a non-MFC C++ application that is hosting the WebBrowser control or in any C++ application that is automating Internet Explorer, you access the *Document* property just like any other COM method—by prepending the name of the property with *get_*. (Note that this property is read-only, so there is no *put_* method for it.) When calling the *get_* method for the *Document* property, you pass in the address of a pointer to an *IDispatch* interface that will be set to the *IDispatch* interface of the document. Here's how you would obtain this property from a non-MFC application:

```
IDispatch* pDisp;
HRESULT hr = m_pInternetExplorer->get_Document(&pDisp);
```

When using this code, you can use the SUCCEEDED macro, which is part of the Win32 API, to determine whether the call to *get_Document* succeeded. You must ensure that *get_Document* succeeded before trying to access the *IDispatch* interface of the document.

> **NOTE**   You must wait for the *DocumentComplete* event to fire before you can safely access the document. If you access the *Document* property before this event has fired, you might experience undesirable results. I'll discuss the *DocumentComplete* event further in Chapter 7.

IWebBrowserApp

The *IWebBrowserApp* interface originally represented only Internet Explorer. Typically, you would create an instance of Internet Explorer using the *InternetExplorer* object. Then you controlled this instance by using the *IWebBrowserApp* interface. (You can still control this instance by using *IWebBrowserApp* today, but you will typically use *IWebBrowser2* instead, as I'll explain shortly.) The *IWebBrowserApp* interface inherits from *IWebBrowser*, so it provides all the functionality of the *IWebBrowser* interface along with its own.

Because *IWebBrowserApp* represents an instance of the Internet Explorer window, its methods and properties typically allow you to control the user interface aspects of the browser window. These methods and properties aren't included in the *IWebBrowser* interface that represents the WebBrowser control: the application that is hosting the control is responsible for providing user interface aspects such as status bars, toolbars, and menu bars. The WebBrowser control is used only to load and display Web pages and other types of files.

IWebBrowserApp has four methods and 10 properties. As with the *IWebBrowser* interface, in the vtable the methods are listed first, followed by the properties.

Methods   The methods of the *IWebBrowserApp* interface are pretty straightforward, as you can see in Table 6-3, but two warrant further discussion: *GetProperty* and *PutProperty*. These methods allow you to store a property in the Internet Explorer property bag so that you can retrieve it later. You'll typically want to do this to store some state information or data from one Web page to the next. (In fact, you can even use these methods when hosting the WebBrowser control by using the *IWebBrowser2* interface.)

TABLE 6-3
IWEBBROWSERAPP METHODS IN VTABLE ORDER

Method	Description
Quit	Forces the Internet Explorer window to close. In other words, it shuts down the instance of Internet Explorer that you are automating.
ClientToWindow	Converts the client coordinates of a point to window coordinates. Client coordinates are relative to the upper left corner of the client area, whereas window coordinates are relative to the upper left corner of the window.
PutProperty	Stores a property in the Internet Explorer property bag, which can be retrieved at a later time by using *GetProperty*.
GetProperty	Retrieves a property that was previously stored in the Internet Explorer property bag by using *PutProperty*.

If you read Chapter 5, you're already familiar with the Internet Explorer property bag. Storing a property in the property bag is as easy as calling the *PutProperty* method and passing it the property's name and value. Retrieving the property is as easy as calling the *GetProperty* method and passing it the name of the property you want to retrieve. The value of that property will be returned if it exists in the property bag.

Calling the methods in Table 6-3 in Visual Basic is pretty simple. The following Visual Basic code saves the *CurrentPicture* property and then retrieves it. (In this next bit of code, *InternetExplorer1* is an *InternetExplorer* object that you declare somewhere in your code.)

```
InternetExplorer1.PutProperty "CurrentPicture", 10
InternetExplorer1.GetProperty("CurrentPicture")
```

Calling the *PutProperty* and *GetProperty* methods in Visual C++ is just as easy, but calling the *PutProperty* method returns an *HRESULT* instead of the value of the property. As with most COM methods, when a value is returned from a method, that value is placed in a variable that is passed to the method. Here's a Visual C++ code example that shows how to use the *PutProperty* and *GetProperty* methods:

```
CSomeClass::PutGetProperty(VARIANT vtCurrentValue, VARIANT* vtNewValue)
{
    HRESULT hr;
    hr = m_pInternetExplorer->PutProperty(L"CurrentPicture",
                              vtCurrentValue);

    if (SUCCEEDED(hr))
    {
        // Notice that vtNewValue is already a pointer, so you
        // don't have to pass the address to GetProperty.
        //
        hr = m_pInternetExplorer->GetProperty(L"CurrentPicture",
                                  vtNewValue);
    }

    return hr;
}
```

The *PutGetProperty* method takes a *VARIANT* that is the current value of the property and a pointer to a *VARIANT* that will receive the value of the property retrieved from the property bag. Then the *PutProperty* method is called to store the *CurrentPicture* property in Internet Explorer's property bag. If that call succeeds, the *GetProperty* method retrieves the value that was just stored. Finally, the *HRESULT* that was returned from calls to the *PutProperty* and *GetProperty* methods is returned. The *PutGetProperty* method isn't extremely useful, but it does demonstrate how to use the *PutProperty* and *GetProperty* methods.

Properties   The *IWebBrowserApp* interface has 10 properties. Short descriptions of these properties are listed in vtable order in Table 6-4. To determine the entire vtable order for *IWebBrowserApp*, append the properties to the methods. (*IWebBrowserApp*'s vtable also includes *IWebBrowser*'s vtable, because *IWebBrowserApp* inherits from *IWebBrowser*. *IWebBrowser*'s methods and properties appear before *IWebBrowserApp*'s methods and properties in the vtable.)

TABLE 6-4
IWEBBROWSERAPP PROPERTIES IN VTABLE ORDER

Property	Description
Name	Returns the name of the object. (For example, when automating Internet Explorer, the *Name* property returns *Microsoft Internet Explorer*.)
HWND	Returns the handle of the Internet Explorer main window.
FullName	Returns the full path of the Internet Explorer executable file (iexplore.exe).
Path	Returns the full path of the Internet Explorer application.
Visible	Retrieves or sets the visibility of the Internet Explorer window. (In other words, you can use this property to determine or control whether Internet Explorer is visible or hidden.)
StatusBar	Shows or hides the Internet Explorer status bar. This property can also be used to determine the current state of the status bar—visible or hidden.
StatusText	Sets or retrieves the text that is shown in the Internet Explorer status bar.
ToolBar	Shows or hides the Internet Explorer toolbar. This property can also be used to determine the current state of the toolbar—visible or hidden.
MenuBar	Shows or hides the Internet Explorer menu bar. This property can also be used to determine the current state of the menu bar—visible or hidden.
FullScreen	Sets or retrieves a value that indicates whether Internet Explorer is currently being displayed in FullScreen mode. In FullScreen mode, Internet Explorer takes up the entire screen.

The properties listed in Table 6-4 are straightforward and easy to use. For example, if you wanted to retrieve the text that is stored in the Internet Explorer status bar from your Visual Basic application, you would use this code:

```
Dim strStatusText
strStatusText = InternetExplorer1.StatusText
```

You retrieve the status text in a Visual C++ application in a similar manner, especially if you are hosting the WebBrowser control using the MFC wrapper class. The following C++ code retrieves the status text for an application that is automating Internet Explorer:

```
BSTR bstrStatusText;
HRESULT hr = m_pInternetExplorer->get_StatusText(&bstrStatusText);
```

IWebBrowser2

Because of the COM rule that all interfaces are immutable (they can never change), to add new functionality to a COM interface, you must create a new interface. This new interface can inherit from other interfaces to extend their functionality. For example, when the need arose to add functionality to the WebBrowser and Internet Explorer interfaces, the developers were required to create a new interface: *IWebBrowser2*.

As mentioned earlier, *IWebBrowser2* inherits from both *IWebBrowser* and *IWebBrowserApp*, plus it provides functionality that isn't included in either. So you should use the *IWebBrowser2* interface for all interaction with either the WebBrowser control or Internet Explorer.

The *IWebBrowser2* interface has four methods and eight properties. As with the *IWebBrowser* and *IWebBrowserApp* interfaces, the properties follow the methods in *IWebBrowser2*'s vtable.

> **NOTE** *IWebBrowser2*'s vtable contains all *IWebBrowser2's* methods and properties, which include the methods and properties of *IWebBrowserApp*, *IWebBrowser*, and any interfaces from which they derive.

Methods   The four methods of the *IWebBrowser2* interface are briefly described, in vtable order, in Table 6-5.

Probably one of the most widely used *IWebBrowser2* interface methods is *ExecWB*. It provides a wrapper around the *Exec* method of the *IOleCommandTarget* interface that is implemented by the WebBrowser. Before the *ExecWB* method was created, you couldn't directly call *IOleCommandTarget::Exec* from Visual Basic, because Visual Basic cannot access the *IOleCommandTarget* interface and accordingly cannot use the method of this interface directly. The *IOleCommandTarget::Exec* method was used a lot in the past, so the WebBrowser developers decided to create *ExecWB* to make things easier.

> **NOTE** In object-oriented programming languages, an expression such as *IOleCommandTarget::Exec* indicates that the *Exec* method is a member of the *IOleCommandTarget* interface. Any method or property of a class or interface can be represented in this way.

TABLE 6-5
IWEBBROWSER2 METHODS IN VTABLE ORDER

Method	Description
Navigate2	Functions basically the same as the *Navigate* method of *IWebBrowser* except that *Navigate2* allows you to navigate to a location that might not be expressed as a URL, such as a Windows shell folder. (A Windows shell folder is represented by a pointer to an item identifier list, or PIDL, in the Windows shell namespace.)
QueryStatusWB	Works as a wrapper function for the *QueryStatus* method of the *IOleCommandTarget* interface implemented in the WebBrowser.
ExecWB	Works as a wrapper function for the *Exec* method of the *IOleCommandTarget* interface implemented in the WebBrowser.
ShowBrowserBar	Shows or hides a specific browser bar. (I'll discuss browser bars further in Chapter 10.) This method applies only to the *InternetExplorer* object.

Why on earth would you want to call the *ExecWB* method, anyway? Because it allows you to access functionality (via *IOleCommandTarget::Exec*) that isn't exposed by the WebBrowser interfaces. You're probably wondering why the developers didn't just implement methods and properties for this extra functionality. Remember that COM interfaces are immutable. Once the vtable of an interface is published, the interface can't be changed. So you can't add functionality without creating a new interface.

The *ExecWB* method allows WebBrowser developers to add functionality without creating new interfaces. Plus, that which is exposed by the WebBrowser via *ExecWB* typically consists of functionality that isn't used often, such as invoking the Save As dialog box for the Web page or zooming the content on the page. The way *ExecWB* works is that you pass it a command ID and any parameters that are necessary for the command you want to invoke. Far too many command IDs exist to list them all here. However, they're included in the *OLECMDID* enumeration in the DocObj.h header file.

> **NOTE** Make sure you're using the latest DocObj.h header file for Internet Explorer 5. All the headers and libraries can be downloaded from the "Downloads/Samples" section of the MSDN Online Web Workshop: *http:// msdn.microsoft.com/workshop*. Incidentally, you need to download and install these headers and libraries if you intend to compile the Visual C++ examples in this and later chapters.

As an example, suppose you want to zoom the contents of a Web page. Internet Explorer enables you to change the size of the text on a Web page from smallest to largest by using the View menu's Text Size submenu. The *ExecWB* method exposes functionality that allows you to change the size of the text displayed in the browser. For the Zoom command, you can specify the values *0*, *1*, *2*, *3*, or *4*, where *0* is the smallest and *4* is the largest. For example, the following code changes the zoom size to the largest (*4*) for a Visual Basic application hosting the WebBrowser control:

```
WebBrowser1.ExecWB OLECMDID_ZOOM, OLECMDEXECOPT_DONTPROMPTUSER, _
                CLng(4), Null
```

In this code, I call the *ExecWB* method, passing it *OLECMDID_ZOOM* constant for the first parameter. This constant specifies that the zoom operation should be executed. The second parameter that is passed in is a constant that tells *ExecWB* not to prompt the user. Alternatively, you could prompt the user by specifying *OLECMDEXECOPT_PROMPTUSER*. (These constants—along with a few more—are included in the *OLECMDEXECOPT* enumeration in DocObj.h.)

The third parameter is an input parameter that specifies the size of the text you want to set. I want to make the text as large as possible, so I specify *4*. Note that I wrap the value in a call to the Visual Basic *CLng* function, which converts the value that I specify to a variant—the required type of this input value. The final parameter is an output parameter that contains any return values. Because return values aren't required in this case, I pass a value of *Null*.

> **NOTE**   The *OLECMDID* and *OLECMDEXECOPT* enumerations are included in the type library for the WebBrowser control. Therefore, you won't need to define constants for their values in your Visual Basic project. The companion CD includes a sample Visual Basic application named VBZoom that demonstrates the use of *ExecWB* with *OLECMDID_ZOOM*, which you can find in the folder \Samples\Chap06\VBZoom.

RETRIEVING THE CURRENT ZOOM VALUE

If you want to retrieve the current zoom value, you can call *ExecWB* with the *OLECMDID_ZOOM* command ID, passing *Null* for the third parameter and a variant variable for the fourth. Upon returning from *ExecWB*, the variable will contain the current zoom value. Here's the Visual Basic code to retrieve the current zoom value:

```
Dim range as Variant
WebBrowser1.ExecWB OLECMDID_ZOOM, OLECMDEXECOPT_DONTPROMPTUSER, _
                Null, range
```

Properties The *IWebBrowser2* interface has eight properties. (Table 6-6 describes them in vtable order.) These properties are pretty straightforward, so I'll explain only one of them—*AddressBar*.

TABLE 6-6
IWebBrowser2 PROPERTIES IN VTABLE ORDER

Property	Description
ReadyState	Returns the ready state of the WebBrowser (in other words, it indicates whether the document is finished loading). Although you can use the *ReadyState* property, using the *DocumentComplete* event to determine whether the document is completely finished loading (that is, all components and the HTML are loaded) is better. (You'll learn how to use *DocumentComplete* in Chapter 7.)
Offline	Returns or sets the value that indicates whether the WebBrowser is operating in offline mode.
Silent	Returns or sets the value that indicates whether the WebBrowser is operating in silent mode. If it is, no dialog boxes will be displayed.
RegisterAsBrowser	Retrieves or sets the value that indicates whether the WebBrowser is registered as the top-level browser.
RegisterAsDropTarget	Retrieves or sets the value that indicates whether the WebBrowser is registered as a drop target for navigation. If the WebBrowser is registered as a drop target, users will be able to drag and drop links into the WebBrowser control that you're hosting or into the Internet Explorer window.
TheaterMode	Retrieves or sets the value that indicates whether Internet Explorer is in theater or normal window mode. In theater mode, Internet Explorer takes up the entire screen like in FullScreen mode, but it also has a minimal set of buttons and other user interface elements. (This property applies only to the *InternetExplorer* object.)
AddressBar	Shows or hides the Internet Explorer address bar. (This property applies only to the *InternetExplorer* object.)
Resizable	Returns or sets the value that indicates whether Internet Explorer can be resized. Using this property, you can prevent the user from changing the size of the Internet Explorer window. (This property applies only to the *InternetExplorer* object.)

WEBBROWSER CONTROL AND
INTERNET EXPLORER DIFFERENCES

As you've seen, whether you're hosting the WebBrowser control or automating Internet Explorer, you use one interface—*IWebBrowser2*—which includes all the methods of *IWebBrowser* and *IWebBrowserApp* and a lot more. Some methods and properties of *IWebBrowser2*, however, don't work unless you're automating Internet Explorer.

For example, if you're hosting the WebBrowser control, user interface features such as the address bar, menu bar, status bar, and toolbar are implemented by your application and not by the WebBrowser control. So properties of *IWebBrowser2* such as *AddressBar*, *MenuBar*, *StatusBar*, and *ToolBar* aren't functional when hosting the WebBrowser control. Because you've created the container application yourself, you should be able to control the user interface features without having to rely on these properties. The properties exist to help you easily communicate with a running instance of Internet Explorer. Some methods and properties apply only to Internet Explorer: these methods include *ShowBrowserBar* and *ClientToWindow*, and these properties include *FullScreen*, *MenuBar*, *Resizable*, *AddressBar*, *StatusBar*, *StatusText*, *TheaterMode*, and *ToolBar*.

The *AddressBar* property allows you to show or hide the Internet Explorer address bar: the toolbar that contains a text box in which you can enter a URL that you want to navigate to in the browser. Being able to show or hide the address bar enables you to completely control your user's navigation experience—you already have properties that allow you to show or hide the other user interface features.

Controlling the user's navigation experience is often helpful if you want to provide Internet browsing for your corporate intranet or for an elementary school, for example. In these environments, you would want to control the user's navigation so that certain inappropriate Web sites weren't available. You could create your own browser by using the WebBrowser control, which I'll show you how to do later. But if you don't have the time or resources to do so, you could automate Internet Explorer instead. Automating Internet Explorer allows you to turn off all user interface features that enable a user to navigate to a Web page, such as the menu bar, toolbar, and address bar. Then you can create a number of Web pages that provide links to which the user can navigate.

Turning off the user interface features is easy. To hide the menu bar, use the *MenuBar* property. To hide the toolbar, use the *ToolBar* property. To hide the address bar, use the *AddressBar* property. To hide each of these user interface features, simply set their associated properties to *False*. For example, here's how you would turn off the menu bar, toolbar, and address bar in a Visual Basic application that is automating Internet Explorer:

```
InternetExplorer1.AddressBar = False
InternetExplorer1.ToolBar = False
InternetExplorer1.MenuBar = False
```

HOSTING THE WEBBROWSER CONTROL

Now let's create some applications in Visual Basic and Visual C++ that host the WebBrowser control. After you complete the sample in this section, you should have a basic understanding of how to create an application that hosts the WebBrowser control. When you see how easy it is to add Web browsing to your applications, I'm sure you'll want to start right away!

Using Visual Basic

In Visual Basic, you can develop a fully functional Web browser of your own in five minutes or less. Follow these steps to create a basic Web browser application:

1. Start Visual Basic.

2. Choose Standard EXE from the New Project dialog box. Visual Basic enters design mode so that you can begin designing the form.

3. The WebBrowser control is not automatically included in the Control Toolbox. To add the WebBrowser control to the Control Toolbox, choose Components from the Project menu. The dialog box in Figure 6-3 will be displayed.

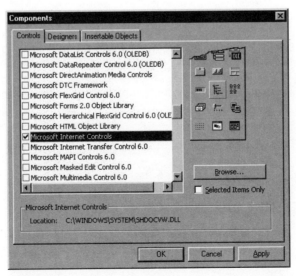

Figure 6-3. *Components dialog box.*

4. Click the Controls tab if the tab isn't already visible. Then check Microsoft Internet Controls in the list box, and click OK to close the dialog box. Visual Basic adds the WebBrowser control icon to the bottom of the Control Toolbox, as shown in Figure 6-4.

WebBrowser control icon

Figure 6-4. *Visual Basic Control Toolbox after adding the WebBrowser control icon.*

5. To add the WebBrowser control to the form, click the WebBrowser control icon in the Control Toolbox and size the control on your form. Once you've added the control to the form, Visual Basic will assign it the name *WebBrowser1*.

6. Increase the size of your form so that you can see more content on Web pages when you navigate to them. Leave some room for the Visual Basic intrinsic controls that you're going to add later. The form should look similar to the one shown in Figure 6-5.

7. Double-click on an empty area of the form to start adding code to its *Load* event. To make the WebBrowser navigate to a Web page, you just need to call one of the navigation methods such as *GoHome*, *GoSearch*, *Navigate*, or *Navigate2*.

8. Call the *GoHome* method to navigate to the user's home page. The code for the *Load* event handler should look like this:

```
Private Sub Form_Load()
    WebBrowser1.GoHome
End Sub
```

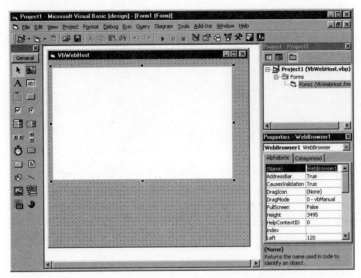

Figure 6-5. *Visual Basic form after adding the WebBrowser control.*

That's it! You're finished. You've created a fully functional Web browser application. By my clock, that took only five minutes. To make sure it works, run your application by clicking the Start button on the Visual Basic toolbar. Your application will load the WebBrowser control and navigate to your home page. Save the project before you proceed, and name it *VbWebHost*.

Although you now have a working Internet application, you'll probably want to add functionality so that the application acts more like a real Web browser application. Add some controls to the form to allow the user to control the navigation. Add a label, a text box for a URL, a Go button, a Back button, a Forward button, and a Stop button. The form should look similar to the one in Figure 6-6 on the following page.

Now assign the properties listed in Table 6-7 on the next page to your controls. When you assign the properties, specify the strings that are on the right side of the equal signs and do not include the quotation marks and equal signs.

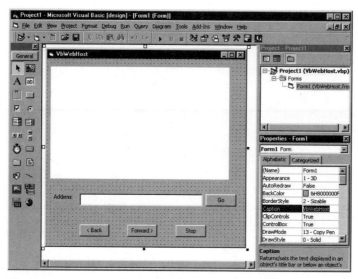

Figure 6-6.   *Visual Basic form after adding controls.*

TABLE 6-7
CONTROL PROPERTIES

Control	*Properties*
Label	Caption = "Address:"
TextBox	Name = txtAddress; Text = "" (In other words, remove the default text.)
Go Button	Name = btnGo; Caption = "Go"
Back Button	Name = btnBack; Caption = "< Back"
Forward Button	Name = btnFwd; Caption = "Forward >"
Stop Button	Name = btnStop; Caption = "Stop"

Now add some code. To make these controls work correctly, use the methods of the WebBrowser control. For example, when the user enters text into the text box and clicks the Go button, use the *Navigate* method to perform the navigation. Of course, you must ensure that the user has indeed entered some text into the text box.

Also, you can use the *GoBack*, *GoForward*, and *Stop* methods to implement the Back, Forward, and Stop buttons. Remember that the *GoBack* and *GoForward* methods have no effect in certain situations. (Chapter 7 demonstrates how to disable Back and Forward buttons when their associated WebBrowser methods have no effect.) After you implement the button controls, your Visual Basic code should look like this:

```
Option Explicit

Private Sub btnBack_Click()
    On Error Resume Next
    WebBrowser1.GoBack
End Sub

Private Sub btnFwd_Click()
    On Error Resume Next
    WebBrowser1.GoForward
End Sub

Private Sub btnGo_Click()
    WebBrowser1.Navigate txtAddress.Text
End Sub

Private Sub btnStop_Click()
    WebBrowser1.Stop
End Sub

Private Sub Form_Load()
    WebBrowser1.GoHome
End Sub
```

Notice that *On Error Resume Next* is specified in the *Click* event handlers for the Back and Forward buttons. When no entries exist in the history list before or after the current URL, these methods return errors. The Visual Basic error handling mechanism is used to handle them.

Now test the code by running the application. After the WebBrowser finishes navigating to your home page, type a URL into the text box and click the Go button. You should have two URLs in the history list. Click the Back button to go back to your home page, and then click the Forward button to move ahead. Click the Stop button while a page is being loaded to ensure that the Stop button works as well.

Printing a Web page

Because users frequently want to print the Web page displayed in their application, you'll want to add printing functionality to your application. In the past, printing a Web page from Visual Basic was cumbersome and unreliable. You had to use the *SendKeys* function to send the accelerator keys that initiated the print operation to the WebBrowser. Now, using the *ExecWB* method, printing Web pages is much easier; plus *ExecWB* is a lot more reliable.

To add printing functionality, first add a Print button to the form. (Use the same procedures that you used to add the Stop, Back, and Forward buttons earlier.) Name this button *btnPrint*, and change the caption to *Print*. The form should look similar to the one displayed in Figure 6-7 on the following page.

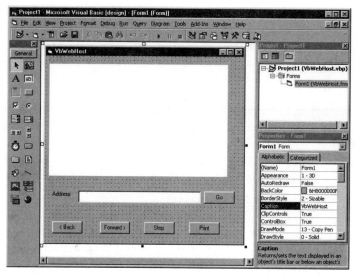

Figure 6-7. *Visual Basic form after adding a Print button.*

Next, double-click the Print button to add code to handle its *Click* event. In the event handler, call the *ExecWB* method, passing it the command ID necessary to print the page: *OLECMDID_PRINT*. As with other calls to *ExecWB*, you should specify whether to prompt the user by passing appropriate value for the second parameter. If you want to prompt the user before printing, specify *OLECMDEXECOPT_PROMPTUSER*; otherwise specify *OLECMDEXECOPT_DONTPROMPTUSER*. For this example, we want to prompt the user before printing. The print command takes no input and returns no output, so you can specify *Null* for the third and fourth parameters. The code for this event handler should look like this:

```
Private Sub btnPrint_Click()
   On Error Resume Next
   WebBrowser1.ExecWB OLECMDID_PRINT, OLECMDEXECOPT_PROMPTUSER, _
                      Null, Null
End Sub
```

Test the new code by running your application, navigating to a Web page, and clicking the Print button. Internet Explorer will display the Print dialog box and let you choose different print options. The sample created by following these steps can be found on the companion CD in the folder \Samples\Chap06\VbWebHost.

Using Visual C++

Creating WebBrowser host applications in Visual C++ is a bit more difficult than in Visual Basic. If you're creating your host application from scratch (without MFC or ATL), hosting the WebBrowser control involves implementing quite a few COM interfaces. You must also create an instance of the WebBrowser control by using the *CoCreateInstance* COM API, specifying *CLSID_WebBrowser* as the CLSID of the object you want to create. And you must "site" the control in your container.

Because creating ActiveX control containers is outside the scope of this book, I'll demonstrate the easy ways to host the WebBrowser control. In this section, I'll show you how to create a WebBrowser host application by using MFC and by using the ActiveX control containment classes that are new in ATL 3.

Using MFC

You can create three types of applications in MFC: single-document interface (SDI), multiple-document interface (MDI), and dialog-based applications. Because building a WebBrowser host in MFC by using the dialog-based approach is similar to creating one in Visual Basic, I'll show you how to create a WebBrowser host by using one of the other approaches—SDI. Once you know how to build a WebBrowser host by using the SDI approach, translating this information to MDI will be pretty easy.

When demonstrating the SDI example in this section, I'll use the WebBrowser (*CWebBrowser2*) wrapper class that the Components And Controls Wizard creates for you. Using this class instead of the built-in MFC *CHtmlView* class will help you better understand how to host the WebBrowser in MFC.

The *CHtmlView* class requires less explanation. To use it, all you have to do is choose *CHtmlView* as the base class of your application in step 6 of the MFC AppWizard when creating your MFC project, as shown in Figure 6-8. After you complete the wizard, the view class for your application will be derived from *CHtmlView*. Then you can call wrapper functions for the different methods of the *IWebBrowser2* interface.

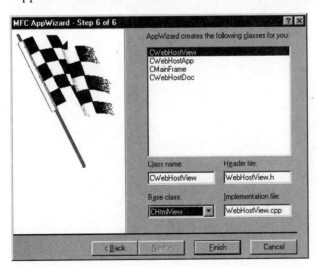

Figure 6-8. *MFC AppWizard - Step 6 of 6 dialog box.*

To create an MFC single-document interface application, start Visual C++ and choose New from the File menu. The New dialog box is displayed, as shown in Figure 6-9.

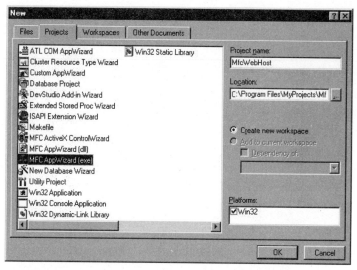

Figure 6-9.   *Visual C++ New dialog box.*

In the Projects tab, select the MFC AppWizard (exe) entry, type a name into the Project Name edit box (such as *MfcWebHost*), and click OK. Step 1 of the MFC AppWizard is displayed. (See Figure 6-10.)

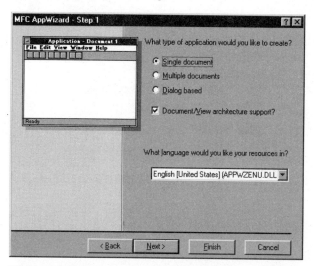

Figure 6-10.   *Step 1 of the MFC AppWizard.*

Select the Single Document option from the dialog box. Then accept the defaults for the remainder of the project settings by clicking the Finish button. Click OK in the New Project Information dialog box that appears. To add the WebBrowser control to your project, select Project/Add To Project/Components And Controls from the Visual C++ menu, as shown in Figure 6-11.

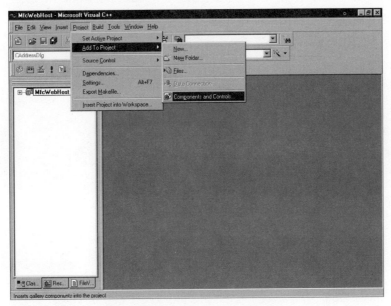

Figure 6-11.   *Selecting Components And Controls.*

Visual C++ gathers information about all the components and controls on your system and displays the Components And Controls Gallery dialog box, as shown in Figure 6-12.

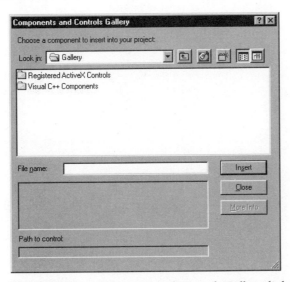

Figure 6-12.   *Components And Controls Gallery dialog box.*

Now double-click Registered ActiveX Controls in the list box. Locate and select Microsoft Web Browser, and click the Insert button. When prompted whether you want to insert this component, click OK. The wizard displays the Confirm Classes dialog box that is shown in Figure 6-13.

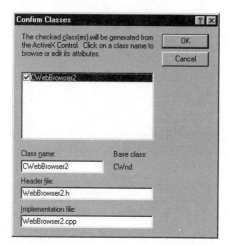

Figure 6-13.   *Confirm Classes dialog box.*

By default, *CWebBrowser2* is selected. The *CWebBrowser2* class is a wrapper class for the WebBrowser control that Visual C++ is going to create for you. Because this class's implementation is specific to MFC, you can use it only in MFC projects. Click the OK button to add *CWebBrowser2* to your project. Then close the Components And Controls Gallery dialog box.

Include the WebBrowser2.h file in the header file for your view class—MfcWebHostView.h:

```
#include "WebBrowser2.h"
```

Create a private or protected data member in your view class, and name it *m_webBrowser*. The declaration of this data member should look similar to this:

```
protected:
    CWebBrowser2 m_webBrowser;
```

Create a message handler for the *WM_CREATE* message. In the event handler, add code to create a new instance of the WebBrowser control by using *m_webBrowser's* *Create* method. (The *Create* method is a member of the wrapper class that was created for you.) The code for the *OnCreate* message handler should look like this:

```
int CMfcWebHostView::OnCreate(LPCREATESTRUCT lpCreateStruct)
{
```

```
    if (CView::OnCreate(lpCreateStruct) == -1)
        return -1;

    // Create WebBrowser control
    //
    if (!m_webBrowser.Create(NULL, WS_CHILD|WS_VISIBLE,
                        CRect(), this, NULL))
    {
        return -1;
    }

    return 0;
}
```

Now create a Windows message handler for the *WM_SIZE* message. Add code to the message handler to change the size of the WebBrowser control when the size of your application changes. If you don't include this code, the WebBrowser control will never appear in the View window. Here's the code for the *OnSize* message handler:

```
void CMfcWebHostView::OnSize(UINT nType, int cx, int cy)
{
    CView::OnSize(nType, cx, cy);


    // Resize WebBrowser control
    //
    m_webBrowser.MoveWindow( 0, 0, cx, cy );
    m_webBrowser.UpdateWindow();
}
```

Override the *OnInitialUpdate* method of the base class to navigate to the user's home page when your application is first created. Here's how the code for the *OnInitialUpdate* message handler should appear:

```
void CMfcWebHostView::OnInitialUpdate()
{
    CView::OnInitialUpdate();

    // Navigate to the user's home page.
    //
    m_webBrowser.GoHome();
}
```

Compile and run the application. It should load the WebBrowser control and navigate to your user's home page. The application should look similar to the one shown in Figure 6-14 on the following page.

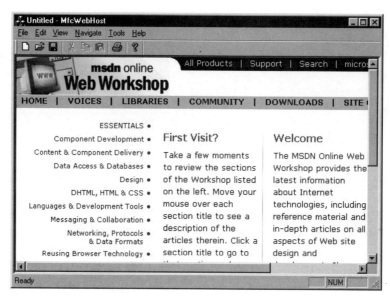

Figure 6-14. *MfcWebHost application.*

Now add some functionality to your application so that it can be used to browse the Internet. Add a Navigate menu that contains submenu items for Go Back, Go Forward, Go Home, Go Search, Go To A Web Page, and Stop. Your new menu should look similar to Figure 6-15.

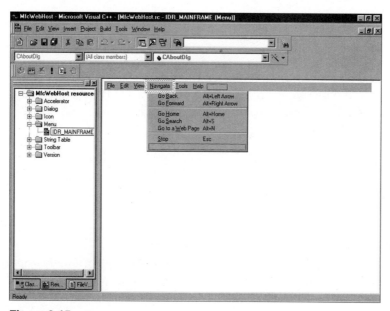

Figure 6-15. *Navigate menu.*

You might want to add accelerator keys for your new menu items, such as the Alt-Left arrow key combination for Go Back. You can use the same accelerator keys that Internet Explorer uses if you like.

> **NOTE** You can find the accelerator keys that Internet Explorer uses by inspecting the menu items on the Internet Explorer View menu. Note that no menu item exists that is similar to our Go To A Web Page menu item. Internet Explorer uses an edit box on the toolbar. You might want to add an edit box for the URL instead of a menu item.

Create menu handlers to implement each menu item. Adding menu handlers to the view class is the easiest way to implement the menu functionality. Use the methods of the WebBrowser control to perform the necessary operations. For example, use the *GoBack* method to implement the Go Back menu item. The code for these event handlers should look like this:

```
void CMfcWebHostView::OnNavigateGoBack()
{
    m_webBrowser.GoBack();
}

void CMfcWebHostView::OnNavigateGoForward()
{
    m_webBrowser.GoForward();
}

void CMfcWebHostView::OnNavigateGoHome()
{
    m_webBrowser.GoHome();
}

void CMfcWebHostView::OnNavigateGoSearch()
{
    m_webBrowser.GoSearch();
}

void CMfcWebHostView::OnNavigateStop()
{
    m_webBrowser.Stop();
}
```

As I mentioned earlier, if the user clicks Go Back or Go Forward and no pages exist before or after the current page in the navigation history, an error message will be displayed. In the next chapter, I'll show you how to disable these menu items when they aren't needed to prevent the error message from being displayed.

The Go To A Web Page menu item is a special case. For this menu item, a dialog box should be displayed that asks for the URL that the user wants to navigate to. (See Figure 6-16 on the next page.)

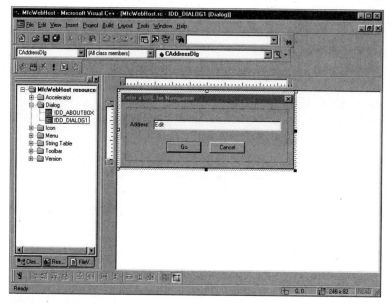

Figure 6-16. *Enter A URL For Navigation dialog box.*

Alternatively, you can create an edit box in the toolbar of your application that will be used for navigation. In this example, I decided to take the dialog approach. When creating this dialog, you can use ClassWizard to create a new dialog class for it. Name this class *CAddressDlg*. The dialog class should contain a *CString* data member named *m_strAddress* that will hold the address that the user entered. If you use ClassWizard to create this data member, the data member will be declared as a public member of the class. Change this data member to a protected data member of the class, and create an accessor method for this member, like so:

```
public:
    const CString& GetAddress() const { return m_strAddress; }

protected:
    CString m_strAddress;
```

Now create a menu handler for the Go To A Web Page menu item. This menu handler should build and display the *CAddressDlg* dialog box. (Make sure you include the header file for the *CAddressDlg* class in the implementation file for the view class—MfcWebHostView.cpp.) After the user enters a URL and clicks OK, the application should navigate to the URL using the WebBrowser's *Navigate* method. The code for the menu handler should look like this:

```
void CMfcWebHostView::OnNavigateGoToAWebPage()
{
    CAddressDlg dlgAddr;
```

```
// Show the dialog box. If the user clicks OK,
// make sure a URL was entered. If one was entered,
// navigate to that URL by using the Navigate method.
//
if (dlgAddr.DoModal() == IDOK)
{
  CString strAddress = dlgAddr.GetAddress();

  if (!strAddress.IsEmpty())
  {
    COleVariant vtEmpty;

    m_webBrowser.Navigate(strAddress, &vtEmpty,
                  &vtEmpty, &vtEmpty, &vtEmpty);
  }
}
}
```

In this code, an instance of the *CAddressDlg* class is created. Then *DoModal* is called to create and show the dialog box. If the user clicks the OK button, the application checks to make sure that a URL was actually entered before navigating to the URL.

Now compile and test your application. Test all the menu items to make sure you can navigate to a Web page, to your home page, to your search page, and backward and forward in the history list. Make sure the Stop menu item works, too. (This example can be found on the companion CD in the folder \Samples\Chap06\MfcWebHost. The file on the CD includes the additional menu items that are implemented later in this chapter.)

Using ATL

In the past, hosting the WebBrowser control in an application written by using the Active Template Libraries (ATL) wasn't any easier than creating a control container manually by using standard C++. But now, the new ActiveX control containment classes that come with ATL 3 (which shipped with Visual C++ 6) allow you to easily host the WebBrowser control in an ATL application or control.

Because implementing in ATL user interface features such as menus and toolbars still involves using the Win32 APIs, the example that I'm going to show you is pretty basic. I just want to demonstrate how to use the new control containment classes to host the WebBrowser control. We won't implement any user interface features whatsoever. This example will be just a frame with a window that contains the WebBrowser control. In Chapter 9, I'll show you a full-blown browser application that is written with ATL and the Win32 APIs.

To create a WebBrowser host application by using ATL, start Visual C++, and follow the steps at the top of the next page.

1. Choose New from the File menu.

2. In the New dialog box, choose ATL COM AppWizard, and enter *AtlWebHost* for the project name.

3. Click OK, choose Executable (EXE) from the Step 1 Of 1 dialog box, and click the Finish button.

4. Click the OK button in the New Project Information dialog box. The wizard will create the basic code for an ATL stand-alone executable application.

5. Add the control to your project that hosts the WebBrowser control. To do this, right-click AtlWebHost Classes in the ClassView pane of your project.

6. From the context menu, choose New ATL Object. The ATL Object Wizard dialog box is displayed.

7. Click Controls in the left pane, and select HTML Control from the right pane, as shown in Figure 6-17.

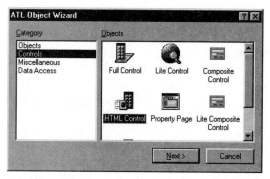

Figure 6-17. *ATL Object Wizard with HTML Control selected.*

8. Click the Next button in the ATL Object Wizard dialog box, and enter a short name for the control, such as *AtlWbHost*. The wizard automatically fills in the rest of the text boxes in the dialog box for you.

9. Keep the defaults for the remainder of the items in the dialog box, and click OK.

The wizard creates the *CAtlWbHost* class for you, which contains boilerplate code to host the WebBrowser control. The key piece of code that instantiates the WebBrowser control is contained in the *OnCreate* method, which is called when the *WM_CREATE* message is sent to the window associated with this class. The code that the wizard inserts for *OnCreate* is shown here:

```
LRESULT OnCreate(UINT /*uMsg*/, WPARAM /*wParam*/, LPARAM /*lParam*/,
                 BOOL& /*bHandled*/)
```

```
{
    CAxWindow wnd(m_hWnd);
    HRESULT hr = wnd.CreateControl(IDH_ATLWBHOST);
    if (SUCCEEDED(hr))
        hr = wnd.SetExternalDispatch(static_cast<IAtlWbHostUI*>(this));
    if (SUCCEEDED(hr))
        hr = wnd.QueryControl(IID_IWebBrowser2, (void**)&m_spBrowser);
    return SUCCEEDED(hr) ? 0 : -1;
}
```

In this code, a window object of type *CAxWindow* is created first. This object provides ActiveX control containment support. Next, the WebBrowser control is created by using the *CreateControl* method of the *CAxWindow* class. Notice that the resource ID of an HTML page is passed to *CreateControl* so that this HTML page will be loaded when the WebBrowser control is created. Then the *SetExternalDispatch* method is invoked. This method pertains to implementing the *IDocHostUIHandler* interface, which I'll discuss in Chapter 9.

If none of the previous method calls have failed, the code uses the *QueryControl* method of *CAxWindow* to query for the *IWebBrowser2* interface. If all goes well, *QueryControl* returns a pointer to the *IWebBrowser2* interface that is stored in the *m_spBrowser* data member. By default, the wizard makes this data member public.

> **NOTE** Being the good object-oriented programmer that I am, I like to change the access-specifier for the *m_spBrowser* data member to a protected data member. You can decide whether you want to do the same thing.

If you compile and run the code that the wizard entered, nothing will happen. You have to add code to create and display the window. To do this, you must first create a method named *Run* in the *CAtlWbHost* class. (The name of this method is irrelevant. You can choose anything that makes sense to you.) This method creates and displays the window for your application, as shown in this code:

```
STDMETHODIMP Run()
{
    //
    // Create and show the window.
    //
    RECT rcClient = { CW_USEDEFAULT, 0, 0, 0 };

    if (Create(GetDesktopWindow(), rcClient, _T("ATL Browser"),
               WS_VISIBLE | WS_OVERLAPPEDWINDOW, 0, (UINT)NULL) == NULL)
    {
        return E_FAIL;
    }

    ShowWindow(SW_SHOWNORMAL);
    return S_OK;
}
```

When the *Create* method is called, a *WM_CREATE* message is sent to the window; consequently, the *OnCreate* method is called. The code to host the WebBrowser control is included in the *OnCreate* method as I showed you earlier.

NOTE   The *Create* method belongs to the *CWindowImpl* class, which is a base class of *CComControl*. *CAtlWbHost* derives directly from *CComControl*, which means that you can call methods of *CWindowImpl* as well.

Next the *Run* method must be called to create and display the window. This call should be made in the AtlWebHost.cpp file directly above the message loop for your application. But before *Run* is called, an instance of the *CAtlWbHost* class must be created. You cannot simply create an instance of this class, like you would do for any other C++ object, by using the *new* operator. You must use the *CreateInstance* method of *CComObject* to create an instance of the class. Locate the message pump for your application in CAtlWebHost.cpp, insert this code to create an instance of the *CAtlWbHost* class, and call the *Run* method:

```
CComObject<CAtlWbHost>* pWbHost;
HRESULT hr = CComObject<CAtlWbHost>::CreateInstance(&pWbHost);

if (SUCCEEDED(hr))
    pWbHost->Run();


// Message pump
MSG msg;
while (GetMessage(&msg, 0, 0, 0))
    DispatchMessage(&msg);
```

If you compile and run the application now, it will work. It loads the WebBrowser control, which navigates to the Web page resource that the wizard automatically inserted into your application. You should navigate somewhere useful, so use the *GoHome* method to navigate to the user's home page. You can call *GoHome* in the *OnCreate* function. After you add the call to *GoHome*, the *OnCreate* function will look like this:

```
LRESULT OnCreate(UINT /*uMsg*/, WPARAM /*wParam*/,
        LPARAM /*lParam*/, BOOL& /*bHandled*/)
{
    CAxWindow wnd(m_hWnd);
    HRESULT hr = wnd.CreateControl(IDH_ATLWBHOST);
    if (SUCCEEDED(hr))
        hr = wnd.SetExternalDispatch(static_cast<IAtlWbHostUI*>(this));
    if (SUCCEEDED(hr))
        hr = wnd.QueryControl(IID_IWebBrowser2, (void**)&m_spBrowser);
```

```
    if (SUCCEEDED(hr))
        m_spBrowser->GoHome();

    return SUCCEEDED(hr) ? 0 : -1;
}
```

When you compile and run your application, the application should look similar to the one shown in Figure 6-18. The sample created can be found on the companion CD in the folder \Samples\Chap06\AtlWebHost.

Figure 6-18. *AtlWebHost application.*

Printing a Web page

Printing a Web page from an MFC application that is hosting the WebBrowser control is just as easy as it is in a Visual Basic application that is hosting the control. All you have to do is call the *ExecWB* method and pass *OLECMDID_PRINT*.

To add printing support to the MfcWebHost example I introduced to you earlier, create a menu handler for the ID_FILE_PRINT menu item. In the menu handler, call the *ExecWB* method of the WebBrowser control, and pass *OLECMDID_PRINT*. You can also specify whether you want the user to be prompted before printing, which we do in the next bit of code. Also, if you want to know whether the user clicked the OK button or the Cancel button, check the return value of *ExecWB*. For the print command, if the user clicked OK to initiate printing, *ExecWB* will return *S_OK*. If the user clicked Cancel, *ExecWB* will return something other than *S_OK*. (I say "something other than *S_OK*" because the value returned isn't representative of the fact that the user clicked the Cancel button.) On the next page is the code for this *OnFilePrint* method that will be called when the user chooses Print from the File menu.

```
void CMfcWebHostView::OnFilePrint()
{
    m_webBrowser.ExecWB(OLECMDID_PRINT, OLECMDEXECOPT_PROMPTUSER,
                        NULL, NULL);
}
```

In addition to printing, the WebBrowser control offers page setup functionality. By using page setup, the user can change different options that pertain to printing such as headers, footers, and page orientation. To implement the page setup functionality, the code calls *ExecWB* and passes *OLECMDID_PAGESETUP*. Create a menu item on the File menu named Page Setup. Then create a menu handler for this menu item, and enter the following code to implement this handler:

```
void CMfcWebHostView::OnFilePageSetup()
{
    m_webBrowser.ExecWB(OLECMDID_PAGESETUP, OLECMDEXECOPT_PROMPTUSER,
                        NULL, NULL);
}
```

Once again, compile and test your application. Try out the printing functionality by choosing Print and Page Setup.

AUTOMATING INTERNET EXPLORER

Automating Internet Explorer opens a world of possibilities for developing Web-based applications. It allows you to customize Internet Explorer to fit your needs without having to create a full-blown application by using Visual Basic or Visual C++. Automation offers other advantages as well: you can change Internet Explorer's user interface by using the methods and properties of its interfaces; you can provide user interface features such as browser bars that you can't easily provide when hosting the WebBrowser control; and you can control navigation.

Automating Internet Explorer is easy. You create a simple application that starts an instance of the browser. Then you control Internet Explorer in the same way you control the WebBrowser control—by using the *IWebBrowser2* interface. I'll show you how easily you can automate Internet Explorer by using Visual Basic and Visual C++.

> **NOTE**   The term *automation* in its truest sense refers to controlling a COM object by using its automation interface—*IDispatch*. But developers who write applications to control Internet Explorer use the terminology *automating Internet Explorer*, even though controlling the browser in this way that might not involve using the *IDispatch* interface directly.

Using Visual Basic

You've already seen how to create a fully functional Visual Basic Web browser application in five minutes by using the WebBrowser control. You can build a fully functional Visual Basic application that automates Internet Explorer in about the same amount of time. Let's build one now.

Start Visual Basic and choose Standard EXE from the New Project dialog box. Then choose References from the Project menu. The References dialog box, shown in Figure 6-19, will be displayed.

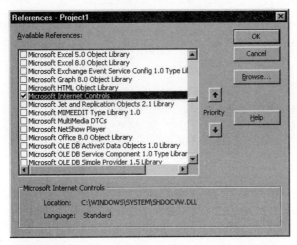

Figure 6-19. *References dialog box.*

Scroll down in the list box, check the Microsoft Internet Controls check box, and click OK (just as you did in the Components dialog box when hosting the WebBrowser control). Now add a command button to the form, name it *btnStart*, and change the caption to *Start IE5*. Then double-click the command button so that you can add code to the event handler for the *Click* event of this button.

When a user clicks the Start IE5 button, you want your application to start a new instance of Internet Explorer 5. The code to make this happen is pretty straightforward. First create a global variable of type *InternetExplorer*. (This is the *InternetExplorer* object that I told you about earlier in this chapter in the section entitled "The WebBrowser Control and Internet Explorer.") Name this variable *InternetExplorer1*.

Now, in the event handler for the *Click* event of *btnStart*, add code to create a new instance of Internet Explorer if an instance hasn't previously been created. You can use either the *CreateObject* Visual Basic function or the *New* keyword. But because you can't perform certain tasks with an object created by a call to *CreateObject*, such as handling events, you should create the *InternetExplorer* object by using the *New* keyword, like this:

```
Set InternetExplorer1 = New InternetExplorer
```

This code creates a new instance of Internet Explorer, but the instance is hidden. To make this instance visible, set the *Visible* property to *True*, as shown at the top of the next page.

```
InternetExplorer1.Visible = True
```

Now you need to navigate to a Web page in this new instance of Internet Explorer. You can do this by calling the *Navigate* method of the *InternetExplorer* object, like this:

```
InternetExplorer1.Navigate "http://www.microsoft.com/"
```

At this point, the entire Visual Basic source code that automates Internet Explorer for this application should look like this:

```
Option Explicit
Dim InternetExplorer1 As InternetExplorer

Private Sub btnStart_Click()
    ' Only create a new instance of Internet Explorer
    ' if one hasn't already been created.
    '
    If Not InternetExplorer1 Is Nothing Then
        Exit Sub
    End If

    Set InternetExplorer1 = New InternetExplorer

    ' Make Internet Explorer visible and navigate
    ' to Microsoft's home page.
    '
    InternetExplorer1.Visible = True
    InternetExplorer1.Navigate "http://www.microsoft.com/"
End Sub

Private Sub Form_Load()
    Set InternetExplorer1 = Nothing
End Sub
```

Go ahead and run your application. Then click the Start IE5 button to run the application and watch Internet Explorer fly! A new instance of Internet Explorer will be started that navigates to Microsoft's home page. That wasn't too difficult, was it? Now let's add some really cool features to the application that allow you to control the instance of Internet Explorer that you create.

First save your project as VbAutoIE.vbp, and save your form as VbAutoIE.frm. Then add some controls to your form, as shown in Figure 6-20. These controls will allow you to show or hide the different user interface features of Internet Explorer such as the address bar, menu bar, status bar, and toolbar. You'll also be able to add text to the status bar.

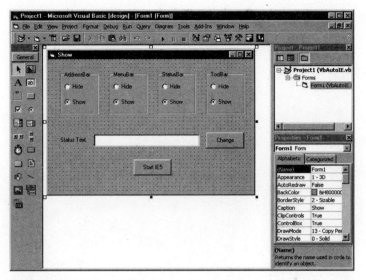

Figure 6-20. *Visual Basic form with controls to customize the Internet Explorer user interface.*

Now set the properties of each of these controls, as shown in Table 6-8. For the Option Buttons control, create four control arrays of option buttons. Each array should contain one Hide and one Show option button, as shown in Figure 6-20. Set the captions of all the top option buttons to *Hide* and all the bottom option buttons to *Show*.

TABLE 6-8
CONTROL PROPERTIES FOR A VISUAL BASIC
PROGRAM AUTOMATING INTERNET EXPLORER

Control	*Properties*
Frame1-4	Captions = *"AddressBar"*, *"MenuBar"*, *"StatusBar"*, and *"ToolBar"*, respectively
Hide Option Buttons	Caption = *"Hide"*; Index = *0*; Value = *False*; Names = *optAddrBar, optMenuBar, optStatusBar,* and *optToolBar*, respectively
Show Option Buttons	Caption = *"Show"*; Index = *1*; Value = *True*; Names = *optAddrBar, optMenuBar, optStatusBar,* and *optToolBar*, respectively
Label	Caption = *"Status Text"*
TextBox	Name = *txtStatusText*. Remove the default text for the *Text* property
CommandButton	Caption = *"Change"*; Name = *btnChange*

Now add code to use the properties of the *InternetExplorer* object to control the browser's user interface features. Take a look at Listing 6-1 to see the Visual Basic code that implements the functions of the controls in the table.

VbAutoIE.bas

```
Option Explicit
Dim InternetExplorer1 As InternetExplorer
Const HideBar = 0
Const ShowBar = 1

Private Sub btnChange_Click()
    On Error Resume Next
    InternetExplorer1.StatusText = txtStatusText.Text
End Sub

Private Sub btnStart_Click()
    ' Only create a new instance of Internet Explorer
    ' if one hasn't already been created.
    '
    If Not InternetExplorer1 Is Nothing Then
        Exit Sub
    End If

    Set InternetExplorer1 = New InternetExplorer

    ' Set the user interface features to match the
    ' entries specified by the user.
    '
    If optAddrBar(ShowBar).Value = True Then
        InternetExplorer1.AddressBar = True
    Else
        InternetExplorer1.AddressBar = False
    End If

    If optMenuBar(ShowBar).Value = True Then
        InternetExplorer1.MenuBar = True
    Else
        InternetExplorer1.MenuBar = False
    End If

    If optToolBar(ShowBar).Value = True Then
        InternetExplorer1.ToolBar = True
    Else
        InternetExplorer1.ToolBar = False
    End If
```

Listing 6-1.

```
   If optStatusBar(ShowBar).Value = True Then
      InternetExplorer1.StatusBar = True
   Else
      InternetExplorer1.StatusBar = False
   End If

   ' Make Internet Explorer visible and navigate
   ' to Microsoft's home page.
   '
   InternetExplorer1.Visible = True
   InternetExplorer1.Navigate "http://www.microsoft.com/"
End Sub

Private Sub Form_Load()
   Set InternetExplorer1 = Nothing
End Sub

Private Sub Form_Unload(Cancel As Integer)
   On Error Resume Next
   InternetExplorer1.Quit
End Sub

Private Sub optAddrBar_Click(Index As Integer)
   On Error Resume Next
   InternetExplorer1.AddressBar = CBool(Index)
End Sub

Private Sub optMenuBar_Click(Index As Integer)
   On Error Resume Next
   InternetExplorer1.MenuBar = CBool(Index)
End Sub

Private Sub optStatusBar_Click(Index As Integer)
   On Error Resume Next
   InternetExplorer1.StatusBar = CBool(Index)
End Sub

Private Sub optToolBar_Click(Index As Integer)
   On Error Resume Next
   InternetExplorer1.ToolBar = Index
End Sub
```

In Listing 6-1, when the form is loaded, the *InternetExplorer1* object is set equal to *Nothing*. (This is how you know that Internet Explorer hasn't been previously started by this application.) When the Start IE5 button is clicked, we check to ensure that an instance of Internet Explorer wasn't previously created. If one was, we return from this method.

NOTE This application can start only one instance of Internet Explorer at any time, even if the user shuts down the browser. I'll show you how to tell when the browser is closed in the next chapter.

If another instance of Internet Explorer wasn't previously created by this application, we create an instance of Internet Explorer 5 by using the *New* keyword. Then we check the current state of each option button in each control array. We set the appropriate Internet Explorer user interface feature according to the current state of each option button. Then we show Internet Explorer by setting its *Visible* property to *True*. Finally we navigate to Microsoft's home page by using the *Navigate* method.

Each time an option button is clicked, we handle the *Click* event of the control array associated with the option button. In the event handler, we show or hide the associated Internet Explorer user interface item by setting the associated *InternetExplorer* property to the *Index* of the selected option button. Because all the properties (except one) for the user interface items that we're interested in take a Boolean value, we use the *CBool* function to convert the *Index* parameter from Integer to Boolean. The *ToolBar* property takes an Integer value, so *ToolBar* can be set equal to *Index*. In each *Click* event handler, we also use *On Error Resume Next*, just in case the user clicked the option buttons without starting Internet Explorer.

In the *Click* event handler for the Change button, we set Internet Explorer's status text to the text entered into the text box. We did so by setting the *StatusText* property to the *Text* property of *txtStatusText*.

When the application is closed, Internet Explorer should shut down if it is still running. To cause Internet Explorer to close, call Internet Explorer's *Quit* method in the *Unload* method for the form. We used the *On Error Resume Next* error handling feature just in case the user previously closed Internet Explorer manually.

Now test your application. Run VbAutoIE, and start a new instance of Internet Explorer by clicking the Start IE5 button. Hide and show all the user interface items by using the option buttons. Also add some text to the status bar by entering the text into the text box and clicking the Change button. The sample created by following these steps can be found on the companion CD in the folder \Samples\Chap06\VbAutoIE.

Using Visual C++ and COM APIs

Although automating Internet Explorer in a Visual C++ application isn't as easy as doing so in a Visual Basic application, it's not terribly difficult, especially if you understand COM and its APIs. And whether you're automating Internet Explorer in MFC, ATL, or standard C++, the method is exactly the same—you use the COM APIs.

We'll convert the VbAutoIE application we built in the previous section to an MFC application. Although we'll use MFC to build the user interface, the way in which we call the Internet Explorer properties, including the way we start Internet Explorer, will work in ATL and standard C++ as well.

Creating an instance of Internet Explorer in Visual C++ involves calling the *CoCreateInstance* COM API function, specifying *CLSID_InternetExplorer* as the first parameter. Creating an instance of Internet Explorer in this way isn't as difficult as manually creating your own ActiveX control container that hosts the WebBrowser control. You don't need to implement the COM interfaces that are necessary for a container or site the object you're creating.

To see how easily you can automate Internet Explorer by using *CoCreateInstance*, let's go ahead and convert VbAutoIE to an MFC application. We'll call this application MfcAutoIE. (Like the other examples in this chapter, this example can be found on the companion CD in the folder \Samples\Chap06\MfcAutoIE.) Start Visual C++, and create a new MFC AppWizard (exe) application named MfcAutoIE. Choose the dialog-based option when prompted, and accept the remainder of the default project settings.

Now add controls to your dialog that match the controls in VbAutoIE. The dialog should look like the one shown in Figure 6-21. Assign intuitive ID names to each control in your dialog. For example, for the radio button group for *AddressBar*, you could assign the ID *IDC_ADDRBAR_HIDE* for the Hide button and the ID *IDC_ADDRBAR_SHOW* for the Show button. Make sure the tab order of the controls matches the order shown in Figure 6-22 on the next page. (The tab order is important because it affects how the radio buttons work.)

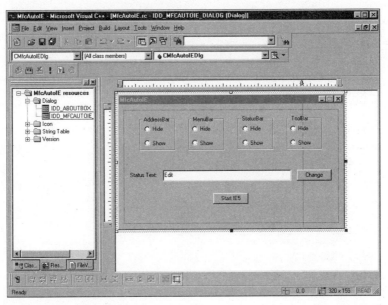

Figure 6-21. *MfcAutoIE dialog.*

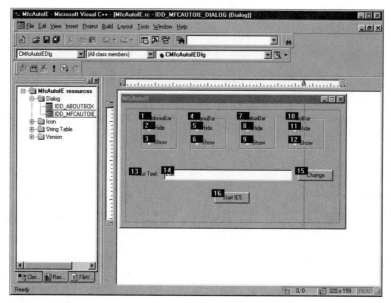

Figure 6-22.   *MfcAutoIE dialog tab order.*

Now set the *Group* property for each of the Hide radio buttons by right-clicking them, choosing Properties, and checking the Group check box. Do not set the *Group* property for the Show radio buttons. Next, create member variables for some of the controls, which are shown in Table 6-9.

TABLE 6-9
MEMBER VARIABLES FOR MFCAUTOIE DIALOG CONTROLS

Control	Type	Member Variable
Hide radio button for AddressBar	*int*	*m_nAddressBar*
Edit box	*CString*	*m_strStatusText*
Hide radio button for MenuBar	*int*	*m_nMenuBar*
Hide radio button for StatusBar	*int*	*m_nStatusBar*
Hide radio button for ToolBar	*int*	*m_nToolBar*

When the member variables in Table 6-9 are created using ClassWizard, their declarations will be inserted into the class definition for *CMfcAutoIEDlg*. These member variables will also be initialized to *–1* in your constructor. Initializing these values to *–1* effectively turns all radio buttons off. In VbAutoIE, I told you to set all the

Show buttons to *true* by default. For this example, we're going to do something a little different. Instead of setting these buttons to *true* by default, we're going to talk about how to determine the current setting of each user interface feature when Internet Explorer is started.

SETTING PROPER DIRECTORY ORDER
BEFORE COMPILING THE MFCAUTOIE EXAMPLE

Before compiling the MfcAutoIE example, you need to perform a few important tasks:

1. Make sure you download the headers and libraries for Internet Explorer 5 from the MSDN Online Web Workshop.

2. In the Directories tab of the Tools/Options menu, make sure to select Library Files from the combo box in the upper right-hand corner and include the directories of the library files for Internet Explorer 5 and Windows 2000 first in the list.

3. Select Include Files from the combo box and place your include file directories in the order indicated in the following list.

   a. *Internet Explorer 5 include directory*. By default this directory is \Workshop\Include.

   b. *A temporary directory named VC6*. You should create this directory under the include directory for the Internet Explorer 5 include files. Next, copy the unknwn.h and unknwn.idl files from the include directory for Microsoft Visual C++ 6 to this temporary directory. Include this new directory as the second item in your include directories list to avoid conflicts between the files in the Microsoft Visual C++ 6 include directory and the files in the Windows 2000 include directory.

   c. *Windows 2000 include directory*. By default this directory is \Workshop\Include\NT5.

   d. *Microsoft Visual C++ 6 include directory*.

   e. *Microsoft Visual C++ 6 ATL include directory*.

   f. *Microsoft Visual C++ 6 MFC include directory*.

Now let's add the code to make it all work. First you should include the ExDisp.h header file in the header file for your dialog—MfcAutoIEDlg.h. ExDisp.h is the header file that contains the interface definition of the WebBrowser interfaces as well as all the class IDs and interface IDs that pertain to the WebBrowser control and Internet Explorer. Make sure you have downloaded the latest version of the Internet Explorer 5 header and library files from MSDN Online Web Workshop.

Create a private or protected data member of type pointer to *IWebBrowser2*, and name it *m_pInetExplorer*. Its declaration should look like this:

```
protected:
    IWebBrowser2* m_pInetExplorer;
```

Now initialize *m_pInetExplorer* to *NULL* in the constructor for the class. You must also initialize COM. Place a call to the *CoInitialize* COM API in the constructor. The constructor code should now look like this:

```
CMfcAutoIEDlg::CMfcAutoIEDlg(CWnd* pParent /*=NULL*/)
    : CDialog(CMfcAutoIEDlg::IDD, pParent),
      m_pInetExplorer(NULL)
{
    //{{AFX_DATA_INIT(CMfcAutoIEDlg)
    m_strStatusText = _T("");
    m_nAddressBar = -1;
    m_nMenuBar = -1;
    m_nStatusBar = -1;
    m_nToolBar = -1;
    //}}AFX_DATA_INIT
    //Note that LoadIcon does not require a subsequent DestroyIcon
    //in Win32.
    m_hIcon = AfxGetApp()->LoadIcon(IDR_MAINFRAME);

    // Initialize COM
    CoInitialize(NULL);
}
```

Create a destructor for the class. In the destructor, use the *CoUninitialize* API function to uninitialize COM. Here's the code for the destructor:

```
CMfcAutoIEDlg::~CMfcAutoIEDlg()
{
    // Uninitialize COM.
    //
    CoUninitialize();
}
```

With the preliminary work behind us, let's implement the controls. First create a Windows message handler for the Start IE5 button. As usual, you can create this message handler by using ClassWizard. In this message handler, create an instance of Internet Explorer by using the *CoCreateInstance* API function. The instance of Internet Explorer that is created will initially be hidden, so you must make it visible by using the *Visible* property. And to navigate to the user's home page, use the *GoHome* method. Here's the code for the message handler:

```
void CMfcAutoIEDlg::OnStartIE5()
{
    // If an instance of Internet Explorer has
    // not already been created, create one.
    // This instance will initially be hidden,
    // so make it visible by using the Visible
    // property. Also, navigate to the user's
    // home page by using the GoHome method.
    //
    if (m_pInetExplorer)
        MessageBox
            (_T("Only one instance of Internet Explorer is allowed."));
    else
    {
        HRESULT hr;
        hr = CoCreateInstance(CLSID_InternetExplorer, NULL, CLSCTX_SERVER,
                        IID_IWebBrowser2, (LPVOID*)&m_pInetExplorer);

        if (SUCCEEDED(hr))
        {
            // Set the radio buttons to their correct values.
            SetRadioButtons();

            m_pInetExplorer->put_Visible(VARIANT_TRUE);
            m_pInetExplorer->GoHome();
        }
    }
}
```

In this code, we first check to see whether an instance of Internet Explorer has already been created. If it has, an error message is displayed. (This example has the same problem as the VbAutoIE example—you can start only one instance of Internet Explorer. In the next chapter, you'll learn how to determine when the browser is closed so that you can reset the data member representing Internet Explorer.) If an instance of Internet Explorer hasn't been created, *CoCreateInstance* is called with *CLSID_InternetExplorer* as the first parameter. (This class ID is defined in ExDisp.h and is the unique identifier of Internet Explorer.)

Then we specify *NULL* for the second parameter because we don't want this object to be aggregated. We want Internet Explorer to run in a separate process, so we specify *CLSCTX_SERVER* for the third parameter. We use the fourth parameter to indicate which interface we want to get from *CoCreateInstance* after the object is created. In this case, we'll almost always want to get *IWebBrowser2*, so we specify *IID_IWebBrowser2* for the fourth parameter. Finally we must pass the address of a variable that will be used to store the returned interface pointer. For this parameter, you must pass the address of a pointer to a *void* type. (Make sure you pass the address of a pointer that points to an interface type.)

If an instance of Internet Explorer was successfully created, a member function named *SetRadioButtons* is called. This is a protected member function that checks the current state of the address bar, menu bar, toolbar, and status bar, and sets the radio button groups accordingly. To check the state of each of these user interface items, we simply retrieve the current value of the property associated with each user interface item.

In C++ applications that use COM without wrapper classes, properties are referenced by using the *get_* and *put_* methods. (Recall that the *get_* form of a property retrieves the current value of that property; the *put_* form of a property sets the current value of the property.) To check the state of the user interface items in question, we simply call the *get_* method of the property associated with each item. All of these *get_* methods except *get_ToolBar* take a pointer to a *VARIANT_BOOL* type that, upon return, indicates whether the user interface item is visible or hidden. If the user interface item is visible, a value of *VARIANT_TRUE* is returned. If the item is hidden, a value of *VARIANT_FALSE* is returned. These values are different from the *TRUE* and *FALSE* values that you're used to.

> **NOTE**   When dealing with variables of type *VARIANT_BOOL* in Visual C++, you must use the values *VARIANT_TRUE* or *VARIANT_FALSE* instead of *TRUE* or *FALSE*. *VARIANT_TRUE* is defined as *0xffff*, whereas *TRUE* is defined as *1*. If you compare *VARIANT_TRUE* to *TRUE*, you'll find they won't match. In Visual Basic applications, you can use *True* or *False* when dealing with variables of type *VARIANT_BOOL*. Visual Basic takes care of the conversion for you.

The *get_ToolBar* method is different from the other property methods in that it takes a pointer to an integer, so if the value of the integer upon return is nonzero, the toolbar is visible. If the value of the integer is *0*, the toolbar is hidden.

> **NOTE**   If a property is read-only, the *put_* form of the property won't exist. The reverse is true as well. If a property is write-only, the *get_* form of the property won't exist.

Here's the code for the *SetRadioButtons* method:

```
void CMfcAutoIEDlg::SetRadioButtons()
{
    VARIANT_BOOL vtBool = VARIANT_TRUE;

    // Get the current state of the AddressBar.
    //
```

```
    m_pInetExplorer->get_AddressBar(&vtBool);
    m_nAddressBar = (vtBool == VARIANT_TRUE) ? 1 : 0;

    // Get the current state of the MenuBar.
    //
    m_pInetExplorer->get_MenuBar(&vtBool);
    m_nMenuBar = (vtBool == VARIANT_TRUE) ? 1 : 0;

    // Get the current state of the StatusBar.
    //
    m_pInetExplorer->get_StatusBar(&vtBool);
    m_nStatusBar = (vtBool == VARIANT_TRUE) ? 1 : 0;

    // Get the current state of the ToolBar.
    // Unlike the other get methods, get_ToolBar
    // takes a pointer to an integer.
    //
    m_pInetExplorer->get_ToolBar(&m_nToolBar);

    UpdateData(FALSE);  // Initializes dialog box with changed values.
}
```

After the call to *SetRadioButtons* method, the next thing we do in the *OnStartIE5* method is set the *Visible* property to *VARIANT_TRUE*. The *Visible* property takes a *VARIANT_BOOL* as its only parameter. Here we want to set this value to true, so we add code to pass *VARIANT_TRUE*. Finally, in the *OnStartIE5* method, the *GoHome* method of the *IWebBrowser2* interface is called to navigate to the user's home page.

The next step in creating this application is to implement Windows message handlers for each of the radio button groups on the dialog. To create a handler method for a radio button group, specify a single method to handle the *BN_CLICKED* message for each of the buttons in the group. For example, open ClassWizard, and locate the ID for the Hide radio button for the *AddressBar* group in the Object ID's list box. (If you entered the ID that I suggested earlier in this section when talking about the radio button group, the ID will be named *IDC_ADDRBAR_HIDE*.) Double-click the *BN_CLICKED* item in the Messages list box.

When prompted for the name of a member function to add to the class, enter the name *OnAddrBarShowHide*. Then locate the ID for the Show radio button for this group (*IDC_ADDRBAR_SHOW*). Double-click the *BN_CLICKED* item in the Messages list box. Again, when prompted, enter the name *OnAddrBarShowHide* for the member function. Now when your user clicks either of the buttons in the group—Hide or Show—the same member function will be called. Then you check the value of the *m_nAddressBar* data member to see which radio button was selected.

Now create message handlers for each of the other radio button groups in the dialog. Name these message handlers *OnMenuBarShowHide*, *OnStatusBarShowHide*, and *OnToolBarShowHide*, respectively, for the *MenuBar* group, the *StatusBar* group, and the *ToolBar* group. The code for these handlers should look like this:

```
void CMfcAutoIEDlg::OnAddrBarShowHide()
{
    UpdateData(TRUE);

    if (m_pInetExplorer)
    {
        VARIANT_BOOL vtShow =
            m_nAddressBar ? VARIANT_TRUE : VARIANT_FALSE;

        m_pInetExplorer->put_AddressBar(vtShow);
    }
}

void CMfcAutoIEDlg::OnMenuBarShowHide()
{
    UpdateData(TRUE);

    if (m_pInetExplorer)
    {
        VARIANT_BOOL vtShow =
            m_nMenuBar ? VARIANT_TRUE : VARIANT_FALSE;

        m_pInetExplorer->put_MenuBar(vtShow);
    }
}

void CMfcAutoIEDlg::OnStatusBarShowHide()
{
    UpdateData(TRUE);

    if (m_pInetExplorer)
    {
        VARIANT_BOOL vtShow =
            m_nStatusBar ? VARIANT_TRUE : VARIANT_FALSE;

        m_pInetExplorer->put_StatusBar(vtShow);
    }
}

void CMfcAutoIEDlg::OnToolBarShowHide()
{
    UpdateData(TRUE);

    if (m_pInetExplorer)
        m_pInetExplorer->put_ToolBar(m_nToolBar);
}
```

Notice in the *OnToolBarShowHide* method that we pass the *m_nToolBar* data member to the *put_ToolBar* method instead of a *VARIANT_BOOL*. We can get away with this because, just like *get_ToolBar*, *put_ToolBar* takes an integer value and not a *VARIANT_BOOL*.

Now create a Windows message handler for the Change button by using ClassWizard. This message handler will set the text in the Internet Explorer status bar to the text entered in the edit box whenever the user clicks the Change button. The code for this message handler should look like this:

```
void CMfcAutoIEDlg::OnChangeStatusText()
{
    UpdateData(TRUE);

    if (m_pInetExplorer)
    {
        _bstr_t bstrStatusText = m_strStatusText.AllocSysString();
        m_pInetExplorer->put_StatusText(bstrStatusText);
    }
}
```

Make sure that the first task you perform in this code is to call *UpdateData* and pass *TRUE*. Doing so updates all data members associated with controls in the dialog, including *m_strStatusText*. If *m_pInetExplorer* isn't *NULL*—meaning that an instance of Internet Explorer has been created—the *StatusText* property is set to the text that the user entered in the edit box. *StatusText* is set the same way as the *Visible* property— by calling the *put_* form of the property function. This function takes a *BSTR* as an input parameter, so the code must call the *AllocSysString* method of the *m_strStatusText* data member to allocate a *BSTR* that can be passed to *put_StatusText*. *AllocSysString* is a *CString* method that returns a *BSTR* representation of the string contained in the *CString* object. The *BSTR* returned from *AllocSysString* is stored in a variable of type *_bstr_t*, one of the COM Compiler Support Classes offered by Visual C++. To use this class, you must include the comdef.h header file in the implementation file for *CMfcAutoIEDlg*— MfcAutoIEDlg.cpp. This class will take care of freeing the *BSTR* when it goes out of scope, so you don't have to call the *SysFreeString* Win32 API function to free the *BSTR* after calling *put_StatusText*.

Hang in there; we're almost finished. To prevent the dialog from closing if the user presses the Enter key, override the *OnOK* method of the base dialog class. In this method you simply do nothing, which prevents the dialog from closing when the user presses Enter. Make sure you don't call the base class *CDialog::OnOK* method; otherwise, the dialog will close.

Now override the *OnCancel* method of the base dialog class, which is called when the user closes the dialog by pressing the Esc key or by clicking the X button in the upper right-hand corner of the dialog. In *OnCancel*, if an instance of Internet

Explorer was previously created, close that instance by calling the *Quit* method of the *InternetExplorer* object. *Quit* can be called even when the user has already manually closed Internet Explorer. If that's the case, the *Quit* method will return *RPC_S_SERVER_UNAVAILABLE*, which indicates that Internet Explorer is no longer available. You can safely ignore this error code. Here's the code for *OnCancel*:

```
void CMfcAutoIEDlg::OnCancel()
{
    if (m_pInetExplorer)
      m_pInetExplorer->Quit();

    CDialog::OnCancel();
}
```

Finally (I bet you can't believe it), you must release the pointer to the *IWebBrowser2* interface for Internet Explorer. You can do this in the destructor for the dialog class. Here's the updated code for the destructor:

```
CMfcAutoIEDlg::~CMfcAutoIEDlg()
{
    // Release the WebBrowser interface pointer
    //
    if (m_pInetExplorer)
    {
       m_pInetExplorer->Release();
       m_pInetExplorer = NULL;
    }

    // Uninitialize COM
    //
    CoUninitialize();
}
```

Now, as usual, compile and run the dialog application. Start an instance of Internet Explorer and test it. Show and hide all the user interface features by using the radio buttons in the dialog. Also add some text to the status bar by entering the text in the edit box and clicking the Change button.

ADDING ADVANCED FUNCTIONALITY

Now that we've covered the basics of hosting the WebBrowser control and automating Internet Explorer, let's get down to the nitty gritty. In this section, I'll show you how to add some advanced functionality to your applications and ActiveX controls. I'll demonstrate how to access the *IWebBrowser2* interface of Internet Explorer from an ActiveX control and even how to get the *WebBrowser* object of a frame on a Web page. Then I'll explain how to implement some functionality in your application that isn't quite as straightforward as you might think. This section is intense. All the code was written by using C++ and COM, and you must have a solid understanding of both to completely understand the topics covered in this section.

Accessing the *IWebBrowser2* Interface of Internet Explorer from an ActiveX Control

The ability to access the *IWebBrowser2* interface of Internet Explorer from an ActiveX control provides you with ultimate control over the browser and your user's browsing experience. This means that you can, for example, invoke the functionality of Internet Explorer from a Web page that you couldn't otherwise access using script. You might want to print or refresh the page or control where your users are navigating. (Knowing when and where your users are navigating requires the use of events, which I will discuss in the next chapter.) The possibilities are endless.

Accessing the *IWebBrowser2* interface of Internet Explorer from an ActiveX control is not straightforward, and you can do it only from within an ActiveX control created with Visual C++. Although you can access the *document* and *window* objects of Internet Explorer from a Visual Basic ActiveX control, as I will show you in Chapter 8, you cannot directly access the *WebBrowser* object itself.

Accessing the *IWebBrowser2* interface of Internet Explorer involves four steps:

1. Include ExDisp.h and shlguid.h in the header file (.h) or implementation file (.cpp) for the class.

2. Call the *IOleClientSite::GetContainer* method of the client site for the control. This method returns a pointer to the *IOleContainer* interface implemented by Internet Explorer.

3. If step 2 succeeds, query the *IOleContainer* pointer for the *IServiceProvider* interface.

4. If step 3 succeeds, call the *QueryService* method of *IServiceProvider* to obtain a pointer to the *IWebBrowser2* interface of Internet Explorer.

    The *QueryService* method takes three parameters. The first parameter specifies the service you want to access. When obtaining a pointer to *IWebBrowser2* in this manner, specify either *SID_SInternetExplorer* or *SID_SWebBrowserApp* for the service. (In actuality, these are both defined to be *IID_IWebBrowserApp*.) The second parameter is the interface ID for the interface pointer you want to receive. For this parameter you should specify *IID_IWebBrowser2*. Finally, for the third parameter you specify the variable in which the returned interface pointer should be stored.

Call any method or property of *IWebBrowser2*. When you're finished, make sure you release any interface pointers you have acquired. Following is sample code that puts these steps to work. I will show you an actual working sample when I talk about printing a Web page from an ActiveX control.

```
//////////////////////////////////////////////////////////
// Begin Step 1

#include <ExDisp.h>
#include <shlguid.h>

// End Step 1
//////////////////////////////////////////////////////////

CSomeClass::SomeMethod(){

//////////////////////////////////////////////////////////
// Begin Step 2

IOleContainer* pContainer;

// m_pClientSite is a pointer to IOleClientSite.
// This is the client site for your control.
//
HRESULT hr = m_pClientSite->GetContainer(&pContainer);
if (FAILED(hr))
    return hr;

// End Step 2
//////////////////////////////////////////////////////////

//////////////////////////////////////////////////////////
// Begin Step 3

IServiceProvider* pServiceProvider;

hr = pContainer->QueryInterface(IID_IServiceProvider,
                                (void**)&pServiceProvider);
pContainer->Release();

if (FAILED(hr))
    return hr;

// End Step 3
//////////////////////////////////////////////////////////
```

```
/////////////////////////////////////////////////////
// Begin Step 4

IWebBrowser2* pWebBrowser;

hr = pServiceProvider->QueryService(SID_SWebBrowserApp,
                        IID_IWebBrowser2,
                        (void**)&pWebBrowser);
pServiceProvider->Release();

if (FAILED(hr))
    return hr;

// End Step 4
/////////////////////////////////////////////////////


/////////////////////////////////////////////////////
// Begin Step 5

// Call some IWebBrowser2 methods and/or properties.

// End Step 5
/////////////////////////////////////////////////////
}
```

Printing a Web page by using an ActiveX control

In versions of Internet Explorer earlier than version 5, one of the most common uses for ActiveX controls that access the *IWebBrowser2* interface of Internet Explorer was to print the contents of a Web page. Although Internet Explorer 5 enables you to print a Web page in script using *window.print*, demonstrating how to create an ActiveX control that prints a Web page is a good way to teach you how to access the *IWebBrowser2* interface of Internet Explorer. Therefore, I will show you how to create an ActiveX control with ATL to perform the printing task. At this point, I'm going to assume that you already know how to create a control with ATL.

Go ahead and start Visual C++, and create a new ATL DLL. You can name your project *AtlPrint* if you want. Next, add a Lite Control to your project using the New ATL Object wizard. You might want to name this control *PrintCtl*. Add a method named *Print* to the *IPrintCtl* interface. Later you will call this method from within script to print the contents of the current Web page.

Before implementing your *Print* method, first include the ExDisp.h and shlguid.h header files in your PrintCtl.cpp implementation file.

Next use the information I just gave you about accessing the *IWebBrowser2* interface of Internet Explorer to get a pointer to the *IWebBrowser2* interface and call

ExecWB to print the current Web page. You might want to use the ATL smart pointer classes—*CComPtr* and *CComQIPtr*—to take some of the hard work out of querying for interfaces and maintaining their reference counts. Here is the code for implementing your *Print* method using these smart pointers:

```
STDMETHODIMP CPrintCtl::Print()
{
    HRESULT hr = E_FAIL;

    if (m_spClientSite)
    {
        CComPtr<IOleContainer> spContainer;

        hr = m_spClientSite->GetContainer(&spContainer);
        ATLASSERT(SUCCEEDED(hr));

        if (SUCCEEDED(hr))
        {
            CComQIPtr<IServiceProvider, &IID_IServiceProvider>
                spServiceProvider(spContainer);

            ATLASSERT(spServiceProvider);

            if (!spServiceProvider)
                hr = E_FAIL;
            else
            {
                CComPtr<IWebBrowser2> spWebBrowser;

                hr = spServiceProvider->QueryService(SID_SInternetExplorer,
                                                     IID_IWebBrowser2,
                                                     (void**)&spWebBrowser);
                ATLASSERT(SUCCEEDED(hr));

                if (SUCCEEDED(hr))
                {
                    spWebBrowser->ExecWB(OLECMDID_PRINT,
                                         OLECMDEXECOPT_PROMPTUSER,
                                         NULL, NULL);
                }
            }
        }
    }

    return hr;
}
```

Now compile your ATL ActiveX control. To test the print function, you must add some script to the sample Web page created for you by the New ATL Object wizard. Listing 6-2 shows the modified HTML code for the sample page that includes script to call the *Print* method. This sample can be found on the companion CD in the folder \Samples\Chap06\AtlPrint.

PrintCtl.htm

```
<HTML>
<HEAD>
    <TITLE>ATL 3.0 test page for object PrintCtl</TITLE>

    <SCRIPT LANGUAGE="VBS">
        Sub btnPrint_onclick
            PrintCtl.Print
        End Sub
    </SCRIPT>
</HEAD>
<BODY>
    <OBJECT ID="PrintCtl"
        CLASSID="CLSID:320B04E4-B55B-11D2-A9BA-444553540001">
    </OBJECT>
    <P>
    <BUTTON ID="btnPrint">Print Page</BUTTON>
</BODY>
</HTML>
```

Listing 6-2.

Accessing the *IWebBrowser2* Interface of Frames When Hosting the WebBrowser Control

A Web page that contains frames contains one *WebBrowser* object per frame. When hosting the WebBrowser control, you'll want to be able to access the *WebBrowser* object from your application so that you can control the frame. This access enables you to control navigation in the frame, refresh the frame, and so on. Once you have a pointer to the *IWebrowser2* interface of the *WebBrowser* object in a frame, you can call any of the *IWebrowser2* interface's methods and properties. (You can also sink events. I will tell you more about sinking events in the next chapter.)

You are able to access the *WebBrowser* object of a frame only from within a Visual C++ application. In Visual Basic, you can access the *document* object of a frame (as I will show you in Chapter 8), but you cannot access the *WebBrowser* object because you cannot access the *IOleContainer* interface of the HTML document that is loaded in the WebBrowser window. Accessing *IOleContainer* is required to access the *WebBrowser* object of the frame. This section details the standard technique that

Visual C++ WebBrowser control hosts can use to access the WebBrowser Object Model of frame windows on a Web page that is loaded inside the WebBrowser control.

The following code demonstrates how to access the *WebBrowser* object of each frame on a Web page to refresh the contents of each frame. The most important piece of the code uses the *IOleContainer::EnumObjects* method of the HTML *document* object to enumerate embeddings on the page. Each of these embeddings represents a control on the page. By querying each control object for the *IWebBrowser2* interface, the code can determine whether the control is a subframe. If a call to *QueryInterface* succeeds for *IWebBrowser2*, the result is a reference to the *WebBrowser* object in the frame. (The data member *m_webBrowser* is of type *CWebBrowser2*—the MFC wrapper class for the WebBrowser control that I showed you earlier.)

```
// Get the IDispatch of the document.
//
LPDISPATCH lpDisp = NULL;
lpDisp = m_webBrowser.GetDocument();

if (lpDisp)
{
    IOleContainer* pContainer;

    // Get the container.
    //
    HRESULT hr = lpDisp->QueryInterface(IID_IOleContainer,
                                        (void**)&pContainer);
    lpDisp->Release();

    if (FAILED(hr))
        return hr;

    // Get an enumerator for the frames.
    //
    IEnumUnknown* pEnumerator;

    hr = pContainer->EnumObjects(OLECONTF_EMBEDDINGS, &pEnumerator);
    pContainer->Release();

    if (FAILED(hr))
        return hr;

    IUnknown* pUnk;
    ULONG uFetched;

    // Enumerate and refresh all the frames.
    //
    for (UINT i = 0; S_OK == pEnumerator->Next(1, &pUnk, &uFetched); i++)
```

```
    {
        // QI for IWebBrowser here to see whether we have
        // an embedded browser.
        IWebBrowser2* pWebBrowser;

        hr = pUnk->QueryInterface(IID_IWebBrowser2, (void**)&pWebBrowser);
        pUnk->Release();

        if (SUCCEEDED(hr))
        {
            // Refresh the frame.
            pWebBrowser->Refresh();
            pWebBrowser->Release();
        }
    }

    pEnumerator->Release();
}
```

Notice in this code that we first get a pointer to the *IDispatch* object of the document by using the *GetDocument* method, which is a member of the *WebBrowser* wrapper class. Then we access the *IOleContainer* interface of the document. The *IOleContainer* interface provides you with the ability to get an enumerator object to enumerate all the embeddings on the page. Then we obtain the enumerator by calling the *EnumObjects* method of *IOleContainer*. *EnumObjects* returns a pointer to an *IEnumUnknown* interface that can be used to enumerate all the embeddings. Next in the code, we loop through all of the embeddings, querying each for the *IWebBrowser2* interface. If the query succeeds, we now have a pointer to the *IWebBrowser2* interface of the frame. We can then call any of its methods or properties. In this case, we call *Refresh* for each frame.

> **WARNING** ActiveX controls hosted on an HTML page can use this technique in a similar manner. However, if you create an ActiveX control to access the WebBrowser control of Internet Explorer or the WebBrowser control of frames on a page, do not mark your control as safe for scripting and initialization.

Invoking the Find, View Source, and Internet Options

By looking at the methods and properties of the WebBrowser control, you can easily see the functionality the control provides. Or can you? Three programmable items provided by the WebBrowser control aren't easily discovered: the Find dialog box, the View Source menu item, and the Internet Options dialog box. If you have used Internet Explorer in the past, you are undoubtedly familiar with these items. The Find dialog box, which enables you to search for text on a Web page, is invoked by pressing Ctrl-F or by choosing Find from the Edit menu.

The View Source menu item, which allows you to view the HTML source code for a Web page, can be invoked by choosing Source from the View menu or by right-clicking on a Web page and choosing View Source. The Internet Options dialog box, shown in Figure 6-23, can be invoked by choosing Internet Options from the Tools menu.

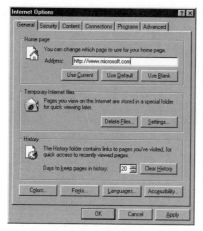

Figure 6-23. *Internet Options dialog box.*

It certainly would be nice to be able to provide your users with these options in your own browser application, but the way you invoke them isn't obvious just by inspecting the methods and properties of the WebBrowser control. You actually invoke these methods by calling the *Exec* method of the *IOleCommandTarget* interface, which is implemented by the WebBrowser. When calling *Exec*, you pass it a special command group GUID named *CGID_IWebBrowser* along with the ID of the command you want to invoke. I mentioned earlier that the *ExecWB* method is a wrapper for the *IOleCommandTarget::Exec* method, but you cannot use *ExecWB* to invoke Find, View Source, or Internet Options because *ExecWB* does not allow you to specify a command group GUID. That means that this technique can be used only in Visual C++ applications—you cannot invoke the commands directly from a Visual Basic application.

> **WARNING** The sample I'm about to show you uses an undocumented command group GUID that is subject to change in the future. Although this sample has been tested to work correctly with Internet Explorer 3.x, 4.x, and 5, there is no guarantee that these techniques will continue to work successfully in future versions. Please use caution when adding this code to an application.

Follow these steps to implement the Find, View Source, and Internet Options commands:

1. Define the command group GUID for the WebBrowser control:

   ```
   DEFINE_GUID(CGID_IWebBrowser,0xED016940L,0xBD5B,0x11cf,0xBA,
       0x4E,0x00,0xC0,0x4F,0xD7,0x08,0x16);
   ```

2. Define the command IDs for Find, View Source, and Internet Options:

   ```
   #define HTMLID_FIND 1
   #define HTMLID_VIEWSOURCE 2
   #define HTMLID_OPTIONS 3
   ```

3. Execute the Find, View Source, and Internet Options commands as needed. For example, you could create a utility method that accepts a command ID and calls *IOleCommandTarget::Exec*, as shown in the following code snippet. (Note that in this MFC code, *m_webBrowser* is an instance of the WebBrowser control. Also, *nCmdID* is one of the IDs defined in step 2.)

   ```
   HRESULT CYourView::ExecCmdTarget(DWORD nCmdID)
   {
       LPDISPATCH lpDispatch = NULL;
       LPOLECOMMANDTARGET lpOleCommandTarget = NULL;
       HRESULT hr = E_FAIL;

       // Get the IDispatch of the document.
       //
       lpDispatch = m_webBrowser.GetDocument();
       ASSERT(lpDispatch);

       if (lpDispatch)
       {
           // Get a pointer for the IOleCommandTarget interface.
           //
           hr = lpDispatch->QueryInterface(IID_IOleCommandTarget,
                                   (void**)&lpOleCommandTarget);
           lpDispatch->Release();

           ASSERT(lpOleCommandTarget);

           if (SUCCEEDED(hr))
           {
               // Invoke the given command id
               // for the WebBrowser control.
               hr = lpOleCommandTarget->Exec
                   (pguidCmdGroup, nCmdID, 0, NULL, NULL);
               lpOleCommandTarget->Release();
           }
       }

       return hr;
   }
   ```

To see this code in action, take a look at the MfcWebHost application we worked on earlier. I updated it with the preceding code to enable users to invoke the Find, View Source, and Internet Options commands. The menu items for these commands exist on the Edit, View, and Tools menus, respectively, as they do in Internet Explorer.

DISTRIBUTING THE WEBBROWSER CONTROL

Now that you know how to create extraordinary applications using the WebBrowser control and Internet Explorer, you are probably wondering which Internet Explorer components you need to ship with your application so that your application is guaranteed to work correctly on systems that might not have Internet Explorer 5 installed. Whether you are hosting the WebBrowser control or automating Internet Explorer, you must ship at least the minimal install of Internet Explorer. To understand why, look again at the architecture diagram shown in Figure 6-1 on page 198. You can see how each component depends on the other—and this diagram reveals only the surface. It does not show the multitude of components involved in providing all the features of the WebBrowser control and Internet Explorer. Because there are so many components involved, you must ensure that your users have at least the minimal install of Internet Explorer for your applications to work.

Don't worry—you don't have to ship each and every component of Internet Explorer. The Internet Explorer 5 installation program allows you to customize your installation so that you ship only those components that are absolutely necessary. In addition, if you use the Internet Explorer Administration Kit (available at *http://ieak.microsoft.com/*) to build your installation program, you can install Internet Explorer silently so that your users are not pestered with a multitude of dialog boxes asking them to confirm different steps in the installation process.

WHAT'S NEXT?

In this chapter, I showed you how easy it is to host the WebBrowser control and automate Internet Explorer in Visual Basic and Visual C++ applications. I showed you the different methods and properties of the WebBrowser that provide you with just about everything you need to create extraordinary Web applications. In the next chapter, I will show you a feature of the WebBrowser control and Internet Explorer that gives you ultimate control—events. You'll learn about the different events of the WebBrowser and how easy it is to use them to control navigation, use your application for any new windows that are created, and know when to enable and disable Back and Forward buttons, plus a whole lot more.

Chapter 7

Internet Explorer Events

In Chapter 6, you created Web-enabled applications by hosting the WebBrowser control and by automating Microsoft Internet Explorer. In both cases, you used the methods and properties of the *IWebBrowser2* interface to create Internet applications quickly and efficiently. As you know, the *IWebBrowser2* interface enables you to navigate to a URL or to a file, move backward and forward in the history list, manipulate the Internet Explorer user interface, and so on. What if I told you it provides even more functionality than that? It's true!

The methods and properties of *IWebBrowser2* give you a certain level of control over navigation and the user interface, but if you can't determine what the WebBrowser is doing and when it is doing it, you still don't have full control. For this reason, the WebBrowser control and Internet Explorer expose events through which you can monitor activity and perform certain actions as necessary. For example, let's say you are creating an application for your corporate intranet, and you want to restrict users from accessing certain Web pages. By handling events in Internet Explorer, you can tell when a user is attempting to navigate to a restricted URL and then cancel that navigation completely.

In this chapter, I'll explain events and how you can handle them in your applications. I'll show you all the events of the WebBrowser control and Internet Explorer, and I'll teach you how to handle them in Microsoft Visual Basic and Microsoft Visual C++ applications. I'll also explain how to handle Internet Explorer events on a Web page by using Microsoft ActiveX controls.

EVENTS AND OUTGOING INTERFACES

As you learned in Chapter 3, whenever a COM object needs to notify a client application that an action has occurred, the COM object sends out a message known as an event. The process of sending the message is referred to as firing an event. But what if an event is fired and nothing is listening? Did the event ever occur? Obviously, the client application that is controlling the COM object has to be listening for these events. When a client application wants to receive events from a COM object, it "advises" the COM object of this fact.

For a COM object to communicate with its client, the object must support one or more outgoing interfaces. A COM object that supports outgoing interfaces is referred to as a connectable object. To be qualified as a connectable object, the object must implement the *IConnectionPointContainer* interface. Through this interface, clients can learn which outgoing interfaces the server supports. Outgoing interfaces are actually implemented by the client and plugged into the COM object through connection points. The part of the client that implements the outgoing interfaces is known as an event sink.

A separate connection point represents each of the outgoing interfaces supported by the server. Each of these connection points can handle only one type of outgoing interface and must support at least the *IConnectionPoint* interface. The diagram in Figure 7-1 depicts the relationship between the connectable object and its client.

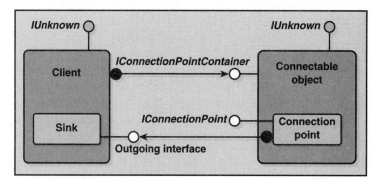

Figure 7-1. *Connectable object and its client.*

The server must implement two interfaces for a client to be able to receive events—*IConnectionPointContainer* and *IConnectionPoint*. We'll take a look at these interfaces now and later examine the different ways to sink events.

IConnectionPointContainer

Every connectable object implements *IConnectionPointContainer*. Through this interface, a client that wants to receive events can find out about the various connection points supported by the connectable object. A client can get a pointer to this interface by calling *QueryInterface* using any other interface that the object supports. (You can call *QueryInterface* using any interface pointer, because all COM interfaces inherit from *IUnknown*.) Then the client can use one of the two methods of the *IConnectionPointContainer* interface, described in Table 7-1, to get a pointer to a connection point.

TABLE 7-1
METHODS OF THE *ICONNECTIONPOINTCONTAINER* INTERFACE

Method	Description
EnumConnectionPoints	Allows the client to get a list of pointers to all the connection points that are supported by the connectable object.
FindConnectionPoint	Lets the client query the connectable object about whether it supports a particular interface. The client specifies the interface identifier (IID) of the connection point it desires. If the connectable object supports this interface, it returns a pointer to the *IConnectionPoint* interface for the appropriate connection point.

IConnectionPoint

Once the client knows which connection points the connectable object supports, the client can establish a connection with the connectable object. The client advises the connectable object about which event sink the object should use for all events. When the client no longer wants to receive events from the connectable object, the client unadvises the object. Table 7-2 on the next page shows the methods of the *IConnectionPoint* interface through which the client can connect to the object. (Most of the time, you'll be concerned with only the first two in the table.)

TABLE 7-2
METHODS OF THE *ICONNECTIONPOINT* INTERFACE

Method	Description
Advise	Establishes a connection between the client and a certain connection point in the connectable object. The client must pass a pointer to the *IUnknown* interface of its event sink. The event sink must implement the *IDispatch* interface to receive events. Typically, the connectable object will call the *Invoke* method of the *IDispatch* interface of the client each time the object fires an event. The *Advise* method returns a cookie that the client must use when breaking the connection through a call to the *Unadvise* method.
Unadvise	Breaks the connection between the client and the connectable object. When calling this method, the client passes the cookie that it received from the call to *Advise*.
GetConnectionInterface	Returns the IID of the outgoing interface managed by the connection point. The *GetConnectionInterface* method lets the client translate from an *IConnectionPoint* interface pointer to an IID.
GetConnectionPointContainer	Retrieves the *IConnectionPointContainer* interface pointer for the connectable object of the connection point.
EnumConnections	Enumerates the current connections for a connectable object.

WAYS TO SINK EVENTS

Depending on which development tool you use to create the client application, you can sink events in different ways. Obviously, sinking events in a Visual Basic application is much different from and easier than sinking events in a C++ application. In C++ applications, you can use different techniques to sink events according to whether you're using ATL, MFC, or standard C++.

Sinking Events in Visual Basic

Visual Basic is the easiest development tool to use when creating most types of applications, so you shouldn't be surprised when I tell you that Visual Basic is the easiest tool to use when sinking events. The ATL and Visual Basic examples that we're about to examine look and act the same, but the ATL example took me about four hours to complete, whereas the Visual Basic example took about 20 minutes. Don't get me wrong—I'm a strong advocate of C++, ATL, and MFC, especially when you're creating your own interfaces. But Visual Basic is a great development tool to use when creating client applications that sink events from servers such as Internet Explorer.

OK, so how do you sink events in a Visual Basic application? When hosting the WebBrowser control, you don't have to do anything special. Visual Basic sets up the event sink for the WebBrowser control on the form. All you have to do is create event handlers for any events that you're interested in.

You create these event handlers just like you create event handlers for any other event (such as the *Form_Load* event). Choose the event you want to handle from the Procedure drop-down list box in the upper right-hand corner of the Visual Basic Integrated Development Environment (IDE) after choosing the object from the Object drop-down list in the upper left-hand corner of the IDE. Then, in the event handler, just add whatever code you want to execute when the event is fired.

To sink events when automating a server, such as Internet Explorer from a Visual Basic application, the procedure is just as straightforward. First set a reference to the type library of the server in the References dialog box, which you can access from the Project/References menu. To set a reference to the type library for Internet Explorer, check the Microsoft Internet Controls option in the References dialog box. If you don't select this type library, Visual Basic won't be able to resolve the reference to the *InternetExplorer* object in your code. Then declare a variable of the type of server you are automating. When you declare this variable, specify the *WithEvents* keyword to tell Visual Basic that you want to receive events from the server. For example, if you were automating Internet Explorer, you would declare a variable like this:

```
Dim WithEvents InternetExplorer1 As InternetExplorer
```

Next create an instance of the server by using the *CreateObject* method or the *New* keyword. Here is an example of using the *CreateObject* method:

```
Set InternetExplorer1 = CreateObject("InternetExplorer.Application.1")
```

Here is an example of using the *New* keyword:

```
Set InternetExplorer1 = New InternetExplorer
```

When you create an instance of the server by using either of these approaches, Visual Basic automatically initializes and manages the event sink for you. It's as simple as that. You don't have to worry about getting a pointer to the connection point container and then finding the connection point that you want. Visual Basic handles it.

After you enter the code to create the server, you insert method calls that correspond to the events that the server is firing. (As mentioned earlier, you can choose these events from the Procedure drop-down list in the Visual Basic IDE after choosing the name of your Internet Explorer object—*InternetExplore1*—from the Object drop-down list.) For example, if you wanted to handle the *DownloadBegin* event that is fired by Internet Explorer, you would declare a method like this:

```
Private Sub InternetExplorer1_DownloadBegin()
    ' Insert your best Visual Basic code here.
End Sub
```

When you no longer want to receive events from the server, just set the Internet Explorer variable to *Nothing*:

```
Set InternetExplorer1 = Nothing
```

Now you're ready to look at the first example of Internet Explorer event sinking, VBIEEvtSpy, which is shown in Figure 7-2. This example has one form that contains a multiline text box and two buttons. One of the buttons starts an instance of Internet Explorer. The other exits from the program and shuts down the running instance of Internet Explorer, if one exists. Each time Internet Explorer fires an event, a description of it is placed in the text box.

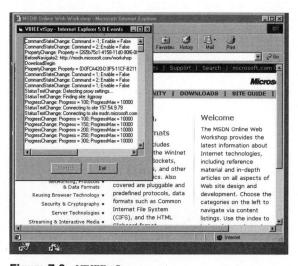

Figure 7-2. *VBIEEvtSpy.*

Writing the code for VBIEEvtSpy is straightforward. First a variable is declared to represent an instance of Internet Explorer. The *WithEvents* keyword is specified when declaring this variable so that the client can receive events from Internet Explorer. When the user clicks the Start IE5 button, the *New* keyword is used to create a new instance of Internet Explorer. Then we make this instance visible and navigate to the user's home page. (This is exactly how we automated Internet Explorer in the last chapter.) Here's the code for the *Click* event handler for the Start IE5 button:

```
Private Sub btnStartIE_Click()
    ' Start a new instance of InternetExplorer
    ' only if one was not previously started.
    '
    If InternetExplorer1 Is Nothing Then
        Set InternetExplorer1 = New InternetExplorer
        InternetExplorer1.Visible = True
        InternetExplorer1.GoHome

        btnStartIE.Enabled = False
    End If
End Sub
```

In this code, just as in the VBAutoIE example in Chapter 6, a new instance of Internet Explorer is started only if one hasn't already been started. But VBIEEvtSpy isn't limited to running only one instance of Internet Explorer each time VBIEEvtSpy is run. In this example, we can detect when the user closes the browser by handling Internet Explorer's *OnQuit* event. When Internet Explorer fires the *OnQuit* event, we set the *InternetExplorer1* object to *Nothing* so that we know it's ready to create another instance of Internet Explorer.

VBIEEvtSpy displays messages in a text box each time the Internet Explorer object fires an event of interest. In the handler functions for the events, a message is printed to the text box to alert the user that an event has been fired. In this example, only a subset of events is handled. You can add event handler functions for any other events that you want to handle. All event handlers perform basically the same task. I'll explain the Internet Explorer events (that is, the WebBrowser control events) later in this chapter. You can find this sample on the companion CD in the folder \Samples\Chap07\VBIEEvtSpy. For now, here's one of the event handlers in this application:

```
Private Sub InternetExplorer1_DownloadComplete()
    strEvents = strEvents + "DownloadComplete" + vbNewLine
    txtEvents.Text = strEvents
End Sub
```

Sinking Events in C++

Sinking events in a C++ application involves a little more work than in a Visual Basic application. But if you're hosting the WebBrowser control in an MFC dialog-based application, you can just choose the events you want to handle by using ClassWizard.

Hosting the WebBrowser control in another type of application or automating Internet Explorer in any C++ application is a bit more difficult but still doesn't require much work. To sink events in a C++ client application, just follow these five steps:

1. Get a pointer to the connection point container (*IConnectionPoint-Container*).

2. Call the *FindConnectionPoint* method of *IConnectionPointContainer* to find the connection point for which you want to sink events. For Internet Explorer, you'll be sinking events for the *DWebBrowserEvents2* connection point interface. (Optionally, you can call *EnumConnectionPoints* to enumerate through all the connection points that a server supports.)

3. Advise the connection point that you want to receive events. When advising, pass a pointer to the *IUnknown* interface of the event sink. Remember that the event sink must implement the *IDispatch* interface to receive events from the WebBrowser. The *Advise* method will return a cookie that you must use when you call the *Unadvise* method.

4. Implement *IDispatch::Invoke* to handle any events that are fired. (Development tools such as MFC and ATL can make this easy for you to do.)

5. When you no longer want to receive events, call *Unadvise*, and pass it the cookie that you received from the call to *Advise*.

These steps might not be obvious if you're developing in Visual Basic or using MFC or ATL, but they are important when creating client applications in standard C++.

The following C++ code allows you to sink events when automating Internet Explorer. Look for the comments that describe which step is being implemented. Assume that the *ConnectEvents* method is called when you want to establish the event sink and that the *Exit* method is called when the program is exited. Also, the class *CSomeClass* inherits from *IDispatch*, and the *m_pIE* data member represents an instance of Internet Explorer that was created through a call to *CoCreateInstance*, as you saw in Chapter 6. (Note that *CSomeClass* is just some arbitrary name of your choosing.)

```
void CSomeClass::ConnectEvents()
{
   IConnectionPointContainer* pCPContainer;

   // Step 1: Get a pointer to the connection point container.
   //
   HRESULT hr = m_pIE->QueryInterface(IID_IConnectionPointContainer,
                                      (void**)&pCPContainer);
```

```
    if (SUCCEEDED(hr))
    {
        // m_pConnectionPoint is defined like this:
        // IConnectionPoint* m_pConnectionPoint;

        // Step 2: Find the connection point.
        //
        hr = pCPContainer->FindConnectionPoint(DIID_DWebBrowserEvents2,
                                               &m_pConnectionPoint);

        if (SUCCEEDED(hr))
        {
            // Step 3: Advise the connection point that you
            // want to sink its events.
            //
            hr = m_pConnectionPoint->Advise(this, &m_dwCookie);
            if (FAILED(hr))
            {
                ::MessageBox(NULL, "Failed to Advise",
                             "C++ Event Sink", MB_OK);
            }
        }

        pCPContainer->Release();
    }
}

void CSomeClass::Exit()
{
    // Step 5: Unadvise. Note that m_pConnectionPoint should
    // be released in the destructor for CSomeClass.
    //
    if (m_pConnectionPoint)
    {
        HRESULT hr = m_pConnectionPoint->Unadvise(m_dwCookie);
        if (FAILED(hr))
        {
            ::MessageBox(NULL, "Failed to Unadvise",
                         "C++ Event Sink", MB_OK):
        }
    }
}
```

Notice that I left out step 4: the implementation of the client's *IDispatch::Invoke* method. I will be talking about this method shortly. The server calls it each time the server fires an event. The server passes to *Invoke* the dispatch ID (DISPID) of the event that it is firing. For Internet Explorer 5, the following DISPIDs are defined in the ExDispID.h header file. (DISPIDs that pertain to Internet Explorer 3.*x* still exist in ExDispID.h for backward compatibility.)

- DISPID_BEFORENAVIGATE2
- DISPID_COMMANDSTATECHANGE
- DISPID_DOCUMENTCOMPLETE
- DISPID_DOWNLOADBEGIN
- DISPID_DOWNLOADCOMPLETE
- DISPID_NAVIGATECOMPLETE2
- DISPID_NEWWINDOW2
- DISPID_ONFULLSCREEN
- DISPID_ONMENUBAR
- DISPID_ONQUIT
- DISPID_ONSTATUSBAR
- DISPID_ONTHEATERMODE
- DISPID_ONTOOLBAR
- DISPID_ONVISIBLE
- DISPID_PROGRESSCHANGE
- DISPID_PROPERTYCHANGE
- DISPID_STATUSTEXTCHANGE
- DISPID_TITLECHANGE

Now we can turn our attention to the mother of all automation methods—*Invoke*. This method takes eight parameters, but we'll discuss only two of them: *dispidMember* and *pDispParams*. (For information about the other six parameters, see the documentation for *IDispatch::Invoke* in MSDN.)

The *dispidMember* parameter tells you which event has been fired. If the client application is sinking events from Internet Explorer, the value of the *dispidMember* parameter corresponds to one of the DISPIDs listed earlier.

The *pDispParams* input parameter is a pointer to a structure that contains, among other items, a count of the number of parameters for the event that is being fired and the actual parameters themselves. Parameters passed to the event handler are stored in *pDispParams->rgvarg* in reverse order as they appear in the parameter list for the event. For example, Internet Explorer fires the *NavigateComplete2* event like this:

```
NavigateComplete2(pDisp, URL)
```

When *Invoke* is called, *pDispParams->cArgs* will contain a value of *2*, with the *URL* parameter in *pDispParams->rgvarg[0]* and the *pDisp* parameter in *pDispParams->rgvarg[1]*. The parameters for the *NavigateComplete2* event are sent in reverse order as they appear in the method signature for *NavigateComplete2* in the preceding line of code. (The term "method signature" is the object-oriented terminology for what you would call a *function prototype* in C.) This is just the way that COM orders input parameters when sending them to the *Invoke* method.

The following code shows a sample implementation of *Invoke* that handles the *NavigateComplete2* event. Notice that this code uses the ATL class *CComVariant* to perform conversion from *VARIANT* to *BSTR*. (The ATL code in the next section demonstrates even more events.)

```
#include <strstrea.h>
STDMETHODIMP CSomeClass::Invoke(DISPID dispidMember,
                                REFIID riid,
                                LCID lcid,
                                WORD wFlags,
                                DISPPARAMS* pDispParams,
                                VARIANT* pvarResult,
                                EXCEPINFO* pExcepInfo,
                                UINT* puArgErr)
{
    USES_CONVERSION;
    strstream strEventInfo;

    if (!pDispParams)
        return E_INVALIDARG;

    switch (dispidMember)
    {
        // The parameters for this DISPID:
        // [0]: URL navigated to - VT_BYREF|VT_VARIANT
        // [1]: An object that evaluates to the top-level or frame
        //      WebBrowser object corresponding to the event.
        //
        case DISPID_NAVIGATECOMPLETE2:
            // Check the argument's type.
            if (pDispParams->rgvarg[0].vt == (VT_BYREF|VT_VARIANT))
            {
```

(continued)

```
        CComVariant varURL(*pDispParams->rgvarg[0].pvarVal);
        varURL.ChangeType(VT_BSTR);

        // strEventInfo is an object of type strstream.
        //
        strEventInfo << "NavigateComplete2: "
                     << OLE2T(vtURL.bstrVal)
                     << ends;

        ::MessageBox(NULL, strEventInfo.str(), "Invoke", MB_OK);
        }
        break;

    default:
        break;
    }

    return S_OK;
}
```

Sinking Events in ATL

Along with providing default implementations of certain COM interfaces, ATL provides two functions—*AtlAdvise* and *AtlUnadvise*—that simplify the job of sinking events for any connectable object.

The *AtlAdvise* function tells a connectable object that the client wants to receive events from it. This function accomplishes steps 1 through 3 of the event sinking steps (described in the "Sinking Events in C++" section). *AtlAdvise* certainly saves you a lot of time and effort. Just like the *IConnectionPoint::Advise* method, *AtlAdvise* returns a cookie that you later use in the call to *AtlUnadvise*. *AtlUnadvise* tells the connectable object that the client no longer wants to receive events.

Let's say, for example, that an ATL application is automating Internet Explorer, so you want to know about any events that are fired by Internet Explorer. To tell Internet Explorer that the client wants to receive events, make the following call to *AtlAdvise*:

```
HRESULT hr = AtlAdvise(m_spInetExplorer, GetUnknown(),
                DIID_DWebBrowserEvents2, &m_dwCookie);
```

Four parameters are passed to *AtlAdvise*. The first parameter is a pointer to the connectable object's *IUnknown* interface. The *m_spInetExplorer* data member is a smart pointer that represents the running instance of Internet Explorer that we're automating. Because the pointer held in *m_spInetExplorer* points to an object that inherits directly or indirectly from *IUnknown*, the compiler automatically converts *m_spInetExplorer* to a pointer to *IUnknown* of the running instance of Internet Explorer.

The second parameter in the call to *AtlAdvise* must be a pointer to the *IUnknown* interface of the object that represents the event sink. The *GetUnknown* method returns this pointer. Remember that the class that represents the event sink must implement *IDispatch* in some way. In this case, the class is inheriting from *IDispatch*.

The third parameter in the call to *AtlAdvise* is the IID of the connection point for which you want to sink events. The IID of the connection point for Internet Explorer events is *DIID_DWebBrowserEvents2*.

The last parameter is a pointer to a DWORD that stores a cookie when the function returns. This cookie will be used in a call to *AtlUnadvise*.

The rest of the code is the same as if this example were a normal C++ application. The client must implement *IDispatch::Invoke* to handle the events that Internet Explorer fires. When your application is finished receiving events from Internet Explorer, just call *AtlUnadvise*, like this:

```
HRESULT hr = AtlUnadvise(m_spInetExplorer,
                         DIID_DWebBrowserEvents2,
                         m_dwCookie);
```

Now let's look at the second example, ATLIEEvtSpy, which you can find on the companion CD in the folder \Samples\Chap07\ATLIEEvtSpy. The ATLIEEvtSpy example behaves almost exactly the same as VBIEEvtSpy, the Visual Basic example we looked at earlier in this chapter. Like VBIEEvtSpy, ATLIEEvtSpy is a dialog-based application that has a list box and two buttons. (See Figure 7-3.)

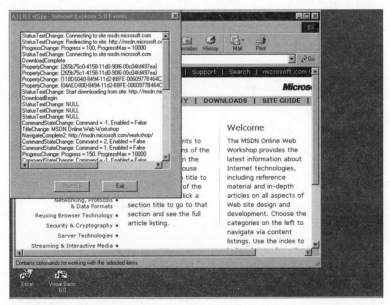

Figure 7-3. *ATLIEEvtSpy.*

When the user clicks the Start IE5 button, the call to the *CoCreateInstance* method creates an instance of Internet Explorer in the message handler for this button. That instance of Internet Explorer is made visible, and the user's home page is loaded into the browser. Here's the code that performs these actions:

```
hr = CoCreateInstance(CLSID_InternetExplorer, NULL, CLSCTX_LOCAL_SERVER,
                      IID_IWebBrowser2, (void**)&m_spInetExplorer);
if (SUCCEEDED(hr))
{
   m_spInetExplorer->put_Visible(TRUE);
   m_spInetExplorer->GoHome();

   ⋮
```

Next, *AtlAdvise* is called to establish the *CIEEvtObj* class as the event sink, like this:

```
hr = AtlAdvise(m_spInetExplorer, GetUnknown(),
               DIID_DWebBrowserEvents2, &m_dwCookie);
```

The *CIEEvtObj* class inherits from *IDispatch*, so the *CIEEvtObj* class can be used as the event sink. The *Invoke* method is implemented in *CIEEvtObj* to handle events. Each time Internet Explorer fires an event, the client displays a message in the list box for events. The following code shows the implementation of *Invoke* for this class:

```
STDMETHODIMP CIEEvtObj::Invoke(DISPID dispidMember,
                               REFIID riid,
                               LCID lcid,
                               WORD wFlags,
                               DISPPARAMS* pDispParams,
                               VARIANT* pvarResult,
                               EXCEPINFO* pExcepInfo,
                               UINT* puArgErr)
{
   _ASSERT(m_spInetExplorer);

   USES_CONVERSION;
   strstream strEventInfo;

   if (!pDispParams)
      return E_INVALIDARG;

   switch (dispidMember)
   {
      //
      // The parameters for this DISPID are as follows:
      // [0]: Cancel flag  - VT_BYREF|VT_BOOL
```

```
// [1]: HTTP headers - VT_BYREF|VT_VARIANT
// [2]: Address of HTTP POST data  - VT_BYREF|VT_VARIANT
// [3]: Target frame name - VT_BYREF|VT_VARIANT
// [4]: Option flags - VT_BYREF|VT_VARIANT
// [5]: URL to navigate to - VT_BYREF|VT_VARIANT
// [6]: An object that evaluates to the top-level or frame
//      WebBrowser object corresponding to the event
//
case DISPID_BEFORENAVIGATE2:
    strEventInfo << "BeforeNavigate2: ";

    if (pDispParams->cArgs >= 5
        && pDispParams->rgvarg[5].vt == (VT_BYREF|VT_VARIANT))
    {
        CComVariant vtURL(*pDispParams->rgvarg[5].pvarVal);
        vtURL.ChangeType(VT_BSTR);

        strEventInfo << OLE2T(vtURL.bstrVal);
    }
    else
        strEventInfo << "NULL";

    strEventInfo << ends;
    break;


//
// The parameters for this DISPID:
// [0]: Enabled state - VT_BOOL
// [1]: Command identifier - VT_I4
//
case DISPID_COMMANDSTATECHANGE:
    strEventInfo << "CommandStateChange: ";

    if (pDispParams->cArgs == 0)
        strEventInfo << "NULL";
    else
    {
        if (pDispParams->cArgs > 1
            && pDispParams->rgvarg[1].vt == VT_I4)
        {
            strEventInfo << "Command = "
                        << pDispParams->rgvarg[1].lVal;
        }

        if (pDispParams->rgvarg[0].vt == VT_BOOL)
```

(continued)

277

```
      {
         strEventInfo << ", Enabled = "
               << ((pDispParams->rgvarg[0].boolVal == VARIANT_TRUE)
                    ? "True" : "False");
      }
   }

   strEventInfo << ends;
   break;

case DISPID_DOCUMENTCOMPLETE:
   strEventInfo << "DocumentComplete" << ends;
   break;

case DISPID_DOWNLOADBEGIN:
   strEventInfo << "DownloadBegin" << ends;
   break;

case DISPID_DOWNLOADCOMPLETE:
   strEventInfo << "DownloadComplete" << ends;
   break;

//
// The parameters for this DISPID:
// [0]: URL navigated to - VT_BYREF|VT_VARIANT
// [1]: An object that evaluates to the top-level or frame
//      WebBrowser object corresponding to the event
//
case DISPID_NAVIGATECOMPLETE2:
   if (pDispParams->rgvarg[0].vt == (VT_BYREF|VT_VARIANT))
   {
      CComVariant vtURL(*pDispParams->rgvarg[0].pvarVal);
      vtURL.ChangeType(VT_BSTR);

      strEventInfo << "NavigateComplete2: "
                  << OLE2T(vtURL.bstrVal)
                  << ends;
   }
   break;

//
// The parameters for this DISPID:
// [0]: Maximum progress - VT_I4
// [1]: Amount of total progress - VT_I4
//
case DISPID_PROGRESSCHANGE:
   strEventInfo << "ProgressChange: ";

   if (pDispParams->cArgs == 0)
      strEventInfo << "NULL";
```

```
      else
      {
          if (pDispParams->cArgs > 1
              && pDispParams->rgvarg[1].vt == VT_I4)
          {
              strEventInfo << "Progress = "
                           << pDispParams->rgvarg[1].lVal;
          }

          if (pDispParams->rgvarg[0].vt == VT_I4)
              strEventInfo << ", ProgressMax = "
                           << pDispParams->rgvarg[0].lVal;
      }

      strEventInfo << ends;
      break;

//
// The parameter for this DISPID:
// [0]: Name of property that changed - VT_BSTR
//
case DISPID_PROPERTYCHANGE:
      strEventInfo << "PropertyChange: ";

      if (pDispParams->cArgs > 0
          && pDispParams->rgvarg[0].vt == VT_BSTR)
      {
          strEventInfo << OLE2T(pDispParams->rgvarg[0].bstrVal);
      }
      else
      {
          strEventInfo << "NULL";
      }

      strEventInfo << ends;
      break;

//
// The parameters for this DISPID:
// [0]: New status bar text - VT_BSTR
//
case DISPID_STATUSTEXTCHANGE:
      LPOLESTR lpStatusText;

      m_spInetExplorer->get_StatusText(&lpStatusText);
      strEventInfo << "StatusTextChange: ";
```

(continued)

```
                if (!strcmp(OLE2T(lpStatusText), ""))
                    strEventInfo << "NULL";
                else
                    strEventInfo << OLE2T(lpStatusText);

                strEventInfo << ends;
                break;

            case DISPID_NEWWINDOW2:
                strEventInfo << "NewWindow2" << ends;
                break;

            //
            // The parameter for this DISPID:
            // [0]: Document title - VT_BSTR
            //
            case DISPID_TITLECHANGE:
                strEventInfo << "TitleChange: ";

                if (pDispParams->cArgs > 0
                    && pDispParams->rgvarg[0].vt == VT_BSTR)
                {
                    strEventInfo << OLE2T(pDispParams->rgvarg[0].bstrVal);
                }
                else
                {
                    strEventInfo << "NULL";
                }

                strEventInfo << ends;
                break;

            // The user has told Internet Explorer to close.
            //
            case DISPID_ONQUIT:
                return Stop();

            default:
                // Note: This class acts only as an event sink, so
                // there's no reason to call the base class version of Invoke.

                strEventInfo << "Unknown Event" << dispidMember << ends;
                break;
        }

    AddEventToList(strEventInfo.str());

    return S_OK;
}
```

Notice that I used the standard C++ library's *strstream* class to build the string to display in the list box. I did this because ATL doesn't provide a string class like the *CString* class that MFC provides. Each time an event is received from Internet Explorer, a string is created that contains the name of the event and any important parameters. Then a helper method of the *CIEEvtObj* class is called to write the string to the list box in the dialog box.

When the user clicks the Exit button or the Close button in the upper right-hand corner of the dialog box, the *AtlUnadvise* function is called to tell Internet Explorer that the client no longer wants to receive events. The following code calls *AtlUnadvise*:

```
STDMETHODIMP CIEEvtObj::Stop()
{
    if (m_spInetExplorer)
    {
        HRESULT hr = AtlUnadvise(m_spInetExplorer,
                            DIID_DWebBrowserEvents2,
                            m_dwCookie);

        if (FAILED(hr))
            ATLTRACE("Failed to Unadvise\n");
    }

    PostQuitMessage(0);
    return S_OK;
}
```

Sinking Events in MFC

MFC provides several handy macros that you can use to sink events when automating a server or hosting a control. In both cases, the class that you use for the event sink must inherit either directly or indirectly from *CCmdTarget*. *CCmdTarget* implements the *IDispatch* interface that is used for sinking events. In addition, you must call the *EnableAutomation* function in your application to initialize the *IDispatch* interface that is contained within *CCmdTarget*.

Sinking events in MFC when automating a COM object

Sinking events in MFC when automating a COM object is relatively easy. All you have to do is write code to call the *AfxConnectionAdvise* helper function to advise the connection point that the client needs to receive events. When the client does not want to receive events, it calls *AfxConnectionUnadvise*. The *AfxConnectionAdvise* and *AfxConnectionUnadvise* functions are defined in the afxctl.h header file.

The *AfxConnectionAdvise* function takes care of querying for the connection point container, finding the connection point, and advising the connection point. This function takes the five parameters listed in Table 7-3 on the next page.

TABLE 7-3
PARAMETERS OF THE *AfxConnectionAdvise* FUNCTION

Parameter	Description
pUnkSrc	A pointer to the *IUnknown* interface of the COM object that fires the events. For example, if you're automating a COM object, *pUnkSrc* is a pointer to the object that is created by a call to *CoCreateInstance*.
pUnkSink	A pointer to the *IUnknown* interface of the event sink.
iid	The IID of the connection point. For Internet Explorer, this is *DIID_DWebBrowserEvents2*.
bRefCount	Passing *TRUE* indicates that creating the connection should cause the reference count of *pUnkSink* to be incremented. Passing *FALSE* indicates that the reference count shouldn't be incremented.
pdwCookie	The identifier of the connection. This identifier is returned by *AfxConnectionAdvise* and should be passed as the *dwCookie* parameter to *AfxConnectionUnadvise* when disconnecting the connection.

The input parameters for *AfxConnectionUnadvise* are the same except that *bRefCount* indicates whether the reference count of *pUnkSink* should be decremented. Also, the final parameter, *pdwCookie*, is changed to *dwCookie*, which contains the value of the cookie.

Handling events is just as easy as setting up the connection. Remember that for an MFC event sink class to be able to receive events, it must inherit in some way from *CCmdTarget*. *CCmdTarget* uses a dispatch map to determine which event handler function to call when it receives an event. You must first declare this dispatch map in the header file and then initialize it in the implementation (.cpp) file. Fortunately, MFC provides a set of macros to help you define and initialize the dispatch map.

To define this dispatch map, simply specify the DECLARE_DISPATCH_MAP macro in the header file for the event sink class. This macro declares the dispatch map and a few functions that *CCmdTarget* uses to access the map. Once you've defined the dispatch map, you'll place a few macros in the implementation file for the dispatch map. The first macro you'll place is the BEGIN_DISPATCH_MAP macro. It takes the name of the event sink class and the name of the base class for the event sink class. For example, if the name of the event sink class is *CEventSink* and it inherits from *CCmdTarget*, the BEGIN_DISPATCH_MAP macro will look like this:

```
BEGIN_DISPATCH_MAP(CEventSink, CCmdTarget)
```

Next you must specify the events that you want to handle and the names of the functions that will handle them. A number of macros are available that you can use to specify the events that you want to handle. To specify these events by their DISPID, use the DISP_FUNCTION_ID macro. This macro takes the six parameters listed in Table 7-4.

TABLE 7-4
PARAMETERS OF THE DISP_FUNCTION_ID MACRO

Parameter	Description
theClass	The name of the event sink class.
szExternalName	The external name of the function.
dispid	The DISPID of the event.
pfnMember	The pointer to a member function that handles the event.
vtRetval	The return value of the member function. This parameter is one of the VARENUM enumerated types defined in the wtypes.h header file.
vtsParams	A space-separated list of one or more *VTS_* constants specifying the function's parameter list. *VTS_* constants are defined in the afxdisp.h header file.

Let's say you want to handle the *DownloadComplete* event fired by Internet Explorer. To tell *CCmdTarget* that you want to handle *DownloadComplete*, use the DISP_FUNCTION_ID macro like this:

```
DISP_FUNCTION_ID(CIE5Events, "DownloadComplete",
                 DISPID_DOWNLOADCOMPLETE, OnDownloadComplete,
                 VT_EMPTY, VTS_NONE)
```

Finally, you must close the dispatch map by using the END_DISPATCH_MAP macro. The completed dispatch map should look like this:

```
BEGIN_DISPATCH_MAP(CEventSink, CCmdTarget)
   DISP_FUNCTION_ID(CIE5Events, "DownloadComplete",
                    DISPID_DOWNLOADCOMPLETE, OnDownloadComplete,
                    VT_EMPTY, VTS_NONE)
END_DISPATCH_MAP()
```

Sinking events in MFC when hosting an ActiveX control

Sinking events when hosting a control is similar to sinking them when automating a COM object. The main difference is that you don't have to advise or unadvise the connection point. *CCmdTarget* handles this for you.

In the case of hosting a control, *CCmdTarget* uses an event sink map instead of a dispatch map. As you might have guessed, MFC provides the macros to define and initialize this event sink map. Declaring the event sink map is just like declaring the dispatch map—specify the DECLARE_EVENTSINK_MAP macro in the header file. In addition to declaring the map, the DECLARE_EVENTSINK_MAP macro declares functions that *CCmdTarget* will use to access the map.

Next you must initialize the event sink in the implementation file. Begin the event sink map with the BEGIN_EVENTSINK_MAP macro. Specify the name of the event sink class and its base class when using this macro. For example, here's how to begin the event sink map for a dialog-based class:

```
BEGIN_EVENTSINK_MAP(CMyDlg, CDialog)
```

Now specify all the events you want to handle and their event handlers by using one of the ON_EVENT* macros. In most cases, you'll simply use ON_EVENT, which takes five parameters, as listed in Table 7-5. For example, if you want to handle WebBrowser control's *DownloadComplete* event, you would specify the following for the ON_EVENT macro:

```
ON_EVENT(CMyDlg, IDC_WEBBROWSER, DISPID_DOWNLOADCOMPLETE,
        OnDownloadComplete, VTS_NONE)
```

If you want one member function to handle a range of events, use the ON _EVENT_RANGE macro.

TABLE 7-5
PARAMETERS OF THE ON_EVENT MACRO

Parameter	Description
theClass	The class to which this event sink map belongs.
id	The resource identifier of the control.
dispid	The dispatch ID of the event fired by the control.
pfnHandler	The pointer to a member function that handles the event. This function should have a *BOOL* return type and parameter types that match the event's parameters. (See the last parameter in this table, *vtsParams*.) The function should return *TRUE* to indicate that the event was handled; otherwise, the function should return *FALSE*.
vtsParams	A sequence of *VTS_* constants that specifies the types of the parameters for the event. These constants are the same ones that are used in dispatch map entries such as *DISP_FUNCTION* and *DISP_FUNCTION_ID*.

You must close the event sink map by using the END_EVENTSINK_MAP macro. The complete definition of the event sink map looks like this:

```
BEGIN_EVENTSINK_MAP(CMyDlg, CDialog)
   ON_EVENT(CMyDlg, IDC_WEBBROWSER, DISPID_DOWNLOADCOMPLETE,
           OnDownloadComplete, VTS_NONE)
END_EVENTSINK_MAP()
```

Now let's examine the final event sink example, MFCIEEvtSpy, which is shown in Figure 7-4. This dialog-based application hosts the WebBrowser control and automates Internet Explorer 5 as well. The example contains two list boxes. The left list box displays events for an instance of Internet Explorer that is being automated, and the right list box displays events for the WebBrowser control that is being hosted in the dialog.

To handle events for the WebBrowser control that is being hosted in the dialog, you use an event sink map. When initializing the event sink map, make an entry for each event that you want to handle. In each entry, specify the method that should be called when the event is fired as well as the list of parameter types that will be passed in to the event handler. For example, to handle the *DocumentComplete* event, you would declare and initialize an event sink map that looked like this:

```
// Declare the event sink map.  This declaration goes
// in the class declaration of CMFCIEEvtSpyDlg in the
// MFCIEEvtSpyDlg.h header file.
//
DECLARE_EVENTSINK_MAP()


// Initialize the event sink map.  These macros
// go in the implementation file - MFCIEEvtSpyDlg.cpp.
//
BEGIN_EVENTSINK_MAP(CMFCIEEvtSpyDlg, CDialog)
    ON_EVENT(CMFCIEEvtSpyDlg, IDC_WEBBROWSER, DISPID_DOCUMENTCOMPLETE,
            OnDocumentComplete, VTS_DISPATCH VTS_PVARIANT)
END_EVENTSINK_MAP()
```

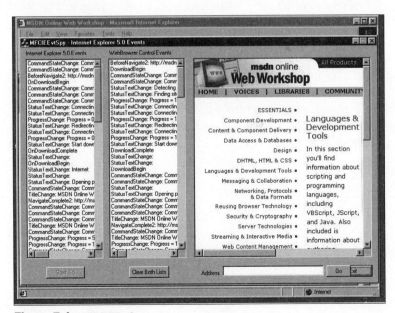

Figure 7-4. *MFCIEEvtSpy.*

When hosting the WebBrowser control in a dialog-based application, you don't usually need to insert the macros manually, because the ClassWizard can do it for you. In a single document interface (SDI) or multiple document interface (MDI) application, however, you'll have to add the macros yourself.

Now that the event sink map is declared, each time the WebBrowser control fires the *DocumentComplete* event, the *OnDocumentComplete* method will be called. In the *OnDocumentComplete* method for the *CMFCIEEvtSpyDlg* class, a string is created that contains the name of the event and the URL to which the user navigated. Then this string is added to the list box that contains the WebBrowser control events. The same actions are performed for many other WebBrowser control events, as you'll see when you look at the MFCIEEvtSpy example on the companion CD. You can find it in the folder \Samples\Chap07\MFCIEEvtSpy.

The following code handles the *DocumentComplete* event. *AddEventToList* is a helper function that merely adds the given string to the specified list box:

```
void CMFCIEEvtSpyDlg::OnDocumentComplete(LPDISPATCH pDisp, VARIANT* URL)
{
    USES_CONVERSION;

    CString strEvt("DocumentComplete: ");
    strEvt += OLE2T(URL->bstrVal);

    AddEventToList(WBListBox, strEvt);
}
```

When the user clicks the Start IE5 button, a new instance of Internet Explorer is created as the result of calling *CoCreateInstance* and passing *CLSID_InternetExplorer*. In addition, *AfxConnectionAdvise* is called to advise the *DWebBrowserEvents2* connection point that it should use the *CIE5Events* class as the event sink for the instance of Internet Explorer that we are automating.

The *CIE5Events* class inherits from *CCmdTarget* and contains the event handlers for events that are fired from the running instance of Internet Explorer. The *CMFCIEEvtSpyDlg* class handles the events that are fired from the WebBrowser control that is being hosted in the dialog.

Here's the code for the Start IE5 button's message handler:

```
void CMFCIEEvtSpyDlg::OnStartIE()
{
    if (m_pInetExplorer == NULL)  // Can start only one instance
    {
        // Create an instance of Internet Explorer.
        //
```

```
            HRESULT hr = CoCreateInstance(CLSID_InternetExplorer,
                                          NULL,
                                          CLSCTX_LOCAL_SERVER,
                                          IID_IWebBrowser2,
                                          (void**)&m_pInetExplorer);
    if (SUCCEEDED(hr))
    {
        // Set up the event sink.
        //
        BOOL bAdvised = AfxConnectionAdvise(m_pInetExplorer,
                            DIID_DWebBrowserEvents2,
                            m_pIE5Events->GetInterface(&IID_IUnknown),
                            TRUE, &m_dwCookie);

        // Disable the Start IE5 button so that the
        // user knows that only one instance of
        // Internet Explorer can be started at a time.
        //
        m_btnStartIE.EnableWindow(FALSE);

        // Make Internet Explorer visible and go home.
        //
        m_pInetExplorer->put_Visible(VARIANT_TRUE);
        m_pInetExplorer->GoHome();
    }
  }
}
```

To handle events for the automated instance of Internet Explorer in the *CIE5Events* class, you must declare a dispatch map in the class declaration for *CIE5Events* and initialize the map in the implementation file. For example, to declare and initialize the dispatch map to handle the *DocumentComplete* event, insert the necessary macros into the header and implementation files for *CIE5Events*:

```
// Declare the dispatch map. This
// declaration is placed in the class declaration
// for the CIE5Events class, which is in the
// CIE5Events.h header file.
//
DECLARE_DISPATCH_MAP()

// Initialize the dispatch map in the
// implementation file for CIE5Events - CIE5Events.cpp.
//
```

(continued)

```
BEGIN_DISPATCH_MAP(CIE5Events, CCmdTarget)
   DISP_FUNCTION_ID(CIE5Events, "DocumentComplete",
                    DISPID_DOCUMENTCOMPLETE, OnDocumentComplete,
                    VT_EMPTY, VTS_DISPATCH VTS_PVARIANT)
END_DISPATCH_MAP()
```

Now whenever the automated instance of Internet Explorer fires the event *DocumentComplete*, the *OnDocumentComplete* method of the *CIE5Events* class will be called. Just like the *OnDocumentComplete* method for *CMFCIEEvtSpy*, the *OnDocumentComplete* method creates a string that contains the name of the event and the URL. This string is added to the list box that contains the events for the automated instance of Internet Explorer. The same action is performed for many of the other events that Internet Explorer fires. Here's the code for the *OnDocumentComplete* method of *CIE5Events*:

```
void CIE5Events::OnDocumentComplete(LPDISPATCH pDisp, VARIANT* URL)
{
   USES_CONVERSION;

   CString strEvt("DocumentComplete: ");
   strEvt += OLE2T(URL->bstrVal);

   m_pParent->AddEventToList(CMFCIEEvtSpyDlg::IE5ListBox, strEvt);
}
```

EVENTS FIRED BY INTERNET EXPLORER 5

As you know, Internet Explorer fires events in the same way as any other COM object—through a connection point. Why on earth does Internet Explorer fire events? Any time Internet Explorer needs to provide information to its clients about current activity, Internet Explorer fires an event through the *DWebBrowserEvents2* connection point. (Prior to version 4, Internet Explorer fired events through the *DWebBrowserEvents* interface. But in versions 4.*x* and 5, Internet Explorer fires events through the *DWebBrowserEvents2* connection point.)

> **NOTE** How can you figure out which events are fired by Internet Explorer? The best source of information is the MSDN Online Web Workshop. Another way to find out which events are fired by Internet Explorer—or any other COM object— is by using the OLE-COM Object Viewer that comes with Visual C++ 5 and 6.

Unlike the standard interfaces of the WebBrowser control and Internet Explorer, the event interfaces have no inheritance hierarchy. The *DWebBrowserEvents* interface is strictly for Internet Explorer 3. If you're hosting the WebBrowser control or automating Internet Explorer 5, you can sink events for this interface—but I wouldn't advise it. The *DWebBrowserEvents2* interface contains methods that are custom-built for Internet Explorer 5. You'll have much more control over the WebBrowser if you sink events for the *DWebBrowserEvents2* interface instead of sinking events for *DWebBrowserEvents*. So don't forget that *2* at the end of the interface name.

Even though *DWebBrowserEvents2* is an event interface, it is just another COM interface like *IWebBrowser2*, so it can contain methods. (The *D* at the beginning of the name simply stands for dispinterface. A dispinterface is an *IDispatch* interface. Unlike a normal interface, a dispinterface has no vtable.) Remember that, like an interface, a dispinterface merely provides the definition of some functionality—it doesn't actually provide the implementation of this functionality. The implementations for the events are provided by the client. For example, in order for the WebBrowser to fire an event, it defines the appropriate method in the *DWebBrowserEvents2* interface. This method is then implemented by the client. But the WebBrowser doesn't call these methods directly. In other words, the WebBrowser doesn't call the *DocumentComplete* method. Because *DWebBrowserEvents2* is a dispinterface, the WebBrowser calls these methods through the client's implementation of *IDispatch::Invoke*. As I mentioned earlier, when the WebBrowser calls the client's implementation of *Invoke*, the WebBrowser passes the DISPID of the event being fired.

> **NOTE** Certain development tools such as Visual Basic, MFC, and ATL allow you to create methods that will be called for the WebBrowser events instead of forcing you to implement *Invoke* yourself, which can be quite cumbersome. These development tools provide the implementation of *Invoke* for you and then call methods based on the DISPID of the event that was fired.

Table 7-6 on the next page lists all the WebBrowser events. (These are the events for both the WebBrowser control and Internet Explorer, although some events apply only when automating Internet Explorer, as I'll explain shortly.) You can easily understand the purpose of most of these events by looking at the table, but I'll discuss a few events in more detail, in the order of their importance.

> **NOTE** Some methods in Table 7-6 include the number *2* at the end of them. Although *DWebBrowserEvents2* doesn't derive from *DWebBrowserEvents*, the methods in *DWebBrowserEvents2* whose names match those methods in *DWebBrowserEvents* were changed (by adding a *2*) to avoid confusion.

Note that several input parameters in Table 7-6 have values of either *VARIANT_TRUE* or *VARIANT_FALSE*. If you write your application using Visual C++, be sure to compare against these values and not against *TRUE* or *FALSE*. If you write your application using Visual Basic, however, you can compare against the traditional *True* or *False* values. Visual Basic takes care of the conversion for you.

Now let's take a look at some of the events a bit more closely.

TABLE 7-6
WEBBROWSER EVENTS

Private Events	Description
BeforeNavigate2	Fired before navigation occurs. (This event is not fired when you refresh the page.)
CommandStateChange	Fired when the enabled state of a command has changed. This event tells you when to enable or disable Back and Forward menu items or buttons.
DocumentComplete	Fired when the entire document is finished loading. If you refresh the page, this event isn't fired.
DownloadBegin	Fired when the download operation for an item has begun. This event is also fired when you refresh the page by using the Refresh button in Internet Explorer or by calling a refresh method such as *IWebBrowser2::Refresh*.
DownloadComplete	Fired when the download operation for an item has completed. This event is also fired when you refresh the page.
NavigateComplete2	Fired after navigation completes. This event corresponds to *BeforeNavigate2*.
NewWindow2	Fired just before a new window is created for displaying a Web page or any other resource.
OnFullScreen	Fired when the *FullScreen* property has changed. This event takes one input parameter of type *VARIANT_BOOL* that indicates whether Internet Explorer is in full-screen mode (*VARIANT_TRUE*) or in normal-screen mode (*VARIANT_FALSE*).
OnMenuBar	Fired when the *MenuBar* property is changed. This event takes one input parameter of type *VARIANT_BOOL* that indicates whether Internet Explorer's menu bar is visible (*VARIANT_TRUE*) or hidden (*VARIANT_FALSE*).
OnQuit	Fired when Internet Explorer is quitting. This event will be fired either when the user closes the browser or when you call the *Quit* method.
OnStatusBar	Fired when the *StatusBar* property is changed. This event takes one input parameter of type *VARIANT_BOOL* that indicates whether Internet Explorer's status bar is visible (*VARIANT_TRUE*) or hidden (*VARIANT_FALSE*).

Private Events	Description
OnTheaterMode	Fired when the *TheaterMode* property is changed. This event takes one input parameter of type *VARIANT_BOOL*. The value of this input parameter is *VARIANT_TRUE* if Internet Explorer is in theater mode and *VARIANT_FALSE* otherwise.
OnToolBar	Fired when the *ToolBar* property is changed. This means that the toolbar was either hidden or made visible. This event takes one input parameter of type *VARIANT_BOOL* that indicates whether Internet Explorer's toolbar is visible (*VARIANT_TRUE*) or hidden (*VARIANT_FALSE*).
OnVisible	Fired when the window for the WebBrowser should be shown or hidden. This event allows the container to act the same way as the Internet Explorer window. *OnVisible* has one input parameter that is of type *VARIANT_BOOL*. The value of the input parameter is *VARIANT_TRUE* if the WebBrowser is visible and *VARIANT_FALSE* otherwise.
ProgressChange	Fired when the progress of a download has been updated. (This topic is discussed in more detail later in the chapter.)
PropertyChange	Fired when a property has changed. Typically, the firing of this event indicates that the *PutProperty* method has been called to add or change the value of a property in the property bag.
StatusTextChange	Fired by Internet Explorer and the WebBrowser control when the text of the status bar has changed even though the WebBrowser control doesn't have a status bar. *StatusTextChange* gives the client a chance to update its status bar with the new text.
TitleChange	Fired when the title of the document becomes available or has changed.

BeforeNavigate2

BeforeNavigate2 does just what it says. It is fired before Internet Explorer navigates to a Web page; therefore, it is fired when the user enters a URL, clicks the Back or Forward button, or performs an action that causes navigation to occur. *BeforeNavigate2* is also fired by the WebBrowser control if you call a navigation method of an instance of the control, such as *Navigate, Navigate2, GoHome,* or *GoSearch*. However, this event is not fired when you refresh the page. If frames are on a page, *BeforeNavigate2* will be fired for each frame as well as for the top-level window. *BeforeNavigate2* has seven input parameters, which are described in Table 7-7.

TABLE 7-7
INPUT PARAMETERS OF THE *BEFORENAVIGATE2* EVENT

Parameter	Description
pDisp	Address of the *IDispatch* interface of the top-level or frame WebBrowser object corresponding to the navigation.
URL	URL to be navigated to.
Flags	Reserved for future use.
TargetFrameName	String that contains the name of the frame in which to display the resource or *NULL* if no named frame is targeted for the resource.
PostData	Address of data to send to the server if the HTTP POST transaction is being used.
Headers	Additional HTTP headers to send to the server (only HTTP URLs). The headers can specify the action required of the server, the type of data being passed to the server, a status code, and so on.
Cancel	Address of a cancel flag. An application can set this parameter to *TRUE* to cancel the navigation operation or to *FALSE* to allow it to proceed.

Notice that most of these parameters match those that you specify in a call to *Navigate* or *Navigate2*. If *BeforeNavigate2* was fired in response to a call to one of these navigation methods, the parameters that you specify are passed to the *BeforeNavigate2* method.

In the handler function for this event, you can cancel the navigation by using the *Cancel* parameter, or you can modify it by using the *pDisp* parameter. To cancel the navigation, set the *Cancel* parameter to *VARIANT_TRUE*. If you want, you can modify the navigation information and then navigate to another location by using the *pDisp* parameter. For example, let's say we want to stop the current navigation, add some header information, and then navigate to the original URL with the added header information. In Visual Basic, we would use the following code to accomplish this:

```
Private Sub WebBrowser1_BeforeNavigate2(ByVal pDisp As Object, _
                                        URL As Variant, _
                                        Flags As Variant, _
```

```
                          TargetFrameName As Variant, _
                          PostData As Variant, _
                          Headers As Variant, _
                          Cancel As Boolean)

    If TypeName(pDisp) = "WebBrowser" And Headers = "" Then
        pDisp.Stop
        pDisp.Navigate URL, Flags, TargetFrameName, PostData, _
                       Headers + "MyHeaders"
        Cancel = True
    End If
End Sub
```

Note several important aspects of this code. First you must check the type of *pDisp* to make sure it is equal to *WebBrowser* because the *BeforeNavigate2* event is fired for all frames that might exist on a Web page. When a page contains frames, *pDisp* might not be a WebBrowser object and therefore any navigation attempt will cause an error.

Second you must check to make sure that the *Headers* parameter is empty to prevent an infinite loop. Remember that *BeforeNavigate2* is fired each time navigation occurs. So if you call *Navigate* in the event handler for the *BeforeNavigate2* event, another *BeforeNavigate2* will be fired. In the preceding code, calling *Navigate* only if the *Headers* parameter is empty prevents an infinite loop. If the *Headers* parameter is empty, *Navigate* is called with a nonempty *Headers* parameter. The next time *BeforeNavigate2* is fired, the *Headers* parameter won't be empty; therefore, we don't call *Navigate* again, preventing an infinite loop.

Third you must call the *Stop* method for *pDisp*. If you don't, the "about: NavigationCanceled" Web page might be displayed after the navigation is first canceled.

CommandStateChange

CommandStateChange is fired when Internet Explorer wants to notify an application that the enabled state of a WebBrowser command has changed. Use this event to determine when to enable or disable the Forward and Back menu items and buttons.

The *CommandStateChange* event's two input parameters, *Command* and *Enable,* warrant special consideration. The *Command* input parameter is the identifier of the command whose enabled state has changed. Two commands for the Forward and Back menu items and buttons—*CSC_NAVIGATEFORWARD* and *CSC_NAVIGATEBACK*, respectively—are of particular interest. (These commands are members of the *CommandStateChangeConstants* enumeration, which is defined in the ExDisp.h header file.) Each time a navigation occurs, the *CommandStateChange* event is fired to tell you whether the Forward or Back menu items and buttons should be enabled or disabled. For example, if no Web pages exist after the current one, the *Command* parameter will be equal to *CSC_NAVIGATEFORWARD*, and the *Enable* parameter will be equal to *VARIANT_FALSE*. (The *CommandStateChangeConstants* enumeration contains a third value—*CSC_UPDATECOMMANDS*—that specifies that the enabled state of a toolbar button might have changed. Typically, you will not be concerned with this value.)

The second parameter of special interest, *Enable*, is *VARIANT_TRUE* if the command is enabled or *VARIANT_FALSE* if the command is disabled.

To show you how to use *CommandStateChange* to enable Forward and Back menu items and buttons, let's update the MfcWebHost example that we created in Chapter 6. Because this example doesn't have Forward or Back buttons, we'll update the menu items for these commands. The Forward and Back menu items in the MfcWebHost example are named Go Forward and Go Back, respectively. Adding buttons to the toolbar is fairly easy, so I'll leave this as an exercise for you to do on your own.

To handle the events in MfcWebHost, you must first enable the event sink because MfcWebHost doesn't currently sink events for the WebBrowser control. Be sure to include the ExDispID.h header file in MfcWebHost.cpp. Declare and initialize the event sink to handle the *CommandStateChange* event:

```
// Event sink map declaration for WebBrowser
// control events. This declaration goes in the
// header file for CMfcWebHostView - MfcWebHostView.h.
//
DECLARE_EVENTSINK_MAP()

// Initialize the event sink map and handle the
// CommandStateChange event.
BEGIN_EVENTSINK_MAP(CMfcWebHostView, CView)
    ON_EVENT(CMFCIEEvtSpyDlg, IDC_WEBBROWSER, DISPID_COMMANDSTATECHANGE,
            OnCommandStateChange, VTS_I4 VTS_BOOL)
END_EVENTSINK_MAP()
```

One important change you need to make to the original example is to change the call to the *Create* method of the WebBrowser control. The second parameter in the ON_EVENT macro indicates the ID of the WebBrowser control you're hosting. The original call to *Create* specified *NULL* for the ID of the WebBrowser. You must declare an ID for the WebBrowser control and change *Create* to specify that this ID is to be used for the WebBrowser control. If you don't, event sinking won't work correctly.

You can define the ID of the WebBrowser control you're hosting in any file in your project. (A good place to do so might be the resource.h header file for the MfcWebHost project.) When defining the ID for the WebBrowser control, go to the resource.h header file and pick a number that is far greater than any of the numbers you are using for resources in your project. For example, the largest number in the resource.h header file for MfcWebHost is *32,779,* so you could define the ID for the WebBrowser control like this:

```
#define IDC_WEBBROWSER  35000
```

The number *35,000* is much higher than the largest ID in resource.h, thus ensuring that the ID numbers won't conflict if you add more resources using ClassWizard. Now change the call to *Create* to use this ID:

```
if (!m_webBrowser.Create(NULL, WS_CHILD|WS_VISIBLE,
                         CRect(), this, IDC_WEBBROWSER))
{
    return -1;
}
```

Next declare the *OnCommandStateChange* method that will be called when the WebBrowser control fires the *CommandStateChange* event. In the class declaration for the *CMfcWebHostView* class, declare *OnCommandStateChange*:

```
void OnCommandStateChange(long lCommand, BOOL bEnable);
```

In the implementation for the *OnCommandStateChange* method, set data members that indicate whether the Go Forward or Go Back items of the Navigate menu (or both) should be enabled or disabled. These data members will be used for the *UPDATE_COMMAND_UI* handlers. Following is the implementation of the *OnCommandStateChange* method:

```
void CMfcWebHostView::OnCommandStateChange(long lCommand, BOOL bEnable)
{
    switch(lCommand)
    {
        // Forward command
        //

        case CSC_NAVIGATEFORWARD:
            m_fForwardEnabled = bEnable;
            break;

        // Back command
        //
        case CSC_NAVIGATEBACK:
            m_fBackEnabled = bEnable;
            break;

        default:
            break;
    }
}
```

Declare the *m_fForwardEnabled* and *m_fBackEnabled* data members as protected members of the *CMfcWebHostView* class. These data members are of type *BOOL*. Also initialize these data members to *TRUE* in the constructor for the *CMfcWebHostView* class.

Now when the *UPDATE_COMMAND_UI* handlers for the Go Forward and Go Back menu items are called, you can enable or disable the appropriate menu item accordingly. Here's the implementation of the *UPDATE_COMMAND_UI* message handlers for the Go Forward and Go Back menu items:

```
void CMfcWebHostView::OnUpdateNavigateGoForward(CCmdUI* pCmdUI)
{
    pCmdUI->Enable(m_fForwardEnabled);
}

void CMfcWebHostView::OnUpdateNavigateGoBack(CCmdUI* pCmdUI)
{
    pCmdUI->Enable(m_fBackEnabled);
}
```

DocumentComplete

Internet Explorer fires *DocumentComplete* when a document is completely finished loading. Only after this event is fired can the document object be safely used. The document object in the case of a Web page with no frames is the *IHTMLDocument2* object, which I'll discuss in the next chapter. When the document is ready to be used, it has reached the *READYSTATE_COMPLETE* state.

Note the following important points about the *DocumentComplete* event:

- In the case of a page with no frames, *DocumentComplete* is fired once after everything is done.

- In the case of a page with multiple frames, *DocumentComplete* is fired multiple times. Not every frame will fire this event, but each frame that fires a *DownloadBegin* event fires a corresponding *DocumentComplete* event.

- The *DocumentComplete* event has a pointer to an *IDispatch* parameter, which is the *IDispatch* of the window for which *DocumentComplete* is fired. This window can be the window contained in a frame as well.

- The top-level frame fires the *DocumentComplete* event after all subframes have fired this event. Therefore, to see whether a page is through downloading, you need to obtain a pointer to the *IUnknown* interface of the *IDispatch* parameter sent to the event handler for the *DocumentComplete* event. Next, compare that pointer to the *IUnknown* interface with the pointer to the *IUnknown* interface of the WebBrowser control that you are hosting or the instance of Internet Explorer you are automating. If these two pointers are the same, the document is completely finished loading. This means that all HTML, images, controls, and so on for the top-level frame and all subframes are finished downloading.

> **NOTE** It is not sufficient to compare the pointer to the *IDispatch* of the WebBrowser control you are hosting to the pointer that is passed into the event handler for the *DocumentComplete* event. According to the rules of COM, the pointer to *IUnknown* is the only interface pointer whose value won't change if the object that the pointer refers to remains unchanged. For example, an object might change the pointer to its *IDispatch* if the *IDispatch* of the object is implemented as a tear-off interface. For more information about tear-off interfaces, refer to MSDN or one of the many COM books offered by Microsoft Press.

Implementing the fourth point in the preceding list in a Visual Basic application that is hosting the WebBrowser control is easy. Just check to see whether the *pDisp* parameter sent to the event handler for the *DocumentComplete* event is a WebBrowser object. Visual Basic will take care of checking the pointers to *IUnknown* of these objects to make sure they refer to the same object. Here is the code to implement this comparison in Visual Basic:

```
Private Sub WebBrowser1_DocumentComplete(ByVal pDisp As Object,
                                    URL As Variant)
   If (pDisp Is WebBrowser1.Object) Then
      MsgBox "The document is finished loading."
   End If
End Sub
```

Implementing the fourth point in a Visual C++ application is a little more difficult, but you can do it! Let's update MfcWebHost to handle the *DocumentComplete* event and display a message when the document is completely finished loading. First add an entry for the *DocumentComplete* event to the event sink map:

```
ON_EVENT(CMfcWebHostView, IDC_WEBBROWSER, DISPID_DOCUMENTCOMPLETE,
        OnDocumentComplete, VTS_DISPATCH VTS_PVARIANT)
```

Next declare the *OnDocumentComplete* method in the class declaration of the *CMfcWebHostView* class:

```
void OnDocumentComplete(LPDISPATCH lpDispatch, VARIANT FAR* URL);
```

Finally, implement the *OnDocumentComplete* method to determine whether the page is finished loading. In the code on the next page, we retrieve the pointer to the *IUnknown* of the WebBrowser control we are hosting. (Note that we can't simply use the pointer to the *IUnknown* that is returned from a call to the *GetControlUnknown* method. The pointer to the *IUnknown* returned from *GetControlUnknown* is not actually the pointer to the *IUnknown* of the WebBrowser control being hosted. What is returned is actually a pointer to the *IOleObject* interface.) Next, we retrieve the pointer to the *IUnknown* of the object that fired the *DocumentComplete* event by calling *QueryInterface* using the *IDispatch* parameter that is sent to the *OnDocumentComplete* method. If the two pointers to the *IUnknown* interface are the same, the page is completely finished loading.

```
void CMfcWebHostView::OnDocumentComplete(LPDISPATCH lpDispatch,
                                        VARIANT FAR* URL)
{
    HRESULT    hr;
    LPUNKNOWN  lpUnknown;
    LPUNKNOWN  lpUnknownWB = NULL;
    LPUNKNOWN  lpUnknownDC = NULL;

    lpUnknown = m_webBrowser.GetControlUnknown();
    ASSERT(lpUnknown);

    if (lpUnknown)
    {
        // Get the pointer to the IUnknown interface of the WebBrowser
        // control being hosted. The pointer to the IUnknown returned from
        // GetControlUnknown is not the pointer to the IUnknown of the
        // WebBrowser control. It's actually a pointer to the IOleObject.
        //
        hr = lpUnknown->QueryInterface(IID_IUnknown,
                                    (LPVOID*)&lpUnknownWB);

        ASSERT(SUCCEEDED(hr));

        if (FAILED(hr))
            return;

        // Get the pointer to the IUnknown of the object that fired this
        // event.
        //
        hr = lpDispatch->QueryInterface(IID_IUnknown,
                                    (LPVOID*)&lpUnknownDC);

        ASSERT(SUCCEEDED(hr));

        if (SUCCEEDED(hr) && lpUnknownWB == lpUnknownDC)
        {
            // The document has finished loading.
            //
```

```
        MessageBox("The document has finished loading.");
    }

    if (lpUnknownWB)
        lpUnknownWB->Release();

    if (lpUnknownDC)
        lpUnknownDC->Release();
    }
}
```

One thing to note from the previous code is that we never release the pointer to the *IUnknown* interface returned from *GetControlUnknown* because this *IUnknown* pointer isn't *AddRef*'ed in the *GetControlUnknown* method. The *GetControlUnknown* method merely returns a pointer to an *IOleObject* data member that is maintained by the control site class—*CControlSite*. If you release this pointer to the *IUnknown* interface, and you shut down the application, an access violation will occur because MFC will try to release the pointer to the *IUnknown* interface one more time after the object has been deleted.

DownloadBegin

The *DownloadBegin* event notifies an application that a navigation operation is beginning. This event is fired shortly after the *BeforeNavigate2* event in a typical navigation scenario, unless the navigation is canceled in the event handler for the *BeforeNavigate2* event. Any animation or busy indicator that the container needs to display should be connected to *DownloadBegin*. Each *DownloadBegin* event has a corresponding *DownloadComplete* event. In the case of a page refresh, *DownloadBegin* and *DownloadComplete* are the only navigation events that are fired.

DownloadComplete

DownloadComplete occurs when a navigation operation finishes, is halted, or fails. Unlike *NavigateComplete2*, which is fired only when a URL is successfully navigated to, *DownloadComplete* is always fired after navigation starts. Any animation or busy indicator that was started in the event handler for *DownloadBegin* should be stopped in the event handler for *DownloadComplete*.

NavigateComplete2

The *NavigateComplete2* event is fired after navigation to a hyperlink is completed for either a window or a frameset element. The firing of this event is the first indication that the document is ready. After this event fires, you can access the document via the *Document* property without receiving an error. But just because you can access the document doesn't mean you can do so safely. You can access elements in the document safely only after the *DocumentComplete* event is fired.

You'll typically handle the *NavigateComplete2* event as soon as you can when you need to access the *document* object but not necessarily the elements within the document, such as when hooking advanced hosting interfaces into the document. (Chapter 9 covers advanced hosting interfaces in detail.) The *NavigateComplete2* event has two parameters—the *IDispatch* of the object that fired the event and the URL that was navigated to.

NewWindow2

The *NewWindow2* event is fired when a user wants to create a new window for displaying a resource. This event precedes the creation of a new window from within the WebBrowser (for example, in response to navigation targeted to a new window or to a scripted *window.open* method).

NewWindow2 is also fired when the *Navigate* or *Navigate2* methods are called and the *navOpenInNewWindow* flag is specified. The *NewWindow2* event isn't fired when the user chooses New Window from the File menu because the Internet Explorer frame implements the menus. (The Internet Explorer frame isn't an HTML frame; it's the frame window.) Therefore, the *WebBrowser* object doesn't know when this new window has been opened. Because *NewWindow2* is sometimes hard to use, let's check out its two parameters: *ppDisp* and *Cancel*.

The *ppDisp* parameter is the address of an interface pointer that, optionally, receives the *IDispatch* interface pointer of a new *WebBrowser* or *InternetExplorer* object, enabling you to either create a new instance of Internet Explorer that you can control from within your navigation or use your application for the new window. This instance is a new, hidden, nonnavigated *WebBrowser* or *InternetExplorer* object. Upon return from the event handler for NewWindow2, the *InternetExplorer* object that fired the *NewWindow2* event will configure and navigate the new object to the target location.

The other parameter, *Cancel*, is the address of a cancel flag. An application can set this parameter to *TRUE* to cancel the navigation operation or set it to *FALSE* to allow the new window operation to proceed. Setting *Cancel* to *TRUE* completely cancels the new window creation and the navigation.

If you do nothing in the event handler for *NewWindow2*, a new *InternetExplorer* object will automatically be created for you to handle the navigation. One reason you might want to handle *NewWindow2* is to control the creation of the new *InternetExplorer* object. Why? Because you might want to limit the number of instances of Internet Explorer, or perhaps you want to handle events from any new instance of Internet Explorer.

The following code handles the *NewWindow2* event; creates a new, hidden, nonnavigated instance of Internet Explorer; and sets the *ppDisp* parameter equal to the new instance. You can add the necessary code for sinking the events of this new instance of Internet Explorer if you want to.

```
void CMyEvtSink::NewWindow2(LPDISPATCH* ppDisp, BOOL* Cancel)
{
    // Note that m_pIE is a class member of type IWebBrowser2*.
    HRESULT hr = CoCreateInstance(CLSID_InternetExplorer, NULL,
                            CLSCTX_LOCAL_SERVER, IID_IWebBrowser2,
                            (void**)&m_pIE);
    if (hr == S_OK)
      *ppDisp = (IDispatch*)pIE;

    // Do not set Cancel to TRUE. If you do,
    // the navigation will be completely canceled.
}
```

Another reason to handle the *NewWindow2* event is that you might want your application to be used for the new window when the user chooses to open a URL in a new window. If you don't handle the *NewWindow2* event so that your application is used for the new window, a new instance of Internet Explorer will be created in response to the new window request.

You can easily add this functionality so that your application is used for the new window to the VbWebHost example from the last chapter. (The entire code for the updated example can be found on the companion CD in the folder \Samples \Chap07\VbWebHostEvt.) Choose *WebBrowser1* from the Object drop-down list in the upper left-hand corner of the code window. Choose *NewWindow2* from the Procedure drop-down list in the upper right-hand corner of the code window. Then implement the *NewWindow2* event by using the following code:

```
Private Sub WebBrowser1_NewWindow2(ppDisp As Object, Cancel As Boolean)
    Dim frmWB As Form1
    Set frmWB = New Form1

    Set ppDisp = frmWB.WebBrowser1.Object
    frmWB.Visible = True

    Set frmWB = Nothing
End Sub
```

In the handler for the *NewWindow2* event, when a new window needs to be created, we create a new copy of *Form1*. This form, rather than a new instance of Internet Explorer, will be used for the navigation. It is very easy to add this functionality to the MfcWebHost sample. (The entire code for this revised example can be found on the companion CD in the folder \Samples\Chap07\MfcWebHostEvt.)

First you must add an entry for the *NewWindow2* event in the event sink map for the view class. (Don't forget to include ExDispID.h in the MfcWebHostView.cpp implementation file, which is needed to resolve *DISPID_NEWWINDOW2*.)

```
ON_EVENT(CMfcWebHostView, IDC_WEBBROWSER, DISPID_NEWWINDOW2,
        OnNewWindow2, VTS_PDISPATCH VTS_PBOOL)
```

Next declare the *OnNewWindow2* method in the class declaration for *CMfcWebHostView*:

```
void OnNewWindow2(LPDISPATCH* ppDisp, BOOL* Cancel);
```

Finally, implement the *OnNewWindow2* method to create a new instance of the MfcWebHost window when a new window is requested, as shown here:

```
void CMfcWebHostView::OnNewWindow2(LPDISPATCH FAR* ppDisp,
                                   BOOL FAR* Cancel)
{
    // Ensure that ppDisp is not NULL.
    // If it is NULL, you probably specified
    // VT_DISPATCH for the first parameter in
    // the ON_EVENT macro for NewWindow2 in
    // the event sink map. The correct parameter
    // type is VT_PDISPATCH.
    //
    ASSERT(ppDisp);
    if (!ppDisp)
        return;

    // Get a pointer to the application object
    // for this application.
    //
    CWinApp* pApp = AfxGetApp();

    // Get the correct document template.
    //
    CDocTemplate* pDocTemplate;
    POSITION pos = pApp->GetFirstDocTemplatePosition();
    pDocTemplate = pApp->GetNextDocTemplate(pos);

    ASSERT(pDocTemplate);

    // Create the new frame.
    CFrameWnd* pNewFrame = pDocTemplate->CreateNewFrame(GetDocument(),
                                          (CFrameWnd*)AfxGetMainWnd());
    ASSERT(pNewFrame);

    // Activate the frame, and set its active view.
    //
```

```
pDocTemplate->InitialUpdateFrame(pNewFrame, NULL);

CMfcWebHostView* pWbView =
                (CMfcWebHostView*)pNewFrame->GetActiveView();

ASSERT(pWbView);

*ppDisp = pWbView->m_webBrowser.GetApplication();
}
```

If you're hosting the WebBrowser control in an SDI or MDI application (the preceding code is an SDI application), implementing the *OnNewWindow2* method is complicated and involves knowing how to work with document templates. However, if you're hosting the WebBrowser control in a dialog-based application, it is a bit easier. Here's how to use your application for the new window if you're hosting the WebBrowser control in a dialog-based application:

```
void CMyDlg::OnNewWindow2(LPDISPATCH FAR* ppDisp, BOOL FAR* Cancel)
{
    m_dlgNewWB = new CMyDlg;
    m_dlgNewWB->Create(IDD_MYDLG_DIALOG);

    *ppDisp = m_dlgNewWB->m_webBrowser.GetApplication();
}
```

Remember to delete *m_dlgNewWB* when you're finished with the new dialog. And don't perform navigation in the *CMyDlg::OnInitDialog* method, because if you do, the code might not work. (Recall that *ppDisp* must point to a new, hidden, nonnavigated *WebBrowser* or *InternetExplorer* object.)

ProgressChange

The *ProgressChange* event notifies your application that the progress of a download operation has been updated. *ProgressChange* has two input parameters:

- *Progress.* Amount of total progress to show, or −1 when the progress is complete

- *ProgressMax.* Maximum progress value

The container can use the information that the *ProgressChange* event provides to display the number of bytes downloaded so far or to update a progress indicator. To calculate the percentage of progress to show in a progress indicator, multiply the value of *Progress* by 100 and divide by the value of *ProgressMax*. If *Progress* is −1, the container can indicate that the operation is finished or hide the progress indicator.

SEQUENCE OF EVENTS

To help you understand when events are fired by the WebBrowser, look at Figure 7-5, which shows the sequence of WebBrowser events during a normal navigation. I've included only the events that pertain to navigating to a Web page that doesn't contain frames. (I didn't include events such as *ProgressChange*, *CommandStateChange*, *OnToolBar*, and so on.) Not all of these events are always fired. But *BeforeNavigate2* and *DocumentComplete* are fired at least once for every navigation except during a refresh, as I explained earlier.

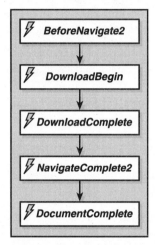

Figure 7-5. *The sequence of events fired by the WebBrowser control during a typical navigation.*

EVENTS USED ONLY WITH INTERNET EXPLORER

Just as some methods and properties of the WebBrowser apply only if you are automating Internet Explorer, some events of the WebBrowser control apply only if you are automating Internet Exporer. The following events do *not* apply if you are only hosting the WebBrowser control:

- *OnQuit*
- *OnVisible*
- *OnToolBar*
- *OnMenuBar*
- *OnStatusBar*

- *OnFullScreen*

- *OnTheaterMode*

Most of these events pertain to user interface items in the browser. Others have to do with closing or displaying Internet Explorer. In some cases, these events will fire despite the fact that you are hosting the WebBrowser control in your application. For example, if you set the *MenuBar* property in your application, even though the WebBrowser control doesn't have a menu bar, the *OnMenuBar* event will fire, but if you show or hide your application's menu bar, the *OnMenuBar* event won't fire. Why? Because you control your menu bar and the WebBrowser control has no knowledge of this or other user interface items. This inconsistency in functionality has been a source of confusion for a long time.

One of these events—*OnQuit*—should never fire when your application hosts the WebBrowser control. For example, look at Table 7-6 on pages 290–91. Notice that the *OnQuit* event is fired when the user shuts down Internet Explorer or when the *Quit* method is called. If you're hosting the control and the user closes your application, the *OnQuit* event won't fire. It fires only when you're automating Internet Explorer and the user manually closes the browser. Also, if you try to call the *Quit* method when hosting the WebBrowser control, an automation error will occur.

HANDLING INTERNET EXPLORER EVENTS FROM ACTIVEX CONTROLS

In the previous chapter, you learned how to create code in your C++ ActiveX controls to access the methods and properties of the *IWebBrowser2* interface implemented by Internet Explorer. As you might have guessed, because you can access the methods and properties of Internet Explorer's *IWebBrowser2* interface, you can also sink events for Internet Explorer's *DWebBrowserEvents2* interface from ActiveX controls. As with accessing the methods and properties, you can sink events in ActiveX controls written only in Visual C++ because you have to access the container object in the same way you accessed it in Chapter 6.

You're probably wondering why you would want to sink Internet Explorer events from an ActiveX control. Well, you might have to if the ActiveX control accesses and changes elements in your document, for instance. (As you'll see in Chapter 8, you will have to make sure that the document can be safely accessed.) Earlier in this chapter in the section titled "*DocumentComplete*," I mentioned that you can't access a document safely until the *DocumentComplete* event has fired. The only way to know that the *DocumentComplete* event has fired from the ActiveX control is to sink events for Internet Explorer and handle the *DocumentComplete* event.

Besides sinking Internet Explorer events because you *have* to, you might also *choose* to. For example, you might want to control the user's navigation experience if you are building an ActiveX control for your corporate intranet or perhaps an elementary school, as I've mentioned in earlier chapters. Any tasks that you can perform when handling events while automating Internet Explorer, you can perform from an ActiveX control.

To illustrate, let's revisit the AtlPrint example from Chapter 6. It allows you to print the document in which AtlPrint's control, PrintCtl, is contained. You probably won't want to print the contents of the document before the document is completely finished loading and, normally, you would want to handle the *DocumentComplete* event to determine when the document is completely finished loading and when it's ready to be used.

When you refresh a page, however, the *DocumentComplete* event is not fired. Because of this and because I want to show you how to use other WebBrowser events, the AtlPrint example handles the *ProgressChange* event to determine whether the page can be printed.

> **NOTE** When the *DocumentComplete* event is not being fired, the *Progress-Change* event is handled to determine whether a page is finished loading. Using *ProgressChange* will work correctly only on a page without frames and probably only on a very simple Web page. The AtlPrint example is here mainly for demonstration purposes. The best way to determine whether the page is finished loading is by handling the *DocumentComplete* event, as I explained earlier. To handle the refresh situation, just look for *DownloadBegin* and *DownloadComplete* events being fired without being wrapped by the *BeforeNavigate2* and *DocumentComplete* events. I will leave this as an exercise for you so that you can learn how to handle the WebBrowser events.

Remember that the *ProgressChange* event has two parameters that tell you the progress of the download operation. The first parameter (the only one we'll discuss) is set to -1 when the progress is complete, which helps you determine whether it's OK to print. (In the next chapter, you'll learn how to use the *DocumentComplete* event in cooperation with the *Document* property to access and change the document.)

To sink Internet Explorer events from the PrintCtl control, you must make a number of changes to AtlPrint. When Internet Explorer loads AtlPrint, you have to set up the event sink, which means you must obtain the *IWebBrowser2* interface implemented by Internet Explorer. (Obtaining the interface is already done in the *Print* method of the *CPrintCtl* class.)

You should move the code that connects to the container and the code that obtains a pointer to its *IWebBrowser2* interface out of the *Print* method. First move the declaration of the *IWebBrowser2* smart pointer from the *Print* method to the class declaration of the *CPrintCtl* class. You'll also have to move the compiler directive that includes the ExDisp.h header file to the PrintCtl.h header file. The declaration of the *IWebBrowser2* smart pointer should look like this:

```
protected:
    CComPtr<IWebBrowser2> m_spWebBrowser;
```

> **NOTE** Obviously, obtaining the *IWebBrowser2* interface should be done only once, when the control is first loaded. Obtaining a pointer to *IWebBrowser2* every time the *Print* method is called is inefficient. To set up the event sink, you have to obtain a pointer to the *IWebBrowser2* interface anyway, so why not just obtain and save this pointer in a data member so that you can use it in the *Print* method as well? This strategy will save you the expense of obtaining this pointer every time the *Print* method is called.

Next override the *SetClientSite* method of *IOleObjectImpl*. The *SetClientSite* method is called when Internet Explorer is notifying the control of its client site. You use this client site (*m_spClientSite*) to access the container and obtain the *IWebBrowser2* interface pointer. In the implementation of *SetClientSite*, you must first call its base class version, like this:

```
IOleObjectImpl<CPrintCtl>::SetClientSite(pClientSite);
```

This code might look a little strange, but remember that *IOleObjectImpl* is a template class. To call its methods, you must specify the required template parameters to indicate to the compiler which instance of the class to use when calling the *SetClientSite* method.

Now move the remaining code that accesses the container and the *IWebBrowser2* interface pointer from the *Print* method to the *SetClientSite* method. The *Print* method should now be pretty empty:

```
STDMETHODIMP CPrintCtl::Print()
{
    ATLASSERT(m_spWebBrowser);

    HRESULT hr = E_FAIL;

    if (m_spWebBrowser)
    {
        hr = m_spWebBrowser->ExecWB(OLECMDID_PRINT,
                                OLECMDEXECOPT_PROMPTUSER, NULL, NULL);
    }

    return hr;
}
```

Add the code to the *SetClientSite* method that sets up the event sink for Internet Explorer events. The implementation of *SetClientSite* should look like this:

> **NOTE**   You can't implement the code to set up the event sink in the *FinalConstruct* method because the client site hasn't been set yet.

```
STDMETHODIMP CPrintCtl::SetClientSite(IOleClientSite* pClientSite)
{
    HRESULT hr = IOleObjectImpl<CPrintCtl>::SetClientSite(pClientSite);

    if (!pClientSite)
    {
        return hr;
    }

    CComPtr<IOleContainer> spContainer;
    m_spClientSite->GetContainer(&spContainer);

    ATLASSERT(spContainer);

    if (SUCCEEDED(hr))
    {
        // Set up the event sink.
        //
        CComQIPtr<IServiceProvider, &IID_IServiceProvider>
            spServiceProvider(spContainer);

        ATLASSERT(spServiceProvider);

        if (spServiceProvider)
        {
            spServiceProvider->QueryService(SID_SInternetExplorer,
                                            IID_IWebBrowser2,
                                            (void**)&m_spWebBrowser);
            ATLASSERT(m_spWebBrowser);

            if (m_spWebBrowser)
            {
                AtlAdvise(m_spWebBrowser, GetUnknown(),
                          DIID_DWebBrowserEvents2, &m_dwCookie);
            }
        }
    }

    return hr;
}
```

Notice in the call to *AtlAdvise* that you'll have to create either a protected or a private data member of type *DWORD* to hold the cookie that is returned from the *AtlAdvise* method. Initialize this data member to *0* in the constructor for the *CPrintCtl* class. Also notice that we hold on to the return value from *IOleObjectImpl::SetClientSite* and use the value as the return value of the *CPrintCtl::SetClientSite* method. This method doesn't check the return values of any of the other methods that are being called because the return value of *CPrintCtl::SetClientSite* should reflect the status of setting the client site.

Finally, we check to see whether the *pClientSite* input parameter is *NULL*. If so, we return from this function because when Internet Explorer unloads the control, it calls *SetClientSite* with *pClientSite* set to *NULL*. This tells you that you are being disconnected from the client site, so the code that obtains a pointer to the *IWebBrowser2* interface of the container doesn't need to be executed.

Because you advised the container that you want to sink events for it, you should be polite and disconnect the sink when you're done, including when the control is being unloaded. To do this, place a call to the *AtlUnadvise* method in the section of code that checks to see whether *pClientSite* is *NULL* in the *SetClientSite* method. Remember that *pClientSite* will be *NULL* when the control is being unloaded. The new section of code should look like this:

```
if (!pClientSite)
{
    ATLASSERT(m_spWebBrowser);

    if (m_spWebBrowser)
        AtlUnadvise(m_spWebBrowser, DIID_DWebBrowserEvents2, m_dwCookie);

    return hr;
}
```

Now that you've established the event sink by using *AtlAdvise*, let's handle some events. To handle events, you must override the *Invoke* method of *IDispatchImpl*. Typically, you would want to create a separate class for your event sink because the DISPIDs of Internet Explorer events could conflict with the DISPIDs of your control. But for this example, you can simply implement the event handlers inside of the *CPrintCtl* class. Implement *Invoke* (as in the code on the next page) to handle the *ProgressChange* event. In the event handler, if the amount of progress is *−1*, set a data member that indicates that the page is ready to be printed.

> **NOTE** Remember that the parameters for methods, properties, and events are sent to *Invoke* in reverse order. Therefore, the *Progress* parameter of the *ProgressChange* event is actually the second parameter in the array of arguments sent to *Invoke*.

```
STDMETHODIMP CPrintCtl::Invoke(DISPID dispidMember,
                               REFIID riid,
                               LCID lcid,
                               WORD wFlags,
                               DISPPARAMS* pDispParams,
                               VARIANT* pvarResult,
                               EXCEPINFO* pExcepInfo,
                               UINT* puArgErr)
{
    if (riid != IID_NULL)
        return DISP_E_UNKNOWNINTERFACE;

    if (!pDispParams)
        return DISP_E_PARAMNOTOPTIONAL;

    switch (dispidMember)
    {
        //
        // The parameters for this DISPID:
        // [0]: Maximum progress - VT_I4
        // [1]: Amount of total progress - VT_I4
        //
        case DISPID_PROGRESSCHANGE:
            if (pDispParams->cArgs != 0)
            {
                // Make sure that you access the
                // correct data member of the rgvarg array.
                // To do this, check the type of data to
                // make sure it is correct.
                //
                if (pDispParams->cArgs > 1
                    && pDispParams->rgvarg[1].vt == VT_I4
                    && pDispParams->rgvarg[0].vt == VT_I4)
                {
                    if (-1 == pDispParams->rgvarg[1].lVal)
                        m_fCanBePrinted = TRUE;
                }
            }

            break;

        default:
            // Call the base class implementation of Invoke
            // so that IPrintCtl methods and properties will
            // work correctly.
            //
```

```
        IDispatchImpl<IPrintCtl, &IID_IPrintCtl,
          &LIBID_ATLPRINTLib>::Invoke(dispidMember, riid, lcid,
                                      wFlags, pDispParams,
                                      pvarResult, pExcepInfo, puArgErr);

      break;
    }

  return S_OK;
}
```

In the handler for the *ProgressChange* event, when the *Progress* parameter (*pDispParams->rgvarg[1].lVal*) is *–1*, we set a data member that tells the control that the document is completely finished loading and that the user can print. Declare this data member as a protected or private member of type *BOOL* belonging to the *CPrintCtl* class. Initialize the data member to *FALSE* in the constructor for the *CPrintCtl* class.

Now when the user tries to print the document by calling the *Print* method, you can check the data member to see whether the document is ready to be printed. Here's the updated code for the *Print* method:

```
STDMETHODIMP CPrintCtl::Print()
{
  if (!m_fCanBePrinted)
  {
    ::MessageBox(NULL, _T("The page is not ready to be printed."),
                 _T("PrintCtl"), MB_OK);
    return E_FAIL;
  }

  ATLASSERT(m_spWebBrowser);

  HRESULT hr = E_FAIL;

  if (m_spWebBrowser)
  {
    hr = m_spWebBrowser->ExecWB(OLECMDID_PRINT,
                                OLECMDEXECOPT_PROMPTUSER, NULL, NULL);
  }

  return hr;
}
```

If the *m_fCanBePrinted* data member is *FALSE*, the code displays a message box that tells the user that the document isn't ready to be printed. If this data member is *TRUE*, the code goes ahead and prints the document. You can find the entire code for the updated AtlPrint example on the companion CD in the folder \Samples \Chap07\AtlPrintEvt.

WHAT'S NEXT?

Now you're an expert at hosting the WebBrowser control and automating Internet Explorer! And you can perform both of these tasks in Visual Basic and Visual C++ applications. Plus, you know how to use the WebBrowser's methods, properties, and events. In the next chapter, you'll build on this experience by using the DHTML Object Model to access and change the contents of Web pages. (I discussed how to do this from scripting in Chapter 3.) In Chapter 8, we'll revisit the DHTML Object Model and see how to access and change the contents of documents from Visual Basic and Visual C++ applications.

Chapter 8

Accessing the DHTML Object Model

In Chapter 3, which introduced the DHTML Object Model (formerly known as the Internet Explorer Object Model), you learned that all objects in the object model fit together in a way that enables you to access and change all HTML elements and data on a Web page. You also learned how to access the object model from JScript and Microsoft Visual Basic Script (VBScript). Chapter 6 showed you how to host the WebBrowser control and automate Microsoft Internet Explorer, and you saw that applications could do either and still access functionality (such as navigating forward and backward in a history list) in the same way.

As you'll see in this chapter, regardless of whether you are hosting the WebBrowser control or automating Internet Explorer, you also access the DHTML Object Model from your applications in the same way. You're going to learn how to access objects in the DHTML Object Model, as well as their methods, properties, events, and collections, from within Microsoft Visual Basic or Microsoft Visual C++ applications that are hosting the WebBrowser control or automating Internet Explorer.

REVISITING THE DHTML OBJECT MODEL

Every HTML element on a Web page is an object. Therefore, each element has methods, properties, events, and even possibly collections. You can use these methods, properties, and so on to manipulate the element or the content contained within the element. Examples of three elements and their related objects and interfaces follow:

Element	Visual Basic Object	Visual C++ Interface
<BODY>	HTMLBodyElement	IHTMLBodyElement
<A>	HTMLAnchorElement	IHTMLAnchorElement
<IMG>	HTMLImgElement	IHTMLImgElement

Most of the major HTML elements have objects and interfaces that apply specifically to them. Some of the minor HTML elements, such as <B> and <I>, use the same interface—*IHTMLElement*—in both Visual Basic and Visual C++ applications. In fact, you can use *IHTMLElement* to refer to all the elements on a Web page.

From within Visual Basic applications, you use an HTML element object in the same way you use any other object. And not surprisingly, because VBScript is a subset of Visual Basic, you access the DHTML Object Model from Visual Basic in the same way you access it from VBScript applications. (The syntax is similar.) As long as you have a reference to the *WebBrowser* object or *InternetExplorer* object in your application, you can retrieve a reference to an HTML document and all the HTML elements contained therein.

Accessing an object or an interface of the DHTML Object Model from within a Visual C++ application is a little more difficult than doing so from within a Visual Basic application. Just remember that every HTML element is an object, and objects have interfaces, so each HTML element on a Web page has an interface. Once you have a pointer to the *IWebBrowser2* interface of the WebBrowser, you can easily get a pointer to the document and any HTML element object it contains. I'll show you how to do this shortly, but first let's see how to access the DHTML Object Model from within Visual Basic.

FOR MORE INFORMATION

In this chapter, you'll learn how to access and change the data on a Web page by using the objects and interfaces in the Internet Explorer DHTML Object Model. You will also learn how to handle events in DHTML. I'm going to show you only a few of the objects, interfaces, and events in the object model that you can access. Far too many exist to cover in one chapter. If you need more information, refer to the MSDN Online Web Workshop or to the book, *Dynamic HTML Reference and Software Development Kit: Comprehensive Reference to DHTML for Microsoft Internet Explorer 5.0*, available from Microsoft Press.

ACCESSING THE DHTML OBJECT MODEL FROM VISUAL BASIC

To help you understand how to obtain or change the data on a Web page, we'll create a simple Visual Basic application that hosts the WebBrowser control. You'll add features to this application as you progress through this section of the chapter. Before you get started, however, you must perform a few preliminary tasks, such as hosting the WebBrowser control or automating Internet Explorer within a Visual Basic application. (You're probably thinking, "Duh, Scott!")

Start Visual Basic, and create a new Standard EXE project. Save the project as VbObjMdl. Add the WebBrowser control to the toolbox by choosing Components from the Project menu and then selecting Microsoft Internet Controls from the Component dialog box. Add the WebBrowser control to your project's main form. Add the typical controls needed to navigate the Web: Address label, Address text box, and Go button. Name the text box *txtAddress*, and name the Go button *btnGo*. The Visual Basic form for your project should look similar to the one shown in Figure 8-1.

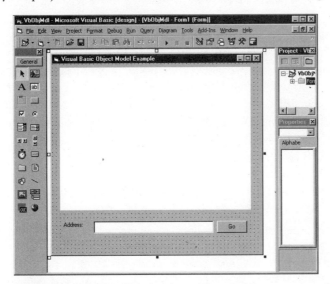

Figure 8-1. *VbObjMdl form after adding WebBrowser control and navigation controls.*

Now add the necessary code to implement the controls on the form. (This code is the typical code you use to navigate to a Web page, as you saw in Chapter 6. You will see the declaration of the *WebDoc* variable later in this section.)

```
Private Sub btnGo_Click()
    On Error Resume Next
    WebBrowser1.Navigate txtAddress.Text
End Sub
```

(continued)

```
Private Sub Form_Load()
   WebBrowser1.GoHome
End Sub
```

To change the data on a Web page or to just read it, you must first obtain a reference to the *document* object. As you learned in Chapter 3, you obtain references to the objects that represent the HTML elements on the Web page through the *document* object. To access the *document* object, you use the WebBrowser's *Document* property. Then you use the *document* object's properties and collections to access all the objects in the DHTML Object Model, including the parent *window* object and all element objects.

But you can't just haphazardly access the *Document* property of the WebBrowser. You must wait until the Web page is completely finished loading before you attempt to access the *document* object. And how do you know when you can safely access it? That's right—after the WebBrowser control's *DocumentComplete* event has fired. Therefore, you need to declare a global variable to hold a reference to the *document* object and set it in the handler method for the WebBrowser control's *DocumentComplete* event.

But wait! Before you declare a global variable that will hold a reference to the *document* object, you must tell Visual Basic where to look when it needs to obtain information about the *document* object's methods, properties, collections, and so forth. If you don't, you will have to declare your variable as type *Object*, which means that Visual Basic's IntelliSense technology won't be able to show you the methods and properties of your object, and you'll have to refer to the actual documentation for the *document* object. (Egad!) If Visual Basic can't find information about an object, it won't display the object's methods, properties, and collections when you type the name of the object and press the period key. Just as you did when automating Internet Explorer in Chapter 6, you tell Visual Basic where to look for information about an object by setting a reference to that object's type library.

> **NOTE**   A type library for a component such as mshtml.dll contains definitions of all the GUIDS; objects; interfaces; and the interfaces' methods, properties, events, and collections that are implemented in the component. In previous versions of Internet Explorer, the type library for MSHTML was contained in mshtml.dll. With Internet Explorer 5, this type library was moved into mshtml.tlb to decrease the size of mshtml.dll and to decrease the size of the minimum installation of Internet Explorer.

The type library for the *document* object and all the HTML element objects on a Web page is contained in a file named mshtml.tlb. (As I mentioned in Chapter 6, these objects are implemented in the MSHTML component.) You set a reference to mshtml.tlb in the References dialog box, which you open by choosing References from the Project menu.

The easiest way to set the reference is to click the Browse button in the References dialog box. By default, Visual Basic displays the Add Reference dialog box that opens in the system directory. (By default, the system directory will be C:\Windows\System for Microsoft Windows 95 and higher systems, and C:\WinNT\ System32 for Microsoft Windows NT or Windows 2000 systems.) After opening the Add Reference dialog box, type in the name of the type library file in the File Name text box, *mshtml.tlb*, and click the Open button. Visual Basic adds a reference to the Microsoft HTML Object Library to the Reference dialog box, as shown in Figure 8-2. (As an alternative to browsing for mshtml.tlb, you can scroll down in the References dialog box and choose Microsoft HTML Object Library.) Click the OK button to finish setting this reference.

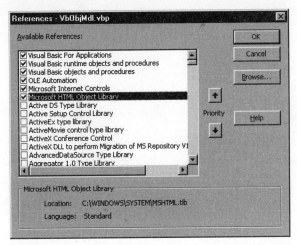

Figure 8-2. *Visual Basic References dialog box with Microsoft HTML Object Library selected.*

Once you've set a reference to the type library for MSHTML, you can use Visual Basic's Object Browser to view all the objects and interfaces in that type library. To display the Object Browser, press F2 or choose Object Browser from the View menu. Then in the upper left-hand drop-down list box where <All Libraries> is displayed, select MSHTML. All the objects and interfaces stored in the MSHTML type library will be displayed, as shown in Figure 8-3.

Now that you've added the MSHTML type library as a reference to your project, you can declare a global variable that will hold a reference to the *document* object returned by the WebBrowser's *Document* property. Name this variable *WebDoc*, and declare it as *HTMLDocument*. The *HTMLDocument* object is defined in the type library for MSHTML and represents the *document* object. *HTMLDocument* is the type of object returned by the WebBrowser's *Document* property. The declaration of this global variable should appear in the code like this:

```
Dim WebDoc As HTMLDocument
```

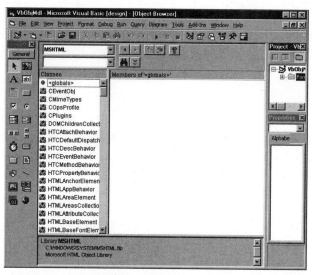

Figure 8-3. *Visual Basic Object Browser displaying the MSHTML type library.*

Next create an event handler for the *DocumentComplete* event, and add the following code to set *WebDoc* to the *document* object returned by the WebBrowser's *Document* property:

```
Private Sub WebBrowser1_DocumentComplete(ByVal pDisp As Object, _
                                         URL As Variant)
    On Error Resume Next
    Set WebDoc = WebBrowser1.Document
End Sub
```

As you can see, whether you are hosting the control or automating Internet Explorer, you'll obtain a reference to the *document* object in the same way.

Later in this section and in the next section, when you add code to obtain and change the data on a Web page, you'll use *WebDoc*. If you use *WebDoc* before you set it to a *document* object, an error will occur. You can avoid this error in two ways. One way is to set *WebDoc* to *Nothing* in the *Form_Load* method and in the *WebBrowser_BeforeNavigate2* event handler. Then you can verify that *WebDoc* is not equal to *Nothing* before trying to use it. The other way is to use one of Visual Basic's error handling statements, *On Error Resume Next*, which involves much less code.

The code in the rest of this section uses the *On Error Resume Next* error handling statement.

Obtaining Data from a Web Page

Obtaining data contained on a Web page—including HTML and the information users enter on a form—is easy in Visual Basic because the DHTML Object Model provides the necessary methods, properties, and collections to do so. In Chapter 3, you learned to obtain the inner and outer HTML of an entire document and of a particular HTML element by using the *innerHTML* and *outerHTML* properties. (You can also use the *innerText* and *outerText* properties to obtain the inner and outer text of a document or an element.) To refresh your memory, add a button to your form, name it *btnBodyHTML*, and change its *Caption* property to *Get Body*. When clicked, the Get Body button displays the HTML contained within the opening <BODY> tag and closing </BODY> tag. Double-click the button to create an event handler for the button's *Click* event. To display the inner HTML for the <BODY> tag, you just access the *innerHTML* property for the object associated with the tag. (This procedure works for any element on the page.)

But how do you obtain a reference to this *body* object? You already have a reference to the *document* object, and by using the methods, properties, and collections of the *document* object, you can easily obtain references to any other object on the page. For example, you can obtain a reference to the *body* object by accessing the *body* property of the *document* object, which enables you to call any of the methods, properties, and collections of the *body* object. To call the *innerHTML* property of the *body* object from the event handler for the btnBodyHTML button, just obtain a reference to the *body* object and call the *innerHTML* property of the *body* object, like this:

```
Private Sub btnBodyHTML_Click()
    On Error Resume Next
    MsgBox WebDoc.body.innerHTML
End Sub
```

This code provides a reference to the *body* object by using the *body* property of the document and then calling *innerHTML*. Remember that in the handler for the *DocumentComplete* event, you set *WebDoc* to the *document* object of the WebBrowser. Now, when the user clicks the Get Body button, the entire HTML in the body section of the Web page will be displayed. Also notice that the code includes the *On Error Resume Next* statement, just in case the user clicks Get Body before the document is completely finished loading. Now run your application and click Get Body. You should see all the HTML contained within the body of the Web page.

The technique you just used to access the *body* object on a Web page works for every element on the page. First you get a reference to the document, and then you access one of its properties or collections to obtain a reference to the object you want. In the preceding code, you saw how to access the *body* object by using the *body* property of the document. However, the *innerHTML* and *outerHTML* properties of the body give you only the HTML that is contained in the body section of the document. It doesn't give you the entire HTML of the page. To access the entire HTML of the page, you must use the new Internet Explorer 5 property, *documentElement*.

To access the entire HTML of the page, add another button to your form that will display the entire contents of the document when clicked. Name this button *btnGetAllHTML*, and change its *Caption* property to *Get All HTML*. Double-click this button to bring up the Code View window and to create the skeleton code for this button's *Click* event handler. In this event handler, add the following code:

```
Private Sub btnGetAllHTML_Click()
    On Error Resume Next
    MsgBox WebDoc.documentElement.outerHTML
End Sub
```

In this code, the *documentElement* property of *WebDoc* is called first to access the object representing the document element. Then the *outerHTML* property of the *document* object we just got is called to get the contents of the entire Web page. Finally, *MsgBox* is called to display the contents of the Web page. Although no <DOCUMENT> tag exists, the *documentElement* property was created to give you access to the entire document as an HTML element. But using the *documentElement* property isn't the only way you can access the entire HTML for a Web page.

Far too many elements exist on the Web page for you to create a specific property for each, so you will occasionally need to use the collections of the *document* object, such as the *All* collection, to obtain references to some of the elements. For example, you can access the entire HTML for a Web page by using the *outerHTML* property of the <HTML> element, but because you can't access <HTML> directly, you have to iterate through the *All* collection of the document, like this:

```
Private Sub btnGetAllHTML_Click()
    On Error Resume Next
    Dim Elem As IHTMLElement

    For Each Elem In WebDoc.All
        If StrComp(Elem.tagName, "HTML", vbTextCompare) = 0 Then
            MsgBox Elem.outerHTML
        End If
    Next
End Sub
```

In this code, we first declare a local variable of type *IHTMLElement*. A variable of this type must be declared because the *All* collection returns a collection of all the elements on the page. Remember, there are objects and interfaces that represent all the elements on the page, and you can use *IHTMLElement* to represent any of those elements. In the code, when we access the elements contained in the *All* collection, we don't know the exact type for the element we are accessing, so we have to declare and use a local variable that has some generic type—*IHTMLElement*.

Notice that in the code we iterate through the *All* collection to look for the <HTML> element. The <HTML> element is usually the first one on the page, and when it is, you can access it by referencing index 0 in the *All* collection. But when it *isn't*, such as the case in which a Web page author adds comments to the top of a Web page, the first element on the page is the HTML comment tag. That's why in the preceding code, we loop through all the elements in the collection looking for the <HTML> tag.

Also notice that we use the *tagName* property of the element in the code. This property can be used to determine whether an element is of a certain type, and it returns the actual tag name of the element without the opening and closing angle brackets (<>). For example, if the element is an <HTML> element, the *tagName* property will return HTML. The preceding code accessed the <HTML> tag, but you can also use the *tagName* property to access any element on the page.

Also notice that in the preceding code, we use the Visual Basic *StrComp* function to compare the *tagName* with the string *"HTML"*. *StrComp* performs a case-insensitive search if you specify the *vbTextCompare* setting for the third parameter. This specification is necessary because no one can guarantee that the string returned from the *tagName* property will be a specific case. Once the <HTML> element is found, the entire contents of the Web page is displayed by using the *outerHTML* property of the <HTML> element.

USING TAGS WITH IDS

If the <HTML> tag in a document has an ID, such as *Html1*, you can obtain a reference to the HTML element object like this:

```
WebDoc.All("Html1")
```

Then you can call the *innerHTML* or *outerHTML* properties as usual. However, most Web page authors don't specify an ID for the <HTML> tag. If you're the creator of the Web page and you need to access the <HTML> tag, you might want to specify an ID for it, because obtaining a reference to the HTML element object using an ID is much more efficient.

In addition to being able to access the HTML for the document or for a specific element on a Web page, you can obtain data that was entered by a user into the form input elements such as a textbox, a checkbox, and a radio button. Once you have a reference to the object that represents the HTML element that you want, you can easily access its methods, properties, and collections. As you might have guessed, the object that represents form input elements is *HTMLInputElement*.

Data entered into a form input element such as a textbox is typically stored in the element's *Value* property. You can specify a default value for an input element by using the VALUE attribute of the <INPUT> tag when you create the page. To obtain the data that is entered into a form input element, you simply use the *Value* property of the *HTMLInputElement* object. This property will reflect the current data entered into the input element. For textboxes, this data will be what the user has entered. For input types such as checkboxes and radio buttons, this value will be what the Web page author specified for the VALUE attribute. In the case of checkboxes and radio buttons, if you just want to know whether they are checked, you can use the *HTMLInputElement* object's *Checked* property.

To see how easily you can obtain the data the user entered, let's modify the example we've been creating. First you need to change the *Form_Load* method. Instead of navigating to the user's home page, you should navigate to a Web page that I've included on the companion CD in the folder \Samples\Chap08\VbObjMdl. This page is called VbObjMdl.htm and it contains an HTML form with a few HTML elements that allow the user to enter data. Copy this Web page to the application directory of the VbObjMdl project, and change the *Form_Load* method to navigate to this page, like this:

```
Private Sub Form_Load()
    WebBrowser1.Navigate App.Path & "\VbObjMdl.htm"
End Sub
```

Next add a button to your form, name it *btnGetFormData*, and change its *Caption* property to *Get Form Data*. Also add a text box to your form that will be used to display all the data the user entered. Name this text box *txtDataValues*, and leave its *Text* property empty. Set its *MultiLine* property to *True*. Your form should now look similar to the one shown in Figure 8-4. (Note that this form already contains the buttons you added earlier as well as a button named Add HTML, which you will add later in this section.)

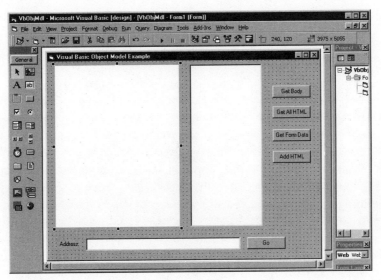

Figure 8-4. *VbObjMdl form after adding Get Form Data button and textbox.*

Now double-click the Get Form Data button to display the Code View window, and create the skeleton code for the Get Form Data button's *Click* event handler. When the Get Form Data button is clicked, the event handler will obtain all the data for the input elements and display it in the text box you just added. Enter the following code in the event handler to implement this functionality:

```
Private Sub btnGetFormData_Click()
   On Error Resume Next

   Dim strData As String
   Dim Elem As HTMLInputElement

   ' Loop through all the elements on the form
   ' and retrieve the data for the input element objects.
   '
   For Each Elem In WebDoc.Forms(0).elements
      strData = strData & "ID: " & Elem.Id & ", "

      If StrComp(Elem.Type, "checkbox", vbTextCompare) = 0 _
         Or StrComp(Elem.Type, "radio", vbTextCompare) = 0 Then

         strData = strData & "Checked: " & Elem.Checked
      Else
         strData = strData & "Value: " & Elem.Value
      End If
```

(continued)

```
        strData = strData & vbCrLf
    Next

    txtDataValues.Text = strData
End Sub
```

In this code, we declare a variable named *Elem* of type *HTMLInputElement* that will hold references to input element objects within the form. Then we use the form's *elements* collection to loop through all the elements on the form. To access the form, you simply use the document's *Forms* collection, which returns all the *form* objects for the Web page. Notice that we reference item 0 in the *Forms* collection, because only one form exists on this page. (Remember that items in collections are indexed starting at 0.)

The form that is returned from the *Forms* collection is a collection as well. Think about it a minute. An HTML form is just a container for input elements, so a *form* object is a collection of input elements. The *form* object has an *item* method, just like other collections, that you can use to access an item in the collection. But using the form's *elements* collection allows you to use the *For Each...Next* loop construct.

Once a reference to an input element exists on the form, we start building the string that will be displayed in the textbox. This string will contain the ID of the element and either the value associated with the element or, if the element is a checkbox or a radio button, the value of the *Checked* property.

As you saw in Chapter 3, most attributes for HTML tags have an associated property that is a member of the object representing the element. For <INPUT> elements, you specify the type of element by using the TYPE attribute; consequently, you determine the type of the input element by using the *Type* property. In the preceding code, if the type of the input element is *checkbox* or *radio*, whether the checkbox or radio button is currently checked is displayed. You can determine whether the checkbox or radio button is checked by using the *HTMLInputElement* object's *Checked* property.

If the input element is not a checkbox or a radio button, the current value of the input element is displayed. This value will be the data inserted by the user or the default value that was specified by using the VALUE attribute.

Now go ahead and test your application. When you run it, the VbObjMdl.htm file should be loaded and displayed, as shown in Figure 8-5. To retrieve the entire HTML of the page and the HTML inside the body of the document, click all the buttons you've added to your form. Also enter some data into the text box, and check the check boxes and radio buttons. Then click the Get Form Data button to retrieve the entered data and display it in the text box.

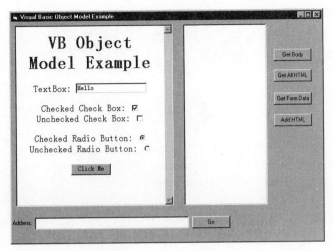

Figure 8-5. *VbObjMdl.*

Dynamically Inserting Data into a Web Page Using Visual Basic

Once you know how to obtain data from a Web page, changing this data—whether it's HTML or data entered by the user—is simple. Most of the properties that you use to retrieve data also allow you to set that data. For example, as you've learned, you use the *innerHTML*, *outerHTML*, *innerText*, and *outerText* properties to retrieve the inner or outer HTML, the text of the entire document, or the text of a specific element. You can also use these properties to change this data.

NOTE Not all properties can be changed—some are read-only. When in doubt, refer to the MSDN Online Web Workshop.

We'll change the VbObjMdl project to allow you to add HTML to the end of the Web page document. First add a new button to your form named *btnAddHTML*, and change its *Caption* property to *Add HTML*. When the Add HTML button is clicked, a form will be displayed that allows the user to enter HTML. This HTML will be appended to the end of the Web page after the form is closed.

Add a new form to your project by selecting Add Form from the Project menu. From the Add Form dialog box, choose the basic form, and then click the Open button to add the form to your project. Change the *Caption* property of your form to *Add HTML*. Then add a text box to the new form, name it *txtHTML*, set its *MultiLine* property to *True*, and clear its *Text* property. Add a button to the form, name it *btnOK*, and set its *Caption* property to *OK*. Your new form should look similar to Figure 8-6.

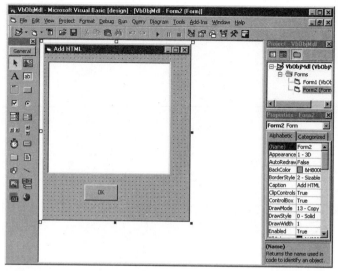

Figure 8-6. *Add HTML form (Form2).*

When the OK button is clicked, the text that is entered into the text box will be added to the end of the Web page being displayed inside the WebBrowser control on the main form. You need to add a little bit of code to make this work correctly. First, in the code window for your main form (Form1), create a public variable named *g_strHTML* of type *String*, like this:

```
Public g_strHTML As String
```

Next go back to Form2, and create a *Click* event handler for the OK button. The code for this button is quite simple. Just set the *g_strHTML* variable of Form1 to the text entered in the text box, and then unload Form2. (Note that if the user just clicks the system Close button, nothing will be added to the Web page. Clicking the system Close button is equivalent to canceling the operation.)

```
Private Sub btnOK_Click()
    Form1.g_strHTML = txtHTML.Text
    Unload Me
End Sub
```

Now that you've written the code to obtain HTML from the user, you have to add the code to display this new form, and add the new HTML to the end of the Web page. Create a *Click* event handler for the Add HTML button. In this event handler, you create and show Form2 as a modal dialog box. When the user clicks the OK button in Form2, the *g_strHTML* variable will be set to the text that was entered into the text box in the dialog box. If the user actually did enter text or HTML, you should call the *insertAdjacentHTML* method to add the HTML to the end of the Web page.

(Remember the *insertAdjacentHTML* method from Chapter 3?) Here's the code to implement the *Click* event handler for the Add HTML button:

```
Private Sub btnAddHTML_Click()
    g_strHTML = ""

    Dim frmHTML As Form2
    Form2.Show vbModal, Me

    If g_strHTML <> "" Then
        WebDoc.body.insertAdjacentHTML "BeforeEnd", g_strHTML
    End If
End Sub
```

Now test the additions you've made to VbObjMdl. Click the Add HTML button to invoke the Add HTML dialog box, and enter some text or HTML into the text box. Then click OK to see the HTML added to the end of the page.

Along with changing the HTML on a page, you can insert or change data in form elements. You already know how to obtain this data, so inserting it into these elements should be a breeze. To add this insertion functionality to the VbObjMdl example, start by adding a text box and a button to Form1. Name the text box *txtNewText*, and leave its *Text* property empty. Name the button *btnChgText1*, and set its *Caption* property to *Change Text1*. When you enter text into the text box and click the Change Text1 button, the text you entered will be inserted into the text box on the VbObjMdl.htm Web page. Your new form should look similar to the one shown in Figure 8-7.

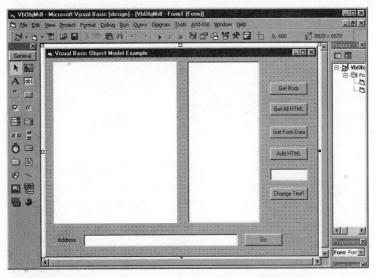

Figure 8-7. *Form1 with new text box and Change Text1 button.*

Now create a *Click* event handler for the Change Text1 button by double-clicking the button. Inside this event handler, set the value of the text box on the Web page to the text that was entered into the *txtNewText* text box. To do this, simply set the *Value* property of the *textbox* object on the Web page to the *Text* property of the *txtNew-Text* textbox on your form. Here's the code for the *Click* event handler for the Change Text1 button:

```
Private Sub btnChgText1_Click()
    On Error Resume Next
    WebDoc.Forms(0).Item("Text1").Value = txtNewText.Text
End Sub
```

This code might look a little complicated because we use object chaining, but it really isn't difficult. Let's examine the code a little more closely. First we get a reference to the form on the Web page by accessing the first item in the *Forms* collection. Because the text box on the Web page has an ID of *Text1*, we can reference the textbox input element by name using the *Item* method of the *form* object. Then, once we have a reference to the *textbox* object, we set the object's *Value* property to the text that was entered into the textbox input element on Form1.

Now run the final version of VbObjMdl. This time, enter some text into the *txtNewText* text box, and click the Change Text1 button. The text you've just entered will be inserted into the text box on the Web page. That's it! You can find the entire code for the final version of VbObjMdl on the companion CD in the folder \Samples\ Chap08\VbObjMdl.

I can't show you all the objects and interfaces of the DHTML Object Model, but the techniques you just learned work with all objects on the Web page. Now let's get down-and-dirty and talk about how to access and change the data on a Web page from a Visual C++ application.

ACCESSING THE DHTML OBJECT MODEL FROM VISUAL C++

As with the Visual Basic example you created earlier, you must perform a few preliminary steps before you can access the object model from within Visual C++. It doesn't matter whether you are hosting the WebBrowser control or automating Internet Explorer in an MFC, an ATL, or a C++ application—you will access the DHTML Object Model the same way—through the *document* object.

In this section, we'll create an MFC dialog-based application that hosts the WebBrowser control. We'll use the MFC wrapper classes for hosting the WebBrowser control, so the method call that retrieves the initial *document* object pointer will be slightly different from the way this pointer is retrieved using other development libraries.

Go ahead and start Visual C++, create a new MFC AppWizard (exe) application, and name it MfcObjMdl. In the Step 1 dialog box, choose Dialog Based. Accept the remainder of the project defaults by clicking the Finish button and then clicking the OK button in the New Project Information dialog box. Visual C++ will automatically display your project's dialog in design mode so that you can add controls to it.

Next add the WebBrowser control to your project by selecting it from the Components And Controls dialog, which you can access via the Project/Add To Project menu. (If you forget how to do this, refer to the section in Chapter 6 starting on page 222.) Add the WebBrowser control to the dialog along with the other controls that you will use for navigation, just as you did for the Visual Basic example. The dialog should look similar to the one shown in Figure 8-8.

Figure 8-8. *MfcObjMdl dialog with WebBrowser control and navigation controls.*

So that the dialog won't close if the user presses the Enter key, change the ID of the Go button to *IDOK*. (The default MFC handler function for a button with the ID *IDOK* automatically closes the dialog. We will add code later to override this message handler and prevent the dialog from closing when the Enter key is pressed.) Use ClassWizard to associate variables with the WebBrowser control and the edit box in the dialog. Name the WebBrowser variable *m_webBrowser* and the edit box variable *m_strAddress*.

Now add the code on the next page to the *OnInitDialog* method for the dialog class to navigate to the user's home page when the application is started.

```
BOOL CMfcObjMdlDlg::OnInitDialog()
{
    ⋮

    m_webBrowser.GoHome();

    ⋮
}
```

Implement the Go button to navigate to the URL that was entered in the edit box. Because the Go button has an ID of *IDOK*, you must name the method *OnOK* so that it will be called when the user presses the Enter key as well as when the user clicks the Go button. Don't call the base class version of this function; if you do, the dialog will be closed when the user presses the Enter key.

```
void CMfcObjMdlDlg::OnOK()
{
    UpdateData();

    if (!m_strAddress.IsEmpty())
    {
        COleVariant vtEmpty;
        m_webBrowser.Navigate(m_strAddress, &vtEmpty, &vtEmpty,
                              &vtEmpty, &vtEmpty);
    }
}
```

Now compile and test the application to make sure it works correctly. When you enter a URL and click the Go button, the application will navigate to the URL you specified.

Before you can start accessing the DHTML Object Model from this application, you must get a pointer to the *document* object. By using the *document* object, you can access the entire contents of the Web page that is loaded into the WebBrowser. Create a data member of the dialog class named *m_pHTMLDocument2* of type *IHTMLDocument2*. This interface is the type that represents the document being displayed in the WebBrowser. Here's how this declaration should appear in the *CMfcObjMdlDlg* class:

```
protected:
    IHTMLDocument2* m_pHTMLDocument2;
```

Initialize this pointer to *NULL* in the constructor for the *CMfcObjMdlDlg* class. Also, in MfcObjMdlDlg.h, include the mshtml.h file, which contains the definition of the *IHTMLDocument2* interface.

```
#include <mshtml.h>
```

USING THE LATEST TECHNOLOGY

Remember to download the latest Internet Explorer 5 headers and libraries from the MSDN Online Web Workshop. Download and install the headers and libraries for Windows 2000 even if you aren't developing for this platform. Some of the headers and libraries that you'll need have been updated and reside in the Windows NT 5 directories that are created when you install them from the MSDN Online Web Workshop. You must place the headers and libraries in the correct order as specified in Chapter 6.

Also note that Internet Explorer 5 has a new interface named *IHTMLDocument3*, which provides some functionality that the *IHTMLDocument2* interface doesn't provide. Unfortunately, *IHTMLDocument3* doesn't inherit from the *IHTMLDocument2* interface, so you must use two separate pointers to access the methods of both interfaces.

Just as you did when you accessed the DHTML Object Model from within Visual Basic, you must wait until the WebBrowser's *DocumentComplete* event has fired before you access the *document* object. Implementing events when hosting the WebBrowser control in an MFC dialog–based application is easy. To implement the *DocumentComplete* event, open ClassWizard, and select the ID of the WebBrowser control from the Object IDs list box on the Message Maps tab, shown in Figure 8-9. If you haven't changed the default ID of the WebBrowser control, the ID will be *IDC_EXPLORER1*.

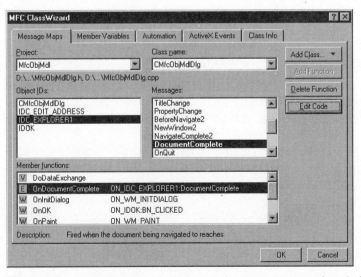

Figure 8-9. *MFC ClassWizard displaying the Message Maps tab with the ID of the WebBrowser control and the* DocumentComplete *event selected.*

Next select DocumentComplete from the Messages list box, which is on the right side of the dialog box. Click the Add Function button to create the event handler. The default name that ClassWizard specifies is *OnDocumentCompleteExplorer1*, but I think that name is rather long. I usually change it to *OnDocumentComplete*. You can change it if you like, or leave it as is. After you specify a name for this event handler, click the OK button. Click the Edit Code button to begin editing the code for this handler method.

In the *DocumentComplete* event's handler method, you're going to retrieve and store the pointer to the document. As in the Visual Basic example you created, you use the *Document* property to obtain this pointer. The MFC class that was created to wrap the WebBrowser control provides a method named *GetDocument* that makes retrieving the *Document* property easy. But unlike what you can do in Visual Basic, you can't call methods of the *document* object directly by using this returned pointer. The pointer that is returned from the *Document* property in Visual C++ applications is actually the pointer to the *IDispatch* interface of the document. You must query for the document interface, *IHTMLDocument2*, before you can directly access the methods and properties of the *document* object. The code that follows shows how the code for the *OnDocumentComplete* method should look.

> **NOTE**   If you are hosting the WebBrowser control by using ATL or standard C++, or if you are automating Internet Explorer, you can obtain a pointer to the *IDispatch* of the document by calling *IWebBrowser2*'s *get_Document* method.

```
void CMfcObjMdlDlg::OnDocumentComplete(LPDISPATCH pDisp, VARIANT FAR* URL)
{
    LPDISPATCH lpDispatch;
    lpDispatch = m_webBrowser.GetDocument();

    if (lpDispatch)
    {
        HRESULT hr = lpDispatch->QueryInterface(IID_IHTMLDocument2,
                                                (LPVOID*)&m_pHTMLDocument2);
        lpDispatch->Release();
        ASSERT(SUCCEEDED(hr));
    }
}
```

Each time you navigate to a new Web page, you should release the document pointer and set it to *NULL*. That way, you can check *m_pHTMLDocument2* to see whether the document has finished loading before you try to use the document pointer. If this pointer is *NULL*, the document hasn't finished loading. If this pointer isn't *NULL*, you should release the pointer and set it to *NULL* in an event handler for the WebBrowser's *BeforeNavigate2* event. Use ClassWizard like you did before to create this event handler. Name this handler method *OnBeforeNavigate2*. Then in this method, release the interface pointer and set it to *NULL*:

```
void CMfcObjMdlDlg::OnBeforeNavigate2(LPDISPATCH pDisp,
                                      VARIANT FAR* URL,
                                      VARIANT FAR* Flags,
                                      VARIANT FAR* TargetFrameName,
                                      VARIANT FAR* PostData,
                                      VARIANT FAR* Headers,
                                      BOOL FAR* Cancel)
{
    if (m_pHTMLDocument2)
    {
        m_pHTMLDocument2->Release();
        m_pHTMLDocument2 = NULL;
    }
}
```

You should also release this pointer when your application is closed. The best place to do this is in the destructor for the *CMfcObjMdlDlg* class. Create the destructor, and release the interface pointer if it isn't *NULL*:

```
CMfcObjMdlDlg::~CMfcObjMdlDlg()
{
    if (m_pHTMLDocument2)
        m_pHTMLDocument2->Release();
}
```

Now that you have a pointer to the *document* object, you're ready to access the data contained in the document and then change it.

Obtaining Data from a Web Page

To see how to retrieve data from the document, let's add the same functionality to MfcObjMdl that we added to the VbObjMdl example. First add a button that will be used to retrieve the inner HTML of the body of the document. Give this button an ID of *IDC_GET_BODY*, and change the caption of the button to *Get Body*. (You might have to resize the WebBrowser control to make room for this and other controls that you're going to add to the dialog.)

Implement a *BN_CLICKED* message handler for the Get Body button in the same way you would for any other button in MFC—by using ClassWizard. Accept the default name of *OnGetBody* for this handler method. In the *OnGetBody* method, you must first obtain a pointer to the *body* object and then retrieve its *innerHTML* property, which returns the inner HTML of the body. Then you can display the inner HTML in a message box. The code to implement the message handler is on the next page.

```
void CMfcObjMdlDlg::OnGetBody()
{
    if (!m_pHTMLDocument2)
        return;

    // Get the body element.
    //
    IHTMLElement* pBody;
    HRESULT hr = m_pHTMLDocument2->get_body(&pBody);

    ASSERT(SUCCEEDED(hr));

    // Get the inner HTML.
    //
    BSTR bstrHTML;
    pBody->get_innerHTML(&bstrHTML);
    pBody->Release();

    USES_CONVERSION;
    MessageBox(OLE2T(bstrHTML), _T("MfcObjMdl"));

    SysFreeString(bstrHTML);
}
```

In this code, we first retrieve a pointer to the body by using the *get_body* method of *IHTMLDocument2*. When *get_body* is called, the address of an *IHTMLElement* pointer is passed to the *get_body* method. You're probably wondering why the address of an *IHTMLBodyElement* pointer isn't passed to the *get_body* method. Although the *IHTMLBodyElement* interface does represent the body of the document, it doesn't inherit from *IHTMLElement*. The *get_body* method returns a pointer to the *IHTML-Element* interface, so an *IHTMLBodyElement* pointer can't be passed. It just won't compile. If you need to use functionality that is specific to the body, you can query the interface returned from *get_body* for the *IHTMLElement* pointer like so:

```
IHTMLBodyElement* pBodyElem;
HRESULT hr = pBody->QueryInterface(IID_IHTMLBodyElement,
                                   (LPVOID*)&pBodyElem);
```

After obtaining a pointer to the body of the document, we call the *get_innerHTML* method to retrieve the inner HTML of the body of the document. The *get_innerHTML* method returns a *BSTR* that contains the inner HTML. Next we use the *MessageBox* function to display the inner HTML. You can use the OLE2T macro to convert the *BSTR* to an *ANSI* character string. To use the OLE2T macro, you must include the afxconv.h file in the MfcObjMdlDlg.cpp file and include the USES_CONVERSION macro in the *OnGetBody* method. Finally, we release the *BSTR* by calling the *SysFreeString* Win32 API function.

That wasn't too hard, was it? Now you can implement the Get All HTML button that displays all the HTML for the document. Add this button to the dialog, and give it an ID of *IDC_GET_ALL_HTML*. Use ClassWizard to create a *BN_CLICKED* message handler named *OnGetAllHTML*. Add code to this message handler method to obtain a pointer to the document element. You can then retrieve and display the entire HTML for the document by using the *outerHTML* property. Here's the code to implement the *OnGetAllHTML* message handler method:

```
void CMfcObjMdlDlg::OnGetAllHtml()
{
    if (!m_pHTMLDocument2)
        return;

    IHTMLDocument3* pHTMLDoc3;
    HRESULT hr = m_pHTMLDocument2->QueryInterface(IID_IHTMLDocument3,
                                            (LPVOID*)&pHTMLDoc3);
    ASSERT(SUCCEEDED(hr));

    // Get the document element.
    //
    IHTMLElement* pDocElem;

    hr = pHTMLDoc3->get_documentElement(&pDocElem);
    pHTMLDoc3->Release();

    ASSERT(SUCCEEDED(hr));

    // Get the outer HTML.
    //
    BSTR bstrHTML;

    pDocElem->get_outerHTML(&bstrHTML);
    pDocElem->Release();

    USES_CONVERSION;
    MessageBox(OLE2T(bstrHTML), _T("MfcObjMdl"));

    SysFreeString(bstrHTML);
}
```

As in the Visual Basic sample, you use the *documentElement* property to retrieve a pointer to the document element. Because this property is a member of the new Internet Explorer 5 *IHTMLDocument3* interface, you must query the document for this interface before you can obtain a pointer to the document element. In the preceding code, we call the *get_documentElement* method to obtain a pointer to the document element. The *get_documentElement* method returns a pointer to an *IHTMLElement* in the same way that the *get_body* method did. You can use the pointer you have just retrieved to call *get_outerHTML* to retrieve the HTML for the entire page. Then you can display the entire HTML by using the *MessageBox* function.

Now it's time to compile and test your application. Navigate to a Web page, and click the Get All HTML button. A message box will be displayed that contains the entire HTML for the page.

Now that you know how to retrieve the HTML of the page in a Visual C++ application, go ahead and add the functionality to retrieve form data from your application. Before adding new controls to the dialog, copy the MfcObjMdl.htm file from the companion CD in the folder \Samples\Chap08\MfcObjMdl and place it in your application directory. Then change the initial navigation in the *OnInitDialog* method to navigate to this page instead of to the user's home page.

Here's the code to navigate to the MfcObjMdl.htm file in the current directory. This code obtains the name of the current directory by using the *GetCurrentDirectory* Win32 API function.

```
BOOL CMfcObjMdlDlg::OnInitDialog()
{
    ⋮
    ⋮
    // Get the length of the buffer for the current directory.
    //
    DWORD dwLen;
    dwLen = ::GetCurrentDirectory(0, NULL);

    // Create a new string, and get the current directory.
    //
    char* pszCurDir;
    pszCurDir = new char[dwLen + 1];
    ::GetCurrentDirectory(dwLen, szCurDir);

    // Format the string to add the HTML file to the end.
    //
    CString strURL;
    strURL.Format("%s\\MfcObjMdl.htm\n", pszCurDir);
    delete pszCurDir;

    // Navigate to MfcObjMdl.htm.
    //
    COleVariant vtEmpty;
    m_webBrowser.Navigate(strURL, &vtEmpty, &vtEmpty, &vtEmpty, &vtEmpty);

    return TRUE;   // Return TRUE unless you set the focus to a
                   // control.
}
```

Now add a list box and button to the dialog. Use ClassWizard to create a data member for the list box control named *m_lstFormData* of type *CListBox*. Also, on the Styles tab in the Properties dialog for the control, uncheck the Sort Property check box. Name the button *IDC_GET_FORM_DATA*, and change its caption to *Get Form Data*.

Compile your application again, and run it to make sure that it loads the MfcObj-Mdl.htm file. At this point, it should look similar to the application in Figure 8-10.

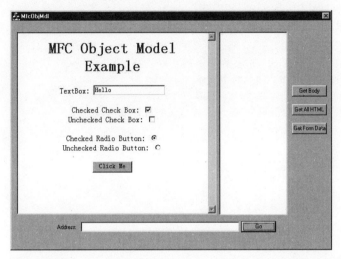

Figure 8-10. *MfcObjMdl dialog after adding list box and Get Form Data button.*

Next use ClassWizard to create a *BN_CLICKED* message handler for the Get Form Data button. Accept the default name of *OnGetFormData* for this message handler. In this message handler, use the *all* collection of the form to retrieve the data the user entered into the form (just as you did in the Visual Basic example). The following code implements this functionality. The *OnGetFormData* method shown in the code is quite long, so I broke it into steps. Each step is indicated by a comment in the code, and I'll explain each of these in turn. You can find the code on the companion CD in the folder \Samples\Chap08\MfcObjMdl.

```
void CMfcObjMdlDlg::OnGetFormData()
{
    // 1) Get a pointer to the forms collection.
    //
    IHTMLElementCollection* pElemColl;
    HRESULT hr = m_pHTMLDocument2->get_forms(&pElemColl);

    if (FAILED(hr))
        return;

    // 2) Get the first form in the collection.
    //
```

(continued)

```
LPDISPATCH lpDispatch = NULL;
COleVariant vtEmpty;
COleVariant vtIdx(0L, VT_I4);

hr = pElemColl->item(vtIdx, vtEmpty, &lpDispatch);
pElemColl->Release();

if (FAILED(hr) || !lpDispatch)
   return;

// 3) Get a pointer to the form itself - IHTMLFormElement.
// This pointer is actually a collection of all the
// input elements in the form.
//
IHTMLFormElement* pFormElem;

hr = lpDispatch->QueryInterface(IID_IHTMLFormElement,
                                (LPVOID*)&pFormElem);
lpDispatch->Release();

if (FAILED(hr))
   return;

// 4) Get and store the number of elements
// in the form.
//
long lLen = 0;
pFormElem->get_length(&lLen);

// 5) Loop through all the elements in the collection
// and retrieve the data entered by the user.
//
IHTMLElement* pElem;
IHTMLInputElement* pInpElem;
BSTR bstrData;
CString strFormData;

USES_CONVERSION;

m_lstFormData.ResetContent();

for (long i = 0; i < lLen; i++)
{
   // 6) Retrieve an item from the collection.
   //
```

```
vtIdx = i;
lpDispatch = NULL;
hr = pFormElem->item(vtIdx, vtEmpty, &lpDispatch);

if (FAILED(hr) || !lpDispatch)
  break;

// 7) Query for IHTMLElement.
//
hr = lpDispatch>QueryInterface(IID_IHTMLElement,
                               (LPVOID*)&pElem);
lpDispatch->Release();

if (FAILED(hr))
  break;

// 8) Get the ID of the element.
//
pElem->get_id(&bstrData);

strFormData = CString("ID: ") + CString(bstrData) + CString(", ");
SysFreeString(bstrData);

// 9) Query for IHTMLInputElement.
//
hr = pElem->QueryInterface(IID_IHTMLInputElement,
                           (LPVOID*)&pInpElem);
pElem->Release();

if (SUCCEEDED(hr))
{
   // 10) Get the type of the input element.
   //
   pInpElem->get_type(&bstrData);

   // If the type of the input element is checkbox
   // or radio button, retrieve the value of the
   // checked property. Otherwise, retrieve the
   // value of the input element.
   //
   if ( !_stricmp(OLE2T(bstrData), _T("checkbox"))
     || !_stricmp(OLE2T(bstrData), _T("radio")))
```

(continued)

339

```
        {
            // 11) Determine whether the checkbox or radio
            // button is checked.
            //
            VARIANT_BOOL vboolChecked;
            pInpElem->get_checked(&vboolChecked);

            if (vboolChecked == VARIANT_TRUE)
                strFormData += "Checked: True";
            else
                strFormData += "Checked: False";
        }
        else
        {
            // 12) Get the value and add it to the string.
            //
            SysFreeString(bstrData);

            pInpElem->get_value(&bstrData);
            strFormData += CString("Value: ") + bstrData;
        }

        SysFreeString(bstrData);
        pInpElem->Release();
    }

    m_lstFormData.AddString(strFormData);
    }

    pFormElem->Release();

    UpdateData(FALSE);
}
```

Here's how to work your way through the code. The following numbers correspond to the numbers in the code comments:

1. Get a pointer to the *forms* collection by calling the *get_forms* method of the *document* object.

2. Because at most one form exists on this Web page, the first form in the collection will be the form we need. If no forms exist on the page, the *item* method will return *S_OK*, but the pointer returned from the *lpDispatch* parameter will be *NULL*. That's why this *OnGetFormData* method checks *lpDispatch* and returns if *lpDispatch* is *NULL*.

3. Get a pointer to the form as represented by the *IHTMLFormElement* interface. To obtain this interface pointer, simply query *lpDispatch*. The returned interface pointer is actually a pointer to a collection of all the input elements on the page.

4. Get the number of elements in the collection by calling the *get_length* method.

5. Loop through all the elements in the collection, and retrieve the data entered by the user. In this loop, the ID of the element is retrieved. Also, if the type of the element is *checkbox* or *radio*, the state of the checkbox or radio button is retrieved. If the input element is something other than a checkbox or radio button, the value of the input element is retrieved.

6. Retrieve an item from the collection of input elements by using the *form* object's *item* method.

7. To retrieve the ID of the element, you must first have a pointer to an *IHTMLElement* because the *get_id* method that returns the ID of the element is a member of this interface. Therefore, query *lpDispatch* for this interface. Store the returned pointer in a local variable named *pElem*.

8. Call *get_id* to get the ID of the element. Add this ID to *strFormData*, which is the string that will be added to the list box.

9. Query *pElem* for *IHTMLInputElement,* because the *get_type, get_checked,* and *get_value* methods are members of the *IHTMLInputElement* interface that will be called in the remainder of this code.

10. Get the type of the input element by calling *get_type*. This type will be used to determine which text to add to *strFormData*. If the type of the input element is *checkbox* or *radio*, a string is added to *strFormData*, indicating whether the checkbox or radio button is checked. If the type of the input element isn't *checkbox* or *radio*, the value of the input element is added to *strFormData*.

11. If the type of the input element is *checkbox* or *radio*, use the *get_checked* method to determine the state of the checkbox or radio button. This method returns *VARIANT_TRUE* if either of these are checked or *VARIANT_FALSE* otherwise. If the checkbox or radio button is checked, add *"Checked: True"* to *strFormData* and *"Checked: False"* otherwise.

12. If the type of input element is something other than *checkbox* or *radio*, get the value of the input element by calling *get_value* and add this value to *strFormData*.

Dynamically Inserting Data into a Web Page Using VC++

Now that you've worked so hard to implement the *OnGetFormData* method, dynamically changing the data on a Web page will be easy. Following our original Visual Basic example, add a button that will allow you to enter HTML text to be appended to the Web page. Name this button *IDC_ADD_HTML*, and change its caption to *Add HTML*. When the user clicks the Add HTML button, a dialog for entering HTML or text will be displayed. When the user clicks the OK button in this dialog, the HTML or text that was entered will be added to the Web page.

Before you implement the *BN_CLICKED* message handler for the Add HTML button, you must create the dialog that will allow users to enter HTML or text. Create a new dialog resource in Visual C++ that contains a multiline edit box and an OK button. Then set the Want Return style in the Properties dialog for the edit box so that when the user presses the Enter key while typing text into the edit box, a carriage return will be inserted. And change the title of the dialog to *Add HTML*. The new dialog should look similar to the one shown in Figure 8-11.

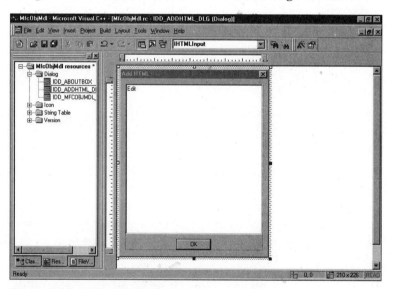

Figure 8-11. *Add HTML dialog.*

Now use ClassWizard to create a new dialog class for this dialog, and name this class *CHtmlDlg*. Also use ClassWizard to associate a *CString* variable with the edit box. Name this variable *m_strHTML*.

Now go back to the MfcObjMdl dialog, and use ClassWizard to implement a message handler for the *BN_CLICKED* message of the Add HTML button. Name this method *OnAddHtml*. In this method, create a new instance of the Add HTML dialog class, and then call its *DoModal* method to display it as a modal dialog. (Remember to include the header file for this dialog.) When the *DoModal* method returns, if the user entered HTML into the edit box and clicked the OK button, add the HTML to the end of the Web page by using the *insertAdjacentHTML* method. Here's the code to implement the *OnAddHtml* method:

```
void CMfcObjMdlDlg::OnAddHtml()
{
    CHtmlDlg dlgHTML;

    if (dlgHTML.DoModal() == IDOK)
    {
        if (!dlgHTML.m_strHTML.IsEmpty())
        {
            // Get the body element from the document.
            //
            IHTMLElement* pBody;
            HRESULT hr = m_pHTMLDocument2->get_body(&pBody);

            if (FAILED(hr))
                return;

            // Insert the HTML entered at the end of
            // the Web page.
            //
            pBody->insertAdjacentHTML(L"BeforeEnd",
                                  dlgHTML.m_strHTML.AllocSysString());
            pBody->Release();
        }
    }
}
```

This code should look familiar to you because you have seen most of it in the section on obtaining data from a Web page. After the user clicks the OK button, if HTML or text was entered we retrieve the body element from the *document* object using the *get_body* method. Then we call the *insertAdjacentHTML* method to insert the HTML right before the end of the body of the document.

Now compile and test your application. Invoke the Add HTML dialog, and enter some HTML or text. When you click the OK button, the HTML or text you entered will be added to the end of the Web page.

Hang in there, we're almost finished! To completely implement this example, you just need to add the controls and code so that you can change the contents of the textbox element on the MfcObjMdl.htm Web page. Add a new edit box and button to the dialog. The dialog should look similar to the one shown in Figure 8-12. Use ClassWizard to associate a *CString* variable with the edit box, and name this variable *m_strNewText*. Also give the button an ID of *IDC_CHANGE_TEXT1*, and change its caption to *Change Text1*.

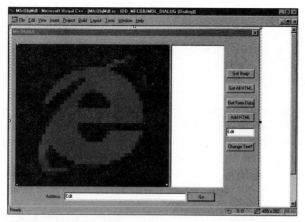

Figure 8-12. *MfcObjMdl dialog after adding the edit box and Change Text1 button.*

Next use ClassWizard to create a *BN_CLICKED* message handler for the Change Text1 button. Name this handler method *OnChangeText1*. In this method, you will simply change the value of the Web page textbox that has the ID *Text1*. Here's the code to implement the *OnChangeText1* method. The code can also be found on the companion CD in the folder \Samples\Chap08\MfcObjMdl.

```
void CMfcObjMdlDlg::OnChangeText1()
{
    UpdateData();

    if (m_strNewText.IsEmpty())
        return;

    // 1) Get a pointer to the forms collection.
    //
    IHTMLElementCollection* pElemColl;
    HRESULT hr = m_pHTMLDocument2->get_forms(&pElemColl);

    if (FAILED(hr))
        return;

    // 2) Get the first form in the collection.
    //
    LPDISPATCH lpDispatch = NULL;
    COleVariant vtEmpty;
    COleVariant vtIdx(0L, VT_I4);

    hr = pElemColl->item(vtIdx, vtEmpty, &lpDispatch);
    pElemColl->Release();
```

```
    if (FAILED(hr) || !lpDispatch)
        return;

    // 3) Get a pointer to the form--IHTMLFormElement.
    // This pointer is actually a pointer to a collection of all the
    // input elements on the form.
    //
    IHTMLFormElement* pFormElem;

    hr = lpDispatch->QueryInterface(IID_IHTMLFormElement,
                                    (LPVOID*)&pFormElem);
    lpDispatch->Release();

    if (FAILED(hr))
        return;

    // 4) Retrieve an item from the collection.
    //
    COleVariant vtName(_T("Text1"));

    lpDispatch = NULL;

    hr = pFormElem->item(vtName, vtEmpty, &lpDispatch);
    pFormElem->Release();

    if (FAILED(hr) || !lpDispatch)
        return;

    // 5) Query for the IHTMLInputElement so that
    // its value can be changed.
    //
    IHTMLInputElement* pInpElem;

    hr = lpDispatch->QueryInterface(IID_IHTMLInputElement,
                                    (LPVOID*)&pInpElem);
    lpDispatch->Release();


    if (FAILED(hr))
        return;

    // 6) Set the value of the textbox
    // to the text entered into the edit box.
    //
    pInpElem->put_value(m_strNewText.AllocSysString());
    pInpElem->Release();
}
```

You've already seen most of this code, so I'll explain only the step that is different—step 6. In this step, we call the *put_value* method of the input element object to change the contents of the textbox on the Web page to what was entered into the edit box on the MfcObjMdl dialog.

Now compile and test your application. Change the text in the text box on the Web page to make sure that it works. That wasn't too painful, was it? By now, you can see the power of the DHTML Object Model. But wait, there's more! In Chapter 7, you learned how to sink events when you are hosting the WebBrowser control or automating Internet Explorer. The objects in the DHTML Object Model also fire events, and you can write event handlers for them in your applications. That's the topic of the next section.

HANDLING DHTML OBJECT EVENTS

Because you already know how to sink events when hosting the WebBrowser control or when automating Internet Explorer, sinking events for the objects in the DHTML Object Model should be a breeze. Almost every element on a Web page fires events. In fact, the DHTML Object Model fires far too many events to explain them all in this chapter. So instead of discussing every event that is fired, I'll just show you how to sink the events.

Sinking Events for DHTML Objects in Visual Basic

To see how easily you can sink events for HTML element objects in Visual Basic applications, let's update the VbObjMdl example to sink events for two of the objects in the object model—the *document* object and the Click Me button on the VbObjMdl.htm Web page. (All the example code to be mentioned in this section can be found on the companion CD in the folder \Samples\Chap08\VbObjMdl.)

Creating the event sink for the document involves two simple steps. The first step is to change the declaration of the *WebDoc* variable to include the *WithEvents* keyword:

```
Dim WithEvents WebDoc As HTMLDocument
```

As you learned in Chapter 7, the *WithEvents* keyword tells Visual Basic that an object is able to sink events. The event sink is connected to the event source when you set *WebDoc* equal to the *document* object in the event handler for the *DocumentComplete* event.

The second step is to choose which event or events you want to handle from the Procedures drop-down list in the upper right-hand corner of the Visual Basic IDE. For this simple example, choose the *ondblclick* event of the *WebDoc*, which is fired whenever the user double-clicks anywhere in the document. When the *ondblclick* event is fired, a message box should appear that shows the user the coordinates of the document that was double-clicked. You can obtain these coordinates by using the *event* object. (Remember this object from way back in Chapter 3?) Here's the code to implement the event handler for the *ondblclick* event:

```
Private Function WebDoc_ondblclick() As Boolean
    On Error Resume Next

    MsgBox "X: " & WebDoc.parentWindow.event.clientX _
        & " Y: " & WebDoc.parentWindow.event.clientY
End Function
```

Notice that the code must use the *parentWindow* property of the *document* object to get the parent *window* object before accessing the *event* object. Remember that the *event* property of the *window* object is the one that provides access to the *event* object. The *event* object has two properties of interest in this event handler: *clientX* and *clientY*. These properties return the *x*-coordinate and the *y*-coordinate of the location of the mouse pointer when this event was fired. These coordinates are relative to the top of the client area of the window.

Sinking events for the Click Me button is a little more complicated. First you must declare a new variable of type *HTMLInputElement*. Don't forget to specify the *WithEvents* keyword:

```
Dim WithEvents btnClickMe As HTMLInputElement
```

Next, in the event handler for the *DocumentComplete* event, you must set the *btnClickMe* variable equal to the input element object for the Click Me button. This is where the event sink for the *btnClickMe* variable is connected to the event source. Here's how the *DocumentComplete* event handler for the *WebBrowser1* sets the *btnClickMe* variable:

```
Private Sub WebBrowser1_DocumentComplete(ByVal pDisp As Object, _
                                    URL As Variant)

    On Error Resume Next
    Set WebDoc = WebBrowser1.Document

    Set btnClickMe = WebDoc.Forms(0).Item("Btn1")
End Sub
```

Now all you have to do is choose which events you want to handle. For this simple example, just handle the *onclick* event and display a message box that tells the user that the button was clicked. The following code implements the event handler for the *onclick* event in your application:

```
Private Function btnClickMe_onclick() As Boolean
    MsgBox "The Click Me Button was Clicked!!"
End Function
```

Sinking Events for DHTML Objects in Visual C++

Sinking events for objects in the DHTML Object Model from your Visual C++ applications involves a little extra code, but it's really not that much trouble. In this section, we'll update the MfcObjMdl example to sink events for the *document* object. (To put your knowledge to the test, I'll let you update the example to sink events for the Click Me button and handle its *onclick* event on your own.)

To set up the event sink for the *document* object, you must first create an event sink class. (Remember the MfcIEEvtSpy example from Chapter 7? This event sink class is similar to the *CIE5Events* class in the MfcIEEvtSpy example.) Create a new class named *CHTMLDocEvents*. Then add the code to set up the event sink, and create a handler method for the *ondblclick* event. (If you're a little rusty at event sinking, you might want to review the section in Chapter 7 titled "Sinking Events in MFC." It starts on page 281.)

Now I'll outline the changes you should make to the HTMLDocEvents.h header file. First create a forward declaration for the *CMfcObjMdlDlg* class. You need this forward declaration so that you can create a data member to hold a pointer to the parent class that will be passed into the constructor. Here is the code for the forward declaration:

```
class CMfcObjMdlDlg;
```

Change the declaration of the constructor to accept a pointer to the parent class. This class is named *CHTMLDocEvents* and its parent class is *CMfcObjMdlDlg*.

```
CHTMLDocEvents(CMfcObjMdlDlg* pParent = NULL);
```

Add a protected data member to the class to hold the pointer to the parent class that is passed to the constructor.

```
protected:
    CMfcObjMdlDlg* m_pParent;
```

Now declare a method that will handle the *ondblclick* event.

```
VARIANT_BOOL OnDblClick ();
```

Finally, declare the dispatch map that will be used to specify the events you want to handle and their associated event handlers.

```
DECLARE_DISPATCH_MAP()
```

OK, we're finished making changes to the HTMLDocEvents.h header file. Next we have to make changes to the HTMLDocEvents.cpp implementation file. First include the MfcObjMdlDlg.h and mshtmdid.h header files in HTMLDocEvents.cpp. The mshtmdid.h header file defines the dispatch IDs that you will use when initializing the dispatch map.

Next change the constructor for the *CHTMLDocEvents* class to accept and store a pointer to the parent. You must also call *EnableAutomation*. This call will be needed by the parent class when the event sink is connected to the event source.

```
CHTMLDocEvents::CHTMLDocEvents(CMfcObjMdlDlg* pParent /* = NULL */)
    : m_pParent(pParent)
{
    EnableAutomation();  // Needed in order to sink events.
}
```

Now initialize the dispatch map, and specify the events you want to handle. The DISP_FUNCTION_ID macro specifies the event you want to handle and the method to call when this event is fired. In this case, you want the *OnDblClick* method to be called when the document fires the *ondblclick* event. The dispatch ID for the *ondblclick* event is *DISPID_HTMLDOCUMENTEVENTS_ONDBLCLICK*, which is defined in mshtmdid.h:

```
BEGIN_DISPATCH_MAP(CHTMLDocEvents, CCmdTarget)
    DISP_FUNCTION_ID(CHTMLDocEvents, "ondblclick",
                    DISPID_HTMLDOCUMENTEVENTS_ONDBLCLICK,
                    OnDblClick, VT_EMPTY, VTS_NONE)
END_DISPATCH_MAP()
```

Implement the *OnDblClick* event handler to obtain the *event* object, and display a message box to show the client coordinates of the mouse pointer when the *ondblclick* event was fired. The following code shows why you need a pointer to the parent object. This pointer gives you access to the HTML document pointer stored in the parent. (For this code to work correctly, you'll have to specify that *CHTMLDocEvents* is a friend of *CMfcObjMdlDlg* in the class declaration of *CMfcObjMdlDlg*.)

```
VARIANT_BOOL CHTMLDocEvents::OnDblClick()
{
    if (!m_pParent || !m_pParent->m_pHTMLDocument2)
        return VARIANT_TRUE;

    IHTMLWindow2* pParentWindow;
    IHTMLDocument2* pDocument = m_pParent->m_pHTMLDocument2;

    HRESULT hr = pDocument->get_parentWindow(&pParentWindow);

    if (SUCCEEDED(hr))
    {
        IHTMLEventObj* pEvtObj;

        hr = pParentWindow->get_event(&pEvtObj);
        pParentWindow->Release();
```

(continued)

```
        if (SUCCEEDED(hr))
        {
            long clientX = 0L, clientY = 0L;

            pEvtObj->get_clientX(&clientX);
            pEvtObj->get_clientY(&clientY);
            pEvtObj->Release();

            CString strText;
            strText.Format("X: %ld Y: %ld", clientX, clientY);

            ::MessageBox(NULL, strText, _T("MfcObjMdl"), MB_OK);
        }
    }

    return VARIANT_TRUE;
}
```

OK, now that we've finished changing the HTMLDocEvents.cpp implementation file, the last task is to make a few changes to *CMfcObjMdlDlg* to set up the event sink. Include the HTMLDocEvents.h header file in the MfcObjMdlDlg.h header file. And make the *CHTMLDocEvents* class a friend of the *CMfcObjMdlDlg* class by placing the following code within the class definition of *CMfcObjMdlDlg*:

```
friend class CHTMLDocEvents;
```

Next declare a protected data member of type *CHTMLDocEvents*. This data member will be used when establishing the event sink. Also, declare a *DWORD* variable that will be used when disconnecting the event sink:

```
protected:
    CHTMLDocEvents* m_pHTMLDocEvents;
    DWORD m_dwCookie;
```

Now, in the constructor for *CMfcObjMdlDlg*, initialize the cookie data member and create a new instance of the *CHTMLDocEvents* class. The constructor should now look like this:

```
CMfcObjMdlDlg::CMfcObjMdlDlg(CWnd* pParent /*=NULL*/)
    : CDialog(CMfcObjMdlDlg::IDD, pParent),
      m_pHTMLDocument2(NULL),
      m_dwCookie(0L)
{
    //{{AFX_DATA_INIT(CMfcObjMdlDlg)
    m_strAddress = _T("");
    m_strNewText = _T("");
    //}}AFX_DATA_INIT
    // Note that LoadIcon does not require a subsequent DestroyIcon
    // in Win32.
```

```
m_hIcon = AfxGetApp()->LoadIcon(IDR_MAINFRAME);

m_pHTMLDocEvents = new CHTMLDocEvents(this);
}
```

Now you're ready to connect the event sink to the document. In the *OnDocument-Complete* event handler, call *AfxConnectionAdvise* to connect the event sink. This process is almost exactly the same as the process you used to set up the event sink when automating Internet Explorer in Chapter 7. (Be sure to include the afxconv.h header file in MfcObjMdlDlg.cpp. This header file is needed for the *AfxConnection-Advise* function.)

```
// Connect the event sink for the document.
//
AfxConnectionAdvise(m_pHTMLDocument2,
                    DIID_HTMLDocumentEvents2,
                    m_pHTMLDocEvents->GetInterface(&IID_IUnknown),
                    TRUE, &m_dwCookie);
```

Because the document is destroyed when the user navigates to a new Web page or closes the application, disconnecting the event sink is recommended, although it isn't absolutely necessary. Disconnecting the event sink ensures that all interfaces are decremented and all objects are deleted cleanly. To disconnect the event sink, place a call to *AfxConnectionUnadvise* before the call to *AfxConnectionAdvise* in the event handler for *DocumentComplete*. You should disconnect the event sink only if it has been previously established. After adding the call to *AfxConnectionUnadvise*, your *OnDocumentComplete* method should look like this:

```
void CMfcObjMdlDlg::OnDocumentComplete(LPDISPATCH pDisp, VARIANT FAR* URL)
{
    LPDISPATCH lpDispatch;
    lpDispatch = m_webBrowser.GetDocument();

    if (lpDispatch)
    {
        HRESULT hr = lpDispatch->QueryInterface(IID_IHTMLDocument2,
                                                (LPVOID*)&m_pHTMLDocument2);

        lpDispatch->Release();

        ASSERT(SUCCEEDED(hr));

        // Disconnect the event sink, if needed.
        //
        if (m_pHTMLDocEvents)
        {
            if (m_dwCookie)
```

(continued)

```
        {
            AfxConnectionUnadvise(m_pHTMLDocument2,
                            DIID_HTMLDocumentEvents2,
                    m_pHTMLDocEvents->GetInterface(&IID_IUnknown),
                            TRUE, m_dwCookie);
            m_dwCookie = 0L;
        }
    }

    // Connect the event sink for the document.
    //
    AfxConnectionAdvise(m_pHTMLDocument2,
                    DIID_HTMLDocumentEvents2,
                    m_pHTMLDocEvents->GetInterface(&IID_IUnknown),
                    TRUE, &m_dwCookie);
    }
}
```

To disconnect the event sink when the application is closed, override the *On-Cancel* method of *CDialog* and call *AfxConnectionUnadvise*, like this:

```
void CMfcObjMdlDlg::OnCancel()
{
    if (m_pHTMLDocEvents)
    {
        // Disconnect the event sink.
        //
        if (m_dwCookie)
        {
            AfxConnectionUnadvise(m_pHTMLDocument2,
                            DIID_HTMLDocumentEvents2,
                        m_pHTMLDocEvents->GetInterface(&IID_IUnknown),
                            TRUE, m_dwCookie);
        }
    }

    CDialog::OnCancel();
}
```

You also need to delete the pointer to *CHTMLDocEvents*. You can safely do this in the destructor for the *CMfcObjMdlDlg* class. After you add the code to delete this pointer, the destructor should look like the following:

```
CMfcObjMdlDlg::~CMfcObjMdlDlg()
{
    if (m_pHTMLDocument2)
        m_pHTMLDocument2->Release();

    delete m_pHTMLDocEvents;
}
```

Now compile and test your application. When a Web page is loaded, double-click in the WebBrowser window. A dialog box should appear that indicates the coordinates of the mouse pointer when this event was fired. Navigate to a new Web page, and try it again.

The examples in this section are pretty basic. Now that you know how to sink events in Visual Basic and Visual C++, the possibilities are endless. For example, you might want to sink events with the *form* object so that your application can validate data entered by the user before it's submitted to your server. You can perform hundreds of tasks with the events fired by the objects in the DHTML Object Model. You're bound only by the limits of your imagination.

ACCESSING THE DHTML OBJECT MODEL FROM A VISUAL BASIC ACTIVEX CONTROL

After discovering the power of the DHTML Object Model, you probably won't be surprised that you can also access this functionality from ActiveX controls on a Web page. In Chapter 6, I showed you how to access the *IWebBrowser2* interface of Internet Explorer from Visual C++ ActiveX controls. Through this interface, you can access the *document* object by using the WebBrowser's *Document* property. And once you have a pointer to the document, you can access any object in the object model, including the *window* object and all the HTML elements on the page. You can also sink events for the objects in the object model from your applications.

Because you already know how to obtain a pointer to the *IWebBrowser2* interface (discussed in Chapter 6), and you also know how to access the objects in the DHTML Object Model, I won't bother showing you how to access the DHTML Object Model from the Visual C++ ActiveX controls again. I'll leave that up to you. I will show you how to access the objects in the object model from a Visual Basic ActiveX control. As you've probably already guessed, you can accomplish this task easily. To see how, we're going to check out a really cool example. This example ActiveX control is named PageController, and it's shown in Figure 8-13 on the next page.

To run PageController, first use Regsvr32.exe to register the SampleControl.ocx file, which is included on the companion CD in the following folder: \Samples\ Chap08\PageController. Next open the PageController.htm file (which is also in the \PageController folder) in Internet Explorer.

PageController provides a lot of functionality. First of all, it allows you to view all the HTML tags on the Web page. When you click the Walk The DOM! button, PageController builds a tree of all the HTML tags on the page and displays this tree in the left-hand tree-view window. When you click a branch in the tree, PageController highlights the section of the Web page that is associated with that HTML tag. For example, if you click the <H1> tag in the tree-view, the heading that reads "ActiveX Control Sample—Page Controller" is highlighted.

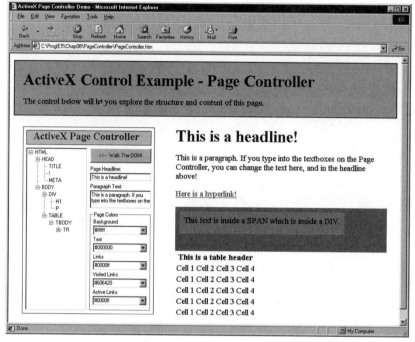

Figure 8-13. *PageController.*

Besides being able to walk the object model, after you've clicked the Walk The DOM! button you can change various elements on the Web page including the headline, paragraph text, and different page colors. But wait—there's more! PageController also sinks events for the *document* object. When you click on an area in the document after you click the Walk The DOM button, a message box is displayed that tells you the HTML tag and ID that are associated with the area that you clicked.

> **NOTE**   This message box won't be displayed if you click the PageController control. Remember event bubbling from Chapter 3? Well, PageController catches events that bubble up to the document level. ActiveX controls written in Visual Basic don't bubble events to the document, so you won't see an event fired when you click the control.

The PageController control consists of a lot of Visual Basic code, much of which we've already covered. So I won't bore you by discussing it all again. Instead, I want to show you how to do something we haven't talked about yet—accessing the object model from an ActiveX control. You already know how to do this if you are hosting the WebBrowser control or automating Internet Explorer.

You start by obtaining a pointer to the *document* object. Retrieving this pointer from an ActiveX control is a little different, but still quite easy. Just create a variable of type *HTMLDocument*, and set it equal to the *Parent* property of the Visual Basic

UserControl object. That's exactly what PageController does. It first defines an *HTML-Document* variable. Then, when you click the Walk The DOM! button, PageController sets this variable equal to *UserControl.Parent*. Here's the code to do this, minus some additional code that actually walks the object model:

```
Private WithEvents myDoc As HTMLDocument

Private Sub btnDomWalker_Click()
    ' Set a reference to the document object.
    Set myDoc = UserControl.Parent
End Sub
```

That's all there is to it. Now the *myDoc* variable refers to the *document* object of the Web page. You'll notice that this code uses the *WithEvents* keyword when defining the *myDoc* variable so that the application can sink events for the *document* object.

The previous code is the most important piece of this example. You must obtain a reference to the *document* object before you can access or change any other element in the object model. The example code is located on the companion CD in the folder \Samples\Chap08\PageController. Take a few moments to look over the code for PageController. Most of this code should be familiar to you because you've already read about it in this chapter.

WHAT'S NEXT?

At this point, you can host the WebBrowser control, automate Internet Explorer, sink events, and access the DHTML Object Model from your applications. In the next chapter, you'll learn about the coolest functionality that the WebBrowser control provides—advanced hosting interfaces. You'll use this advanced functionality to customize user interface elements of the WebBrowser control and to customize users' navigation experience. Hold on, here we go!

Chapter 9

Advanced
Hosting Interfaces

During the time that I was a member of the Internet Client Development group of Microsoft Developer Support, I had the chance to work with customers who were creating some really cool applications using the WebBrowser control. Often these people wanted to know how to manage certain aspects of the WebBrowser control, such as its user interface, as well as learn what the WebBrowser could download and execute.

For example, one customer was struggling with an application she had written that was hosting the WebBrowser control. When her users right-clicked in the WebBrowser window and selected View Source from the context menu, they could view her source code. She, however, wanted to hide her source code from them. Our customer also wanted her users to use only her application for Internet and intranet browsing. But when her users pressed Ctrl-O, they could display the Open dialog box, type in a URL, and press Enter to invoke a new instance of the Microsoft Internet Explorer window.

Taking charge of the WebBrowser control's user interface, extending the DHTML Object Model, and controlling what the WebBrowser control can download and execute are all tasks that Internet Explorer's advanced hosting interfaces can manage for you. This chapter explains these advanced hosting interfaces, including *IDocHostUIHandler*, *ICustomDoc*, and *IDocHostShowUI*, and explains how to use a special ambient property, *DISPID_AMBIENT_DLCONTROL*, to control what users can download and execute when hosting the WebBrowser control. The information you learn in this chapter will give you the appropriate level of control to solve problems like the one I just described, as well as many others.

Unfortunately, the full ability to control tasks is available to you only if you are hosting the WebBrowser control in a Microsoft Visual C++ application, but you can integrate a subset of this functionality into Microsoft Visual Basic applications indirectly by using a Visual C++ COM object named *WBCustomizer*. In this chapter, you'll learn about *WBCustomizer*, which I created for customers, and see how to integrate its functionality into Visual Basic applications. Microsoft doesn't support this COM object, but you can create a similar COM object or update the one I created to accomplish whatever you want. First let's take a look at the advanced hosting interfaces.

IDocHostUIHandler

If you want to have power over user interface features such as menus, toolbars, scrollbars, context menus, and 3-D borders in an application that is hosting the WebBrowser control, simply implement the *IDocHostUIHandler* interface. Each time the WebBrowser control loads a new Web page, the MSHTML component calls the *QueryInterface* method of its host and asks for the *IDocHostUIHandler* interface.

NOTE   Remember that the WebBrowser control hosts the MSHTML component, as you learned in Chapter 6.

During certain points in the execution of your application, MSHTML will call methods of your *IDocHostUIHandler* implementation to enable you to control some of the WebBrowser control's user interface features. Table 9-1 lists all the *IDocHostUIHandler* methods, some of which correspond to methods of standard COM interfaces. Your implementation of these methods is called from their default implementations in the MSHTML component, which is hosted in the WebBrowser control.

TABLE 9-1
METHODS OF THE *IDocHostUIHandler* INTERFACE

Methods	Description
EnableModeless	Called from the MSHTML implementation of *IOleInPlaceActiveObject::EnableModeless*. This method enables or disables modeless dialog boxes when the container creates or destroys a modal dialog box.
FilterDataObject	Called on the host application by MSHTML to allow the host to replace MSHTML's data object. This method allows the host to block certain clipboard formats or support additional clipboard formats.

Methods	*Description*
GetDropTarget	Called by MSHTML when it is being used as a drop target to allow the host to supply an alternative implementation of the *IDropTarget* interface.
GetExternal	Called by MSHTML to obtain the host's *IDispatch* interface. Internet Explorer calls this method when script on a Web page attempts to access methods or properties of the hosting application. (More on this shortly.)
GetHostInfo	Called by MSHTML to retrieve the user interface capabilities of the WebBrowser host application.
GetOptionKeyPath	Returns the Registry key under which MSHTML stores user preferences.
HideUI	Called when MSHTML removes its menus and toolbars.
OnDocWindowActivate	Called from the MSHTML implementation of *IOleInPlaceActiveObject::OnDocWindowActivate* when the document window is being activated or deactivated.
OnFrameWindowActivate	Called from the MSHTML implementation of *IOleInPlaceActiveObject::OnFrameWindowActivate* when the top-level frame window is being activated or deactivated.
ResizeBorder	Called from the MSHTML implementation of *IOleInPlaceActiveObject::ResizeBorder* when the border is being resized.
ShowContextMenu	Called when MSHTML is about to show its context menu. You can cancel the context menu or show your own, as you'll see shortly.
ShowUI	Allows the host application to replace MSHTML menus and toolbars, which are typically displayed only if you are hosting the MSHTML component directly.
TranslateAccelerator	Called from the MSHTML implementation of *IOleInPlaceActiveObject::TranslateAccelerator* or *IOleControlSite::TranslateAccelerator* when the user presses an accelerator key or key combination, such as Backspace, Ctrl-F, or F1, while focus is set to the HTML document window.
TranslateUrl	Called by MSHTML to give the host an opportunity to modify the URL to be loaded. Unless you are hosting the MSHTML component directly, this method might not be useful to you when you are hosting the WebBrowser control. When hosting the WebBrowser, you can use the *BeforeNavigate2* event, as you did in Chapter 7.
UpdateUI	Called by MSHTML to notify the host that the command state has changed.

Let's take a look at the methods I've found to be the most important to customers: *GetHostInfo*, *ShowContextMenu*, *TranslateAccelerator*, and *GetExternal*. I'll discuss *GetExternal* in the context of extending the DHTML Object Model.

GetHostInfo

The *GetHostInfo* method is called whenever a new Web page is loaded. *GetHostInfo* is the primary method used to manage the user interface of the WebBrowser control. It receives a pointer to a *DOCHOSTUIINFO* structure, which has the following definition as declared in the mshtmhst.h header file:

```
typedef struct _DOCHOSTUIINFO
    {
    ULONG cbSize;
    DWORD dwFlags;
    DWORD dwDoubleClick;
    OLECHAR __RPC_FAR *pchHostCss;
    OLECHAR __RPC_FAR *pchHostNS;
    }   DOCHOSTUIINFO;
```

You must first set the first data member of the *DOCHOSTUIINFO* structure, *cbSize*, to the size of the structure. Then, to control the user interface, fill in the second data member, *dwFlags*, with certain flags that specify the hosting application's user interface capabilities. These flags enable and disable the 3-D border, scrollbars, script, and a lot more. The following *DOCHOSTUIFLAG* enumeration defines the flags that can be used to specify which user interface features to enable or disable. Table 9-2 also describes these flags.

```
typedef
enum tagDOCHOSTUIFLAG
    {   DOCHOSTUIFLAG_DIALOG   = 0x1,
    DOCHOSTUIFLAG_DISABLE_HELP_MENU   = 0x2,
    DOCHOSTUIFLAG_NO3DBORDER   = 0x4,
    DOCHOSTUIFLAG_SCROLL_NO   = 0x8,
    DOCHOSTUIFLAG_DISABLE_SCRIPT_INACTIVE   = 0x10,
    DOCHOSTUIFLAG_OPENNEWWIN   = 0x20,
    DOCHOSTUIFLAG_DISABLE_OFFSCREEN   = 0x40,
    DOCHOSTUIFLAG_FLAT_SCROLLBAR   = 0x80,
    DOCHOSTUIFLAG_DIV_BLOCKDEFAULT   = 0x100,
    DOCHOSTUIFLAG_ACTIVATE_CLIENTHIT_ONLY   = 0x200,
    DOCHOSTUIFLAG_OVERRIDEBEHAVIORFACTORY   = 0x400,
    DOCHOSTUIFLAG_CODEPAGELINKEDFONTS   = 0x800,
    DOCHOSTUIFLAG_URL_ENCODING_DISABLE_UTF8   = 0x1000,
    DOCHOSTUIFLAG_URL_ENCODING_ENABLE_UTF8   = 0x2000
    }   DOCHOSTUIFLAG;
```

TABLE 9-2
FLAGS DEFINED IN THE *DOCHOSTUIFLAG* ENUMERATION

Value	*Description*
DOCHOSTUIFLAG_DIALOG	The MSHTML component disables text selection, enabling the application that is hosting the WebBrowser control to act like a dialog.
DOCHOSTUIFLAG_DISABLE_HELP_MENU	The MSHTML component will not add the Help menu item to the container's menu.
DOCHOSTUIFLAG_NO3DBORDER	MSHTML will not use 3-D borders.
DOCHOSTUIFLAG_SCROLL_NO	MSHTML will not use scrollbars.
DOCHOSTUIFLAG_DISABLE_SCRIPT_INACTIVE	MSHTML does not execute any script when loading pages.
DOCHOSTUIFLAG_OPENNEWWIN	MSHTML opens a Web page in a new window when a link is clicked rather than loading it into the same browser window.
DOCHOSTUIFLAG_DISABLE_OFFSCREEN	This flag has not been implemented.
DOCHOSTUIFLAG_FLAT_SCROLLBAR	The document will have flat scrollbars instead of 3-D scrollbars.
DOCHOSTUIFLAG_DIV_BLOCKDEFAULT	MSHTML inserts <DIV> tags if a return is entered in edit mode. Without this flag, the <P> tag is used.
DOCHOSTUIFLAG_ACTIVATE_CLIENTHIT_ONLY	MSHTML becomes UI-active only if the mouse is clicked on the client area of the window. It will not become UI-active if the mouse is clicked on a nonclient area such as a scrollbar.
DOCHOSTUIFLAG_OVERRIDEBEHAVIORFACTORY	MSHTML asks the host application before a behavior is obtained from a URL specified on the page.
DOCHOSTUIFLAG_CODEPAGELINKEDFONTS	The *CODEPAGELINKEDFONTS* flag provides font selection capability for Microsoft Outlook Express. If this flag is enabled, the displayed characters are inspected to determine whether the current font supports the code page. (This flag assumes that the user is using Microsoft Outlook Express 4 and Internet Explorer 5.)

(continued)

FLAGS DEFINED IN THE *DOCHOSTUIFLAG* ENUMERATION *continued*

Value	Description
DOCHOSTUIFLAG_URL_ENCODING_DISABLE_UTF8	The *DISABLE_UTF8* flag controls how non-native URLs are transmitted over the Internet. Non-native URLs contain characters that are outside the multibyte encoding of the URL. If this flag is set, the URL is sent to the server without using UTF-8 encoding.
DOCHOSTUIFLAG_URL_ENCODING_ENABLE_UTF8	The *ENABLE_UTF8* flag controls how non-native URLs are transmitted over the Internet. Non-native URLs contain characters that are outside the multibyte encoding of the URL. If this flag is set, URLs are sent to the server using UTF-8 encoding.

The third data member of the *DOCHOSTUIINFO* structure, *dwDoubleClick*, indicates which action should occur in response to a double-click event. The values that you can specify for this data member are contained in the *DOCHOSTUIDBLCLK* enumeration, as shown here and described in Table 9-3:

```
typedef enum tagDOCHOSTUIDBLCLK {
    DOCHOSTUIDBLCLK_DEFAULT          = 0,
    DOCHOSTUIDBLCLK_SHOWPROPERTIES   = 1,
    DOCHOSTUIDBLCLK_SHOWCODE         = 2
} DOCHOSTUIDBLCLK ;
```

TABLE 9-3
FLAGS DEFINED IN THE *DOCHOSTUIDBLCLK* ENUMERATION

Value	Description
DOCHOSTUIDBLCLK_DEFAULT	Performs the default action
DOCHOSTUIDBLCLK_SHOWPROPERTIES	Shows the item's properties
DOCHOSTUIDBLCLK_SHOWCODE	Shows the page's source

The *DOCHOSTUIINFO* structure's final two data members are *pcbHostCss* and *pcbHostNS*. The *pcbHostCss* data member allows the host application to supply rules for cascading style sheets (CSS) that will affect the page contained in the WebBrowser. The CSS rules then get filtered down through the CSS inheritance chain on the page depending on what the page says is allowed to be overridden. The *pcbHostNS* data member allows the host to supply a namespace declaration for custom tags on the

Web page. (For more information about these two data members, refer to the MSDN Online Web Workshop.)

Now that you understand the *DOCHOSTUIINFO* structure's data members, look at the following code. It shows a typical implementation of the *GetHostInfo* method:

```
STDMETHOD(GetHostInfo)(DOCHOSTUIINFO FAR *pInfo)
{
    pInfo->cbSize  = sizeof(DOCHOSTUIINFO);

    // Turn off the 3-D border and scrollbar.
    pInfo->dwFlags |= DOCHOSTUIFLAG_NO3DBORDER|DOCHOSTUIFLAG_SCROLL_NO;

    return S_OK;
}
```

ShowContextMenu

Remember the customer I told you about at the beginning of this chapter who didn't want to allow her users to view the source code of her Web pages? She was hosting the WebBrowser control in her application but wasn't offering a View Source menu item. The only way her users could view the source of her Web pages was by right-clicking on the Web page and choosing View Source from the WebBrowser's context menu.

To work around this user-access problem in an application that is hosting the WebBrowser control and that has implemented the *IDocHostUIHandler* interface, you can use the *ShowContextMenu* method. The MSHTML component calls the *ShowContextMenu* method any time a context menu will be displayed. Your application can choose not to display the default context menu by returning *S_OK* from your implementation of *ShowContextMenu*. (The context menu that is displayed when you right-click in the document window is actually created by the MSHTML component. Returning *S_OK* from your implementation of *ShowContextMenu* tells MSHTML not to show the default context menu.) You can also display your own context menu at this point, if you want to. The following code demonstrates how to turn off the default context menu by using the *ShowContextMenu* method:

```
STDMETHOD(ShowContextMenu)(DWORD dwID,
                           POINT FAR* ppt,
                           IUnknown FAR*  pcmdtReserved,
                           IDispatch FAR* pdispReserved)
{
    if (m_bEnableCtxMenus)
        return S_FALSE;      // Show context menus.
    else
        return S_OK;         // Do not show context menus.
}
```

As an alternative, you can show your own context menu instead of the default context menu that the MSHTML component displays. The following code, which is included on the companion CD in the folder \Samples\Chap09\AtlBrowser, implements a context menu that replaces the default. (The AtlBrowser example is also included in this folder. AtlBrowser is a WebBrowser control host that we will discuss in detail in the section titled "AtlBrowser.")

```
STDMETHOD(ShowContextMenu)(DWORD dwID, POINT FAR* ppt,
                           IUnknown FAR* pcmdtReserved,
                           IDispatch FAR* pdispReserved)
{
    ATLTRACE("IDocHostUIHandler::ShowContextMenu\n");

    if (m_bEnableCtxMenus)
        return S_FALSE;        // Show standard context menus.
    else
    {
        IOleWindow* pWnd = NULL;
        HRESULT hr = pcmdtReserved->QueryInterface(IID_IOleWindow,
                                                   (void**) &pWnd);

        if (SUCCEEDED(hr))
        {
            HWND hwnd;

            if (SUCCEEDED(pWnd->GetWindow(&hwnd)))
            {
                HMENU menu = ::CreatePopupMenu();
                ::AppendMenu(menu, MF_STRING, IDM_SAVEPICTURE,
                            "&Save Picture As..." );
                ::AppendMenu(menu, MF_STRING, IDM_SAVEBACKGROUND,
                            "Save &Background As..." );

                long myRetVal = ::TrackPopupMenu(menu,
                            TPM_RIGHTBUTTON | TPM_LEFTALIGN | TPM_RETURNCMD,
                            ppt->x, ppt->y, NULL, hwnd, NULL);

                // Send the command to the browser.
                //
                LRESULT myResult = ::SendMessage(hwnd, WM_COMMAND,
                                                 myRetVal, NULL);
            }

            pWnd->Release();
        }
    }

    return S_OK; // We've shown our own context menu.
}
```

Test the code by compiling and running AtlBrowser. Then deselect the Context Menus menu item on the UI Control menu, and right-click on an image or on the background of the application to show the customized context menu. You can see the Save Picture As and Save Background As context menu items on the customized context menu.

When creating your own context menu, the *ShowContextMenu* method's input parameters are helpful. The first parameter, *dwID*, is the ID of the context menu to be displayed. The values for this ID are defined in the mshtmhst.h header file, as follows:

```
#define CONTEXT_MENU_DEFAULT        0
#define CONTEXT_MENU_IMAGE          1
#define CONTEXT_MENU_CONTROL        2
#define CONTEXT_MENU_TABLE          3
// in browse mode
#define CONTEXT_MENU_TEXTSELECT     4
#define CONTEXT_MENU_ANCHOR         5
#define CONTEXT_MENU_UNKNOWN        6
```

The second parameter, *ppt*, is a *POINT* structure that contains the *x*-coordinate and *y*-coordinate for the context menu. The third parameter, *pcmdtReserved*, is a pointer to an *IOleCommandTarget* interface that can be used to query command status and execute commands on this object. The preceding code uses this pointer to query for the *IOleWindow* implementation of the WebBrowser. The fourth parameter, *pdispReserved*, is a pointer to the *IDispatch* of the element that was right-clicked to display a context menu. (For Internet Explorer 4, the value of this parameter was always *NULL*.)

Notice that the code on page 364 uses two of the menu items that are on the default context menu—Save Picture As and Save Background As. You can use many of the default context menu items by specifying their IDs when creating your own menu items. When these items are selected from the context menu, the default Internet Explorer implementation of these items will be invoked. This code specifies *IDM_SAVEPICTURE* and *IDM_SAVEBACKGROUND* to add these items to the context menu. You can find these and other menu IDs in the mshtmcid.h header file.

TranslateAccelerator

Another method of the *IDocHostUIHandler* interface helped my customer solve her other problem. Remember, I mentioned that besides viewing her source code, users were able to press Ctrl-O to execute the Open dialog box and then type in a URL, which caused a new instance of the Internet Explorer window to open. Users could also start a new instance of Internet Explorer by pressing Ctrl-N.

Here's where the *TranslateAccelerator* method comes to the rescue. This method is called from MSHTML's implementation of *IOleInPlaceActiveObject::Translate-Accelerator* or *IOleControl::TranslateAccelerator*. By using your implementation of

IDocHostUIHandler::TranslateAccelerator, you can turn off all accelerator keys or just specific ones that you choose. To turn off all accelerator keys, simply return *S_OK* from the *TranslateAccelerator* method, like this:

```
STDMETHOD(TranslateAccelerator)(LPMSG lpMsg,
                                const GUID FAR* pguidCmdGroup,
                                DWORD nCmdID)
{
    if (m_vbEnableAllAccels == VARIANT_TRUE)
        return S_FALSE;
    else
        return S_OK;
}
```

The same technique applies if you want to turn off a specific accelerator key. When your implementation of *TranslateAccelerator* is called, you check the *LPMSG* structure that you receive to determine whether the user pressed the accelerator key that you want to block. If *TranslateAccelerator* was called in response to a key that you want to block, you just return *S_OK*. The following code turns off specific accelerator keys:

```
STDMETHOD(TranslateAccelerator)(LPMSG lpMsg,
                                const GUID FAR* pguidCmdGroup,
                                DWORD nCmdID)
{
    //
    // If accelerators are turned on, return S_FALSE
    // so that Internet Explorer 5 will perform its
    // default behavior. Check the accelerator to see whether
    // it is in the list of accelerators that are turned off.
    // Return S_OK if the accelerator is in the list.
    //
    if (m_vbEnableAllAccels == VARIANT_TRUE
        || (GetKeyState(VK_CONTROL) >= 0
        && GetKeyState(VK_SHIFT) >= 0 && GetKeyState(VK_MENU) >= 0))
    {
        // Ignore WM_CHAR. The wParam for WM_CHAR is the ASCII code
        // for the character. We want only virtual key codes.
        //
        if (lpMsg->message != WM_CHAR
            && AcceleratorDisabled(lpMsg->wParam))
        {
            return S_OK;
        }

        return S_FALSE;
    }

    return S_OK;
}
```

```
bool CWBCustomizer::AcceleratorDisabled(short nKeyCode)
{
    short nVirtExtKey = 0;

    //
    // Get the virtual key that is pressed to pass it to FindAccelerator.
    //
    if (GetKeyState(VK_CONTROL) < 0)
        nVirtExtKey = VK_CONTROL;
    else if (GetKeyState(VK_MENU) < 0)
        nVirtExtKey = VK_MENU;
    else if (GetKeyState(VK_SHIFT) < 0)
        nVirtExtKey = VK_SHIFT;

    list<ACCELERATOR>::iterator it = FindAccelerator
                                        (nKeyCode, nVirtExtKey);
    if (it != m_disabledAccelerators.end())
    {
        //
        // The accelerator is disabled if it is found in the list
        // AND if no virtual key is present for the accelerator in the
        // list and the Ctrl, Alt, or Shift keys are not pressed
        // OR the virtual key is present and that virtual key is pressed.
        //
        if ((!it->nVirtExtKey && GetKeyState(VK_CONTROL) >= 0
            && GetKeyState(VK_MENU) >= 0 && GetKeyState(VK_SHIFT) >= 0)
            || GetKeyState(it->nVirtExtKey) < 0)
        {
            return true;
        }
    }

    return false;
}


list<CWBCustomizer::ACCELERATOR>::iterator
CWBCustomizer::FindAccelerator(short nKeyCode, short nVirtExtKey)
{
    list<ACCELERATOR>::iterator it;

    // Search the list for the accelerator.
    for (it = m_disabledAccelerators.begin();
        it != m_disabledAccelerators.end(); ++it)
    {
        //
        // If the key code is found in the list, check to see
        // whether the virtual key code matches the one passed in to this
        // function.
        //
```
(continued)

```
        if (it->nKeyCode == nKeyCode && it->nVirtExtKey == nVirtExtKey)
            break;
    }

    return it;
}
```

This code comes from the *WBCustomizer* object example that you'll encounter in the "*ICustomDoc*" section of this chapter. (You can find all code for *WBCustomizer* on the companion CD in the folder \Samples\Chap09\WBCustomizer.) In *WBCustomizer*, the Standard Template Library (STL) list class maintains a list of all disabled accelerator keys. When *TranslateAccelerator* is called, the code searches the list of disabled accelerator keys for the key or keys that were pressed. If those keys are found in the list, *TranslateAccelerator* returns *S_OK* to disable them. If those keys aren't found in the list, *TranslateAccelerator* returns *S_FALSE*.

Extending the DHTML Object Model

Besides allowing you to manage the WebBrowser control's user interface, the *IDocHostUIHandler* interface lets you extend the DHTML Object Model so that you can access methods and properties of the WebBrowser host application from within script on a Web page. For example, if you have a method in the host application named *SayHello*, you can call it from a Web page that is loaded by your application, like this:

```
<SCRIPT LANGUAGE="VBScript">
    Sub Window_onLoad
        window.external.SayHello
    End Sub
</SCRIPT>
```

When the WebBrowser control encounters a call to *window.external.SayHello*, it tries to resolve the *SayHello* method by performing a few steps. First it calls the *IDocHostUIHandler::GetExternal* method implemented in your host application to get a pointer to your application's implementation of the *IDispatch* interface. Then the WebBrowser control calls your *IDispatch::GetIDsOfNames* method to retrieve the dispatch ID (DISPID) of the *SayHello* method. Finally it calls your *IDispatch::Invoke* method and passes it the dispatch ID of *SayHello*.

In your implementation of *Invoke*, you simply handle the *DISPID* for the *SayHello* method. When you receive this *DISPID*, you can do whatever you want, such as call the *SayHello* method. The following code implements *GetExternal* and *Invoke*. (This code also comes from the AtlBrowser sample, which we'll look at in more detail shortly.) Because AtlBrowser is implemented by using ATL and inherits from *IDispatchImpl*, ATL implements the *GetIDsOfNames* method for you, so you need to implement only *GetExternal* and override *Invoke*:

```
STDMETHOD(GetExternal)(IDispatch** ppDispatch)
{
    *ppDispatch = this;
    return S_OK;
}

STDMETHODIMP CAtlBrCon::Invoke(DISPID dispidMember, REFIID riid,
                               LCID lcid, WORD wFlags,
                               DISPPARAMS* pDispParams,
                               VARIANT* pvarResult, EXCEPINFO* pExcepInfo,
                               UINT* puArgErr)
{
    switch (dispidMember)
    {
        case DISPID_SAYHELLO:
            SayHello();

        default:
            return DISP_E_MEMBERNOTFOUND;
    }

    return S_OK;
}
```

To see this code in action, compile and run AtlBrowser and navigate to the AtlBrowser.htm. When you click the Say Hello button, Internet Explorer invokes the *SayHello* method, which displays a message box such as the one shown in Figure 9-1.

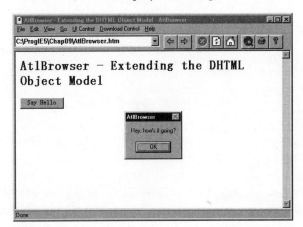

Figure 9-1. *AtlBrowser after navigating to AtlBrowser.htm and clicking the Say Hello button.*

AtlBrowser

The AtlBrowser example demonstrates how to implement the advanced hosting interfaces, including extending the DHTML Object Model, as I just showed you. AtlBrowser also implements the *IDocHostUIHandler* interface.

AtlBrowser is a WebBrowser control host that is built by using ATL, but it doesn't use the new ATL control hosting classes. AtlBrowser hosts the WebBrowser control using plain vanilla C++ and uses ATL for certain features such as message maps and smart pointers. To implement *IDocHostUIHandler*, AtlBrowser contains a class named *CAtlBrCon*, which implements the container for the WebBrowser control. To implement *IDocHostUIHandler*, *CAtlBrCon* simply inherits from the interface, contains an entry for the interface in its COM map, and implements all the methods of *IDocHostUIHandler*. (You'll see how to implement this interface by using the ATL control hosting classes.)

Some of the *IDocHostUIHandler* methods implemented in *CAtlBrCon* just return *E_NOTIMPL* by using the ATLTRACENOTIMPL macro. This macro prints a trace message in debug mode and returns *E_NOTIMPL* to indicate that the method isn't implemented. In release mode, *E_NOTIMPL* is returned, but no trace message is printed.

To enable users to change certain user interface features of the WebBrowser on the fly—such as 3-D borders, scrollbars, and context menus—AtlBrowser contains a menu named UI Control. The Context Menus menu item is implemented by using *IDocHostUIHandler::ShowContextMenu*, as shown here:

```
STDMETHOD(ShowContextMenu)(DWORD dwID, POINT FAR* ppt,
                           IUnknown FAR* pcmdtReserved,
                           IDispatch FAR* pdispReserved)
{
   ATLTRACE("IDocHostUIHandler::ShowContextMenu\n");

   if (m_bEnableCtxMenus)
      return S_FALSE;         // Show context menus.
   else
      return S_OK;            // Do not show context menus.
}
```

In this code, *m_bEnableCtxMenus* is a data member of the *CAtlBrCon* class that is set to the current state of the context menus: on (*TRUE*) or off (*FALSE*). When you click the Context Menus menu item, you toggle the value of this data member, which effectively toggles the state of the context menus. In the *ShowContextMenu* method shown in the preceding code, if context menus are on, *S_FALSE* is returned. If context menus are off, *S_OK* is returned.

Most of the remaining menu items on the UI Control menu are implemented by using the *IDocHostUIHandler::GetHostInfo* method. (One of the menu items on the UI Control menu, Use AtlBrowser Help, is implemented by using the *IDocHostShowUI* interface.) A data member of the *CAtlBrCon* class is used to maintain the status of each user interface item on this menu. When you select or deselect one of these menu items, the *DOCHOSTUIINFO* value corresponding to that user interface menu item is either added to or removed from this data member. For example, if you wanted to turn off scrollbars on the fly, you would deselect the Scrollbars menu item. The *DOCHOSTUIINFO* value, which specifies that no scrollbars should be used, is then added to this data member, as in the following code:

```
LRESULT CAtlBrCon::OnUIFlag(WORD, WORD wID, HWND, BOOL&)
{
    // Is the menu item checked?
    BOOL bIsChecked = (::GetMenuState(m_hMenu, wID,
                        MF_BYCOMMAND) == MF_CHECKED) ? TRUE : FALSE;

    bIsChecked = !bIsChecked;

    //
    // If the menu item is not checked, add its corresponding UI flag
    // to the DWORD that holds the Download Control constants.
    // To add it, OR it to the current value.  To remove it,
    // XOR it if it is not 0.  (XOR'ing something with 0 results
    // in that something.  For example, 128 ^ 0 = 128.)
    //
    //
    switch(wID)
    {
    case ID_UICONTROL_SCROLLBARS:
        m_dwDocHostUIFlags = bIsChecked ?
                        (m_dwDocHostUIFlags ^ DOCHOSTUIFLAG_SCROLL_NO)
                        : (m_dwDocHostUIFlags | DOCHOSTUIFLAG_SCROLL_NO);
        break;

    default:
        return 0;
    }

    //
    // Navigate to the current URL so that the
    // change takes effect.
    //
```

(continued)

```
CComBSTR bstrURL;
CComVariant vtEmpty;

m_spWebBrowser->get_LocationURL(&bstrURL);
m_spWebBrowser->Navigate(bstrURL, &vtEmpty, &vtEmpty,
                         &vtEmpty, &vtEmpty);

::CheckMenuItem(m_hMenu, wID, bIsChecked ? MF_CHECKED : MF_UNCHECKED);
return 0;
}
```

The *OnUIFlag* method is called when one of the menu items on the UI Control menu is selected. (*OnUIFlag* is linked to these menu items using the COMMAND_ RANGE_HANDLER macro.) When this method is called, the current checked state of the menu item is determined and then reversed. In other words, if the item was already checked when you selected it, it is then unchecked, and vice versa.

If you check the Scrollbars menu item by selecting it from the menu, meaning that you want scrollbars to be displayed, the *DOCHOSTUIFLAG_SCROLL_NO* value is XOR'ed to the *m_dwDocHostUIFlags* data member. Consequently, the value *DOCHOSTUIFLAG_SCROLL_NO* is removed from the data member. If you uncheck the Scrollbars menu item, the *DOCHOSTUIFLAG_SCROLL_NO* value is OR'ed to the *m_dwDocHostUIFlags* data member. The *DOCHOSTUIFLAG_SCROLL_NO* value is then added to the *m_dwDocHostUIFlags* data member.

Notice that the code calls *IWebBrowser2::Navigate* after setting the *m_dwDocHostUIFlags* data member to force the change made to the scroll bar to take effect. The reason for calling *IWebBrowser2::Navigate* is that these user interface features can be set only in the *IDocHostUIHandler::GetHostInfo* method, and this method is called by the MSHTML component only when you first navigate to a page. Remember, MSHTML is created and destroyed each time you navigate to a new Web page.

To force a new instance of MSHTML to be created to load the new user interface settings, you must call *IWebBrowser2::Navigate*. Merely refreshing the page by using *IWebBrowser2::Refresh* won't do the trick: you must re-navigate to the page. If you won't be changing your application's user interface features on the fly, which is typically the case, you can just set these features one time in your implementation of *IDocHostUIHandler::GetHostInfo*.

Each time you navigate to a Web page, the MSHTML component calls your implementation of *IDocHostUIHandler::GetHostInfo*. In this method, you specify the user interface features of your application by setting the *dwFlags* member of the *DOCHOSTUIINFO* structure that is passed to this method by pointer. In AtlBrowser, we simply set the *dwFlags* data member to the *m_dwDocHostUIFlags* data member of the *CAtlBrCon* class.

```
STDMETHOD(GetHostInfo)(DOCHOSTUIINFO FAR *pInfo)
{
    ATLTRACE(_T("IDocHostUIHandler::GetHostInfo"));

    pInfo->cbSize     = sizeof(DOCHOSTUIINFO);
    pInfo->dwFlags    = m_dwDocHostUIFlags;
    pInfo->dwDoubleClick = DOCHOSTUIDBLCLK_DEFAULT;

    return S_OK;
}
```

ICUSTOMDOC

After telling my customer about *IDocHostUIHandler*, I thought all her problems were solved. But there was one more problem. Her application was created using Visual Basic, which means that she couldn't implement *IDocHostUIHandler*. That's where the *ICustomDoc* interface saves the day.

The MSHTML component implements the *ICustomDoc* interface to allow you to implement the *IDocHostUIHandler* interface in a COM object that is not a WebBrowser host. To specify your implementation of *IDocHostUIHandler*, which MSHTML should use when it needs user interface information, you simply query MSHTML (represented by the *IHTMLDocument2* interface) for the *ICustomDoc* interface and call its only method, *SetUIHandler*. To this method, you pass a pointer to your implementation of *IDocHostUIHandler*.

However, this approach has a few caveats. Certain *IDocHostUIHandler* methods are called by MSHTML only if the object implementing *IDocHostUIHandler* also implements *IOleClientSite*—in other words, only if the object is a host application. A couple of these methods are *GetHostInfo* and *GetExternal*. *ShowContextMenu* and *TranslateAccelerator* are called even if the host doesn't implement *IOleClientSite*.

Also remember that the *IDocHostUIHandler* methods are called by MSHTML, and *ICustomDoc* is implemented by the MSHTML component. Because a new version of MSHTML is loaded each time you navigate to a new Web page, you must query the document for *ICustomDoc* and call the *SetUIHandler* method each time a new page is loaded. You shouldn't call this method until the WebBrowser control fires its *NavigateComplete2* event.

Here's how you would set your implementation of *IDocHostUIHandler* by using *SetUIHandler*. (Note that *m_spWebBrowser* is a smart pointer for the WebBrowser control.)

```
if (m_spWebBrowser)
{
   CComPtr<IDispatch> spDoc;
   m_spWebBrowser->get_Document(&spDoc);

   if (spDoc)
   {
      CComQIPtr<ICustomDoc, &IID_ICustomDoc> spCustomDoc(spDoc);
      if (spCustomDoc)
         spCustomDoc->SetUIHandler(this);
   }
}
```

WBCUSTOMIZER OBJECT

When I was with the Internet Client Development group of Microsoft Developer Support, I discovered that a lot of developers who were creating Visual Basic applications that host the WebBrowser control wanted to disable context menus and specific accelerator keys. As you know, you can do this by using two methods of *IDocHostUIHandler*: *ShowContextMenu* and *TranslateAccelerator*. But you can't implement *IDocHostUIHandler* in Visual Basic.

That's why I created *WBCustomizer*, a COM object created by using ATL. It implements *IDocHostUIHandler* for use in Visual Basic applications and allows you to enable or disable context menus, all accelerators, or only specific ones.

WHERE TO GET THE *WBCUSTOMIZER* OBJECT

You can get the *WBCustomizer* object from the companion CD and many other sources as well, such as the Microsoft Visual Basic Web Site at *http://msdn.microsoft.com/vbasic*, and Knowledge Base article number Q183235, which you can access at *http://support.microsoft.com/support/kb/articles/q183/2/35.asp*. The Knowledge Base article includes source code for the *WBCustomizer* COM object, the COM object compiled in release mode with minimum dependencies, and a Visual Basic example that demonstrates how to use *WBCustomizer*.

To compile both examples discussed in this Knowledge Base article, you must install headers and libraries for Internet Explorer 5, as I explained in earlier chapters, and you must place the headers and libraries in the correct order as specified in Chapter 6.

Let's look at how *WBCustomizer* works and how to use it in Visual Basic applications. (You can also use *WBCustomizer* as an example if you want to implement the functionality of controlling user interface features in your own COM objects or applications.) *WBCustomizer* exposes three properties: *WebBrowser*, *EnableContextMenus*, and *EnableAllAccelerators*. *EnableAccelerator* is its only method.

The *WebBrowser* property is crucial. It must be set so that the *WBCustomizer* object can connect its implementation of *IDocHostUIHandler* to the WebBrowser control you are hosting.

The *EnableContextMenus* and *EnableAllAccelerators* properties do just what they say: they enable or disable context menus and all accelerators, respectively.

The *EnableAccelerator* method allows you to enable or disable specific accelerator keys. It takes the key code of the accelerator key, the extended key code for Ctrl, Alt, or Shift, and the state of the key. The state of the accelerator key is *True* or *False* depending on whether you want to enable or disable it.

To use *WBCustomizer* in a Visual Basic application, follow these steps:

1. Register WBCustomizer.dll on your system by using Regsvr32, as follows:

   ```
   regsvr32 WBCustomizer.dll
   ```

2. Set a reference to Microsoft WebBrowser Customizer Sample Object in your Visual Basic application.

3. Declare a variable of type *WBCustomizer*, as follows:

   ```
   Dim CustomWB As WBCustomizer
   ```

4. In the *Form_Load* event handler, create a new instance of the *WBCustomizer* object, as follows:

   ```
   Set CustomWB = New WBCustomizer
   ```

5. To do its work, *WBCustomizer* needs a reference to the WebBrowser control that is on the form. Set this reference by using the *WebBrowser* property of *WBCustomizer*, as follows:

   ```
   Set WBCustomizer.WebBrowser = WebBrowser1
   ```

6. Turn context menus on or off by setting the *EnableContextMenus* property to *True* or *False*. A value of *True* turns context menus on. *False* turns them off.

7. Turn all accelerator keys on or off by setting the *EnableAllAccelerators* property to *True* or *False*. A value of *True* turns on all accelerators. A value of *False* turns them all off. Only those accelerators that require Ctrl, Shift, or Alt key combinations will be turned off. Those that don't require one of these keys, such as Tab, F1, and so forth, must be turned off manually, as described in step 8.

8. Turn specific accelerator keys on or off by using the *EnableAccelerator* method. The following parameters apply to this method:

❑ *nKeyCode*. The key code constant that specifies an accelerator key (*vbKeyTab*, *vbKeyN*, *vbKeyO*, and so on).

❑ *nVirtExtKey*. The virtual key code of an extended key, such as *vbKeyControl*, *vbKeyAlt*, or *vbKeyShift*. This parameter is optional and has a default value of *0*.

❑ *bState*. The state of the accelerator key. *True* turns the accelerator key on, and *False* turns it off. This parameter has a default value of *True*.

VBCustomWB is a Visual Basic sample application that uses *WBCustomizer*. Figure 9-2 shows this application in action. As you can see, VBCustomWB has check boxes that you can use to enable or disable the context menus and accelerators. You can easily customize this application to fit your own needs.

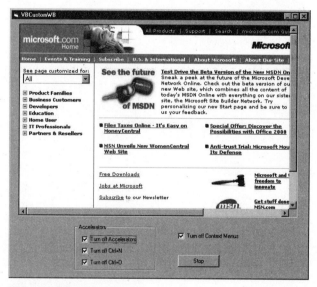

Figure 9-2. *VBCustomWB.*

IDOCHOSTSHOWUI

IDocHostShowUI, another advanced hosting interface that a WebBrowser hosting application can implement, allows you to manage message boxes and help for the WebBrowser control. When the WebBrowser control needs to display a message box, MSHTML calls the *ShowMessage* method of your *IDocHostShowUI* implementation. You can turn off the message box by returning *S_OK*. (Or leave it alone by returning *S_FALSE*.)

The *ShowMessage* method's input parameters include information about the message that you can use when displaying your own message. For instance, maybe the WebBrowser control is displaying a confusing message to your users. You can trap this confusing message in the *ShowMessage* method, and then display a different message that pertains to your users. Table 9-4 describes the input parameters of the *ShowMessage* method.

TABLE 9-4
INPUT PARAMETERS OF THE *SHOWMESSAGE* METHOD

Parameter	Description
hwnd	Handle to the owner window.
lpstrText	Text for the message box.
lpstrCaption	Caption for the message box.
dwType	Type flags. These flags correspond to the constants for the Win32 API's *MessageBox* function.
lpstrHelpFile	Name of a help file associated with this message.
dwHelpContext	Help context identifier.
plResult	Button clicked by the user. The allowable values for this parameter are taken from the Win32 API's *MessageBox* function. If you show your own message box, set this parameter to the return value of the *MessageBox* function.

IDocHostShowUI also gives you control over help that the WebBrowser control displays. For instance, when the user presses the F1 key, MSHTML calls your implementation of *IDocHostShowUI::ShowHelp*. Again, you can turn off the WebBrowser's help by returning *S_OK* and display your own help instead of MSHTML's default help. (Or you can allow the default help to be displayed by returning *S_FALSE*.)

The AtlBrowser example that we looked at earlier in this chapter contains a menu item on the UI Control menu called Use AtlBrowser Help. When you select this menu item, you are effectively telling AtlBrowser to show its own help and return *S_OK* from the *ShowHelp* method.

Try running AtlBrowser and pressing the F1 key. When you do, MSHTML queries AtlBrowser for *IDocHostShowUI* and calls *ShowHelp*. If the Use AtlBrowser Help menu item is selected, AtlBrowser displays its About dialog box and returns *S_OK*. If this menu item isn't selected, AtlBrowser returns *S_FALSE* to allow MSHTML to display its own help.

Here's the implementation of *ShowHelp* in the *CAtlBrCon* class:

```
STDMETHOD(ShowHelp)(HWND hwnd, LPOLESTR pszHelpFile, UINT uCommand,
                    DWORD dwData, POINT ptMouse,
                    IDispatch *pDispatchObjectHit)
```

(continued)

```
{
    ATLTRACE(_T("IDocHostShowUI::ShowHelp\n"));

    if (m_bAtlBrowserHelp)
    {
        CAboutBox dlg(m_hWnd);
        dlg.DoModal();
        return S_OK;
    }

    return S_FALSE;
}
```

CONTROLLING DOWNLOAD AND EXECUTION

Along with letting you manage its user interface, the WebBrowser control lets you determine what it can download and execute. For example, you can decide to prevent the WebBrowser control from downloading images, video, script, ActiveX controls, and so on. You can also prevent the WebBrowser control from executing script, ActiveX controls, and Java applets.

To control what the WebBrowser control can download and execute, your host application must implement a special dispatch ID referred to as *DISPID_AMBIENT_DLCONTROL*. In your implementation of *IDispatch::Invoke*, you handle *DISPID_AMBIENT_DLCONTROL* in a *case* statement. When *Invoke* is called with its *dispidMember* parameter set to this ID, you set the *pvarResult* parameter to a combination of flags that indicate what can or cannot be downloaded, executed, or both. Table 9-5 shows the complete list of these flags.

TABLE 9-5
DOWNLOAD CONTROL VALUES

Value	*Description*
DLCTL_DLIMAGES	Images will be downloaded from the server.
DLCTL_VIDEOS	Any video clips that are contained in the document will be played.
DLCTL_BGSOUNDS	Background sounds associated with the document will be played.
DLCTL_NO_SCRIPTS	Scripts will not be executed.
DLCTL_NO_JAVA	Java applets will not be executed.
DLCTL_NO_RUNACTIVEXCTLS	ActiveX controls will not be executed.
DLCTL_NO_DLACTIVEXCTLS	ActiveX controls will not be downloaded.
DLCTL_DOWNLOADONLY	The page will be downloaded but not displayed.

Value	*Description*
DLCTL_NO_FRAMEDOWNLOAD	Frames will not be downloaded, but the frameset page will be downloaded and parsed. The frameset will also be ignored, and no frame tags will be rendered.
DLCTL_RESYNCHRONIZE	Files in the cache will be ignored, and the server will be asked for updated information. The cached information will be used if the server indicates that the cached information is up-to-date. Using this value causes the *BINDF_RESYNCHRONIZE* flag to be set when making requests through URLMON.
DLCTL_PRAGMA_NO_CACHE	The request will be forced through to the server, and the proxy will be ignored, even if the proxy indicates that the data is up-to-date. Using this value causes the *BINDF_PRAGMA_ NO_CACHE* flag to be set when making requests through URLMON.
DLCTL_NO_BEHAVIORS	Behaviors are disabled in the document.
DLCTL_NO_METACHARSET	HTML character sets reflected by META elements are suppressed in the document.
DLCTL_URL_ENCODING_DISABLE_UTF8	This is the same as the *DOCHOSTUIFLAG_URL_ ENCODING_DISABLE_UTF8* flag in Table 9-2. The difference between these two flags is that the flag in Table 9-2 is used only when the MSHTML component is first instantiated, and the download flag in Table 9-5 is used whenever the WebBrowser needs to perform a download.
DLCTL_URL_ENCODING_ENABLE_UTF8	This is the same as the *DOCHOSTUIFLAG_URL_ ENCODING_ENABLE_UTF8* flag in Table 9-2. The difference between the two flags described in the entry above applies to these two flags as well.
DLCTL_FORCEOFFLINE	Always operates in offline mode. Using this value causes the *BINDF_OFFLINEOPERATION* flag to be set even if the computer is connected to the Internet when making requests through URLMON.
DLCTL_NO_CLIENTPULL	No client pull operations will be performed.
DLCTL_SILENT	No user interface will be displayed. Using this value causes the *BINDF_SILENTOPERATION* flag to be set when making requests through URLMON.

(continued)

DOWNLOAD CONTROL VALUES *continued*

Value	Description
DLCTL_OFFLINEIFNOTCONNECTED	Operates in offline mode if not connected to the Internet. Using this value causes the *BINDF_GETFROMCACHE_IF_NET_FAIL* flag to be set if the computer is connected to the Internet when making requests through URLMON.
DLCTL_OFFLINE	Same as *DLCTL_OFFLINEIFNOTCONNECTED*.

The code on the next page implements *Invoke*, which handles *DISPID_AMBIENT_DLCONTROL* to allow the download of images, videos, and background sounds, but turns off the execution of script.

```
STDMETHODIMP CAtlBrCon::Invoke(DISPID dispidMember, REFIID riid,
                               LCID lcid, WORD wFlags,
                               DISPPARAMS* pDispParams,
                               VARIANT* pvarResult,
                               EXCEPINFO* pExcepInfo,
                               UINT* puArgErr)
{
   switch (dispidMember)
   {
      case DISPID_AMBIENT_DLCONTROL:
         *pvarResult = DLCTL_DLIMAGES | DLCTL_VIDEOS
                     | DLCTL_BGSOUNDS | DLCTL_NO_SCRIPTS;
         break;

      default:
         return DISP_E_MEMBERNOTFOUND;
   }

   return S_OK;
}
```

The AtlBrowser example implements download control as well as the functionality of controlling the user interface features that I showed you earlier. To let you specify download control options on the fly, AtlBrowser provides a menu named Download Control that allows you to enable or disable some of its menu items.

In the same way a data member is used by other AtlBrowser menu items to control user interface features, a data member is used to keep track of which items listed in Table 9-5 should be enabled or disabled. When MSHTML needs to know what to download, it calls AtlBrowser's implementation of *Invoke*, passing *DISPID_AMBIENT_DLCONTROL* for the *dispidMember* input parameter. AtlBrowser then handles this dispatch ID and sets the *pvarResult* return value to the value of the data member that specifies which items should be downloaded. The following code performs this function:

```
case DISPID_AMBIENT_DLCONTROL:
    {
        CComVariant vtResult(static_cast<long>(m_dwDLControl));
        *pvarResult = vtResult;
    }

    break;
```

Note that AtlBrowser automatically allows the download of images, videos, and background sounds by initializing the *m_dwDLControl* data member in the constructor for *CAtlBrCon*, like so:

```
CAtlBrCon::CAtlBrCon() :
    m_dwDLControl(DLCTL_DLIMAGES|DLCTL_VIDEOS|DLCTL_BGSOUNDS),

    ⋮
{
}
```

You might want to try out this download control feature using AtlBrowser. Also try adding some of the items in Table 9-5 that aren't implemented by AtlBrowser.

WHAT'S NEXT?

The advanced hosting interfaces let you control the user interface of the WebBrowser control as well as what the WebBrowser control can download and execute when you are hosting it. As usual, implementing this functionality in your applications is easy. And in doing so, you have total control over the browsing experience that you provide to your users.

In the next chapter, you'll learn how to implement an Internet Explorer feature known as Web Accessories. Web Accessories allows you to enhance the user interface of the browser, further enabling you to provide an even richer browsing experience for your users.

Chapter 10

Web Accessories

In previous chapters, you took advantage of Microsoft Internet Explorer functionality either by hosting the WebBrowser control or by automating Internet Explorer. Reusing Internet Explorer technology in either of those ways is great because each gives you ultimate control over all aspects of Internet Explorer, including browsing and the user interface.

But what if you want to enhance the browser without creating your own hosting application or automating Internet Explorer? Suppose you want the Tip Of The Day to be displayed in the browser when users start Internet Explorer so that they can learn how to use its features as time goes on. Or perhaps you want to create a calculator application that users can start with the click of a button. Such an application could assist staff in your accounting department or people who shop online. To implement this functionality without having to create your own browser application or automate Internet Explorer, you can use new technology known as Web Accessories.

What are Web Accessories, you ask? They are extensions to Internet Explorer that you can create to enhance your users' browsing experience. Web Accessories can be basic Web content that you create by using standard HTML, DHTML, and script, or full-blown COM-based applications written in Microsoft Visual C++ or Microsoft Visual Basic.

To build Web Accessories, you use browser extensions. A browser extension might be a menu item or a toolbar button that you create and add to Internet Explorer and that, when selected, executes your application. Or it might be an Explorer Bar similar to the Internet Explorer Search band or Favorites band (see Figure 10-1 and Figure 10-2 on the following pages). This new terminology might seem a bit confusing, but it's really quite simple: Web Accessories are browser enhancements to Internet Explorer that developers can create by using browser extensions.

In this chapter, I will show you how to create Web Accessories using the four different types of browser extensions: Explorer Bars, toolbar buttons, main menu items, and context menu items.

UNDERSTANDING EXPLORER BARS AND DESK BANDS

Chapter 1 provides an overview of Explorer Bars, but let's review that information again now. Explorer Bars are child windows that are parented by the Internet Explorer browser window. When you start an Explorer Bar, the bar appears inside the browser window either vertically or horizontally. Vertical Explorer Bars are known as Explorer bands, and horizontal Explorer Bars are known as Communication bands, or simply Comm bands. You will also work with Desk bands, which are a technology included with the shell that is installed by Microsoft Windows 98 and 2000. (Desk bands are also installed by Internet Explorer 4 and later versions when you install the desktop update.)

Explorer Bands

Internet Explorer 5 automatically installs four different vertical Explorer Bars (also referred to as Explorer bands): Search, Favorites, History, and Folders.

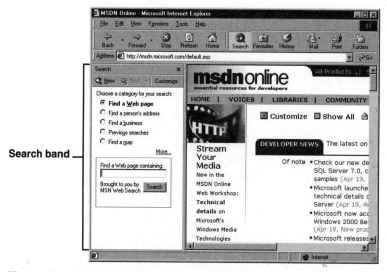

Figure 10-1. *Search band.*

The Search band, shown in Figure 10-1, allows you to quickly access your favorite search site, such as Yahoo, AltaVista, Excite, and so forth. You can easily customize which search engines are available by clicking the Customize button in the Search band and then making your selections. You start the Search band by clicking the Search button on the Internet Explorer toolbar or by selecting Search from the View/Explorer Bar menu.

The Favorites band, shown in Figure 10-2, allows you to view, select, and organize your favorite URLs by clicking the Add button and the Organize button provided in the band. The Favorites band provides easy access to your favorite URLs; you don't have to choose the URLs from the Favorites menu. You start the band by clicking the Favorites button on the Internet Explorer toolbar or by selecting Favorites from the View/Explorer Bar menu.

Figure 10-2. *Favorites band.*

Figure 10-3 on the following page shows the History band, which allows you to view URLs that you have previously visited. From this band, you can open or delete an item in the history list or add it to your favorites. You can start this Explorer band by clicking the History button on the Internet Explorer toolbar or by selecting History from the View/Explorer Bar menu, just as you would to start the Search and Favorites bands.

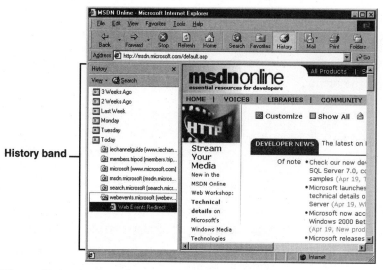

Figure 10-3. *History band.*

The last Explorer band that Internet Explorer 5 installs for you is the Folders band, as shown in Figure 10-4. It allows you to navigate to different folders on your system or on the network, just as you would if you were using Microsoft Windows Explorer. Unlike the other Explorer bands, the Folders band doesn't have a button on the Internet Explorer toolbar by default, but you can add a button for it by right-clicking the Internet Explorer toolbar and choosing Customize. As an alternative, you can select the Folders band from the View/Explorer Bar menu.

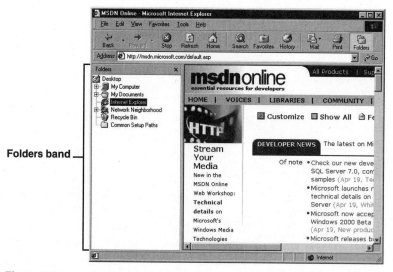

Figure 10-4. *Folders band.*

Comm Bands

Internet Explorer 5 installs one default horizontal Explorer Bar (also known as the Comm band): Tip Of The Day. Another Comm band, the Discuss band, is installed with Office 2000 and allows you to participate in discussions with others about a Web page. You can add remarks to the Web page, edit and reply to existing remarks, and so on.

The Tip Of The Day Comm band (shown at the bottom of the screen in Figure 10-5) provides handy, daily tips that help you learn more about using Internet Explorer. As a matter of fact, as I was writing this book and testing out the Tip Of The Day band, I learned that you can press Alt-D to move the cursor to the Address bar. I encourage you to give the Tip Of The Day band a try. The tips are quite informative.

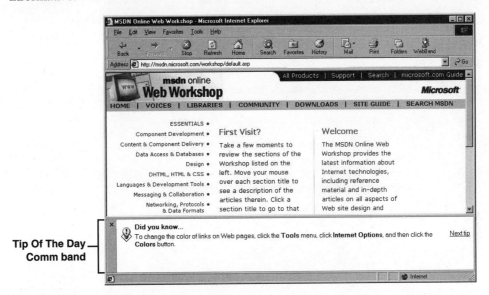

Tip Of The Day Comm band

Figure 10-5. *Tip Of The Day band.*

Desk Bands

As I mentioned, Desk bands are installed by Internet Explorer 4 and later versions as part of the shell that is installed with Windows 98 and Windows 2000 when you install the desktop update. You can create Desk bands in much the same way you create Explorer Bars.

Instead of being connected to the Internet Explorer window as Explorer Bars are, Desk bands are connected to the desktop, and you can use them only if you have activated the Active Desktop. You start Desk bands by right-clicking the Active Desktop task bar and selecting the Desk band from the Toolbars submenu.

> **NOTE** The terminology might seem a little confusing. Just remember that Explorer Bars are the technology that includes Explorer bands and Comm bands. Desk bands are a technology in and of themselves. Also, you'll sometimes hear Explorer Bars and Desk bands referred to as band objects, so don't be confused. I'll use the term Explorer Bar when referring to Explorer bands and Comm bands, but I'll use the term *band object* when referring to all three.

CREATING EXPLORER BARS USING DHTML AND SCRIPT

Creating Explorer Bars for Internet Explorer 5 is relatively easy, especially if you already know how to create Web pages. You just need to add a few keys and values to the Registry to tell Internet Explorer where to obtain your Web page and how to display it—vertically, as an Explorer band, or horizontally, as a Comm band.

To show your Web page as an Explorer Bar in Internet Explorer, perform the following steps:

1. Create a globally unique identifier (GUID) that will be used for your Web page. Use the Guidgen.exe program that is included with Microsoft Visual Studio.

2. From the Create GUID dialog box, select the Registry Format radio button, as shown in Figure 10-6. Then click the Copy button to copy the new GUID to the clipboard.

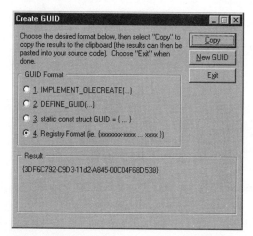

Figure 10-6. *The Create GUID dialog box.*

3. Run the Regedit application, and create a new key under *HKEY_CLASSES_ROOT\CLSID*. Name it by using the GUID you created in step 1. The new key should look like this:

```
HKEY_CLASSES_ROOT\CLSID\<GUID Created In Step 1>
```

4. Set the *Default* value of this key to the name of your Explorer Bar that you want to appear in Internet Explorer's View/Explorer Bar menu.

5. Create a new subkey beneath the key you created in step 3, and name this key *Implemented Categories*. This key will tell Internet Explorer how to display your Explorer Bar—vertically or horizontally. The new key should look like this:

```
HKEY_CLASSES_ROOT\CLSID\<GUID Created In Step 1>\Implemented
    Categories
```

6. Create a subkey beneath the key you created in step 5, and name it by using the category ID (CATID) of the type of Explorer Bar you want to create.

The following table shows the CATIDs that you can use to specify an Explorer band or a Comm band. (You can't specify a Desk band by using this technique.)

Category ID (CATID)	*Purpose*
{00021493-0000-0000-C000-000000000046}	Explorer band (vertical)
{00021494-0000-0000-C000-000000000046}	Comm band (horizontal)

At this point, the keys you've created should look similar to those shown in Figure 10-7. Of course, the GUID you created in step 1 will be different.

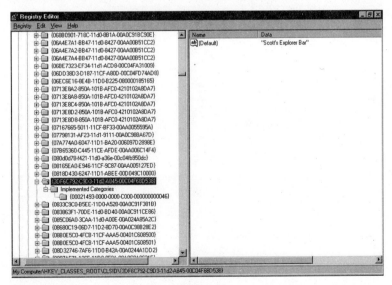

Figure 10-7. *New Registry keys after step 6.*

7. Create a new key under the key you created for your GUID in step 3, and name it *InProcServer32*. The new key should look like this:

```
HKEY_CLASSES_ROOT\CLSID\<GUID Created In Step 1>
\InProcServer32
```

8. The value of the key you created in step 7 will tell Internet Explorer how to start your Explorer Bar. Because you are creating an Explorer Bar to contain a Web page that you've created, set the *Default* value of the *InProcServer32* key to the full path of shdocvw.dll. (The shdocvw.dll file is located in the \Windows\System directory for Microsoft Windows 95 and later versions, and the \WinNT\System32 directory for Microsoft Windows NT systems.)

    If you were creating an Explorer Bar in C++ and COM, you would set this value to the path of the Explorer Bar's DLL file. (More on this in the next section.)

9. Create a new string value under the *InProcServer32* key named *ThreadingModel*. Set the value of *ThreadingModel* to *Apartment*. The Registry keys should look similar to those in Figure 10-8.

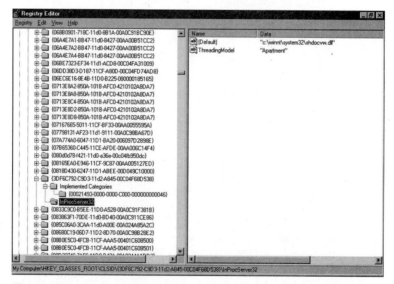

Figure 10-8. *Registry keys after step 9.*

10. Create a new key under the GUID key that you created in step 3, and name this key *Instance*. This key is required for Explorer Bars that display Web pages but is optional for Explorer Bars created by using C++ and COM. The new key should look like this:

```
HKEY_CLASSES_ROOT\CLSID\<GUID Created In Step 1>\Instance
```

11. Create a new string value named *CLSID* under the *Instance* key. Set the value of *CLSID* as follows:

    ```
    {4D5C8C2A-D075-11d0-B416-00C04FB90376}
    ```

12. Create a new key named *InitPropertyBag* under the *Instance* key. Again, this key is required only if you are creating an Explorer Bar that displays a Web page. The new key should look like this:

    ```
    HKEY_CLASSES_ROOT\CLSID\<GUID Created In Step 1>
    \Instance\InitPropertyBag
    ```

13. Create a new string value under the *InitPropertyBag* key that you just created. Name this string *URL*, and set its value to the location of the Web page that you want displayed in the Explorer Bar. Now the Registry key structure should look similar to Figure 10-9.

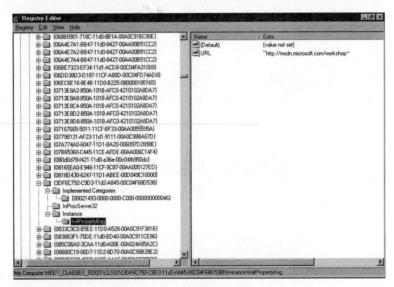

Figure 10-9. *Registry key structure after step 13.*

If you'd like to specify the default size of your Explorer Bar when it is first displayed, follow these additional steps:

14. Create a new key by using the GUID you created in step 1. This key will be created beneath another branch of the Registry, and it should look like this:

    ```
    HKEY_LOCAL_MACHINE\Software\Microsoft\Internet
        Explorer\Explorer Bars\<GUID Created In Step 1>
    ```

15. Create a new binary value named *BarSize* under the key you created in the previous step. Set the value of *BarSize* to an 8-byte, binary value in hexadecimal notation that specifies the default size for your Explorer Bar.

Internet Explorer interprets the value in pixels. For instance, setting the value to *41 00 00 00 00 00 00 00* is equal to 65 pixels. To determine the hexadecimal value that you should use for *BarSize*, just convert from decimal to hexadecimal the number of pixels that you want your Explorer Bar to be.

Now you have a working Explorer Bar that displays a Web page. Although performing all these steps might be cumbersome if you do it manually, you can easily create an ActiveX control that will do it for you. Then you can put this ActiveX control on a Web page so that your Explorer Bar will be installed when users navigate to your Web site.

To test your Explorer Bar, select the View/Explorer Bar menu. The name you provided in step 4 will appear on that menu. Just select it as you would any other Explorer Bar. You can also add a button to Internet Explorer's toolbar, as you'll see later in this chapter.

> **TIP** To initiate navigation in the main Internet Explorer window when users click a link on the Web page in your Explorer Bar, set *TARGET=_main* as follows:

```
<A HREF="http://msdn.microsoft.com/workshop" TARGET=_main>
```

CREATING EXPLORER BARS AND DESK BANDS USING C++ AND COM

Creating Explorer Bars and Desk bands by using C++ and COM is a bit more involved than creating them by using DHTML and script, as you might imagine. However, C++ and COM give you a lot more power and flexibility. For example, you might want to know when users are navigating in the main Internet Explorer window. To achieve this, you would have to sink events for the WebBrowser of the main Internet Explorer window, which is possible only when using C++.

When you use C++ and COM to create an Explorer band, Comm band, or Desk band, the process is almost the same for each type of band object: you create a DLL that implements a few required interfaces and possibly other optional interfaces. The main difference is the way you register the band object. As in the previous section, when you create keys in the Registry to build Explorer Bars, the value of the CATID that you specify beneath the *Implemented Categories* key determines the type of band object.

> **NOTE** Remember that the term band object encompasses both Explorer Bars and Desk bands.

When registering your band object, you can choose from the three CATIDs listed in the following table to specify which type of band object you want to create. The values in the table can be used when registering your band object. (These constants are defined in the Internet Explorer 5 shlguid.h header file, which you can download from the MSDN Online Web Workshop.)

CATID Constant	Value	Description
CATID_InfoBand	{00021493-0000-0000-C000-000000000046}	Explorer band
CATID_CommBand	{00021494-0000-0000-C000-000000000046}	Comm band
CATID_DeskBand	{00021492-0000-0000-C000-000000000046}	Desk band

Implementing the Required DLL Functions

Because a band object is a DLL, you must implement a few DLL functions: *DllMain*, *DllGetClassObject*, *DllCanUnloadNow*, and *DllRegisterServer*. To allow your users to easily unregister your band object by using Regsvr32.exe, you should also implement *DllUnregisterServer*. You implement *DllMain*, *DllGetClassObject*, and *DllCanUnloadNow* in the same way you would implement them with any COM DLL, so we'll look at only the two that are important for band objects: *DllRegisterServer* and *DllUnregisterServer*.

Because you already know which Registry keys need to be created for your band object, you should easily be able to understand the code that I will show you. When implementing *DllRegisterServer*, you must call the necessary Registry functions to create the keys discussed earlier in the section "Creating Explorer Bars Using DHTML and Script," including registering the CLSID for your band object and the component category.

The following code is taken from the WebBand example and shows how you might want to implement *DllRegisterServer*:

```
STDAPI DllRegisterServer(void)
{
    // Register the Explorer Bar object.
    if (!RegisterServer(CLSID_WBExplorerBar, TEXT("&WebBand Search")))
        return SELFREG_E_CLASS;

    // Register the Component Categories for the Explorer Bar object.
    if (!RegisterComCat(CLSID_WBExplorerBar, CATID_InfoBand))
        return SELFREG_E_CLASS;

    return S_OK;
}
```

WebBand Example

Throughout the rest of this chapter, we'll examine the code from the WebBand application included on the companion CD in the folder \Samples\Chap10\ WebBand. WebBand, shown in Figure 10-11 on page 419, is an example of a vertical Explorer band that hosts the WebBrowser control. Although WebBand demonstrates how to create an Explorer band, the concepts apply to Comm and Desk bands as well. (WebBand is similar to the Internet Explorer 5 Search band.)

To use WebBand, copy the WebBand.htm and Results.htm files from the companion CD to the root directory for your Internet server (for example, C:\InetPub\wwwroot). If you want to place these files in a different directory, you must change the definition of *STARTUP_URL* in the WBExplorerBar.cpp file to point to the new location.

After compiling and registering WebBand.dll, start Internet Explorer 5, and choose WebBand Search from the View/Explorer Bar menu. WebBand will load WebBand.htm, which contains a form with an edit box, Submit button, and a couple of links to other Web pages.

When you type some text in the edit box and click the Submit button, the Results.htm file will be loaded into the current window. If you click one of the links on the WebBand.htm Web page, the URL will be loaded into the main Internet Explorer window.

This code consolidates the Registry function calls into two private functions: *RegisterServer* and *RegisterComCat*. These functions take care of registering the CLSID and component categories for the WebBand Explorer Bar. Here's the implementation of these two functions:

```
typedef struct
{
    HKEY    hRootKey;
    LPTSTR  szSubKey;   // TCHAR szSubKey[MAX_PATH];
    LPTSTR  lpszValueName;
    LPTSTR  szData;     // TCHAR szData[MAX_PATH];

} DOREGSTRUCT, *LPDOREGSTRUCT;

BOOL RegisterServer(CLSID clsid, LPTSTR lpszTitle)
{
    int     i;
    HKEY    hKey;
    LRESULT lResult;
    DWORD   dwDisp;
```

```
    TCHAR   szSubKey[MAX_PATH];
    TCHAR   szCLSID[MAX_PATH];
    TCHAR   szModule[MAX_PATH];
    LPWSTR  pwsz;

    // Get the CLSID in string form.
    StringFromIID(clsid, &pwsz);

    if (pwsz)
    {
#ifdef UNICODE
        lstrcpy(szCLSID, pwsz);
#else
        WideCharToMultiByte(CP_ACP, 0, pwsz, -1, szCLSID,
                            ARRAYSIZE(szCLSID), NULL, NULL);
#endif

        // Free the string.
        LPMALLOC pMalloc;

        CoGetMalloc(1, &pMalloc);
        pMalloc->Free(pwsz);

        pMalloc->Release();
    }

    // Get this application's path and filename.
    GetModuleFileName(g_hInst, szModule, ARRAYSIZE(szModule));

    DOREGSTRUCT ClsidEntries[] =
    {
        HKEY_CLASSES_ROOT, TEXT("CLSID\\%s"),
            NULL, lpszTitle,
        HKEY_CLASSES_ROOT, TEXT("CLSID\\%s\\InprocServer32"),
            NULL, szModule,
        HKEY_CLASSES_ROOT, TEXT("CLSID\\%s\\InprocServer32")
            TEXT("ThreadingModel"), TEXT("Apartment")
        NULL, NULL, NULL, NULL
    };

    // Register the CLSID entries.
    for (i = 0; ClsidEntries[i].hRootKey; i++)
    {
        // Create the subkey string. For this case, insert
        // the file extension.
        //
        wsprintf(szSubKey, ClsidEntries[i].szSubKey, szCLSID);
```

(continued)

```
            lResult = RegCreateKeyEx(ClsidEntries[i].hRootKey, szSubKey,
                            0, NULL, REG_OPTION_NON_VOLATILE,
                            KEY_WRITE, NULL, &hKey, &dwDisp);

        if (ERROR_SUCCESS == lResult)
        {
            TCHAR szData[MAX_PATH];

            // If necessary, create the value string.
            wsprintf(szData, ClsidEntries[i].szData, szModule);

            lResult = RegSetValueEx(hKey, ClsidEntries[i].lpszValueName,
                            0, REG_SZ, (LPBYTE)szData,
                            lstrlen(szData) + 1);
            RegCloseKey(hKey);

            if (ERROR_SUCCESS != lResult)
                return FALSE;
        }
        else
        {
            return FALSE;
        }
    }

    return TRUE;
}

BOOL RegisterComCat(CLSID clsid, CATID CatID)
{
    ICatRegister* pcr;
    HRESULT hr = S_OK ;

    CoInitialize(NULL);

    hr = CoCreateInstance(CLSID_StdComponentCategoriesMgr,
                        NULL,
                        CLSCTX_INPROC_SERVER,
                        IID_ICatRegister,
                        (LPVOID*)&pcr);

    if (SUCCEEDED(hr))
    {
        hr = pcr->RegisterClassImplCategories(clsid, 1, &CatID);
        pcr->Release();
    }

    CoUninitialize();

    return SUCCEEDED(hr);
}
```

In this code, the *RegisterServer* function is pretty straightforward. It uses an array of *DOREGSTRUCT* structures that contain the necessary information to be entered into the Registry. The *DOREGSTRUCT* structure is defined at the beginning of this code. After initializing the array of *DOREGSTRUCT* structures, the code loops through the array and calls *RegCreateKeyEx* to create the Registry keys and *RegSetValueEx* to set Registry values. (These functions are both Win32 API functions.) When initializing the array of *DOREGSTRUCT* structures, make sure that the Registry information is listed in top-down order. In other words, the *CLSID* key must be created before any of its subkeys.

The *RegisterComCat* function is a little more interesting. Instead of calling the Win32 Registry functions to register the component category information, the code uses the Component Categories Manager. This COM object takes care of registering the component categories for you. After initializing COM, the code creates an instance of the Component Categories Manager by calling *CoCreateInstance* and passing *CLSID_StdComponentCategoriesMgr*.

When calling *CoCreateInstance*, the code also passes the interface ID *IID_ICatRegister* as the fourth parameter to request a pointer to the *ICatRegister* interface. Then the code calls the *RegisterClassImplCategories* method of *ICatRegister*, passing the CLSID of the WebBand Explorer Bar and the CATID of the type of band that you want to create. The *RegisterClassImplCategories* method registers the component category for your band object.

So that your users can unregister your band object, you should also implement the *DllUnregisterServer* function. This implementation isn't required, but it enables your users to use Rregsvr32.exe to unregister your band object, which will keep them happy. Imagine having to manually unregister all ActiveX controls or COM objects on your system. I know that wouldn't make me happy!

Implementing the *DllUnregisterServer* function is pretty easy, as the following WebBand code demonstrates:

```
STDAPI DllUnregisterServer(void)
{
   // Register the Component Categories for the Explorer Bar object.
   if (!UnRegisterComCat(CLSID_WBExplorerBar, CATID_InfoBand))
      return SELFREG_E_CLASS;

   // Register the Explorer Bar object.
   if (!UnRegisterServer(CLSID_WBExplorerBar))
      return SELFREG_E_CLASS;

   return S_OK;
}
```

Notice that this code unregisters the component categories first, before it unregisters the CLSID for your band object, because the component category information is stored as the *Implemented Categories* subkey of your CLSID. You can't delete a key from the Registry by using the Win32 API functions if that key has subkeys.

The *UnRegisterComCat* function is similar to the *RegisterComCat* function. It uses the Component Categories Manager to unregister the component categories:

```
BOOL UnRegisterComCat(CLSID clsid, CATID CatID)
{
    ICatRegister* pcr;
    HRESULT hr = S_OK ;

    CoInitialize(NULL);

    hr = CoCreateInstance(CLSID_StdComponentCategoriesMgr,
                          NULL,
                          CLSCTX_INPROC_SERVER,
                          IID_ICatRegister,
                          (LPVOID*)&pcr);

    if (SUCCEEDED(hr))
    {
        hr = pcr->UnRegisterClassImplCategories(clsid, 1, &CatID);
        pcr->Release();
    }

    CoUninitialize();

    return SUCCEEDED(hr);
}
```

As you can see, the only difference between this code and the code for the *RegisterComCat* function is that *UnRegisterComCat* calls *ICatRegister::UnRegisterClassImplCategories* to unregister the component categories.

The implementation of the function *UnRegisterServer* is similar to the function *RegisterServer*:

```
BOOL UnRegisterServer(CLSID clsid)
{
    TCHAR   szSubKey[MAX_PATH];
    TCHAR   szCLSID[MAX_PATH];
    LPWSTR  pwsz;

    // Get the CLSID in string form.
    StringFromIID(clsid, &pwsz);

    if (pwsz)
    {
```

```
#ifdef UNICODE
    lstrcpy(szCLSID, pwsz);
#else
    WideCharToMultiByte(CP_ACP, 0, pwsz, -1, szCLSID,
                        ARRAYSIZE(szCLSID), NULL, NULL);
#endif

    // Free the string.
    LPMALLOC pMalloc;

    CoGetMalloc(1, &pMalloc);

    pMalloc->Free(pwsz);
    pMalloc->Release();
}

DOREGSTRUCT ClsidEntries[] =
{
    HKEY_CLASSES_ROOT, TEXT("CLSID\\%s\\InprocServer32"),
        NULL, NULL,
    //
    // Remove the Implemented Categories key, just in case
    // UnRegisterClassImplCategories doesn't remove it.
    //
    HKEY_CLASSES_ROOT, TEXT("CLSID\\%s\\Implemented Categories"),
        NULL, NULL,
    HKEY_CLASSES_ROOT, TEXT("CLSID\\%s"), NULL, NULL,
        NULL, NULL, NULL, NULL
};

// Delete the CLSID entries.
for (int i = 0; ClsidEntries[i].hRootKey; i++)
{
    wsprintf(szSubKey, ClsidEntries[i].szSubKey, szCLSID);
    RegDeleteKey(ClsidEntries[i].hRootKey, szSubKey);
}

return TRUE;
}
```

This code uses the *RegDeleteKey* Win32 API function to delete the *CLSID* key and its subkeys. Notice that the *DOREGSTRUCT* array is set up to delete all subkeys before their parent keys. This is required.

Implementing Required Interfaces

Besides implementing the required DLL functions (and of course *IUnknown*), you must implement a few interfaces: *IDeskBand*, *IDockingWindow*, *IOleWindow*, *IObjectWithSite*, and *IPersistStream*.

IDeskBand

The *IDeskBand* interface is specific to band objects. You implement it just as you would any other interface. The WebBand example is written by using standard C++, so a class named *CWBExplorerBar* implements *IDeskBand* by inheriting from it and implementing its one method, *GetBandInfo*. Internet Explorer uses *GetBandInfo* to specify the identifier and viewing mode of your band object as well as to obtain information about your band object. The *GetBandInfo* method is defined in the shlobj.h header file as follows:

```
HRESULT GetBandInfo(DWORD dwBandID, DWORD dwViewMode, DESKBANDINFO* pdbi);
```

The first parameter of this method is the identifier of the band as assigned by the container—Internet Explorer, in most cases. The second parameter is the view mode, which can have one of the values shown in Table 10-1. You should save the values stored in the first and second parameters in data members of the class that implement *IDeskBand*.

TABLE 10-1
DWVIEWMODE CONSTANTS

Value	*Description*
DBIF_VIEWMODE_NORMAL	Your band object is being displayed in a horizontal band.
DBIF_VIEWMODE_VERTICAL	Your band object is being displayed in a vertical band.
DBIF_VIEWMODE_FLOATING	Your band object is being displayed in a floating band.
DBIF_VIEWMODE_TRANSPARENT	Your band object is being displayed in a transparent band.

Internet Explorer will request information from your band object by using the third parameter of this method—*pdbi*. This parameter is a pointer to a *DESKBANDINFO* structure, which is defined as follows:

```
typedef struct {
    DWORD       dwMask;
    POINTL      ptMinSize;
    POINTL      ptMaxSize;
    POINTL      ptIntegral;
    POINTL      ptActual
    WCHAR       wszTitl[256];
    DWORD       dwModeFlags;
    COLORREF    crBkgnd;
} DESKBANDINFO;
```

Internet Explorer uses the *dwMask* member of this structure to specify what information it is requesting. This data member can contain one or more of the flags listed in Table 10-2.

TABLE 10-2
dwMask VALUES

Value	Description
DBIM_ACTUAL	*ptActual* is being requested. This data member receives the ideal size you would like your band object to be. It is not guaranteed to be this size.
DBIM_BKCOLOR	*crBkgnd* is being requested. This data member receives the background color of your band object. *DBIM_BKCOLOR* is ignored if the *dwModeFlags* data member doesn't contain the *DBIMF_BKCOLOR* flag.
DBIM_INTEGRAL	*ptIntegral* is being requested. This data member receives the sizing step value of the band object, which specifies in which increments the band will be resized. This data member is ignored if *dwModeFlags* doesn't contain *DBIMF_VARIABLEHEIGHT*.
DBIM_MAXSIZE	*ptMaxSize* is being requested. This data member receives the maximum size of your band object.
DBIM_MINSIZE	*ptMinSize* is being requested. This data member receives the minimum size of your band object.
DBIM_MODEFLAGS	*dwModeFlags* is being requested. This data member receives one or more flags, logically OR'ed together, that define the mode of operation for your band object. The following are the possible values for this data member: **DBIMF_BKCOLOR** Your band object will have the background color defined by the *crBkgnd* data member. **DBIMF_DEBOSSED** Your band object will appear sunken when displayed. **DBIMF_NORMAL** Your band is in normal mode of operation. **DBIMF_VARIABLEHEIGHT** The height of the band object can be changed. The *ptIntegral* data member defines the step value for resizing your band object.
DBIM_TITLE	*wszTitle* is being requested. This data member receives the title of your band object.

This next code listing shows how the WebBand example implements the *GetBandInfo* method:

```
#define MIN_SIZE_X    10
#define MIN_SIZE_Y    10

STDMETHODIMP CWBExplorerBar::GetBandInfo(DWORD dwBandID,
                                         DWORD dwViewMode,
                                         DESKBANDINFO* pdbi)
{
    if (pdbi)
    {
        _dwBandID = dwBandID;
        _dwViewMode = dwViewMode;

        if (pdbi->dwMask & DBIM_MINSIZE)
        {
            pdbi->ptMinSize.x = MIN_SIZE_X;
            pdbi->ptMinSize.y = MIN_SIZE_Y;
        }

        if (pdbi->dwMask & DBIM_MAXSIZE)
        {
            pdbi->ptMaxSize.x = -1;
            pdbi->ptMaxSize.y = -1;
        }

        if (pdbi->dwMask & DBIM_INTEGRAL)
        {
            pdbi->ptIntegral.x = 1;
            pdbi->ptIntegral.y = 1;
        }

        if (pdbi->dwMask & DBIM_ACTUAL)
        {
            pdbi->ptActual.x = 0;
            pdbi->ptActual.y = 0;
        }

        if (pdbi->dwMask & DBIM_TITLE)
        {
            lstrcpyW(pdbi->wszTitle, L"WebBand Search");
        }

        if (pdbi->dwMask & DBIM_MODEFLAGS)
            pdbi->dwModeFlags = DBIMF_VARIABLEHEIGHT;

        if (pdbi->dwMask & DBIM_BKCOLOR)
```

```
    {
        // Use the default background color by removing this flag.
        pdbi->dwMask &= ~DBIM_BKCOLOR;
    }

    return S_OK;
}

    return E_INVALIDARG;
}
```

In addition to implementing the *IDeskBand* interface, because *IDeskBand* inherits from the *IDockingWindow* interface and *IDockingWindow* inherits from the *IOleWindow* interface, you must implement these interfaces as well. Implementing the *IOleWindow* interface's methods is pretty standard, so I won't show you here. (If you're interested, take a look at the WebBand example.)

Implementing most of the *IDockingWindow* interface's methods is pretty standard as well, but its *ShowDW* method warrants some attention. *ShowDW* is called when the Explorer band's window is being shown or hidden. The *ShowDW* method takes one parameter, *fShow*, which is a Boolean value that indicates whether the band object's window is being shown (TRUE) or hidden (FALSE). Here is WebBand's implementation of the *ShowDW* method:

```
STDMETHODIMP CWBExplorerBar::ShowDW(BOOL fShow)
{
    if (_hWnd)
    {
        //
        // Hide or show the window depending on
        // the value of the fShow parameter.
        //
        if (fShow)
            ShowWindow(_hWnd, SW_SHOW);
        else
            ShowWindow(_hWnd, SW_HIDE);
    }

    return S_OK;
}
```

IObjectWithSite

Internet Explorer uses the *IObjectWithSite* interface's *SetSite* method to pass a pointer to the *IUnknown* interface of the band object's site. One way you can use this pointer is to query for various interfaces implemented in the container such as *IWebBrowser2*, *IInputObjectSite*, and *IOleInPlaceObject*. You can then use these interfaces to perform different actions in your band object and to control the container—Internet Explorer.

The following code shows the *IObjectWithSite* interface's *SetSite* method as implemented by the *CWBExplorerBar* class of the WebBand example:

```
STDMETHODIMP CWBExplorerBar::SetSite(IUnknown* pUnkSite)
{
    // If pUnkSite is not NULL, a new site is being set.
    if (pUnkSite)
    {
        //
        // If a pointer to the IInputObjectSite interface is being held,
        // release it.
        //
        if (_pSite)
        {
            _pSite->Release();
            _pSite = NULL;
        }

        // Get the parent window.
        IOleWindow* pOleWindow;

        if (SUCCEEDED(pUnkSite->QueryInterface(IID_IOleWindow,
                      (LPVOID*)&pOleWindow)))
        {
            pOleWindow->GetWindow(&_hwndParent);
            pOleWindow->Release();
        }

        _ASSERT(_hwndParent);
        if (!_hwndParent)
            return E_FAIL;

        if (!RegisterAndCreateWindow())
            return E_FAIL;

        // Get and keep the IInputObjectSite pointer.
        HRESULT hr = pUnkSite->QueryInterface(IID_IInputObjectSite,
                                              (LPVOID*)&_pSite);
        _ASSERT(SUCCEEDED(hr));

        //
        // Get the IWebBrowser2 interface of Internet Explorer
        // so that you can perform such tasks as
        // navigating in the main window and writing to the status bar.
        //
        IOleCommandTarget* pCmdTarget;
```

```
     hr = pUnkSite->QueryInterface(IID_IOleCommandTarget,
                                   (LPVOID*)&pCmdTarget);
     if (SUCCEEDED(hr))
     {
         IServiceProvider* pSP;
         hr = pCmdTarget->QueryInterface(IID_IServiceProvider,
                                         (LPVOID*)&pSP);

         pCmdTarget->Release();

         if (SUCCEEDED(hr))
         {
             if (_pFrameWB)
             {
                 _pFrameWB->Release();
                 _pFrameWB = NULL;
             }

             hr = pSP->QueryService(SID_SWebBrowserApp,
                                    IID_IWebBrowser2,
                                    (LPVOID*)&_pFrameWB);
             _ASSERT(_pFrameWB);

             pSP->Release();
         }
     }
     :



 }

 return S_OK;
}
```

Much of the code in the *SetSite* method pertains to hosting the WebBrowser control in the band object, which we'll look at later in this chapter. But you'll need to include quite a bit of code in this method whether or not you are hosting the WebBrowser control.

The first action that this code performs is to get the *HWND* of the parent window. The code will use it later to perform tasks such as activating the window and determining the window size. To obtain this *HWND*, the code simply queries the *IUnknown* of the site for *IOleWindow* and then calls *IOleWindow*'s *GetWindow* method.

Next a private member function named *RegisterAndCreateWindow* is called to register and create the window for the band object—hence, the name. The implementation of this function is what you would expect when registering a window class and creating a window of that class, as shown on the following page.

```
BOOL CWBExplorerBar::RegisterAndCreateWindow(void)
{
   // If the window doesn't exist yet, create it now.
   if (!_hWnd)
   {
      // Can't create a child window without a parent.
      if (!_hwndParent)
         return FALSE;

      // If the window class hasn't been registered, then do so.
      WNDCLASS wc;
      if (!GetClassInfo(g_hInst, EB_CLASS_NAME, &wc))
      {
         ZeroMemory(&wc, sizeof(wc));
         wc.style          = CS_HREDRAW | CS_VREDRAW | CS_GLOBALCLASS;
         wc.lpfnWndProc    = (WNDPROC)MainWndProc;
         wc.cbClsExtra     = 0;
         wc.cbWndExtra     = 0;
         wc.hInstance      = g_hInst;
         wc.hIcon          = NULL;
         wc.hCursor        = LoadCursor(NULL, IDC_ARROW);
         wc.hbrBackground  = NULL;
         wc.lpszMenuName   = NULL;
         wc.lpszClassName  = EB_CLASS_NAME;

         if (!RegisterClass(&wc))
         {
            // If RegisterClass fails, CreateWindowEx will fail.
         }
      }

      RECT rc;
      GetClientRect(_hWnd, &rc);

      // Create the window. The WndProc will set _hWnd.
      CreateWindowEx(0,
                     EB_CLASS_NAME,
                     NULL,
                     WS_CHILD | WS_CLIPSIBLINGS | WS_BORDER,
                     rc.left,
                     rc.top,
                     rc.right - rc.left,
                     rc.bottom - rc.top,
                     _hwndParent,
                     NULL,
                     g_hInst,
                     (LPVOID)this);
   }
```

```
    return (NULL != _hWnd);
}
```

The next action that is performed in the *SetSite* method is querying the site's *IUnknown* interface for a pointer to the site's implementation of *IInputObjectSite*. This pointer is stored in a data member of the class that will later be used to alert the container when the focus has changed to the band object.

The remainder of the *SetSite* method's code gets a pointer to the *IWebBrowser2* interface of the container (Internet Explorer) and creates and sites an instance of the WebBrowser control that will be hosted in the WebBand Explorer Bar. I'll talk more about this later in this chapter in the section on hosting the WebBrowser control in a band object.

IPersistStream

Internet Explorer calls the methods of your band object's implementation of *IPersistStream* to allow your band object to load or save persistent data. If you don't have any data to load or save, your code must still return *S_OK* from the *Load* and *Save* methods, and it can return *S_FALSE* from the *IsDirty* method.

Implementing Optional Interfaces

You can implement a number of optional interfaces in any ActiveX control or COM object, and a band object is no exception. The interfaces discussed in the following sections are of particular importance for band objects.

IInputObject

The *IInputObject* interface must be implemented by your band object if your band object is going to receive user input. This implementation is necessary, for instance, if your band is hosting the WebBrowser control and you want to allow users to type information into form controls and use accelerator keys such as Backspace and Delete. The WebBand example hosts the WebBrowser control, so the *IInputObject* interface is of particular importance. Internet Explorer implements the *IInputObjectSite* interface and uses the *IInputObject* interface to manage user input focus.

If you implement the *IInputObject* interface in your band object, you must implement its three methods: *UIActivateIO*, *HasFocusIO*, and *TranslateAcceleratorIO*. If you aren't hosting the WebBrowser control, the code for these methods is pretty straightforward, as shown next. But if you are hosting the WebBrowser control, these methods become a little more complex. (See the Appendix for details about the changes to these methods.)

```
STDMETHODIMP CExplorerBar::UIActivateIO(BOOL fActivate, LPMSG pMsg)
{
    if (fActivate)
        SetFocus(m_hWnd);

    return S_OK;
}

STDMETHODIMP CExplorerBar::HasFocusIO(void)
{
    if (m_fFocus)
        return S_OK;

    return S_FALSE;
}

STDMETHODIMP CExplorerBar::TranslateAcceleratorIO(LPMSG pMsg)
{
    return S_FALSE;
}
```

IContextMenu

Implement the *IContextMenu* interface if you want to add items to the context menu that is displayed when you right-click your band object. (If you are hosting the WebBrowser control, the context menu is displayed when you click your band object's title bar.)

IContextMenu has three methods: *QueryContextMenu*, *InvokeCommand*, and *GetCommandString*. The *QueryContextMenu* method is called when the context menu is about to be displayed. In the implementation of *QueryContextMenu*, you can add your context menu items. For example, the WebBand example adds the Refresh menu item and the Open In New Window menu item. WebBand implements the *QueryContextMenu* method like this:

```
STDMETHODIMP CWBExplorerBar::QueryContextMenu(HMENU hmenu,
                                              UINT indexMenu,
                                              UINT idCmdFirst,
                                              UINT idCmdLast,
                                              UINT uFlags)
{
    if (!(CMF_DEFAULTONLY & uFlags))
    {
        InsertMenu(hmenu, indexMenu, MF_STRING | MF_BYPOSITION,
                idCmdFirst + IDM_REFRESH, "&Refresh");

        InsertMenu(hmenu, indexMenu + 1, MF_STRING | MF_BYPOSITION,
                idCmdFirst + IDM_OPENINWINDOW, "&Open in Window");
```

```
        return MAKE_HRESULT(SEVERITY_SUCCESS, 0,
                            USHORT(IDM_OPENINWINDOW + 1));
    }

    return MAKE_HRESULT(SEVERITY_SUCCESS, 0, USHORT(0));
}
```

The *InvokeCommand* method is called when the user selects one of your context menu items. This method is passed a pointer to a structure that contains information about which menu item was selected, including the ID of the menu item. In this method, you can execute whatever code corresponds to the selected menu item.

Here is WebBand's implementation of the *InvokeCommand* method. Notice that the menu items pertain to the WebBrowser's Refresh operation and Open In New Window operation:

```
STDMETHODIMP CWBExplorerBar::InvokeCommand(LPCMINVOKECOMMANDINFO lpici)
{
    switch (LOWORD(lpici->lpVerb))
    {
        case IDM_REFRESH:
            _pWebBrowserOC->Refresh();
            break;

        case IDM_OPENINWINDOW:
            {
                BSTR bstrURL;

                HRESULT hr = _pWebBrowserOC->get_LocationURL(&bstrURL);
                if (SUCCEEDED(hr))
                {
                    _variant_t vtEmpty;
                    _variant_t vtFlags((long)
                                    (navOpenInNewWindow|navNoHistory));

                    hr = _pWebBrowserOC->Navigate(bstrURL, &vtFlags,
                                                  &vtEmpty, &vtEmpty,
                                                  &vtEmpty);
                }

                break;
            }

        default:
            return E_INVALIDARG;
    }

    return NOERROR;
}
```

The *IContextMenu* interface's last method is *GetCommandString*. It is called when Internet Explorer needs help text or a language-independent command name. The help text is typically displayed in Internet Explorer's status bar. (For more information about the *GetCommandString* method, refer to the MSDN documentation or *GetCommandString*'s implementation in the WebBand example.)

Sending Commands to the Container

A band object can send commands to its container to tell the container that the band object's information has changed or to tell the container to maximize the band object. To send commands to the container, query the container for its implementation of the *IOleCommandTarget* interface. You can use the pointer to the *IUnknown* interface that was received in the *SetSite* method or any interface pointer obtained from this *IUnknown* pointer. Then the code should call the *IOleCommandTarget* interface's *Exec* method to send a command to the container.

When calling the *Exec* method, specify *CGID_DeskBand* for the command group and the ID of your band object that you received in the *GetBandInfo* method for the *pvaIn* parameter of *Exec*. Currently, four commands exist that you can send to your container. (These commands are defined in the shlobj.h header file.)

- *DBID_BANDINFOCHANGED*. This command tells the container that the band object's information has changed and that the container should call the band object's *GetBandInfo* method to obtain the updated information.

- *DBID_SHOWONLY*. This command turns other bands on or off. The *vt* member of *pvaIn* should be set to *VT_UNKNOWN*, and the *punkVal* member should be set to one of the following values:

  - *Pointer to* IUnknown *of the current band*. All bands should be hidden except for this band.

  - *0*. Hide every band.

  - *1*. Show every band.

- *DBID_MAXIMIZEBAND*. This command tells the container to maximize your band object.

- *DBID_PUSHCHEVRON*. This command can be used to programmatically display a chevron menu, the type of menu button that contains chevron characters (>>). This menu button is typically displayed on a toolbar when not enough room exists to display all the items on the toolbar. For this command ID, the *nCmdExecOpt* parameter should be set to the ID of the band. The *vt* member of *pvaIn* should be set to *VT_I4*. The *lVal* member of *pvaIn* gets handed back to the band as an *lParam*, which contains the menu notification (*RBN_CHEVRONPUSHED*) to display the chevron drop-down menu.

Implementing the Windows Procedure for the Band Object

You probably wouldn't expect to have to implement a Windows procedure for a band object because it exists in a DLL. But because band objects use child windows for their display, a Windows procedure is required to handle Windows messages. The WebBand example handles a normal set of Windows messages, as shown here:

```
LRESULT CALLBACK MainWndProc(HWND hWnd, UINT uMessage,
                               WPARAM wParam, LPARAM lParam)
{
    if (uMessage == WM_NCCREATE)
    {
        LPCREATESTRUCT lpcs = (LPCREATESTRUCT)lParam;
        SetWindowLong(hWnd, GWL_USERDATA, (LONG)lpcs->lpCreateParams);
    }

    CWBExplorerBar* pThis = reinterpret_cast<CWBExplorerBar*>
                                (GetWindowLong(hWnd, GWL_USERDATA));
    if (pThis)
        return pThis->WndProc(hWnd, uMessage, wParam, lParam);
    else
        return DefWindowProc(hWnd, uMessage, wParam, lParam);
}

LRESULT CWBExplorerBar::WndProc(HWND hWnd, UINT uMessage,
                                  WPARAM wParam, LPARAM lParam)
{
    switch (uMessage)
    {
    case WM_NCCREATE:
    {
        // Set the window handle.
        _hWnd = hWnd;
    }
    break;

    case WM_PAINT:
        return OnPaint();

    case WM_COMMAND:
        return OnCommand(wParam, lParam);

    case WM_SETFOCUS:
        return OnSetFocus();
```

(continued)

```
        case WM_KILLFOCUS:
            return OnKillFocus();

        case WM_SIZE:
            return OnSize();

        case WM_DESTROY:
            Cleanup();
            return 0;
    }
    return DefWindowProc(hWnd, uMessage, wParam, lParam);
}
```

Notice that WebBand uses two functions to handle Windows messages: they keep the code clean and minimize the number of static data members and static member functions. Using this technique, only one global function and no static variables are needed. If the main Windows procedure, *MainWndProc*, were a member of the *CWBExplorerBar* class, it would have to be static. Therefore, any data members accessed in the *MainWndProc* method would have to be static or accessed through the *pThis* local variable.

Two messages in the Windows procedure that are of particular interest are *WM_SETFOCUS* and *WM_KILLFOCUS*. The handlers for these messages inform the site that the focus has changed. This is when the pointer to the *IInputObjectSite* interface that you saved in the *SetSite* method comes into play. In the handlers for these messages, you call *IInputObjectSite::OnFocusChangeIS* to inform the site that the focus has changed.

The following code shows the implementation for these message handlers:

```
LRESULT CWBExplorerBar::OnSetFocus(void)
{
    FocusChange(TRUE);
    return 0;
}


LRESULT CWBExplorerBar::OnKillFocus(void)
{
    FocusChange(FALSE);
    return 0;
}


void CWBExplorerBar::FocusChange(BOOL fFocus)
{
    // Inform the input object site that the focus has changed.
    //
    if (_pSite)
        _pSite->OnFocusChangeIS(static_cast<IDockingWindow*>(this), fFocus);
}
```

Hosting the WebBrowser Control in a Band Object

Because a band object is just a COM object, it can contain ActiveX controls like any other COM object. If you want to host the WebBrowser control in your band object, all you have to do is implement the correct interfaces and call the right methods to create and site the WebBrowser control.

At a minimum, to contain ActiveX controls, your band object should implement the following interfaces: *IOleClientSite*, *IOleInPlaceSite*, and *IOleControlSite*. Most of the methods of these interfaces are implemented by using boilerplate code, so we won't look at them here. In fact, most of them can return only *E_NOTIMPL* or *S_OK*. (Take a look at the WebBand example if you're interested in implementing these methods.)

However, one method deserves more attention: *IOleControlSite::OnFocus*. This method is called when the control being hosted by your band object receives or loses the focus. Just as in the message handler for *WM_SETFOCUS*, when *IOleControlSite:: OnFocus* is called you must inform the site that the focus has changed by calling *IInputObjectSite::OnFocusChangeIS*. If you don't inform the site that focus has changed, you'll experience problems with accelerator keys on Web pages that contain text boxes and text areas. (The Appendix discusses problems with band object accelerator keys in more detail.) Here's the implementation code for the *OnFocus* method:

```
STDMETHODIMP CWBExplorerBar::OnFocus(BOOL fGotFocus)
{
    if (_pSite)
        _pSite->OnFocusChangeIS(static_cast<IInputObject*>(this),
                                fGotFocus);

    return S_OK;
}
```

After implementing the interfaces that your band object requires so that it can be an ActiveX control host, you must call the methods to create and site the control. These actions usually occur in the *SetSite* method, so let's take another look at that method now. This time, the code shows how to create and site the WebBrowser control:

```
STDMETHODIMP CWBExplorerBar::SetSite(IUnknown* pUnkSite)
{
    // If pUnkSite is not NULL, a new site is being set.
    if (pUnkSite)
```

(continued)

```
{
    ⋮
    // Create and initialize the WebBrowser control that we are hosting.
    hr = CoCreateInstance(CLSID_WebBrowser, NULL, CLSCTX_INPROC,
                          IID_IOleObject, (LPVOID*)&_pIOleObject);
    if (hr != S_OK)
        return E_FAIL;

    if (_pIOleObject->SetClientSite(this) != S_OK)
        return E_FAIL;

    // Get the rectangle of the client area.
    RECT rcClient = { CW_USEDEFAULT, 0, 0, 0 };
    GetClientRect(_hWnd, &rcClient);

    MSG msg;

    // In-place activate the WebBrowser control.
    hr = _pIOleObject->DoVerb(OLEIVERB_INPLACEACTIVATE, &msg,
                              this, 0, _hWnd, &rcClient);
    _ASSERT(SUCCEEDED(hr));

    if (FAILED(hr))
        return E_FAIL;

    //
    // Get the pointer to the WebBrowser control.
    //
    hr = _pIOleObject->QueryInterface(IID_IWebBrowser2,
                                      (LPVOID*)&_pWebBrowserOC);
    _ASSERT(_pWebBrowserOC);

    if (FAILED(hr))
        return E_FAIL;
    else
    {
        // Set up an event sink for the WebBrowser events.
        if (_pWebBrowserOC)
            AdviseWBEventSink();

        //
        // QI for the in-place object to set the size.
        //
        if (_pIOleIPObject)
        {
            _pIOleIPObject->Release();
            _pIOleIPObject = NULL;
        }
```

```
        hr = _pWebBrowserOC->QueryInterface(IID_IOleInPlaceObject,
                                            (LPVOID*)&_pIOleIPObject);
        _ASSERT(_pIOleIPObject);

        if (FAILED(hr))
            return E_FAIL;

        hr = _pIOleIPObject->SetObjectRects(&rcClient, &rcClient);
        _ASSERT(SUCCEEDED(hr));

        // Navigate to the sample search page.
        _variant_t vtEmpty;
        _bstr_t bstrURL(STARTUP_URL);

        _pWebBrowserOC->Navigate(bstrURL, &vtEmpty, &vtEmpty,
                                 &vtEmpty, &vtEmpty);

        // Get the HWND of the WebBrowser control.
        //
        IOleWindow* pWnd;

        if (SUCCEEDED(_pWebBrowserOC->QueryInterface(IID_IOleWindow,
                                                     (LPVOID*)&pWnd)))
        {
            pWnd->GetWindow(&_hwndWB);
            pWnd->Release();
        }
    }
}

    return S_OK;
}
```

First this code creates an instance of the WebBrowser control—nothing new to you by now. When calling *CoCreateInstance* to create the control, a pointer to the *IOleObject* interface of the host is obtained so that the *IOleObject* interface's *SetClientSite* method can then be called to set the client site for the control. Then the *IOleObject::DoVerb* method is called to in-place activate the WebBrowser control.

Next the pointer to the *IOleObject* interface is queried for a pointer to *IWebBrowser2*. This pointer will be used later to navigate within the band object and perform any other task that you would normally expect of this type of pointer, such as setting up an event sink (which is done next in the *SetSite* method).

Next the pointer to the *IWebBrowser2* interface is queried for *IOleInPlaceObject*, which sets the size of the WebBrowser control by calling the *SetObjectRects* method of *IOleInPlaceObject*.

The *IWebBrowser2::Navigate* method is then called to navigate to a Web page. Finally the pointer to *IWebBrowser2* is queried for *IOleWindow* so that the *GetWindow* method can be called to get the *HWND* of the WebBrowser control. This *HWND* will be used in the *IInputObject::HasFocusIO* method to determine whether the WebBrowser control or any of its child windows has the focus. (This is discussed in more detail in the Appendix.)

You must perform one last task to make this all work. In the handler for the *WM_SIZE* message, the code must call *IOleInPlaceObject::SetObjectRects* to resize the WebBrowser control window when your band object's window is resized. If the code doesn't call this method, the WebBrowser control will always be the same size. The following code shows WebBand's implementation of the message handler for *WM_SIZE*:

```
LRESULT CWBExplorerBar::OnSize(void)
{
   HRESULT hr = E_FAIL;

   if (_pIOleIPObject)
   {
      RECT rcClient;
      GetClientRect(_hWnd, &rcClient);

      hr = _pIOleIPObject->SetObjectRects(&rcClient, &rcClient);
      _ASSERT(SUCCEEDED(hr));
   }

   return hr;
}
```

ADDING TOOLBAR BUTTONS

Now that you know all about band objects, let's add some buttons to Internet Explorer's toolbar so that you'll be able to run any application on your system with the click of a button. You can execute Explorer Bars, COM objects, scripts, and normal executable applications directly from Internet Explorer's toolbar, allowing you to easily start your favorite applications or scripts without having to search through a maze of menus or folders on your hard disk. Adding toolbar buttons also makes Explorer Bars easier to use because you won't have to search for them on Internet Explorer's menus.

Just as when you created an Explorer Bar in DHTML and script, you must add the information in the Registry before you can add toolbar buttons to the Internet Explorer user interface. Because adding this information manually can be cumbersome, you might want to have an ActiveX control or the setup program for an application or a band object update the Registry for you. To update the Registry, follow these steps:

1. Create a new GUID as you did when creating a DHTML Explorer Bar on pages 388–92.

2. Use this newly created GUID as the name of a new key you create under the key *HKEY_LOCAL_MACHINE\Software\Microsoft\Internet Explorer\ Extensions*. The new key should look like this:

    ```
    HKEY_LOCAL_MACHINE\Software\Microsoft\Internet
        Explorer\Extensions\<Your New GUID>
    ```

3. Optionally, you can create a new string value under the key you created in step 2 that will cause your toolbar button to appear on the Internet Explorer toolbar by default. Name this new string value *Default Visible*. (Notice that this name is two words.) Set *Default Visible* to *Yes* to show the button by default; otherwise, set it to *No*.

    By default, new buttons aren't displayed on the Internet Explorer toolbar. They are included on the left side of the Customize Toolbar dialog box.

4. Create a new string value under the key you created in step 2, and name it *ButtonText*. It should point to the label you want for the new toolbar button.

5. Create a new string value under the key you created in step 2. Name this string value *HotIcon*. Set the value of *HotIcon* to the full path of the file that contains the icon that you want displayed when the mouse hovers over the button.

    The value of *HotIcon* can point directly to an .ico file that contains the icon or to a resource in a DLL or other resource file. (For more on icons, see the sidebar following these steps.)

6. Create a new string value under the key you created in step 2, and name it *Icon*.

7. Set the value of *Icon* to the full path of the file that contains the icon for the button.

    Optionally, you can provide support for multiple native languages. For more information about adding this support, refer to the MSDN Online Web Workshop.

REFERENCING ICONS

Icons that are stored in a resource such as a DLL can be referenced by providing the path to the resource and the ID of the icon in the following format: *"path,resourceID"*. For instance, if the icon is stored in a DLL named YourDll.dll and has a resource ID of *104*, you would reference it like this: "YourDll.dll,104".

For more information about creating icons for Internet Explorer and a style guide about toolbar buttons, refer to the MSDN Online Web Workshop Toolbar Button Style Guide: *http://msdn.microsoft.com/workshop/browser/ext/overview/ toolbar_style.asp*.)

At this point, the Registry key and values you added should resemble those shown in Figure 10-10. (The button won't actually show on the toolbar until you add more information about the action to take when the button is clicked.)

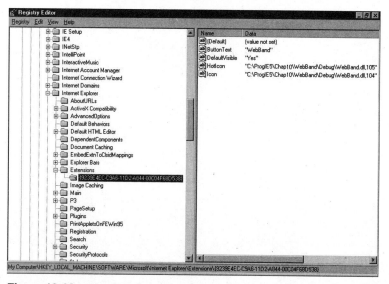

Figure 10-10. *Initial Registry key and values.*

Now that you've entered the preliminary Registry information for the new toolbar button, you must enter some additional Registry information. The information will vary depending on what will be run when the toolbar is clicked.

Displaying Explorer Bars

To create a toolbar button that displays an Explorer Bar when clicked, follow these additional steps:

1. Create a new string value under the GUID key (*HKEY_LOCAL_MACHINE\ Software\Microsoft\Internet Explorer\Extensions*<Your New GUID>) that you created in the steps in the previous section. Name this string value *CLSID*. Set the value of *CLSID* to the following:

   ```
   {E0DD6CAB-2D10-11D2-8F1A-0000F87ABD16}
   ```

2. Create a new string value under the same key, and name it *BandCLSID*. Set the value of *BandCLSID* to the CLSID of your Explorer Bar.

   The WebBand example includes the necessary code to register the toolbar information. If you compile and register WebBand and start Internet Explorer, you will see the WebBand icon on the toolbar, as shown in Figure 10-11.

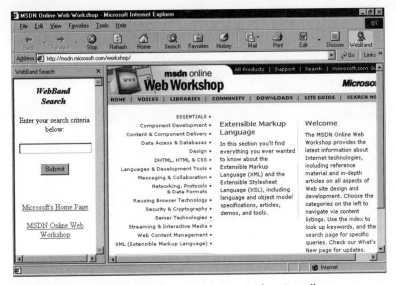

Figure 10-11. *WebBand button on Internet Explorer's toolbar.*

Running COM Objects

If you are creating a toolbar button to run a COM object, follow these additional steps:

1. After registering your COM object and performing the initial steps to update the Registry, create a new string value named *CLSID* under the GUID key you created in the initial steps. Set the value of *CLSID* to the following:

   ```
   {1FBA04EE-3024-11D2-8F1F-0000F87ABD16}
   ```

2. Create a new string value under the GUID key named *ClsidExtension*. Set the value of *ClsidExtension* to the CLSID of the COM object that you want to run. This COM object must implement *IOleCommandTarget*.

The *Exec* method of this interface will be called with *nCmdID* equal to *1* when the button is clicked and *2* when the menu item associated with this COM object is selected. (You'll implement the menu item shortly.) If your COM object needs to access the DHTML Object Model of the page that Internet Explorer is displaying, the COM object must implement *IObjectWithSite*. If the COM object implements *IObjectWithSite*, when the *SetSite* method is called the method will be passed a pointer to the *IShellBrowser* interface implemented in Internet Explorer.

Running Scripts

You can also create a toolbar button that runs script when it is clicked. In addition to the initial steps to update the Registry, you need to follow these steps:

1. Create a new string value under the GUID key that you created in the initial steps. Name this string value *CLSID*, and give it the following value:

    ```
    {1FBA04EE-3024-11D2-8F1F-0000F87ABD16}
    ```

2. Create a new string value named *Script* beneath the GUID key. Set the value of *Script* to the full path of the file that contains the script that you want to run. Make sure that no *Exec* string value exists. The *Script* and *Exec* values can't coexist.

    NOTE   Script that is run from a toolbar button or a menu item has an HTML window; therefore, it can access *window* and *document* object methods such as *alert*. But if you try to use methods that aren't in the DHTML Object Model, such as VBScript's *MsgBox* function, you will receive a run-time error.

Running Executable Files

Finally, you can also create buttons that run executable files that exist on your system. Along with the initial steps to update the Registry, perform the following steps:

1. Create a new string value under the GUID key that you created in the initial steps. Name this string value *CLSID*, and give it the following value:

    ```
    {1FBA04EE-3024-11D2-8F1F-0000F87ABD16}
    ```

2. Create a new string value named *Exec* beneath the GUID key. Set the value of *Exec* to the full path of the .exe file that you want to run. Make sure that no *Script* string value exists. These two values can't coexist.

ADDING MAIN MENU ITEMS

Besides adding toolbar buttons, you can also add menu items that correspond to COM objects, scripts, and executable files. You don't need to add menu items for Explorer Bars manually because they are automatically added for you when you register your Explorer Bar.

The menu items that you create are added to Internet Explorer's Tools menu. The steps to create menu items are almost identical to the steps you must follow to create toolbar buttons. To create menu items, follow the steps for creating a toolbar button on pages 416–19, plus these additional three steps. If you don't want a toolbar button to be created, just omit the step to add the *ButtonText* string value.

1. Create a new string value named *MenuText* under your GUID key. The value of *MenuText* is the text that will appear on the Tools menu. Unlike normal menu items, this text doesn't support any underlining for shortcut keys because there is no way to prevent conflicts with menu shortcuts.

2. If you want text to appear in Internet Explorer's status bar when the menu item is highlighted, create a new string value named *MenuStatusBar* under the GUID key. The value of *MenuStatusBar* is the text that will appear in Internet Explorer's status bar when your menu item is highlighted.

3. If you want the new menu item to exist on Internet Explorer's Help menu instead of on the Tools menu, under your GUID key, create a new string value named *MenuCustomize*. Set the value of *MenuCustomize* to *Help*. If you set the value of *MenuCustomize* to anything other than *Help*, the menu item will appear under the Tools menu.

ADDING CONTEXT MENU ITEMS

To wrap up our work with browser extensions, let's add menu items to Internet Explorer's standard context menu, the menu that is displayed when you right-click in the document window. You can add context menu items that execute script files located at a specific URL. Just as with adding toolbar buttons or menu items, creating context menu items involves adding some information to the Registry.

To add menu items to the Internet Explorer context menu, follow these steps:

1. Create a new key under the following Registry key:

```
HKEY_CURRENT_USER\Software\Microsoft\Internet Explorer\MenuExt
```

2. Give the new key the name of the item as you want it to appear in the context menu. Include an ampersand character (&) before the letter of your menu item that you want used as a shortcut key. The new key will look like this:

```
HKEY_CURRENT_USER\Software\Microsoft\Internet
    Explorer\MenuExt\<Your Menu Text>
```

3. Set the default value of this new key to the URL of the script file that you want to execute when this context menu item is selected. This script can obtain the *window* object of the parent window from the *menuArguments* property of the *external* object. For example, if you want to obtain the URL of the current document, use the *menuArguments* property, like this:

```
alert(window.external.menuArguments.document.location.href);
```

That's it. You're finished! Couldn't be much simpler. Now you might want to add a few optional values to your key to be more specific about when your menu item should be displayed and how the script should be run. For example, you might want to specify that your context menu item is displayed in the default context menu or only when the user right-clicks on a link. To specify when your context menu item should be displayed, create a new binary value under the context menu item key you created in step 1. The name of this binary value should be *Contexts*, and the value of *Contexts* should be one of the values listed in Table 10-3.

TABLE 10-3
CONTEXTS BINARY VALUES

Context	Value	Description
Default	0x01	The menu item is displayed in the default context menu.
Images	0x02	The menu item is displayed in the context menu for images.
Controls	0x04	The menu item is displayed in the context menu for ActiveX controls.
Tables	0x08	The menu item is displayed in the context menu for tables.
Text Selection	0x10	The menu item is displayed in the context menu for selected text.
Anchor	0x20	The menu item is displayed in the context menu for anchors (also known as hyperlinks).

Furthermore, you can combine these values to specify more than one context by logically OR'ing values together. For example, if you wanted the menu item to be displayed for the context menus for text selection and anchors, you would set the value of *Contexts* to *30*.

> **NOTE**   Don't enter the *0x* portion of the value in the Registry. The *0x* just appears in the table so that you know that these are hexadecimal values.

Besides being able to specify in which context menu you want the menu item to display, you can also specify how you want the script to run. You can create a *DWORD* value that is named *Flags* under your menu item key. Currently, only one value can be specified for *Flags*: *0x01*. This value causes the script to be run as if it had been called via the *showModalDialog* method, in which case your script will not be able to access the *window* object of the parent through the *menuArguments* property of the *external* object.

That's it! Now that you've read this chapter, you can create your own Web Accessories by using different types of browser extensions. You can also download a number of Web Accessories from Microsoft's Web site—such as those created by Microsoft developers and a few created by third-party vendors—from *http://www.microsoft.com/windows/ie/webaccess*. Some of the Web Accessories are Explorer Bars that enhance your navigation experience. Others include a quick search tool, a context menu item to list all the links on a page, a context menu item that lets you zoom images on your Web page, and many more. I encourage you to download them all and give them a try.

WHAT'S NEXT?

In this chapter, you learned how to customize Internet Explorer to fit your needs and the needs of your users. By creating Web Accessories, you can customize Internet Explorer to make it easier to use.

In the next chapter, we'll check out the hottest new Internet Explorer 5 technology—Behaviors. Behaviors allow you to create components that you can reuse from one Web page to the next. You can create these components by using only DHTML and script or by using C++ and COM.

Chapter 11

DHTML
Behaviors and
HTML Components

In Chapter 2, you learned how to enhance Web pages and create Web-based applications by using Microsoft JScript and Microsoft VBScript. But one of the biggest problems with writing script is reusability. If you want to reuse your script, you can copy it from one HTML file to another, but if you have a lot of files in which you want to use this script, this task can be quite overwhelming. You can also place all your script in a separate file and include the file in an HTML file by using the SRC attribute of the <SCRIPT> tag. Although this approach will work in most respects, it doesn't allow you to easily attach event handlers to specific elements on the Web page, and it doesn't allow your script component to expose an object model of its own and fire events.

Once again, Microsoft Internet Explorer 5 comes to the rescue! One of its best new features is DHTML Behaviors—lightweight components that encapsulate specific functionality, or behavior, on a Web page. You can easily attach a DHTML Behavior (or Behavior, for short) to any HTML element on a Web page, thereby enhancing the element's default behavior. Because a Behavior's methods, properties, and events appear to be part of the HTML element to which the Behavior is attached, the Behavior extends the element's object model.

Furthermore, DHTML Behaviors allow you to separate the dynamic functionality of a Web page from its content and design, ensuring the integrity of a Web page—a critical advantage when the content author, designer, and engineer are all working independently on a Web site. Although cascading style sheets (CSS), which Internet Explorer 3 introduced a few years ago, allowed you to separate the design of a Web page from its content and dynamic functionality, you couldn't separate the dynamic functionality from the content.

DHTML Behaviors also make the dynamic functionality of your Web pages more manageable. To change the dynamic functionality, you have to change only the script that resides in the DHTML Behavior component instead of changing the script that resides on every single Web page. For example, the DHTML Ledger application discussed in Chapter 3 is implemented entirely in DHTML and script. As you can see from the code on the companion CD, the amount of code is overwhelming! (The location for this code is \Samples\Chap03\DHTML Ledger.) Luckily, DHTML Behaviors allow you to remove script from the HTML document and place it in a separate component that you can attach to individual elements in the document and reuse across multiple pages. Using a DHTML Behavior, you need only one line of code to reuse the Ledger component, as shown here:

```
<DIV ID=sheet1 STYLE="behavior:url(ledger.htc)"></DIV>
```

One line of code is much easier to deal with—wouldn't you agree? Along with making the page simpler to manage, Behaviors allow you to propagate changes to all pages that are using the DHTML Ledger Behavior, an example application that you'll see later in this chapter. You'll also learn about default Behaviors, using DHTML Behaviors created with HTCs, and Binary DHTML Behaviors. You'll have the opportunity to create your own Behaviors as well.

USING DEFAULT BEHAVIORS

Internet Explorer installs a number of its own default Behaviors, as shown in Table 11-1. Two categories of these default Behaviors are of particular importance to Web developers: client capabilities and persistence. The next two sections cover these Behaviors in detail. For more information about the other default Behaviors, refer to the MSDN Online Web Workshop.

TABLE 11-1
INTERNET EXPLORER'S DEFAULT BEHAVIORS

Behavior	Description
AnchorClick	Enables browser navigation to a folder.
anim	Defines an instance of the Microsoft DirectAnimation viewer in an HTML page that can be used to render DirectAnimation objects and play DirectAnimation sounds. (For more information about the Microsoft DirectAnimation viewer, refer to MSDN Online: *http://msdn.microsoft.com.*)
animation	Defines a timed animation element.
audio	Defines a timed audio element.
clientCaps	Provides information about the features supported by the current instance of Internet Explorer and enables installation of browser components on demand.
download	Provides a means to download a file. You can also use this Behavior to indicate a specified callback function that will be called when download is complete.
homePage	Contains information about a user's home page.
httpFolder	Contains scripting features that enable browser navigation to a folder view.
img	Defines a timed image element.
media	Defines a generic, timed media element.
par	Defines a new timeline container. All HTML descendents of this element will have independent, or parallel, timing.
saveFavorite	Enables an object to save data in a Favorites list.
saveHistory	Enables an object to save data in the browser history.
saveSnapshot	Enables an object to save data in a snapshot.
seq	Defines a new timeline container for sequentially timed elements.
time	Provides an active timeline. By using this Behavior, you can set any HTML element to appear at a given time, last for a specified duration, and repeat the behavior if desired.
userData	Enables an object to persist data in user data.
video	Defines a timed video element.

When using the default Behaviors in HTML, you specify the ID of the Behavior, preceded by the pound sign (#). You must also include the *#default* ID before the ID of the Behavior to tell Internet Explorer that the ID of the Behavior you are specifying is a default Behavior implemented by Internet Explorer. For example, you would use the following syntax to attach the *time* Behavior to the <BODY> tag:

```
<BODY ID="oTimeBehavior" STYLE="behavior:url(#default#time)">
```

Client Capabilities

When designing a Web site, you typically want to support users whose systems have different capabilities. For example, users will be accessing your Web site via different types of Internet connections: modem, LAN, and so forth. If they're connecting to your Web site via modem, which is usually slower than a LAN connection, you might want to limit the number and types of graphics displayed on the page, for example.

Also, certain Internet Explorer features might be disabled on a user's machine, such as support of Java applications. In versions earlier than Internet Explorer 5, if you wanted everyone to be able to access your Web sites, you had to design the sites to work correctly with the lowest common denominator system. For instance, maybe you couldn't include high-resolution graphics, Java applets, or any of the other cool Internet Explorer features on your Web site. Or maybe you designed your Web site to work only on systems that used a certain type of Internet connection and that had Java enabled, thus denying low-end users the pleasure of enjoying your Web site.

clientCaps

To address these issues, Internet Explorer 5 includes a default Behavior named *clientCaps*. The *clientCaps* Behavior allows you to determine the capabilities of the client system when your Web site is accessed; furthermore, it allows you to display different data depending on how the client system is configured. For example, if the user is hooked up to the Internet via a LAN connection, you can display high-resolution graphics. On the other hand, if the user is connected via a modem, you might want to display lower-resolution graphics.

As with the other default Behaviors that Internet Explorer 5 installs, you attach the *clientCaps* Behavior by using the *#default* ID, followed by the ID of the *clientCaps* Behavior. You use the following code to attach this default Behavior to the <BODY> tag on your Web page:

```
<BODY ID="oClientCaps" STYLE="behavior:url(#default#clientCaps)">
```

Once you've added the *clientCaps* Behavior to an HTML element, you can access the properties of the object to which the Behavior is attached (in this case, the *body* object, which is represented by the *oClientCaps* ID) to determine the different capabilities of the client system. Table 11-2 lists the properties of the *clientCaps* Behavior.

TABLE 11-2
PROPERTIES OF THE *CLIENTCAPS* DEFAULT BEHAVIOR

Property	Description
availHeight	Returns the height of the working area of the system's screen, in pixels, excluding the Microsoft Windows taskbar
availWidth	Returns the width of the working area of the system's screen, in pixels, excluding the Windows taskbar
bufferDepth	Returns the number of bits per pixel used for colors on the offscreen bitmap buffer
colorDepth	Returns the number of bits per pixel used for colors on the destination device or buffer
connectionType	Specifies the type of connection currently being used (LAN, modem, or offline)
cookieEnabled	Returns whether client-side cookies are enabled
cpuClass	Returns a string that indicates the class of the CPU being used (*x86*, *Alpha*, or *Other*)
height	Returns the vertical resolution of the screen in pixels
javaEnabled	Indicates whether the Microsoft virtual machine is enabled
platform	Returns a string that indicates the platform on which the browser is running—for example, the Microsoft Windows 32-bit platform, the Microsoft Windows 16-bit platform, or the Microsoft Windows CE platform
systemLanguage	Returns the default language that the system is using (For a list of language codes, refer to the following document in the MSDN Online Web Workshop: *http://msdn.microsoft.com/ workshop/author/dhtml/reference/language_codes.asp.*)
userLanguage	Returns the current user language
width	Returns the horizontal resolution of the screen, in pixels

The *clientCaps* Behavior also includes a number of methods that you can use to determine information about the particular components of the client's system to be installed. Table 11-3 on the following page lists these methods.

To see how to use the *clientCaps* Behavior, take a look at the ClientCaps Web page shown in Figure 11-1 on the next page. The ClientCaps example, which you can find on the companion CD in the folder \Samples\Chap11, enables you to determine any of the capabilities of the client system on which the browser is running.

TABLE 11-3
METHODS OF THE *CLIENTCAPS* DEFAULT BEHAVIOR

Method	Description
addComponentRequest	Adds a component to the queue of components to be installed; specify one of the component IDs listed on *http://msdn.microsoft.com/workshop/author/behaviors/ reference/methods/installable.asp*
clearComponentRequest	Clears the queue of all component download requests
compareVersions	Compares two version numbers retrieved by using the *getComponentVersion* method
doComponentRequest	Downloads all the components that have been queued by using the *addComponentRequest* method
getComponentVersion	Returns the version of the specified component; for this method and the *isComponentInstalled* method, specify a component from the list of detectable component identifiers listed on *http://msdn.microsoft.com/workshop/ author/behaviors/reference/methods/detectable.asp*
isComponentInstalled	Returns a Boolean value indicating whether the specified component is installed

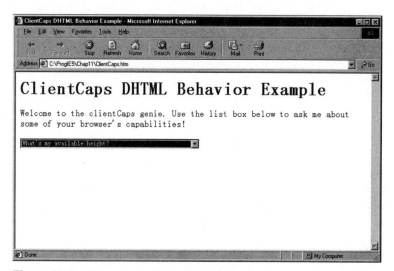

Figure 11-1. *ClientCaps DHTML Behavior example.*

In this example, the *clientCaps* Behavior is attached to the <BODY> tag, as you saw earlier. The ClientCaps example contains a drop-down list box that has option items for each of the client capabilities listed in Table 11-2 and these two methods listed in Table 11-3: *getComponentVersion* and *isComponentInstalled*. When the user selects an item in the list, the *queryGenie* function is called.

In the *queryGenie* function, the currently selected item is interrogated. The *select* object's *selectedIndex* property is used to determine the selected item, and a *switch* statement is used for the *selectedIndex* property to determine which client capability to display to the user. For example, to determine which type of connection the user activated to hook up to the Internet, you can use the *connectionType* property, like this:

```
case 5:
   answer = "Your connection type is " + oClientCaps.connectionType + ".";
   break;
```

The ClientCaps example also demonstrates how to determine whether the Microsoft VRML Viewer is installed by using the *isComponentInstalled* method of the *clientCaps* Behavior. (For more information about the Microsoft VRML Viewer, visit the Microsoft VRML home page: *http://www.microsoft.com/VRML.*)

```
case 14:
   answer = "You ";
   if (oClientCaps.isComponentInstalled("x-vrml", "mimetype") == false)
   {
      answer = answer + "do not ";
   }

   answer = answer + "have the Microsoft VRML Viewer installed.";
   break;
```

The ClientCaps application demonstrates how to determine the version of an installed component as well. For example, it determines what version of the Microsoft Media Player is installed by using the *getComponentVersion* method:

```
case 15:
   var version;
   version = oClientCaps.getComponentVersion(
               "{22d6f312-b0f6-11d0-94ab-0080c74c7e95}",
               "componentid");
   if (version != null)
   {
      answer = "You have version " + version
            + " of the Microsoft Media Player installed.";
   }
```

(continued)

```
else
{
    answer = "You do not have the Microsoft Media Player installed.";
}
break;
```

Persistence

Persistence is another important category of default Behaviors. How many times have you navigated to a customizable Web page and changed it to fit your preferences, only to lose those preferences when you navigated away from the page or shut down the browser? By using Internet Explorer 5's four default persistence Behaviors (discussed at length in the following sections), you can save the state and information of a page in different ways, as the following list shows:

- *saveFavorite*. Persists the current state of the Web page when it is saved as a favorite in the Favorites list.

- *saveHistory*. Persists the state of the Web page when the user navigates away from it.

- *saveSnapshot*. Allows you to persist form values, styles, dynamic content, and scripting variables when the user has saved a Web page using Internet Explorer's Save As menu item. The values being persisted are included in the saved document.

- *userData*. Allows you to persist information across sessions by writing to an XML data store. This information is saved when the page is unloaded and restored whenever the page is reloaded.

  NOTE   XML is outside the scope of this book. For more information, refer to the MSDN Online Web Workshop.

To learn about how each of these persistence Behaviors is used, check out another example named LinkBuilder, which is on the companion CD in the folder \Samples\Chap11. (See Figure 11-2.) This example allows you to save link information by using the various persistence Behaviors.

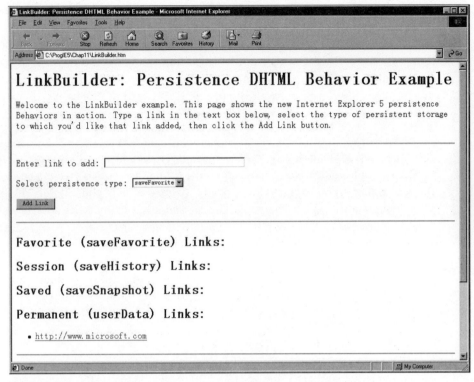

Figure 11-2. *LinkBuilder persistence DHTML Behavior example.*

saveFavorite

The *saveFavorite* Behavior requires that you specify the <META> tag, the *style* block, and the CLASS attributes in order to persist an object. The ID attribute is also recommended for performance reasons. The LinkBuilder example specifies these elements as follows:

```
<HTML>
<HEAD>
   <META NAME="SAVE" content="favorite">
   <STYLE>
      .saveFavorite {behavior:url(#default#saveFavorite);}
   </STYLE>
</HEAD>

<BODY>
   <UL ID="oLinks0" CLASS="saveFavorite"></UL>
</BODY>
</HTML>
```

In this code, the <META> and <STYLE> tags are used to specify that the Web page is persistent and that it uses the *saveFavorite* Behavior. CLASS is included as an attribute of the <UL> tag, and it specifies the type of persistence that the element is using. That's all you need to do. Now when you save the page as a favorite, all information that is part of the <UL> tag is saved with the Favorites. (The LinkBuilder application dynamically inserts HTML into the <UL> tag by using the *insertAdjacentHTML* and *innerHTML* properties discussed in Chapter 3.)

saveHistory

The *saveHistory* Behavior requires the same three elements as the *saveFavorite* Behavior. The LinkBuilder example uses the *saveHistory* Behavior to save the links you've entered so that if you navigate away from a page, the links you entered will be displayed when you return to the page. This Behavior has many other uses as well. For example, it persists information for the current browser instance, so if you shut down Internet Explorer, the information you persisted will appear the next time you start the browser and navigate to your page.

The following HTML shows the *saveHistory* Behavior implementation in the LinkBuilder example:

```
<HTML>
<HEAD>
   <META NAME="SAVE" content="history">
   <STYLE>
      .saveHistory {behavior:url(#default#saveHistory);}
   </STYLE>
</HEAD>

<BODY>
   <UL ID="oLinks1" CLASS="saveHistory"></UL>
</BODY>
</HTML>
```

Note that the *style* block typically contains all the Behaviors that you're using for the current Web page. In other words, you'll have only one *style* block on your page. Or, instead of the *style* block, you can use an inline STYLE attribute (as you'll see in the section "Using Behaviors Created with HTML Components").

saveSnapshot

The *saveSnapshot* Behavior allows you to save form data directly within the page. This data is then persisted when you save the Web page by using Internet Explorer's Save As dialog box. The *saveSnapshot* Behavior requires the same elements as the other two Behaviors we've just looked at. However, the ID attribute in this Behavior isn't optional; it's required. Here's the HTML that implements the *saveSnapshot* Behavior in the LinkBuilder example:

```
<HTML>
<HEAD>
   <META NAME="SAVE" content="snapshot">
   <STYLE>
      .saveSnapshot {behavior:url(#default#saveSnapshot);}
   </STYLE>
</HEAD>

<BODY>
   <UL ID="oLinks2" CLASS="saveSnapshot"></UL>
</BODY>
</HTML>
```

userData

The *userData* Behavior persists session data from one session to the next. A session is a connection between a browser and a server. Sessions are generally used for virtual shopping Web sites or search engines. Session data consists of session files and variables that contain user identification, activity, and other information. These session files and variables are typically used in CGI scripts or Active Server Pages to save the state or other information of a session on the server. By using the new Internet Explorer *userData* Behavior, you can persist this data on the client side instead of on the server side.

> **NOTE**   The *userData* Behavior is an excellent replacement for client-side cookies. Just like the *userData* Behavior, cookies can save session information; however, client-side cookies suffer from a 4-KB data limit. The *userData* Behavior doesn't have this upper limit. If you're currently using client-side cookies, consider using the *userData* Behavior instead.

The *userData* Behavior requires three elements to function properly: a *style* block or STYLE attribute, an ID attribute, and a CLASS attribute that are applied to the object whose data you want to persist. The following code shows these three elements as they are included in the LinkBuilder example. (The META element isn't needed for the *userData* Behavior as it is for the other persistence Behaviors.)

```
<HTML>
<HEAD>
   <STYLE>
      .userData {behavior:url(#default#userData);}
   </STYLE>
</HEAD>

<BODY>
   <UL ID="oLinks3" CLASS="userData" ></UL>
</BODY>
</HTML>
```

Unlike the other persistence Behaviors, the data to be stored with the *userData* Behavior isn't stored automatically when you shut down (or save) the page, nor is it loaded automatically when you restore the page. To save the data, you must use the *setAttribute* method to store the data in an attribute, and then call the *save* method to save the data in an arbitrary XML store. You'll typically call these methods when you're unloading the current page (in other words, in the *onunload* event handler of the *window* object.) The following VBScript code stores user data information as it is implemented in the LinkBuilder example:

```
Sub window_onunload()
    Dim elem

    Set elem = document.all.oLinks3
    elem.setAttribute "sInnerHTML", elem.innerHTML
    elem.save "oXMLBranch"
    Set elem = Nothing
End Sub
```

In this code, the call to *setAttribute* sets the data for an attribute. The first parameter to *setAttribute* is the attribute name. You can use any name you want, keeping in mind that you'll use this name when retrieving the data later. The *save* method is then used to save the data to an arbitrary XML data store.

When this Web page is reloaded, you'll probably want to load the data that was previously stored by using the *userData* Behavior. First call the *load* method to load the XML data store that you previously saved, and then call the *getAttribute* method to retrieve the data that you previously saved when calling the *setAttribute* method. Typically, you'll want to call these methods in the *onload* event handler of the *window* object because *onload* is fired when the Web page is finished loading.

The following code loads user data as it is implemented in the LinkBuilder example:

```
Sub window_onload()
    Dim elem

    Set elem = document.all.oLinks3
    elem.load "oXMLBranch"

    If Not IsNull(elem.getAttribute("sInnerHTML")) Then
        elem.innerHTML = elem.getAttribute("sInnerHTML")
    End If

    Set elem = Nothing
End Sub
```

When calling the *load* method, this code specifies the name of the XML store that was specified in the call to the *save* method in the *window_onunload* event handler. Also, when calling the *getAttribute* method to retrieve the actual data, the code specifies the same attribute name that was specified when *setAttribute* was called.

OK, we're finished looking at DHTML default Behaviors. Now let's see how you can implement Behaviors yourself and even create your own. We'll work with HTML Components (HTCs) by using DHTML and script.

USING BEHAVIORS CREATED WITH HTML COMPONENTS

HTML Components (HTCs) are components that encapsulate script and can be attached to HTML elements on a Web page. But they are more than that, as you'll see when you create your own DHTML Behaviors with HTCs. Using Behaviors created with HTCs is simple. Either you use the new scripting methods, or you use the new CSS behavior attribute. (Microsoft has proposed this attribute as an addition to the CSS standard.)

Attaching Behaviors to HTML Elements

You can use the new *addBehavior* method to add a Behavior to an HTML element and the new *removeBehavior* method to remove it. When you call *addBehavior*, the Behavior is appended to a list of Behaviors that are attached to the element. When you call *removeBehavior*, the Behavior is detached from the list. You can also attach a Behavior to an element by setting the *behavior* property of the *style* object, but doing so will effectively hide any Behaviors that you attach by using the CSS behavior attribute.

Let's look at an example. To add an HTC Behavior to an anchor tag by using scripting, you can use the *addBehavior* method in JScript, as follows:

```
var iID = anchor1.addBehavior("BehaveYourself.htc");
```

In this line of code, the ID of the anchor tag is *anchor1*. By using the *addBehavior* method, the Behavior implemented in the BehaveYourself.htc file is added to the list of Behaviors attached to the anchor tag. The *addBehavior* method returns an ID that you can use later to detach the Behavior, like so:

```
anchor1.removeBehavior(iID);
```

Now let's see how to attach a Behavior by setting the *behavior* property of the *style* object. The JScript code on the next page demonstrates this.

```
anchor1.style.behavior = "url(BehaveYourself.htc)";
```

Notice that when setting the value of the *behavior* property, you use the *url* property to tell Internet Explorer that the value of the *behavior* property points to a URL.

> **NOTE** Although you can attach Behaviors by using script or the CSS behavior attribute, for simplicity we'll use the CSS technique for the remainder of this chapter.

The other technique for attaching Behaviors is to use the CSS behavior attribute. The value of the behavior attribute points to the .htc file that contains a Behavior implemented as an HTC (or to the ID of a Binary DHTML Behavior implemented by using C++ and COM, as you'll see in the section "Using Binary DHTML Behaviors"). When attaching a Behavior in this way, you set the value of the behavior attribute to the URL of the Behavior.

Using the CSS behavior attribute, you can attach an HTC to an HTML element as a Behavior in three ways. First you can attach it directly to an HTML element: (If you want to apply multiple behaviors to an element, specify a space-delimited list of URLs for the behavior attribute. See MSDN for more information.)

```
<A HREF="myfile.htm" STYLE="behavior:url(myBehavior.htc)">Text</A>
```

The second way is to use a CSS *style* block, as shown here:

```
<HEAD>
    <STYLE>
        A { behavior:url(myBehavior.htc) }
    </STYLE>
</HEAD>
```

Finally you can use the CSS *style* block in combination with the CLASS attribute of an HTML element, like this:

```
<HEAD>
    <STYLE>
        .myClass {behavior:url(myBehavior.htc) }
    </STYLE>
</HEAD>

<BODY>
    <DIV ID="oDiv1" CLASS="myClass"></DIV>
</BODY>
```

> **NOTE** If you specify both the STYLE attribute and the CLASS attribute for an HTML element, the STYLE attribute takes priority.

That's it. Now you can use the HTC as an extension of the element to which it is attached. Hence, if the HTC exposes methods, properties, or events (or all three), you can access them as if they were methods, properties, and events of the element to which the Behavior is attached.

For example, the DHTML Ledger Behavior (discussed in detail in the next section) exposes a method called *hide* that hides the ledger. By using the ID of the <DIV> tag to which the Behavior is attached, you can call *hide* as you would any other method of the <DIV> tag. (Note that *sheet1* is the ID of a <DIV> tag in the DHTML Ledger Behavior sample.)

```
sheet1.hide();    // JScript
sheet1.hide       ' VBScript
```

Handling events is just as easy. For example, the DHTML Ledger Behavior has an *onhide* event that is fired whenever the window is hidden. You handle this event as you would any other DHTML event. Here's the VBScript code for *onhide*'s event handler:

```
<SCRIPT LANGUAGE="VBScript">
   Sub sheet1_onhide
     MsgBox "The ledger was hidden."
   End Sub
</SCRIPT>
```

Remember that the object associated with *onhide* is the object to which the Behavior is attached. Because the DHTML Ledger Behavior is attached to the <DIV> tag (as in the preceding code), the *onhide* event is fired on behalf of the <DIV> tag.

Creating Behaviors in Script by Using HTCs

What fun would Behaviors be if you couldn't create your own? If you could use only the default Behaviors that Internet Explorer installs, you could do a lot, but your accomplishments would ultimately be limited. The easiest way to create Behaviors for Internet Explorer 5 is by using DHTML and script as HTCs.

To develop an HTC, you must first create a file that has the .htc extension. Next you must insert the basic skeleton HTML that indicates that the .htc file is an HTML Component. This HTML consists of the <COMPONENT> tag and the <SCRIPT> tag. (The <COMPONENT> tag is optional, but I recommend that you use it to specify that this file is an HTML Component.) The following is the base HTML that you need for your HTC:

```
<PUBLIC:COMPONENT>
   <SCRIPT>
   </SCRIPT>
</PUBLIC:COMPONENT>
```

After defining the base HTML for your HTC, you can then define and implement your methods, properties, and events by using the correct HTML tags. You enter the script to implement these methods, properties, and events within the *script* block, as you'll see next.

Exposing methods from an HTC

To implement a method in an HTC, you use the <METHOD> tag. Let's look at the Ledger Behavior example. (Actually we have already seen parts of this example application.) The DHTML Ledger from Chapter 3 has been converted to a Behavior implemented as an HTC and included on the companion CD in the folder \Samples\Chap11\Ledger Behavior. (See Figure 11-3.)

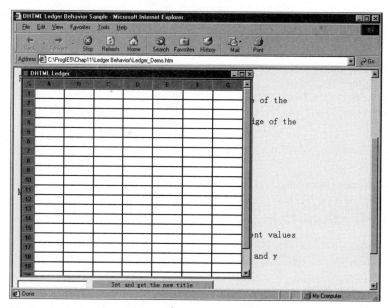

Figure 11-3. *DHTML Ledger Behavior.*

This example includes an HTC named ledger.htc. One of the methods this HTC exposes is named *show*. As you might have guessed, the *show* method displays the ledger, and a method named *hide* hides the ledger. These methods are defined by using the <METHOD> tag, as shown in the following code:

```
<PUBLIC:METHOD  NAME = "show" />
<PUBLIC:METHOD  NAME = "hide" />
```

The HTML defines the *show* and *hide* methods by using the NAME attribute of the <METHOD> tag. The NAME attribute specifies the name by which the method is referred to in the document that contains this HTC. The <METHOD> tag also has two optional attributes: INTERNALNAME and ID. The INTERNALNAME attribute specifies the name by which this method is referred to in the component, so you can specify different names for the method depending on how it is being called: externally by the containing document, or internally by the HTC.

If the INTERNALNAME attribute is omitted, the value of the NAME attribute is used to refer to the method internally as well as externally. The ID attribute identifies the <METHOD> tag within the component. By using this ID, you can access an HTC method from script as an object.

After using the <METHOD> tag to define the methods of the HTC, you must implement the methods to make them work. Implementing the methods in an HTC is the same as implementing them on a normal Web page. The following JScript code implements the *show* and *hide* methods in the DHTML Ledger Behavior example. (The *show* and *hide* methods call internal functions that show and hide the HTC. You'll see the implementation of these functions shortly.)

```
function show()
{
    window_open();
}

function hide()
{
    window_close();
}
```

After defining and implementing the methods, you can access them as if they were methods of the object to which this HTC is attached. For instance, to hide the ledger, you just call the *hide* method by using the name of the object to which the HTC is attached (*sheet1*), like this in JScript:

```
sheet1.hide();
```

Exposing properties from an HTC

Adding properties to an HTC is just as easy as adding methods. To add a property to an HTC that can be accessed from the containing Web page, you use the <PROPERTY> tag. In addition to having the NAME, ID, and INTERNALNAME attributes that the <METHOD> tag has, the <PROPERTY> tag has the optional attributes shown in Table 11-4.

TABLE 11-4
OPTIONAL ATTRIBUTES OF THE <PROPERTY> TAG

Attribute	Description
GET	The value of this attribute specifies the function to be called whenever the value of the defined property is retrieved. If you specify a GET attribute without specifying a PUT attribute, this property is read-only.
PERSIST	The value of this attribute specifies whether the defined property should be persisted as part of a particular page. This is a Boolean value.
PUT	The value of this attribute specifies the function to be called whenever the value of the defined property is set. If you specify a PUT attribute without specifying a GET attribute, this property is write-only. Also, you should call the *fireChange* method associated with the <PROPERTY> tag so that you can notify the containing document that the property has changed.
VALUE	The value of this attribute specifies the default value for the defined property.

The DHTML Ledger Behavior example defines several properties, one of which is *title*. The *title* property corresponds to the title that is listed in the ledger's title bar. Check out this definition for the *title* property in ledger.htc:

```
<PUBLIC:PROPERTY NAME = "title"      PUT = "put_title"
                 GET  = "get_title"  ID  = "Title1" />
```

In the definition of the *title* property, the NAME attribute specifies the name that the containing document uses to access the property. This name is used whether you are setting or retrieving this property. For example, to set the value of the *title* property in the document containing the Ledger Behavior, you can use this JScript code:

```
sheet1.title = "This is a new title.";
```

To retrieve the value of the *title* property, you can use this JScript code:

```
var strTitle = sheet1.title;
```

The PUT and GET attributes specify the names of the methods that will be called when you set or retrieve the value of the *title* property from the containing document. These methods are automatically called for you. (Internet Explorer will display an error message if you try to call them yourself because these function names are internal to the HTC.)

In addition to specifying the PUT and GET attributes, you can also specify the ID attribute. Specifying the ID attribute enables the HTC to access the <PROPERTY>

tag directly and call this tag's *fireChange* method when the value of the defined property is changed.

Next you have to implement the methods specified by the PUT and GET attributes. Otherwise, not much will happen, and you'll receive an error when trying to access the *title* property. Implementing these methods is as easy as implementing any other method in script, as you can see from this implementation of the *put_title* and *get_title* methods in the Ledger Behavior example:

```
function put_title(strTitle)
{
   window.document.all(uniqueID + "_title").innerHTML = strTitle;
   window.document.all(uniqueID + "_min_title").innerHTML = strTitle;

   Title1.fireChange();
}

function get_title()
{
   return window.document.all(uniqueID + "_title").innerHTML;
}
```

In the *put_title* method, the title of the ledger is changed, and the *title* property's *fireChange* method is called by using the property's ID—*Title1*. Calling *fireChange* alerts the containing document of the property change. When you call the *fireChange* method, the element to which this Behavior is attached fires the *onpropertychange* event. When the element fires *onpropertychange*, it sets the *propertyName* of the *event* object to the name of the property, which is *title* in this case.

Firing events from an HTC

An HTML Component can fire events as well as expose methods and properties. When an HTC fires an event, the event appears to the containing document as having been fired by the element to which the HTC is attached. Let's see how an HTC fires events in the DHTML Ledger Behavior example. This example contains the *onshow* and *onhide* events, which are fired when the *show* and *hide* methods are called. These events are defined by using the <EVENT> tag, like this:

```
<PUBLIC:EVENT  NAME="onshow"  ID="evt_onshow" />
<PUBLIC:EVENT  NAME="onhide"  ID="evt_onhide" />
```

The <EVENT> tag has only two attributes: NAME and ID. The NAME attribute specifies the name of the event as it appears to the containing document. This name is used when handling the event. For example, to handle the events specified by the NAME attribute, which are *onshow* and *onhide* in this case, you can add two inline event handlers to the <DIV> tag to which the Ledger Behavior is attached.

```
<DIV ID=sheet1 STYLE="behavior:url(ledger.htc)" state=minimized
    onshow="alert('The ledger was shown.')"
    onhide="alert('The ledger was hidden.')">
</DIV>
```

When handling HTC events, you must use either inline event handlers, as shown in the preceding code, or the <SCRIPT FOR="…" EVENT="…"> syntax.

The events that the HTC fires appear to be fired by the element itself, but in an HTC, the *fire* method actually fires the events. The *fire* method is a member of the *event* object that is created when you specify the <EVENT> tag. You can reference this object by using the value that you specify for the ID attribute.

When the window is shown or hidden in the DHTML Ledger HTC, two private methods are called: *window_open* and *window_close*. When these methods are called, the window is either shown or hidden. In the *window_open* method, the *onshow* event is fired; in the *window_close* method, the *onhide* event is fired. Here's the code for these two methods that shows you how to fire the *onshow* and *onhide* events:

```
function window_open()
{
    // Fire the onshow event.
    var myEvent = createEventObject();
    evt_onshow.fire(myEvent);

    style.display = "";
}

function window_close()
{
    // Fire the onhide event.
    var myEvent = createEventObject();
    evt_onhide.fire(myEvent);

    style.display = "none";
}
```

This code shows that the name of the *onshow* event object is *evt_onshow*, and the name of the *onhide* event object is *evt_onhide*. In either case, you use the *fire* method to fire the corresponding event.

When you call the *fire* method, you can optionally send an *event* object with the event to provide specific information about the event—for example, the *x*-coordinate and the *y*-coordinate of the mouse pointer. To create an *event* object, you use the *createEventObject* method, which simply returns a new *event* object. You can set the different properties of the *event* object, and then send the object along with the event you are firing. (If you're having trouble remembering the *event* object, reread the section in Chapter 3 starting on page 97.)

Accessing the Containing Document's DHTML Object Model

An HTC can access the DHTML Object Model of the document in which the HTC is being used. Through the wonders of DHTML, the HTC can access all the methods and properties of all the objects in the document. Consequently, the HTC can handle events that are fired by the objects in the document.

Because the HTC appears to the document as though it were part of the element to which the HTC is attached, your HTC has access to the *window* object of the containing document. This means that you can obtain the *document* object and, from there, any other object on the page. For example, if you want to insert some HTML into the body of the containing document from an HTC, you can call the *insertAdjacentHTML* method like this:

```
window.document.body.insertAdjacentHTML("BeforeEnd", "SomeTextOrHTML");
```

Being able to access the *document* object means that you can apply what you learned about DHTML in Chapter 3 to Web pages that contain HTCs. Internet Explorer also gives you quick and easy access to the HTML element to which the HTC is attached through the new *element* object. By using this *element* object, you can call any of the methods and properties of the containing element.

For instance, the DHTML Ledger Behavior example employs a little chicanery. To pass the initial state of the ledger to the HTC (minimized or maximized), this example uses the STATE attribute of the <DIV> tag, as shown here:

```
<DIV ID=sheet1 STYLE="behavior:url(ledger.htc)" state=minimized>
</DIV>
```

"Wait a minute!" you say. "No STATE attribute exists for the <DIV> tag!" That's right. Remember that any attribute that Internet Explorer doesn't recognize will be ignored. However, you can obtain the value of the STATE attribute from the HTC attached to the <DIV> tag by using the *element* object. In the DHTML Ledger HTC, the value of STATE is used to determine the initial state of the window, as the following code shows:

```
// Show the window.
element.style.display = "";
if (element.state == "minimized")
{
    window_minimize();
}
```

In this code, the *element* object is used to obtain the *style* object and set its *display* property to the empty string, effectively hiding the window. Then the *element* object is used again to determine the initial state in which to show the window. If the STATE attribute is set to *minimized*, the internal *window_minimize* function is called. This function shows the ledger window in a minimized state.

The *element* object as used in the preceding code is optional. Remember that the HTC is attached to an HTML element. If you call a method or access a property without specifying the *element* object, Internet Explorer assumes that the method or the property is a member of the element to which the Behavior is attached. Therefore, you can also write the previous code like this:

```
// Show the window.
style.display = "";
if (state == "minimized")
{
    window_minimize();
}
```

Accessing the methods and properties of the element to which the Behavior is attached without specifying the *element* object is actually slightly more efficient—when you specify the *element* object, Internet Explorer (actually, the MSHTML component) must make a trip out to the *document* object to locate the *element* object. If you don't specify the *element* object, this trip to the *document* object is unnecessary; but using the *element* object makes your code a little easier to read. As with most decisions, there's a trade-off. In this case, the trade-off is between readability and performance. I'll leave the decision up to you.

Attaching to the containing document's events from an HTC

As mentioned, an HTC can attach event handlers to events in the document in which the HTC is being used. You can attach event handlers to elements in the document in two ways. The first way is by using the <ATTACH> tag. The <ATTACH> tag allows you to attach event handlers for any event of the element to which the Behavior is attached, or to the parent document or parent window of the element.

Using the <ATTACH> tag is quite simple. For example, the DHTML Ledger example attaches two event handlers by using the <ATTACH> tag: the *onmousemove* event of the document and the *onload* event of the window. The event handlers are attached to these events by using the following HTML:

```
<PUBLIC:ATTACH EVENT="onmousemove" FOR="document" ONEVENT=drag()   />
<PUBLIC:ATTACH EVENT="onload" FOR="window" ONEVENT=create_window() />
```

The <ATTACH> tag has four attributes, three of which are used in the preceding code. The first attribute is EVENT, and it is required because it specifies the name of the event you want to handle.

The second attribute, FOR, specifies the object to which you want to attach the event handler. The value of FOR can be *document*, *element*, or *window*. FOR is optional, and if you don't specify it, the event handler will be attached to the element to which the Behavior is attached.

The third attribute is ONEVENT. It is used to specify the inline script or function to be executed when the specified event is fired. In the previous HTML code, the *drag* function is called when the *onmousemove* event is fired (allowing you to reposition the window), and the *create_window* method is called when the *onload* event is fired.

The final attribute is ID. It has the same meaning as the ID attribute in other tags you've seen.

When an event fires on the element, document, or window to which you've attached an event handler in the HTC, the event handler that is specified in the containing document is called first. If multiple Behaviors are attached to an element and multiple event handlers for the same event have been attached to the element, these event handlers will be called in random order after the event handler specified in the containing document is called.

The other way to attach an event handler to an element is by using the *attachEvent* method. One advantage of using *attachEvent* over the <ATTACH> tag is that you can attach event handlers to many more objects—in fact, to just about any object in the DHTML Object Model.

> **NOTE** For a full list of objects that support the *attachEvent* method, refer to the documentation for the *attachEvent* method in the MSDN Online Web Workshop.

The *attachEvent* method is easy to use. You simply call it off the object to which you want to attach an event handler. You pass the name of the event you want to handle as the first parameter and a reference to the event handler function as the second parameter. As an example, look at the following code from the DHTML Ledger example, which uses the *attachEvent* method to attach the event handlers *parse_click* and *release_mouse* to two events. Specifically, the code attaches the *parse_click* function to the *onmousedown* event for the element to which the Behavior is attached, and the *release_mouse* function is attached to the *onmouseup* event of the document.

```
attachEvent("onmousedown", parse_click);
window.document.attachEvent("onmouseup", release_mouse);
```

If you want to detach event handlers, you can use the *detachEvent* method. For example, to detach the *parse_click* and *release_mouse* event handlers that were attached by using the *attachEvent* method, you would call *detachEvent* like this:

```
detachEvent("onmousedown", parse_click);
window.document.detachEvent("onmouseup", release_mouse);
```

HTC Disadvantages

Although Behaviors are easy to implement as HTCs, using HTCs to create Behaviors has a few disadvantages. First, because your HTC is written in DHTML and script, users can view and reuse your source code. If you're planning to market your HTC, and someone downloads and reuses your source code for free, the hours of hard work you spent creating your Behavior are basically given away for free. If you're creating Behaviors for use on your corporate intranet, however, you probably don't have to worry about this issue.

> **NOTE**   To solve the problem of users copying your script, you could encode it. Encoding is a little complicated, and it's outside the scope of this book. For more information about script encoding, visit the Microsoft Scripting Technologies Web site: *http://msdn.microsoft.com/scripting.*

Another drawback to HTCs is that because they are integrated into a document, the security restrictions that normally apply to an HTML document also apply to HTCs. Hence, HTCs can't implement script that accesses resources on another domain or system, such as the file system of the local machine.

USING BINARY DHTML BEHAVIORS

As you'll see in this section, Binary DHTML Behaviors don't suffer from the restrictions that HTCs do. Binary DHTML Behaviors are just normal COM objects that you can create based on C++ libraries such as ATL or MFC. (You can also create Binary DHTML Behaviors using standard C++.) Using Binary DHTML Behaviors is just as easy as using Behaviors implemented as HTCs, except that one extra step is required. Because a Binary DHTML Behavior is a binary component, you must insert it into a Web page by using the <OBJECT> tag, as shown in the following code. (This code comes from a Binary Behavior example named AtlBehave that we'll discuss in more detail later in this section.)

```
<OBJECT
   ID=behave1
   CLASSID="clsid:140D550D-2290-11D2-AF61-00A0C9C9E6C5"
   CODEBASE="atlbehave.cab">
</OBJECT>
```

The format of the <OBJECT> tag for inserting a Binary DHTML Behavior is exactly the same as its format for inserting an ActiveX control and other COM objects. And because you are required to use the <OBJECT> tag to insert Binary DHTML Behaviors into a Web page, the security mechanism that Internet Explorer applies to the Binary DHTML Behavior is the same as the mechanism that it applies to ActiveX controls and other COM objects. If the Binary DHTML Behavior isn't safe for scripting, initialization, or both, Internet Explorer will display the same security dialog box you've seen in Chapters 5 and 6.

As you know, when inserting an ActiveX control or COM object into a Web page by using the <OBJECT> tag, you can use the ID attribute to specify an identification marker for that object. When specifying the name of the Behavior for the CSS behavior attribute of the STYLE attribute, instead of specifying the filename for the Behavior, you use the ID that you specified for the <OBJECT> tag, as shown here:

```
<SPAN ID=target STYLE="behavior:url(#behave1); font-size:xx-large">
    This text has an attached Behavior.
    Move the cursor here to see the effect.
</SPAN>
```

Notice that besides specifying the ID of the Binary Behavior, you must also specify the pound sign (#). The pound sign tells Internet Explorer that the ID is for the Binary Behavior on the current page and is not the name of a file that contains the implementation of an HTC Behavior. (Note that you shouldn't give your Binary DHTML Behavior an ID of *default*. If you do, the ID will conflict with the ID of the default DHTML Behaviors.)

To demonstrate how to implement Binary DHTML Behaviors and how to sink events for HTML elements from a Binary DHTML Behavior, let's look at AtlBehave, a Binary Behavior example created using ATL. The AtlBehave example, which is shown in Figure 11-4, can be found on the companion CD in the folder \Samples\Chap11\AtlBehave.

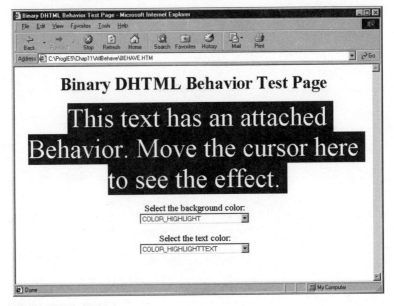

Figure 11-4. *AtlBehave.*

Before compiling the AtlBehave example, you must install headers and libraries for Internet Explorer 5 and place the headers and libraries in the correct order as specified in Chapter 6.

Implementing Binary DHTML Behaviors in C++

As with any other COM object, you must implement some interfaces for Binary Behaviors, and the container must implement some other interfaces. The required and optional interfaces implemented by a Binary DHTML Behavior and those that are implemented by the container are listed in Table 11-5.

TABLE 11-5
INTERFACES IMPLEMENTED BY THE BINARY DHTML BEHAVIOR AND THE CONTAINER

Interface	Description	Where Implemented
IElementBehavior	Receives notifications from the container (MSHTML) concerning the activities of DHTML Behaviors. This interface is an event sink, and it's required.	Behavior
IElementBehaviorCategory	Provides Behaviors with a way to identify their categories. Using categories, you can locate all related Behaviors. This interface is optional.	Behavior
IElementBehaviorFactory	Provides the container (MSHTML) with implementations of Behaviors. This interface is the class factory for a Behavior, and it's required.	Behavior
IElementBehaviorSite	Provides a means of communication between a Behavior and the container (MSHTML). This is the site interface for the Behavior. This interface is required.	Container
IElementBehaviorSiteCategory	Provides Behaviors a means of finding related Behaviors. This interface is optional.	Container
IElementBehaviorSiteOM	Provides event services to Behaviors. These event services allow Behaviors to create events, fire events, and so on. This interface is required if the container wants to provide event services.	Container

Although all the interfaces listed in Table 11-5 are important, we'll look at only those interfaces that you'll normally use when creating Binary Behaviors. We'll discuss *IElementBehaviorFactory* and *IElementBehavior* first. *IElementBehaviorSite* and *IElementBehaviorSiteOM* will be covered when we talk about *IElementBehavior*'s *Init* method.

IElementBehaviorFactory

Probably the most important Behavior interface is *IElementBehaviorFactory*. Through this interface, the container (MSHTML, in the case of Internet Explorer) creates an instance of a Behavior. Then the container obtains a pointer to the Behavior's *IElementBehavior* interface with which the container will communicate. The *IElementBehaviorFactory* interface has one method that is used for creating the Binary DHTML Behavior and obtaining a pointer to the Behavior's *IElementBehavior* interface: *FindBehavior*. The following code from the AtlBehave example shows an implementation of the *FindBehavior* method. Table 11-6 on the next page shows the four parameters of the *FindBehavior* method.

```
STDMETHODIMP
CFactory::FindBehavior(BSTR pchNameSpace,
                       BSTR pchTagName,
                       IElementBehaviorSite* pUnkArg,
                       IElementBehavior** ppBehavior)
{
    HRESULT hr;
    CComObject<CBehavior>* pBehavior;

    // Create a Behavior object.
    hr = CComObject<CBehavior>::CreateInstance( &pBehavior );

    if (SUCCEEDED(hr))
    {
        hr = pBehavior->QueryInterface(__uuidof(IElementBehavior),
                                       (void**)ppBehavior );
    }

    return hr;
}
```

The implementation of the *FindBehavior* method as shown in the preceding code is typical of any class factory creation technique. First an instance of the *CBehavior* class is created by using the *CreateInstance* method. In this example, *CBehavior* is the class that implements the *IElementBehavior* interface. Then *QueryInterface* is called to obtain a pointer to the *IElementBehavior* interface that is implemented in the *CBehavior* class. This pointer is returned to the container via the *ppBehavior* method parameter.

TABLE 11-6
PARAMETERS OF THE *FINDBEHAVIOR* METHOD

Parameter	Description
bstrBehavior	String that contains the name of the Behavior for which the container is searching.
bstrBehaviorURL	String that contains the URL of the Behavior for which the container is searching.
pSite	Pointer to the container's implementation of the *IElementBehaviorSite* interface.
ppBehavior	Pointer to the *IElementBehavior* interface that is implemented by the Binary DHTML Behavior. After creating an instance of the Behavior, the *FindBehavior* method should query for the *IElementBehavior* interface and return the pointer to the container through this interface.

IElementBehavior

Another important interface that the Binary DHTML Behavior must implement is *IElementBehavior*. This interface is an event sink that receives notifications from the container (MSHTML) concerning the activities of Behaviors on a Web page. The *IElementBehavior* interface contains three methods, shown in Table 11-7 in vtable order.

TABLE 11-7
METHODS OF THE *IELEMENTBEHAVIOR* INTERFACE

Method	Description
Init	Called immediately after the container obtains the *IElementBehavior* interface by calling the *IElementBehaviorFactory::FindBehavior* method. A pointer to the *IElementBehaviorSite* interface of the container is passed to the implementation of the *Init* method.
Notify	Called with information about the parsing of the document and the Behavior component. The *Notify* method is the actual event sink for the Behavior. It is passed one of the values contained in the BEHAVIOR_EVENT enumeration defined in the mshtml.h header file. Just as when implementing the *IDispatch::Invoke* method for other event sinks, the *Notify* method typically contains a *switch* statement to handle the Behavior events of interest.
Detach	Called before the document is unloaded.

The following code implements the *Init* method in the AtlBehave example:

```
STDMETHODIMP
CBehavior::Init(IElementBehaviorSite* pBehaviorSite)
{
    // Cache the IElementBehaviorSite interface pointer.
    m_spSite = pBehaviorSite;

    // Cache the IElementBehaviorSiteOM interface pointer.
    HRESULT hr = m_spSite->QueryInterface(__uuidof(IElementBehaviorSiteOM),
                                    (void**)&m_spOMSite);

    ATLASSERT(SUCCEEDED(hr));

    if (SUCCEEDED(hr))
        m_spOMSite->RegisterEvent(L"ondocumentready", 0, NULL);

    return S_OK;
}
```

This implementation is quite simple. The *Init* method receives a pointer to the *IElementBehaviorSite* interface that is implemented in the container. This site pointer is saved in the *m_spSite* data member that will be used in this and other methods in the Behavior.

Next the *IElementBehaviorSite* interface pointer is queried for a pointer to the *IElementBehaviorSiteOM* interface, which is saved in the *m_spOMSite* data member. This data member will be used to register and fire an event.

Registration of the event occurs in the next step of the *Init* method when the code calls the *RegisterEvent* method of the *IElementBehaviorSiteOM* interface. All events must be registered before they can be fired. Also, registration of events must occur in the *Init* method. If you try to register an event elsewhere, you'll receive an error.

The *RegisterEvent* method takes three arguments. The first is the name of the event that you want to fire. The second argument is reserved, so you should specify *0* for this parameter. The third argument is a pointer to a *long* value that receives a cookie that can be used in later event calls. In the call to *RegisterEvent* in the previous code, only the name of the event is specified.

IElementBehaviorSite

As you saw, the *IElementBehaviorSite* interface that is implemented by the container is sent to the Behavior's *Init* method. The *IElementBehaviorSite* interface is the means by which the Binary DHTML Behavior communicates with the document. This interface contains one method, *GetElement*, which returns a pointer to the *IHTMLElement* interface that is implemented by the element to which a Binary DHTML Behavior is attached.

Calling the *GetElement* method is analogous to using the *element* object in an HTC. Through the *IHTMLElement* interface that is returned from *GetElement*, you can access methods, properties, and events of the element to which a Behavior is attached. Therefore, you can also access methods, properties, and events of any other object in the DHTML Object Model for the Web page.

IElementBehaviorSiteOM

By using the pointer to the *IElementBehaviorSite* interface received in the *Init* method, you can query for the *IElementBehaviorSiteOM* interface, as shown in the implementation of *Init* in the previous code. *IElementBehaviorSiteOM* provides event services to the Behavior, and through it, you can perform tasks such as creating event objects and firing events, just as you can with HTCs. The methods of the *IElementBehaviorSiteOM* are listed in Table 11-8.

TABLE 11-8
METHODS OF THE *IELEMENTBEHAVIORSITEOM* INTERFACE

Method	Description
CreateEventObject	Creates a new *event* object that can be used when calling the *FireEvent* method to pass event information to event handlers.
FireEvent	Fires an event.
GetEventCookie	Returns the ID that identifies the Behavior event to the container (MSHTML).
RegisterEvent	Registers a Behavior event with the container (MSHTML). This method must be called before MSHTML will recognize events fired by a Binary DHTML Behavior. When using the *IElementBehaviorSiteOM* interface to code event handlers for events fired by Binary DHTML Behaviors, use inline event handlers or the <SCRIPT FOR="…" EVENT="…"> syntax.
RegisterName	Registers a Behavior name with the container (MSHTML).
RegisterUrn	Registers a Uniform Resource Name (URN) with the container (MSHTML).

The next method of the *IElementBehavior* interface that is implemented by the *CBehavior* class is *Notify*. This method is the event sink for the Behavior, and it has the following two input parameters:

■   *lEvent*. Identifies the event being sent to the Behavior from the container—MSHTML. The value of this input parameter can be any of the constants defined in the BEHAVIOR_EVENT enumeration declared in the mshtml.h header file.

■ *pVar.* Reserved.

Here's the implementation of the *Notify* method as included in the AtlBehave example:

```
STDMETHODIMP
CBehavior::Notify(LONG lEvent, VARIANT* pVar)
{
   HRESULT hr = S_OK;
   CComPtr<IHTMLElement> spElem;

   switch (lEvent)
   {
   // End tag of element has been parsed (We can get at attributes.)
   case BEHAVIOREVENT_CONTENTREADY:
      break;

   // HTML document has been parsed
   // (We can get at the document object model.)
   //
   case BEHAVIOREVENT_DOCUMENTREADY:
      if (m_spSite)
      {
         hr = m_spSite->GetElement(&m_spElem);
         if (SUCCEEDED(hr))
         {
            // Create and connect the event sink.
            hr = CComObject<CEventSink>::CreateInstance(&m_pEventSink);
            if (SUCCEEDED(hr))
            {
               CComPtr<IHTMLStyle> spStyle;
               HRESULT hr;

               hr = m_spElem->get_style(&spStyle);
               if (SUCCEEDED(hr))
               {
                  spStyle->get_color(&m_varColor);
                  spStyle->get_backgroundColor(&m_varBackColor);
               }

               m_pEventSink->m_pBehavior = this;

               hr = AtlAdvise(m_spElem, m_pEventSink,
                              DIID_HTMLElementEvents,
                              &m_dwCookie);
```

(continued)

455

```
            }
          }
        }

        // Fire the ondocumentready event.
        //
        ATLASSERT(m_spOMSite);
        if (m_spOMSite)
        {
            LONG lCookie;

            hr = m_spOMSite->GetEventCookie(L"ondocumentready", &lCookie);
            ATLASSERT(SUCCEEDED(hr));

            if (SUCCEEDED(hr))
            {
                IHTMLEventObj* pEvtObj;

                hr = m_spOMSite->CreateEventObject(&pEvtObj);
                ATLASSERT(SUCCEEDED(hr));

                if (SUCCEEDED(hr))
                {
                    hr = m_spOMSite->FireEvent(lCookie, pEvtObj);
                    ATLASSERT(SUCCEEDED(hr));

                    pEvtObj->Release();
                }
            }
        }

        break;

    case BEHAVIOREVENT_APPLYSTYLE:
        break;

    case BEHAVIOREVENT_DOCUMENTCONTEXTCHANGE:
        break;

    default:
        break;
    }

    return S_OK;
}
```

The only event that is handled is *BEHAVIOREVENT_DOCUMENTREADY*, which indicates that the document is finished loading. In this event handler, the *style* object is retrieved from the element to which the Behavior is attached. Then the text and background color are retrieved. Next an event sink is connected to the element to handle the element's events. Finally the *ondocumentready* event is fired to the containing document.

This code is a little overkill, but it does demonstrate how to fire an event from a Binary DHTML Behavior. Before firing the event, the *GetEventCookie* method must be called to retrieve the event ID. (The event ID that is returned as the third parameter of the *RegisterEvent* method could have been stored as a data member, but I wanted to show you how to use as many of the methods in *IElementBehaviorSiteOM* as possible.) Next *CreateEventObject* is called to create an event object. Finally *FireEvent* is called to fire the event by using the cookie and the *event* object obtained earlier.

The final method of the *IElementBehavior* interface that is implemented by the *CBehavior* class is *Detach*. The *Detach* method is called when the document is being unloaded. The implementation of *Detach* is simple—typically, you just perform cleanup by releasing any interface pointers and freeing any memory that was dynamically allocated. The following code implements the AtlBehave example's *Detach* method:

```
STDMETHODIMP
CBehavior::Detach(void)
{
    // Release cached interface pointers.
    ATLASSERT(m_pEventSink);
    m_pEventSink->Release();

    ATLASSERT(m_spElem);
    m_spElem.Release();

    ATLASSERT(m_spOMSite);
    m_spOMSite.Release();

    return S_OK;
}
```

Now that you know how to implement Binary DHTML Behaviors, let's take a look at some other Behavior examples to round out our discussion.

USING OTHER BEHAVIOR EXAMPLES

Many ready-made Behaviors are at your disposal. The MSDN Online Web Workshop provides a Behaviors library that contains lots of examples, including *calendar*, *coolbar*, *menu*, and *tooltip*. The Behaviors library is updated all the time, and it is available at this URL: *http://msdn.microsoft.com/workshop/author/behaviors/library/ behaviorslibrary.asp.*

In addition to the examples that we've used in this chapter, two others that I haven't discussed are available on the companion CD in the folder \Samples\Chap11. The first is the table-of-contents builder Behavior, which is shown in Figure 11-5. It allows you to build a table of contents based on the headings on your Web page. When using this Behavior, you specify a HEADINGS attribute for the HTML element to which you are attaching the Behavior. The value of the HEADINGS attribute is a semicolon-separated list of the heading levels for which you want to create a table of contents. You can also specify other attributes such as the name that appears in the title bar of the table of contents window. To attach the table-of-contents builder Behavior to a <DIV> tag and to specify that a table of contents be built for all H1 and H2 tags, you would insert code into your Web page that looks like this:

```
<DIV STYLE="behavior:url(Toc.htc)" headings="H1;H2" titlebar="Contents">
</DIV>
```

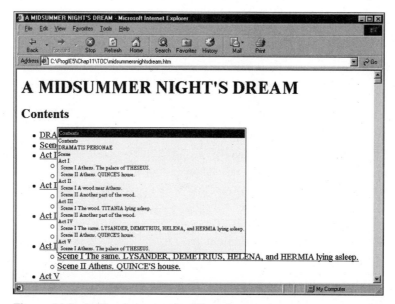

Figure 11-5. *Table-of-contents builder Behavior.*

HTML Spy is another Behavior on the companion CD and is shown in Figure 11-6. An HTML Application that uses a Behavior to spy on the contents of a Web page, HTML Spy demonstrates a lot of the concepts that we've discussed in this book, including HTAs, the DHTML Object Model, mouse capture, and Behaviors.

Figure 11-6. *HTML Spy Behavior.*

To use HTML Spy, double-click htmlSpy.hta in Windows Explorer, or type its name at the command line. Either enter a URL in the HTML Spy's address bar after you launch this application or specify the URL via the command line when you launch it, and then press Enter. (This URL must be preceded by the correct protocol specifier: *http://*, *file://*, or some other.) Next click the Spy icon and, while keeping the left mouse button pressed, start moving the pointer over the client area of the target frame window (the window that contains the Web page to which you just navigated). As you hover over an HTML element, a ToolTip will display the element's *tagName* and identifiers.

Once you find an element of interest, release the left mouse button. Detailed information about the HTML element that you selected will be displayed in the right-hand window. The information that is displayed at the top of the right-hand window is a list of all attributes of the HTML element. Below the list of attributes is a hierarchy chart for that element with the element you selected highlighted in red letters. If you click on an item in this parent chain list with the left mouse button, the item will expand to show the item's immediate children.

Holding down the ALT key while clicking the left mouse button on an item in the parent chain list will display a complete list of all the item's children. The corresponding object for the item clicked will be highlighted in red letters in the target frame window. You can toggle the list by clicking or ALT-clicking the list again.

WHAT'S NEXT

In this chapter, you created DHTML Behaviors implemented as HTCs and binary components. Now you know how valuable Behaviors can be to the development of Web sites. DHTML Behaviors allow you to separate the dynamic functionality from the content and design of your Web site. They also allow you to create components that you can reuse in the Web sites that you might build in the future.

In the next chapter, I'll introduce you to an Internet Explorer technology that can enhance the navigation experience of your users—Browser Helper Objects (BHOs). BHOs are DLLs you create that will attach themselves to every new instance of Internet Explorer.

Chapter 12

Browser
Helper Objects

In Chapter 6, you learned how to develop applications that automate Microsoft Internet Explorer. You created instances of Internet Explorer in those applications by using *CoCreateInstance* with *CLSID_InternetExplorer*.

What if you wanted to connect to instances of Internet Explorer that are already running to gain full control over Internet Explorer from your application? Then you could tell Internet Explorer where to go and what to do. Maybe you want to handle Internet Explorer events or access the DHTML Object Model. You might want to control just about any Internet Explorer action.

To control Internet Explorer in versions 3 and earlier, you had to use the somewhat cumbersome, difficult, and limited technique named Dynamic Data Exchange (DDE). One of DDE's limitations was that you couldn't receive events from Internet Explorer. Instead of receiving events, you could receive notifications, which aren't as robust. If you could connect to a running instance of Internet Explorer using COM, you could control it and receive events from it. But Internet Explorer isn't like normal automation servers such as Microsoft Word or Microsoft Excel—it doesn't register itself in the Running Object Table, so you can't find and bind to running instances of it.

To connect to running instances of Internet Explorer, you can use a Browser Helper Object (BHO), which is a DLL that Internet Explorer loads whenever a new instance of Internet Explorer is started. The BHO is effectively connected to Internet Explorer, so it can control Internet Explorer's actions and listen to the events that

Internet Explorer is firing. In this chapter, you'll learn how to use and create BHOs to gain control over Internet Explorer and how to handle Internet Explorer events in your BHOs.

HOW INTERNET EXPLORER STARTS A BHO

Each time a new instance of Internet Explorer starts, it checks the Registry for the following key:

```
HKEY_LOCAL_MACHINE\SOFTWARE\Microsoft\Windows\CurrentVersion
   \Explorer\Browser Helper Objects
```

If Internet Explorer finds this key in the Registry, it looks for one or more CLSIDs listed below the key, as shown in Figure 12-1.

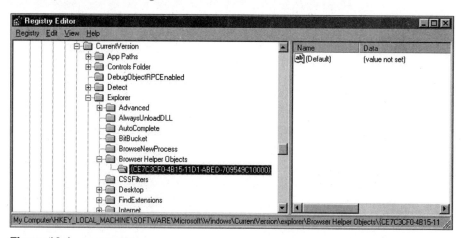

Figure 12-1. *Registry keys.*

The CLSID keys under the *Browser Helper Objects* key tell Internet Explorer which BHOs to load. You can create a *CLSID* key for your BHO manually by editing the Registry yourself, or you can have the registration code for your BHO insert this key for you.

For each CLSID that is listed below the *Browser Helper Objects* key, Internet Explorer calls *CoCreateInstance* to start an instance of the Browser Helper Object in the same process space as the browser. In other words, Internet Explorer starts the BHO as an in-proc server. If the BHO has registered its CLSID and implements the *IObjectWithSite* interface, the BHO is started by Internet Explorer and is passed a pointer to the *IWebBrowser2* interface of Internet Explorer. Through this interface, the BHO can control and receive events from Internet Explorer in the same way that you've seen in earlier chapters.

Remember that as long as the BHO is built correctly, it will be loaded each time a new instance of Internet Explorer is started. So if you have the Microsoft Active Desktop installed, the BHO will be loaded each time you open a folder, a subfolder, or a browser window. If you no longer want the BHO to be loaded, you must remove the Registry keys that are associated with it. Again, you can do this manually by editing the Registry yourself, or you can have the unregistration code of your Browser Helper Object do it for you.

CREATING A BHO

To create a Browser Helper Object, you can use any development language that supports COM. In this chapter, we'll use Microsoft Visual C++ and ATL to create a Browser Helper Object named IEHelper.

IEHelper

When loaded, IEHelper creates a window that displays all the events that are fired by Internet Explorer. IEHelper also provides an edit box into which you can enter a URL. After typing in the URL, you can click the Navigate button to go to the URL you've just entered. You can also click the Go Back and Go Forward buttons to move backward and forward in the navigation history. (See Figure 12-2.)

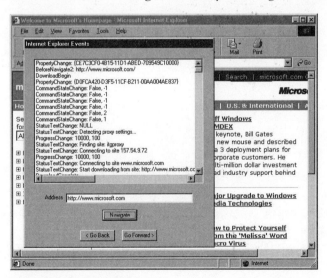

Figure 12-2. *IEHelper.*

To create a BHO, first create a new project by using Visual C++'s ATL COM AppWizard, which you can access from the New dialog box shown in Figure 12-3.

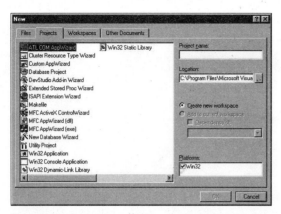

Figure 12-3. *New dialog box, from which you can access the ATL COM AppWizard.*

A Browser Helper Object must be a DLL because it is loaded into the same process space as Internet Explorer. So in step 1 of the ATL COM AppWizard, shown in Figure 12-4, choose Dynamic Link Library (DLL) as the server type, and then click the Finish button. Click OK in the New Project Information dialog box that appears.

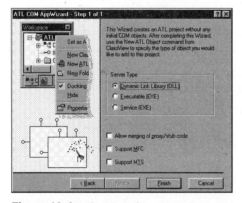

Figure 12-4. *Choosing the server type.*

Next we'll create a simple ATL object. In the ClassView pane of your project, right-click your project name and choose New ATL Object. Then click the Simple Object icon, shown in Figure 12-5, and click the Next button to open the ATL Object Wizard Properties dialog box.

On the Names tab (shown in Figure 12-6), enter *IEHlprObj* in the Short Name field. Retain the defaults for all the other fields, and click OK.

We won't go into how to create the window that displays Internet Explorer's events and provides navigation buttons. The code to perform these actions is standard Win32 code and can be seen by loading the IEHelper example from the companion

CD in the folder \Samples\Chap12\IEHelper. Now let's concentrate on how to implement the *IObjectWithSite* interface in a Browser Helper Object.

Figure 12-5. *Creating a simple ATL object.*

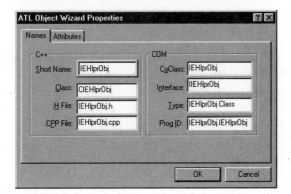

Figure 12-6. *ATL Object Wizard Properties dialog box.*

Implementing *IObjectWithSite*

After creating the IEHlprObj simple ATL object, we must change the default implementation of the *CIEHlprObj* class to implement the *IObjectWithSite* interface. It is through the *SetSite* method of the *IObjectWithSite* interface that we receive a pointer to the *IWebBrowser2* interface of Internet Explorer. Without this interface, you will not be able to communicate with or control Internet Explorer. In fact, if you don't implement this interface, Internet Explorer will not even load your Browser Helper Object.

Implementing the *IObjectWithSite* interface in ATL is easy. Just change the declaration of *CIEHlprObj* so that *CIEHlprObj* will inherit from *IObjectWithSiteImpl*, and add *IObjectWithSite* to your COM map by using the COM_INTERFACE_ENTRY_IMPL macro. The code on the next page shows the changed declaration of the *CIEHlprObj* class and its COM map.

```
///////////////////////////////////////////////////////////////////
// CIEHlprObj
class ATL_NO_VTABLE CIEHlprObj :
   public CComObjectRootEx<CComSingleThreadModel>,
   public CComCoClass<CIEHlprObj, &CLSID_IEHlprObj>,
   public IObjectWithSiteImpl<CIEHlprObj>,
   public IDispatchImpl<IIEHlprObj,
                        &IID_IIEHlprObj,
                        &LIBID_IEHELPERLib>
{
   :
   :
   BEGIN_COM_MAP(CIEHlprObj)
      COM_INTERFACE_ENTRY(IIEHlprObj)
      COM_INTERFACE_ENTRY(IDispatch)
      COM_INTERFACE_ENTRY_IMPL(IObjectWithSite)
   END_COM_MAP()
   :
   :

};
```

Next you must override the *SetSite* method of the *IObjectWithSite* interface. When
Internet Explorer loads the Browser Helper Object, it calls your *IObjectWithSite::SetSite*
method and passes a pointer to its *IWebBrowser2* interface. The implementation
of the *SetSite* method is straightforward. All you need to do is save a copy of this
IWebBrowser2 interface pointer so that you can use it later. This process, shown in
the following code, is as easy as copying the *IWebBrowser2* interface pointer to a class
member or a global variable. The code also shows a partial implementation of the
SetSite method.

```
STDMETHODIMP CIEHlprObj::SetSite(IUnknown *pUnkSite)
{
   USES_CONVERSION;
   HRESULT hr = E_FAIL;

   if (!pUnkSite)
      ATLTRACE("\nSetSite(): pUnkSite is NULL\n\n");
   else
   {
      // Make sure Internet Explorer is the one calling SetSite
      // by querying pUnkSite for the IWebBrowser2 interface.
      //
      m_spWebBrowser2 = pUnkSite;

      if (!m_spWebBrowser2)
      {
         hr = E_FAIL;
      }
```

```
        else
        {
            ⋮
        }
    }

    return hr;
}
```

HANDLING INTERNET EXPLORER EVENTS IN A BHO

In IEHelper's implementation of the *SetSite* method, IEHelper advises Internet Explorer that it wants to receive all the events that Internet Explorer fires. To receive events from Internet Explorer, you must implement the *IDispatch* interface.

By default, simple ATL objects inherit from *IDispatchImpl*, so you can use *AtlAdvise* to have Internet Explorer alert you when it fires events. The only *IDispatchImpl* method that you must override to receive events is the *Invoke* method. Internet Explorer will call your *Invoke* method each time it fires an event.

To stop receiving events, you can call the *AtlUnadvise* method. When Internet Explorer informs you that it is quitting, you call *AtlUnadvise* by passing *DISPID_QUIT* to the *Invoke* method. The following code overrides the *Invoke* method. As you can see, a lot of this code is for handling the Internet Explorer events and writing their names to the IEHelper events window.

```
STDMETHODIMP CIEHlprObj::Invoke(DISPID dispidMember, REFIID riid,
                                LCID lcid, WORD wFlags,
                                DISPPARAMS* pDispParams,
                                VARIANT* pvarResult,
                                EXCEPINFO*  pExcepInfo, UINT* puArgErr)
{
    USES_CONVERSION;
    strstream strEventInfo;

    if (!pDispParams)
        return E_INVALIDARG;

    //
    // Get the current URL.
    //
    LPOLESTR lpURL = NULL;
    m_spWebBrowser2->get_LocationURL(&lpURL);
```

(continued)

```
switch (dispidMember)
{
    //
    // The parameters for this DISPID are as follows:
    // [0]: Cancel flag   - VT_BYREF|VT_BOOL
    // [1]: HTTP headers - VT_BYREF|VT_VARIANT
    // [2]: Address of HTTP POST data   - VT_BYREF|VT_VARIANT
    // [3]: Target frame name - VT_BYREF|VT_VARIANT
    // [4]: Option flags - VT_BYREF|VT_VARIANT
    // [5]: URL to navigate to - VT_BYREF|VT_VARIANT
    // [6]: An object that evaluates to the top-level or frame
    //      WebBrowser object corresponding to the event
    //
    case DISPID_BEFORENAVIGATE2:
        strEventInfo << "BeforeNavigate2: ";

        if (pDispParams->cArgs >= 5 &&
            pDispParams->rgvarg[5].vt == (VT_BYREF|VT_VARIANT))
        {
            CComVariant varURL(*pDispParams->rgvarg[5].pvarVal);
            varURL.ChangeType(VT_BSTR);

            strEventInfo << OLE2T(varURL.bstrVal);
        }
        else
            strEventInfo << "NULL";

        strEventInfo << ends;
        break;

    //
    // The parameters for this DISPID:
    // [0]: URL navigated to - VT_BYREF|VT_VARIANT
    // [1]: An object that evaluates to the top-level or frame
    //      WebBrowser object corresponding to the event
    //
    case DISPID_NAVIGATECOMPLETE2:
        if (pDispParams->rgvarg[0].vt == (VT_BYREF|VT_VARIANT))
        {
            CComVariant varURL(*pDispParams->rgvarg[0].pvarVal);
            varURL.ChangeType(VT_BSTR);

            strEventInfo << "NavigateComplete2: "
                         << OLE2T(varURL.bstrVal)
                         << ends;
        }
        break;

    //
    // The parameters for this DISPID:
```

```
    // [0]: New status bar text - VT_BSTR
    //
    case DISPID_STATUSTEXTCHANGE:
        LPOLESTR lpStatusText;

        m_spWebBrowser2->get_StatusText(&lpStatusText);
        strEventInfo << "StatusTextChange: ";

        if (!strcmp(OLE2T(lpStatusText), ""))
            strEventInfo << "NULL";
        else
            strEventInfo << OLE2T(lpStatusText);

        strEventInfo << ends;
        break;

    //
    // The parameters for this DISPID:
    // [0]: Maximum progress - VT_I4
    // [1]: Amount of total progress - VT_I4
    //
    case DISPID_PROGRESSCHANGE:
        strEventInfo << "ProgressChange: ";

        if (pDispParams->cArgs == 0)
            strEventInfo << "NULL";
        else
        {
            if (pDispParams->rgvarg[0].vt == VT_I4)
                strEventInfo << pDispParams->rgvarg[0].lVal;

            if (pDispParams->cArgs > 1 &&
                pDispParams->rgvarg[1].vt == VT_I4)
            {
                strEventInfo << ", " << pDispParams->rgvarg[1].lVal;
            }
        }

        strEventInfo << ends;
        break;

    case DISPID_DOCUMENTCOMPLETE:
        strEventInfo << "DocumentComplete" << ends;
        break;

    case DISPID_DOWNLOADBEGIN:
        strEventInfo << "DownloadBegin" << ends;
        break;
```

(continued)

```
case DISPID_DOWNLOADCOMPLETE:
   strEventInfo << "DownloadComplete" << ends;
   break;

//
// The parameters for this DISPID:
// [0]: Enabled state - VT_BOOL
// [1]: Command identifier - VT_I4
//
case DISPID_COMMANDSTATECHANGE:
   strEventInfo << "CommandStateChange: ";

   if (pDispParams->cArgs == 0)
     strEventInfo << "NULL";
   else
   {
      if (pDispParams->rgvarg[0].vt == VT_BOOL)
      {
         strEventInfo << ((pDispParams->rgvarg[0].boolVal ==
                           VARIANT_TRUE) ? "True" : "False");
      }

      if (pDispParams->cArgs > 1 &&
          pDispParams->rgvarg[1].vt == VT_I4)
      {
         strEventInfo << ", " << pDispParams->rgvarg[1].lVal;
      }
   }

   strEventInfo << ends;
   break;

case DISPID_NEWWINDOW2:
   strEventInfo << "NewWindow2" << ends;
   break;

//
// The parameters for this DISPID:
// [0]: Document title - VT_BSTR
//
case DISPID_TITLECHANGE:
   strEventInfo << "TitleChange: ";

   if (pDispParams->cArgs > 0 &&
       pDispParams->rgvarg[0].vt == VT_BSTR)
   {
      strEventInfo << OLE2T(pDispParams->rgvarg[0].bstrVal);
   }
```

```
        else
        {
            strEventInfo << "NULL";
        }

        strEventInfo << ends;
        break;

    //
    // The parameters for this DISPID:
    // [0]: Name of property that changed - VT_BSTR
    //
    case DISPID_PROPERTYCHANGE:
        strEventInfo << "PropertyChange: ";

        if (pDispParams->cArgs > 0 &&
            pDispParams->rgvarg[0].vt == VT_BSTR)
        {
            strEventInfo << OLE2T(pDispParams->rgvarg[0].bstrVal);
        }
        else
        {
            strEventInfo << "NULL";
        }

        strEventInfo << ends;
        break;

    //
    // The parameters for this DISPID:
    // [0]: Address of cancel flag - VT_BYREF|VT_BOOL
    //
    case DISPID_QUIT:
        strEventInfo << "Quit" << ends;

        ManageConnection(Unadvise);
        m_dlgEvents.DestroyWindow();
        break;

    default:
        strEventInfo << "Unknown Event" << dispidMember << ends;
        break;
    }

    m_dlgEvents.AddEventToList(strEventInfo.str());

    return S_OK;
}
```

The code here shouldn't be new to you. We examined most of it in Chapter 7 when we discussed sinking events in ATL. You can refer to Chapter 7 if you have any questions about it.

CONTROLLING INTERNET EXPLORER BY USING A BHO

In addition to using a BHO to receive events from Internet Explorer, you can use a BHO to control Internet Explorer's behavior. By using the pointer to the *IWebBrowser2* interface that you saved in the *SetSite* method, you can call any of *IWebBrowser2*'s methods, including *Navigate*, *GoBack*, and *GoForward*, to name a few.

IEHelper demonstrates how to control Internet Explorer by providing navigation buttons. When you enter a URL into the Address edit box and click the Navigate button, IEHelper calls the *Navigate* method of *IWebBrowser2*, as shown here:

```
void CIEHlprObj::Navigate(LPTSTR szURL)
{
    CComBSTR bstrURL(szURL);
    CComVariant vtEmpty;

    m_spWebBrowser2->Navigate(bstrURL, &vtEmpty, &vtEmpty,
                              &vtEmpty, &vtEmpty);
}
```

You can also click the Go Back and Go Forward buttons to navigate backward and forward in the history list. When you click one of the two buttons, IEHelper calls either the *GoBack* method or the *GoForward* method of the *IWebBrowser2* interface, as shown here:

```
void CIEHlprObj::GoBack()
{
    m_spWebBrowser2->GoBack();
}

void CIEHlprObj::GoForward()
{
    m_spWebBrowser2->GoForward();
}
```

By now, this code should be pretty familiar to you. If you have further questions about it, refer to Chapter 6.

REGISTERING AND UNREGISTERING A BHO

For Internet Explorer to be able to load IEHelper, IEHelper must be registered as a Browser Helper Object in the Registry. You can edit the Registry manually, or you can change the default Registry script that the ATL Object Wizard creates to include the needed Registry information. To simplify this process for the user, we'll change the default Registry script. This way, any time you register or unregister a Browser Helper Object by using Regsvr32, the Registry is updated automatically.

First you must add information to the bottom of the IEHlprObj.rgs file to create a key for the CLSID of IEHlprObj. You will also use this Registry script to remove the Registry entries when you unregister a Browser Helper Object. The following code shows how the completed Registry script will look. Replace the CLSID for IEHlprObj with the CLSID for your object.

```
HKCR
{
    IEHlprObj.IEHlprObj.1 = s 'IEHlprObj Class'
    {
        CLSID = s '{CE7C3CF0-4B15-11D1-ABED-709549C10000}'
    }
    IEHlprObj.IEHlprObj = s 'IEHlprObj Class'
    {
        CurVer = s 'IEHlprObj.IEHlprObj.1'
    }
    NoRemove CLSID
    {
        ForceRemove {CE7C3CF0-4B15-11D1-ABED-709549C10000}
            = s 'IEHlprObj Class'
        {
            ProgID = s 'IEHlprObj.IEHlprObj.1'
            VersionIndependentProgID = s 'IEHlprObj.IEHlprObj'
            ForceRemove 'Programmable'
            InprocServer32 = s '%MODULE%'
            {
                val ThreadingModel = s 'Apartment'
            }
        }
    }
}

HKLM
{
    SOFTWARE
```

(continued)

```
{
    Microsoft
    {
        Windows
        {
            CurrentVersion
            {
                Explorer
                {
                    'Browser Helper Objects'
                    {
                        {CE7C3CF0-4B15-11D1-ABED-709549C10000}
                    }
                }
            }
        }
    }
}
```

This code is just basic Registry script. It specifies the keys that should be created automatically when registering your Browser Helper Object and those that should be deleted when unregistering your BHO. If you need more information about Registry scripts, please refer to one of the great ATL books offered by Microsoft Press, *Inside ATL*, by George Shepherd and Brad King (1999). If you need more information about the Windows Registry, take a look at *Inside the Microsoft Windows 98 Registry* by Günter Born (Microsoft Press, 1998). As always, another great source of information is the MSDN Online Libraries (*http://msdn.microsoft.com/*).

To register IEHelper, run the Regsvr32 utility as follows:

```
regsvr32 IEHelper.dll
```

To unregister IEHelper, run Regsvr32 like this:

```
regsvr32 /u IEHelper.dll
```

See? Didn't I tell you that Browser Helper Objects are a lot easier to use than DDE to control running instances of Internet Explorer? And they provide much greater functionality, too. As this chapter shows, you can control Internet Explorer and even handle Internet Explorer events by using BHOs.

WHERE DO YOU WANT TO GO TODAY (OR TOMORROW)?

So we've finally reached the end. I think I'm going to cry...I'll miss you all so much! At least I know that now you're empowered to create Web-based applications by using the Internet Explorer development platform. I challenge you to create the most imaginative applications you can think of using Internet Explorer technologies. You can take advantage of DHTML, HTML Applications, the WebBrowser control, and everything else you've learned about in this book to make your applications the best in the business. I hope to hear about the new and exciting applications that you create based on Internet Explorer!

Appendix

Troubleshooting and Support Resources

You will no doubt encounter obstacles when developing Internet Explorer applications. Because keystroke problems are so common and so difficult to figure out when hosting the WebBrowser control, this appendix covers the keystroke problems that you might come across when hosting the WebBrowser control in MFC, ATL, or standard C++ applications. For information about other issues, refer to one of the reference sources described later in this appendix or contact Microsoft Developer Support, as explained at the end of this appendix.

KEYSTROKE PROBLEMS

When hosting the WebBrowser control in MFC, ATL, or standard C++ applications, you might run into trouble with certain accelerator keys such as Backspace, Delete, and Tab. Problems usually occur when users type into intrinsic controls such as text boxes that reside on Web pages loaded by the WebBrowser control. Why? Because the intrinsic controls on a Web page don't automatically receive the messages generated by these accelerator keys. When the WebBrowser control receives an accelerator key message, it doesn't automatically pass it to child controls on a Web page. You must somehow alert the WebBrowser control to pass these messages to the intrinsic controls on your Web page.

Invariably, the solution is the same whether you're hosting the WebBrowser control in MFC, ATL, or standard C++ applications: call the *TranslateAccelerator* method of the *IOleInPlaceActiveObject* interface that is implemented by the WebBrowser control. Where and how to call this method, however, isn't always clear. In this section, I'll discuss the proper time and place to call *TranslateAccelerator* to work around keystroke problems.

MFC

As you know, you can create three types of applications in MFC: dialog-based, single document interface (SDI), and multiple document interface (MDI). The way you handle the keystroke problem depends on whether you are hosting the WebBrowser control in a dialog-based application or in an SDI or MDI application.

MFC dialog-based applications

When you host the WebBrowser control in an MFC dialog-based application, the *TranslateAccelerator* method is automatically called for you, so you won't encounter keystroke problems. However, you need to understand how MFC works when you are hosting the WebBrowser control in a dialog-based application to help you diagnose and solve keystroke problems that you might run into when hosting the control in an MFC SDI or MDI application.

In an MFC application, MFC manages the Windows message pump for you. In a dialog-based application in particular, the *IsDialogMessage* method is called in the message pump. One of the tasks performed by the *IsDialogMessage* method is calling *TranslateAccelerator* for any control in the dialog. *IsDialogMessage* passes to the *TranslateAccelerator* method the *MSG* structure that was received from a call to the *GetMessage* function in the message pump.

MFC manages the message pump by creating an instance of a class named *COccManager*, which manages all the OLE controls in the dialog. The *IsDialogMessage* method is a member of the *COccManager* class.

The *IsDialogMessage* method gets a handle to the window that has the focus. If this window is a control, the *TranslateAccelerator* method is called on that control to give it a chance to process the message. If this window isn't a control, *IsDialogMessage* keeps calling the *GetParent* method until it finds an ActiveX control or until it reaches the top-level parent. If it finds a control, it calls *TranslateAccelerator* on that control.

MFC SDI and MDI applications

You will typically encounter keystroke problems in MFC SDI and MDI applications because the *IsDialogMessage* method isn't called automatically as it is in dialog-based applications. Hence, you'll have to call *IsDialogMessage* yourself to fix keystroke problems. But where do you call it?

In the message pump, MFC gives your application a chance to process a message before the message is processed by the default window procedure. To allow you to process a message, MFC calls the *PreTranslateMessage* method, which is a virtual method of the *CWnd* class. If you implement *PreTranslateMessage* in any of your *CWnd*-derived classes, MFC will call it automatically.

> **NOTE** *CWinApp* also has a *PreTranslateMessage* method. You can override it in the *CWinApp*-derived class for your application.

An MFC SDI or MDI application typically has a view class that derives from *CView*. In turn, *CView* derives from *CWnd*. If you implement *PreTranslateMessage* in your view class, MFC will call your implementation of *PreTranslateMessage* through the wonders of polymorphism. To solve the keystroke problems in an MFC SDI or MDI application, you just need to call *IsDialogMessage* from within *PreTranslate-Message*, as shown in the following code. Knowledge Base article Q165074 explains this solution in detail.

```
BOOL CMyView::PreTranslateMessage(MSG* pMsg)
{
   if (IsDialogMessage(pMsg))
      return TRUE;
   else
      return CWnd::PreTranslateMessage(pMsg);
}
```

But sometimes this solution doesn't work. Suppose you have an application that resembles Microsoft Internet Explorer in that it has an edit box that can be used for entering a URL. If the focus is set to that edit box, each time the user presses Tab, the focus will shift around in the application window but will never move to controls on the Web page inside the WebBrowser control window. The desired behavior would be for the focus to shift from control to control in your application as well as in the WebBrowser window.

To make the desired Tab functionality work, you might have to pass the Tab key–related message directly to the WebBrowser control by calling *Translate-Accelerator* in the *PreTranslateMessage* method for your *CMainFrame* class. The following code shows how to perform this call. In this code, *ID_URL_NAME* is the resource ID of an edit box used for entering a URL in the application.

```
BOOL CMainFrame::PreTranslateMessage(MSG* pMsg)
{
   if (pMsg->message == WM_KEYDOWN)
   {
      if (!(::IsChild(m_wndToolBar.GetDlgItem
            (ID_URL_NAME)->GetSafeHwnd(), pMsg->hwnd))
         || pMsg->wParam == VK_TAB)
      {
         LPDISPATCH lpDispatch = NULL;

         lpDispatch = ((CMyView*)
                     GetActiveView())->m_webBrowser.GetDocument();

         ASSERT(lpDispatch);

         // Query the IDispatch interface for the
         // IOleInPlaceActiveObject interface.
         //
         IOleInPlaceActiveObject* pIOIPAO = NULL;

         lpDispatch->QueryInterface(IID_IOleInPlaceActiveObject,
                                    (void**)&pIOIPAO);
         lpDispatch->Release();

         ASSERT(pIOIPAO);

         // Pass the keydown message to
         // IOleInPlaceActiveObject::TranslateAccelerator.
         //
         HRESULT hr = pIOIPAO->TranslateAccelerator(pMsg);
         pIOIPAO->Release();

         // TranslateAccelerator will return S_FALSE if it
         // doesn't process the message.
         //
         if (S_OK == hr)
            return TRUE;
      }
   }

   return CFrameWnd::PreTranslateMessage(pMsg);
}
```

This code can also fix problems with other accelerator keys such as Backspace and Delete, though such keystroke problems seldom affect these keys.

> **NOTE** If you are hosting the WebBrowser control in a DLL, calling *Translate-Accelerator* is a bit more involved. Refer to the Knowledge Base article Q175502 for more information.

ATL and Standard C++

When you host the WebBrowser control in an ATL application or an application using standard C++, solving keystroke problems can be rather simple. You just need to query the WebBrowser control for the *IOleInPlaceActiveObject* interface, and call its *TranslateAccelerator* method. Typically, you call *TranslateAccelerator* in your handler function for the *WM_KEYDOWN* message. The following ATL code shows you how to call the *TranslateAccelerator* method to fix keystroke problems:

```
// WM_KEYDOWN handler method
//
LRESULT CMyClass::OnKeydown(UINT uMsg, WPARAM wParam, LPARAM lParam,
                            BOOL& bHandled)
{
    // m_spWebBrowser is a data member of type IWebBrowser2.
    // Using CComQIPtr in this way queries m_spWebBrowser
    // for the IOleInPlaceActiveObject interface, which is
    // then stored in the pIOIPAO variable.
    //
    CComQIPtr<IOleInPlaceActiveObject,
            &IID_IOleInPlaceActiveObject> pIOIPAO(m_spWebBrowser);

    HRESULT hr = S_FALSE;

    if (pIOIPAO)
    {
        MSG msg;
        msg.message = uMsg;
        msg.wParam = wParam;
        msg.lParam = lParam;

        hr = pIOIPAO->TranslateAccelerator(&msg);
    }

    return hr;
}
```

The standard C++ code below also demonstrates how to call the *Translate-Accelerator* method to fix keystroke problems:

```
// WM_KEYDOWN handler method
//
LRESULT CMyClass::OnKeydown(UINT uMsg, WPARAM wParam, LPARAM lParam,
                            BOOL& bHandled)
{
    IOleInPlaceActiveObject* pIOIPAO;
```

(continued)

```
      HRESULT hr = m_pWebBrowser->QueryInterface(IID_IWebBrowser2,
                                                  (void**)&pIOIPAO);

      if (SUCCEEDED(hr))
      {
         MSG msg;
         msg.message = uMsg;
         msg.wParam = wParam;
         msg.lParam = lParam;

         hr = pIOIPAO->TranslateAccelerator(&msg);
         pIOIPAO->Release();
      }

      return hr;
}
```

Sometimes your application won't automatically be sent *WM_KEYDOWN* messages for accelerator keys. When it isn't, you must send *WM_KEYDOWN* to your window manually. The following message pump sends all keyboard messages to your application's window:

```
while (GetMessage(&msg, NULL, 0, 0))
{
   TranslateMessage(&msg);

   // Send all keyboard messages to the window of your
   // application. hwndApp is the window handle of
   // your application.
   //
   if (msg.message >= WM_KEYFIRST && msg.message <= WM_KEYLAST)
      ::SendMessage(hwndApp, msg.message, msg.wParam, msg.lParam);

   DispatchMessage(&msg);
}
```

Win32 SDK Modal Dialog

It would be nice if you could create Win32 SDK dialogs by using one of the following Win32 API dialog box functions: *DialogBox*, *DialogBoxIndirect*, *DialogBoxIndirectParam*, or *DialogBoxParam*. These functions are especially helpful when you're creating modal dialogs because they handle the message pump for your application. However, using them creates a dilemma when you're trying to fix keystroke problems—where do you put the call to *TranslateAccelerator*? I don't recommend that you use the Win32 dialog box functions to create your modal dialog that hosts the WebBrowser control. Let's look at why.

When the focus is set to a control on a dialog, the control is sent the *WB_ GETDLGCODE* message. Typically, a control responds to this message by returning *DLGC_WANTALLKEYS*. Then the control is given a chance to handle all keys the user entered.

The WebBrowser control, however, responds to the *WM_GETDLGCODE* message by returning *DLGC_WANTARROWS | DLGC_WANTCHARS*. Therefore, it won't handle certain keys such as Tab and Delete. To work around this, you need to have control of the message pump so that you can call *TranslateAccelerator* (as I explained earlier). To control the message pump, you should create the dialog window yourself.

> **NOTE** You can use MFC or ATL to create a Win32 dialog. In addition, if you need a modal dialog that just displays a Web page, you can use the *show-ModalDialog* method provided by Internet Explorer.

If you don't want to fix your keystroke problems by creating the dialog window manually, you have one other option: a Windows hook. By using a Windows hook, you can retrieve all keyboard messages for the current thread and then call *TranslateAccelerator* so that accelerator keys will be processed.

But this approach has one problem. When the focus is on the WebBrowser control and you attempt to change the focus between controls on the Web page by pressing Tab, the focus will never leave the WebBrowser window. You can tab between controls on the Web page or between controls in your application, but you can't do both.

Follow these four steps to set up a Windows hook to work around keystroke problems in a Win32 SDK dialog:

1. Declare the hook procedure in your header file.

```
static LRESULT CALLBACK GetMsgHookProc(int nCode, WPARAM wParam,
                                       LPARAM lParam);
```

2. During initialization, set the hook procedure by calling *SetWindowsHookEx*. Also, make sure to save the returned hook handle so that you can unhook the hook procedure when your application is shutting down or when you no longer need it.

```
// Declare this global handle in
// one of your project files.
//
HHOOK g_hook;

// Place this code inside an initialization
// method in your implementation file (.cpp).
//
g_hook = SetWindowsHookEx(WH_GETMESSAGE, GetMsgHookProc,
                          NULL, GetCurrentThreadId());
```

3. Implement the hook procedure, and call *TranslateAccelerator*.

```
LRESULT CALLBACK CYourClass::GetMsgHookProc(int nCode,
                                            WPARAM wParam,
                                            LPARAM lParam)
{
    LPCKFSEARCH pThis = (LPCKFSEARCH)
                        GetWindowLong(hwndMain, DWL_USER);

    if (pThis && nCode >= 0)
    {
        MSG* pMsg = (MSG*)lParam;

        // m_pOleInPlaceActObj is an IoleInPlaceActiveObject
        // data member of the view class that is initialized
        // after the WebBrowser control is loaded.

        if (pThis->m_pOleInPlaceActObj)
            pThis->m_pOleInPlaceActObj->TranslateAccelerator(pMsg);

        // This next bit of code causes the tab to work in the
        // WebBrowser window. If you don't implement this code,
        // tabbing will happen only in the dialog. You can tab
        // either in the dialog or in the WebBrowser window,
        // but not in both.


        if (pMsg->wParam == VK_TAB)
            ZeroMemory(pMsg, sizeof(MSG));
    }

    return CallNextHookEx(g_hook, nCode, wParam, lParam);
}
```

4. When your application is shutting down or when you no longer need the hook, unhook the hook procedure by using this code:

```
UnhookWindowsHookEx(g_hook);
```

Band Objects

When hosting the WebBrowser control in band objects—Explorer Bars (Explorer bands and Comm bands) and Desk bands—fixing keystroke problems is a little more complicated than merely calling *TranslateAccelerator*; you not only have to call this method, but you must also deal with focus issues. The WebBrowser control has to know that your band object currently has the focus; otherwise, the accelerator keys won't be processed. You must perform a number of tasks to make the accelerator keys work correctly.

Don't forget to implement the *IOleControlSite* interface when hosting the WebBrowser control in a band object, just as you would when hosting the WebBrowser control in a standard application. Implementing *IOleControlSite* is extremely important, as its *OnFocus* method is called when the focus is set to the WebBrowser control. When *OnFocus* is called, you must query the WebBrowser control for the *IInputObjectSite* interface and call its *OnFocusChangeIS* method, which tells the WebBrowser control that your band object now has the focus.

The following code demonstrates how to call the *OnFocusChangeIS* method if you are hosting the WebBrowser control in an Explorer Bar. (This code is from the WebBand sample that I showed you in Chapter 10.) Note that in this code, *m_pSite* is a data member of type *IInputObjectSite*, which was retrieved from the WebBrowser control in the Explorer Bar's *IObjectWithSite::SetSite* method. Also note that the Explorer Bar has to implement the *IInputObject* interface.

```
STDMETHODIMP CWBExplorerBar::OnFocus(BOOL fGotFocus)
{
    if (m_pSite)
        m_pSite->OnFocusChangeIS(static_cast<IInputObject*>(this),
                                 fGotFocus);
    return S_OK;
}
```

Now whenever a key is pressed, three actions occur. First, the Explorer Bar's *IInputObject::HasFocusIO* method is called to see whether the Explorer Bar currently has the focus. The Explorer Bar's implementation of *IInputObject::HasFocusIO* should determine whether the WebBrowser control that the Explorer Bar is hosting has the focus or any of the WebBrowser control's children have the focus. The *HasFocusIO* method should return *S_OK* if the WebBrowser control or one of its children has the focus, or *S_FALSE* otherwise. Here's the code for *HasFocusIO*:

```
STDMETHODIMP CWBExplorerBar::HasFocusIO(void)
{
    HWND hwnd = GetFocus();
    HWND hwndTmp = m_hwndWB;  // HWND of the WebBrowser control

    // See whether the focus has been set to any of the children.
    //
    while (hwnd && hwndTmp)
    {
        if (hwnd == hwndTmp)
            return S_OK;

        hwndTmp = ::GetWindow(hwndTmp, GW_CHILD);
    }

    return S_FALSE;
}
```

Second, the Explorer Bar's *IInputObject::UIActivateIO* method is called to tell the Explorer Bar that it is being activated. The Explorer Bar's implementation of this method either UI-activates or in-place activates the WebBrowser control, depending on the value of one of the *IInputObject::UIActivateIO* method's input values: *fActivate*. Note that in the next code sample, *m_pIOleObject* is a pointer to an instance of *IOleObject* that was retrieved from the WebBrowser control in the *SetSite* method of the Explorer Bar.

```
STDMETHODIMP CWBExplorerBar::UIActivateIO(BOOL fActivate, LPMSG lpMsg)
{
    _ASSERT(m_pIOleObject);

    HRESULT hr = E_FAIL;

    if (m_pIOleObject)
    {
        RECT  rc;
        GetClientRect(m_hwndParent, &rc);

        //
        // If the Explorer Bar is being activated, we must UI-activate
        // the WebBrowser control for all accelerators to work.
        //
        if (fActivate)
        {
            hr = m_pIOleObject->DoVerb(OLEIVERB_UIACTIVATE, lpMsg,
                                      this, 0, _hwndParent, &rc);
        }
        else
        {
            hr = m_pIOleObject->DoVerb(OLEIVERB_INPLACEACTIVATE, lpMsg,
                                      this, 0, _hwndParent, &rc);
        }
    }

    return hr;
}
```

Third, the Explorer Bar's *IInputObject::TranslateAcceleratorIO* method is called. Here the Explorer Bar passes the keystroke message to the hosted WebBrowser control by calling *IOleInPlaceActiveObject::TranslateAccelerator*. Calling *TranslateAccelerator* causes accelerator keys such as the Backspace key and the Delete key to be processed by the WebBrowser control.

```
STDMETHODIMP CWBExplorerBar::TranslateAcceleratorIO(LPMSG pMsg)
{
   LPDISPATCH pDisp = NULL;
   IOleInPlaceActiveObject* pIOIPAO;
   HRESULT hr = S_FALSE;

   //
   // Send accelerator messages to the WebBrowser control
   // so that keys such as Backspace and Delete will work correctly.
   // Note that s_ denotes a static data member.
   //
   hr = s_pWebBrowserOC->get_Application(&pDisp);

   if (SUCCEEDED(hr))
   {
      hr = pDisp->QueryInterface(IID_IOleInPlaceActiveObject,
                                 (LPVOID*)&pIOIPAO);
      pDisp->Release();

      if (SUCCEEDED(hr))
      {
         hr = pIOIPAO->TranslateAccelerator(pMsg);
         pIOIPAO->Release();
      }
   }

   return hr;
}
```

You might find the preceding discussion and associated code a little confusing at first. To better understand how band objects work, refer to Chapter 10.

SUPPORT RESOURCES

If you experience trouble when developing Internet Explorer applications, before spending the money to contact Microsoft Developer Support, check out some of the following support resources for help.

Newsgroups

You'll often find free answers to your questions by getting in touch with Internet Explorer newsgroups. Access the news server and look for newsgroups that contain the word *programming* in the name and that begin with *microsoft.public.inetexplorer* or *microsoft.public.inetsdk*. Each newsgroup is specialized for a particular area. For example, the newsgroup for the WebBrowser control is *microsoft.public.inetsdk.programming.webbrowser_ctl*.

Documentation

Programming documentation exists on both CD and the Internet. The best source of information is the MSDN Online Web Workshop, which is available at *http://msdn.microsoft.com/workshop*. If you subscribe to the Microsoft Developer Network, you will receive documentation in CD form each quarter.

Technical Assistance sections of MSDN Workshop

Many different areas of the MSDN Online Web Workshop, such as "Reusing Browser Technology," contain Technical Assistance sections where important information is available to help you diagnose and resolve problems. These sections are maintained by support engineers who have daily contact with customers who are programming for Internet Explorer. I have the great honor of being one of the people who initiated the Technical Assistance area. Jason Strayer was also a key force in initiating this area, as was the rest of the Internet Client Development team. The Technical Assistance areas not only provide answers to commonly asked questions but also provide references to Knowledge Base articles, Peer Support (newsgroups), magazine articles, and so on.

Microsoft Knowledge Base

If you don't find what you need in the newsgroups or documentation, you can search for articles in the Knowledge Base (KB): *http://support.microsoft.com/support/*. If you know the number of the KB article you want, you can go to that article directly. For instance, if you wanted to access KB article Q196339 directly, you would enter the following URL into the Internet Explorer address bar: *http://support.microsoft.com/support/kb/articles/Q196/3/39.asp*. KBs are stored in a folder hierarchy. The base folder consists of the letter *Q* and the first three digits of the article ID. The name of the next folder consists of the fourth digit in the ID. Finally, the name of the file that contains the actual content consists of the last two digits of the ID followed by .asp. You can substitute any article number you want in this way.

One other way to access KB articles is by e-mail. If you send e-mail to *mshelp@microsoft.com* with the KB article number in the subject line, you'll receive the KB article in a return e-mail. However, you won't receive any sample files that are included with the KB article. You must retrieve sample files from the Microsoft Personal Support Center: *http://support.microsoft.com/support/*.

The following table lists the commonly accessed KB articles that will help you troubleshoot when developing for Internet Explorer:

FREQUENTLY ACCESSED KB ARTICLES

Article Number	Title
Q188864	INFO: Internet Explorer *designMode* Property Is Not Supported
Q188015	HOWTO: Access Methods/Properties of Container from Script
Q185567	PRB: FORM Inside of Empty <TABLE> Pair Does Not Generate Submit
Q185538	HOWTO: Cause Navigation to Occur in Same WebBrowser Window
Q185376	BUG: Redirection in Anchor Tag Using Location.href Fails
Q185375	HOWTO: Create a Single EXE Install of Internet Explorer
Q185374	PRB: document_onmouseout Fires When Mouse is Over HTML Form
Q185141	PRB: SIZE Attribute of INPUT Tag Has No Effect for Some Types
Q185140	PRB: Trouble Inserting Non-Displayable HTML into Web Page
Q185128	HOWTO: Insert Event Handler Into Web Page from WebBrowser App
Q185127	HOWTO: Call a script function from a VC WebBrowser application
Q185123	PRB: SELECTED Attribute Not Honored After Refresh
Q185122	HOWTO: Use the TDC in an Active Desktop Item
Q185121	BUG: LPKTool Does Not Display Some Licensed ActiveX Controls
Q184975	BUG: Setting TreeView1.ImageList Causes Err in Internet Explorer
Q184876	HOWTO: Use the WebBrowser Control NewWindow2 Event
Q184801	INFO: Key Commands Firing onClick Different for IE and Netscape
Q184783	HOWTO: Search for Internet Client SDK Articles Using Keywords
Q184782	DOC: ModifyDesktopItem Fails To Modify Friendly Name
Q184780	SAMPLE: IEFavMnu.exe Creates an Internet Explorer 4.0 Favorite
Q184767	PRB: OLE Initialization Error in Internet Explorer
Q184418	BUG: ShellUIHelper Not Registered Without IE4 Desktop Update
Q183977	SAMPLE: Using HTML Layout Content in Internet Explorer 3.02, 4.0
Q183806	INFO: The Different Levels of Font Embedding in IE4
Q183805	PRB: Digitally Signed File Cannot Be Confirmed by IE4
Q183804	HOWTO: Specify Items to Be Cached in a .cdf File
Q183509	PRB: Setting JScript Event Handler Invokes the Handler Function
Q183339	DOC: window.external Supports All Methods of ShellUIHelper
Q183235	SAMPLE: WBCustomizer.dll Implements IDocHostUIHandler for VB
Q183048	PRB: Events Not Firing When IE4 WebBrowser Placed On Web Page
Q183044	HOWTO: Develop with IE3 WebBrowser Control on an IE4 Machine
Q183023	BUG: Cannot Use Out-Of-Proc Server Instantiated in OBJECT Tag
Q182888	HOWTO: Handle Invalid Certificate Authority Error with WinInet
Q182490	BUG: Navigate(2) Causes Access Violation in Shdocvw.dll
Q182484	INFO: Color Management in IE4 Using ColorInfo Filter

(continued)

Article Number	Title
Q182117	PRB: Unresolved External for IID/CLSID from Internet Client SDK
Q182034	HOWTO: Invoke the "Add to Favorites" Dialog Box in IE4
Q181779	DOC: Setting Cancel to TRUE in NewWindow2 Stops Navigation
Q181689	INFO: Purpose and Format of Folder.htt
Q181678	HOWTO: Retrieve the URL of a Web Page from an ActiveX Control
Q181074	PRB: No Filter Applied to <SPAN>,<DIV> If Attributes Unspecified
Q180856	DOC: Page Break Styles Supported Only with Block Elements
Q180366	HOWTO: Determine When a Page Is Done Loading in WebBrowser Ctrl
Q179609	DOC: Window.navigator.connectionSpeed Is Not Supported
Q179421	FIX: WebBrowser Control in CFormView Does Not Repaint Properly
Q179420	PRB: CoGetClassObjectFromUrl Fails with "Generic Trust Failure"
Q179135	BUG: Polygon ATL Sample Fails to Work in Internet Explorer 4.0
Q178853	FILE: HLINKAXD Demonstrates a Hyperlinking Active Document
Q178851	HOWTO: Enumerate Channels in Internet Explorer 4.0
Q178380	FILE: FAVREAD Reads Internet Shortcuts from Favorites Folder
Q178066	INFO: IE Does Not Send Referer Header in Unsecured Situations
Q177877	FILE: Internet Explorer 4.01 Refresh of the Internet Client SDK
Q177555	FIX: PostData is Empty in BeforeNavigate of IE3 WebBrowser
Q177269	PRB: Internet Explorer 4 Keeps Active Document Servers Running
Q177241	HOWTO: Adding to the Standard Context Menus of the WebBrowser
Q176789	PRB: Permission Denied Accessing Web Browser Control in HTML
Q176787	HOWTO: Get WinInet Information from a URL Moniker Binding
Q176347	BUG: IE Can't Open Registered Helper App for URL with Spaces
Q176343	BUG: IBinding::Abort Fails in BindStatusCallback::OnStartBinding
Q175506	PRB: 'Permission Denied' calling window.external.isSubscribed()
Q175504	HOWTO: Determining Whether a User Is Subscribed to a Channel
Q175474	INFO: Header Required Posting HTML Form Encoded Data to ASP Page
Q174866	PRB: CAB SDK Headers Contain Incorrect CB_MAX_DISK Value
Q174864	PRB: ActiveX Control with DLL Extension Doesn't Download
Q174687	HOWTO: Creating Personalized Channels using ASP
Q174546	PRB: <USAGE VALUE="Email"> in a CDF Does Not Send E-mail
Q174393	HOWTO: Getting IHlinkFrame from Within a Hyperlink Target
Q173476	FILE: Active Document Container Apps Must Redistribute ACTXPRXY
Q172998	HOWTO: Use WebBrowser HEADERS Param in Navigate Method

Article Number	Title
Q172064	HOWTO: Submitting Data from an ActiveX Control in a Form
Q169438	PRB: ActiveX Control Does Not Display Correctly on Web Page
Q169437	HOWTO: Debugging Code Download Activity in Internet Explorer 3.x
Q168917	HOWTO: Setting Up Internet Download for Comdlg32.ocx
Q167834	HOWTO: Web Browser Navigation Using a PIDL
Q167658	HOWTO: Automate Internet Explorer to POST Form Data
Q165800	SAMPLE: PostMon.exe Demonstrates Using URL Moniker to POST Data
Q165074	PRB: Keystroke Problems in CView/CWnd WebBrowser Control
Q165072	SAMPLE: MimeType.exe Makes ActiveX Obj. Default MIME Type Player
Q165021	SAMPLE: VFiles.exe Calls WinVerifyTrust & Authenticates Files
Q164119	SAMPLE: SafeCtl.exe Implements IObjectSafety in ActiveX Control
Q163958	PRB: Ccdist.exe Fails to Register Comcat.dll Until Reboot
Q163954	PRB: SignCode Returns "Unable to Sign the Program 0x80070057"
Q163623	FIX: Form.Submit Method Doesn't Use Form.Action Property
Q163282	HOWTO: Using Forward & Back Buttons for WebBrowser Control
Q160920	FIX: Framer Sample Does Not Handle Activation Correctly
Q159923	HOWTO: Using Licensed ActiveX Controls in Internet Explorer
Q159617	HOWTO: Accessing a Secured Resource Using the FTP Protocol
Q156905	SAMPLE: Progress Uses IAuthenticate to Bind to Secured Web Page
Q156904	FIX: Returning User Name and Password from IAuthenticate Fails
Q156732	HOWTO: Print from the Microsoft WebBrowser Control
Q156693	SAMPLE: IEZoom.exe Changes the Font Size of WebBrowser Control

MICROSOFT DEVELOPER SUPPORT

If you need technical assistance with your Internet Explorer applications and you've tried all the resources in this appendix without luck, contact Microsoft Developer Support either by phone or online.

If you want to speak directly to a support engineer in Developer Support, you have several options. These options change depending on the product for which you're seeking help and the type of contract you have—none, priority, premier, and so on. The available options keep changing. For the latest information about your options, navigate to this URL: *http://support.microsoft.com/support/supportnet/default.asp.*

To contact Microsoft Developer Support via the Web, you have several options as well. Navigate to the following URL for the most current information on these contact options and to open a support incident: *http://support.microsoft.com/support/webresponse.asp.*

Here are a few guidelines for getting the most from Developer Support:

- Before you contact Developer Support, make sure to prepare a small sample application, control, or Web page that demonstrates the problem you're having. This sample will enable the support engineer to see the problem and find a solution much faster. These samples are sometimes required.

- Give a detailed description of the problem you're having.

- If you contact Developer Support by phone, mention a few keywords that describe the technologies you are using, such as ATL, the WebBrowser control, or Code Download. These keywords will help your call get routed faster to the correct place.

- If you are implementing any of the topics discussed in this book and you are calling Developer Support for help, mention that you are performing Internet client development.

Index

Note: Italicized page numbers indicate figures or tables.

About the Author...

Scott Roberts has been a developer for about nine years, and during that time he has created many different applications and systems, including telephony applications, point-of-sale applications, and communications and controls systems. In July of 1997, Scott was hired by Microsoft as a developer support engineer for the Internet Client Developer Support Team. He assisted customers who were using Microsoft Internet Explorer to build Microsoft Visual C++ and Microsoft Visual Basic applications, Microsoft ActiveX controls, DHTML Applications, and so on. Scott's specialties included the WebBrowser control, the advanced hosting interfaces, COM, ATL, and C++. Also the content lead for Internet Client Development, he helped to initiate the Technical Assistance area of the MSDN Online Web Workshop. Currently Scott is a contributing editor for *MIND* magazine; with the help of Joshua Trupin (also with *MIND*), Scott started the magazine's FAQ column. This column features articles from developer support engineers about common customer issues.

Scott recently moved over to the development side of Internet Explorer and is now a software design engineer on the Trident Object Model Team. He writes code for the WebBrowser control, HTML applications, the DHTML Object Model, and other aspects of the MSHTML component of Internet Explorer. Scott hopes to help customers behind the scenes by writing solid code for future versions of Internet Explorer.

Scott is also a joint author of *C++ How To* (SAMS Publishing, 1998).

Scott was born in Cincinnati, Ohio, spent some time in the Bay Area, and now lives in Redmond, Washington, with his wife Andrea. Scott and Andrea are expecting their first child and are very busy preparing for the new addition to their family, who should be born by the time this book hits the stores.

Scott Roberts can be contacted at *scottrobe@hotmail.com*.

The manuscript for this book was prepared using Microsoft Word 97. Pages were composed by Microsoft Press using Adobe PageMaker 6.52 for Windows, with text in Garamond and display type in Helvetica Black. Composed pages were delivered to the printer as electronic prepress files.

Cover Graphic Designer
Tim Girvin Design, Inc.

Cover Illustrator
Glenn Mitsui

Interior Graphic Artist
Rob Nance

Principal Compositor
Elizabeth Hansford

Principal Proofreader/Copy Editor
Patricia Masserman

Indexer
Julie Kawabata

Microsoft press online

press On!

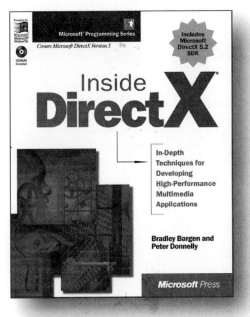

Achieve
dynamic
new effects
on the Web.

MICROSOFT LICENSE AGREEMENT
Book Companion CD

IMPORTANT—READ CAREFULLY: This Microsoft End-User License Agreement ("EULA") is a legal agreement between you (either an individual or an entity) and Microsoft Corporation for the Microsoft product identified above, which includes computer software and may include associated media, printed materials, and "online" or electronic documentation ("SOFTWARE PRODUCT"). Any component included within the SOFTWARE PRODUCT that is accompanied by a separate End-User License Agreement shall be governed by such agreement and not the terms set forth below. By installing, copying, or otherwise using the SOFTWARE PRODUCT, you agree to be bound by the terms of this EULA. If you do not agree to the terms of this EULA, you are not authorized to install, copy, or otherwise use the SOFTWARE PRODUCT; you may, however, return the SOFTWARE PRODUCT, along with all printed materials and other items that form a part of the Microsoft product that includes the SOFTWARE PRODUCT, to the place you obtained them for a full refund.

SOFTWARE PRODUCT LICENSE

The SOFTWARE PRODUCT is protected by United States copyright laws and international copyright treaties, as well as other intellectual property laws and treaties. The SOFTWARE PRODUCT is licensed, not sold.

1. **GRANT OF LICENSE.** This EULA grants you the following rights:

   a. **Software Product.** You may install and use one copy of the SOFTWARE PRODUCT on a single computer. The primary user of the computer on which the SOFTWARE PRODUCT is installed may make a second copy for his or her exclusive use on a portable computer.

   b. **Storage/Network Use.** You may also store or install a copy of the SOFTWARE PRODUCT on a storage device, such as a network server, used only to install or run the SOFTWARE PRODUCT on your other computers over an internal network; however, you must acquire and dedicate a license for each separate computer on which the SOFTWARE PRODUCT is installed or run from the storage device. A license for the SOFTWARE PRODUCT may not be shared or used concurrently on different computers.

   c. **License Pak.** If you have acquired this EULA in a Microsoft License Pak, you may make the number of additional copies of the computer software portion of the SOFTWARE PRODUCT authorized on the printed copy of this EULA, and you may use each copy in the manner specified above. You are also entitled to make a corresponding number of secondary copies for portable computer use as specified above.

   d. **Sample Code.** Solely with respect to portions, if any, of the SOFTWARE PRODUCT that are identified within the SOFTWARE PRODUCT as sample code (the "SAMPLE CODE"):

      i. **Use and Modification.** Microsoft grants you the right to use and modify the source code version of the SAMPLE CODE, *provided* you comply with subsection (d)(iii) below. You may not distribute the SAMPLE CODE, or any modified version of the SAMPLE CODE, in source code form.

      ii. **Redistributable Files.** Provided you comply with subsection (d)(iii) below, Microsoft grants you a nonexclusive, royalty-free right to reproduce and distribute the object code version of the SAMPLE CODE and of any modified SAMPLE CODE, other than SAMPLE CODE, or any modified version thereof, designated as not redistributable in the Readme file that forms a part of the SOFTWARE PRODUCT (the "Non-Redistributable Sample Code"). All SAMPLE CODE other than the Non-Redistributable Sample Code is collectively referred to as the "REDISTRIBUTABLES."

      iii. **Redistribution Requirements.** If you redistribute the REDISTRIBUTABLES, you agree to: (i) distribute the REDISTRIBUTABLES in object code form only in conjunction with and as a part of your software application product; (ii) not use Microsoft's name, logo, or trademarks to market your software application product; (iii) include a valid copyright notice on your software application product; (iv) indemnify, hold harmless, and defend Microsoft from and against any claims or lawsuits, including attorney's fees, that arise or result from the use or distribution of your software application product; and (v) not permit further distribution of the REDISTRIBUTABLES by your end user. Contact Microsoft for the applicable royalties due and other licensing terms for all other uses and/or distribution of the REDISTRIBUTABLES.

2. **DESCRIPTION OF OTHER RIGHTS AND LIMITATIONS.**

   - **Limitations on Reverse Engineering, Decompilation, and Disassembly.** You may not reverse engineer, decompile, or disassemble the SOFTWARE PRODUCT, except and only to the extent that such activity is expressly permitted by applicable law notwithstanding this limitation.

   - **Separation of Components.** The SOFTWARE PRODUCT is licensed as a single product. Its component parts may not be separated for use on more than one computer.

   - **Rental.** You may not rent, lease, or lend the SOFTWARE PRODUCT.

   - **Support Services.** Microsoft may, but is not obligated to, provide you with support services related to the SOFTWARE PRODUCT ("Support Services"). Use of Support Services is governed by the Microsoft policies and programs described in the user manual, in "online" documentation, and/or in other Microsoft-provided materials. Any supplemental software code provided to you as part of the Support Services shall be considered part of the SOFTWARE PRODUCT and subject to the terms and conditions of this EULA. With respect to technical information you provide to Microsoft as part of the Support Services, Microsoft may use such information for its business purposes, including for product support and development. Microsoft will not utilize such technical information in a form that personally identifies you.

- **Software Transfer.** You may permanently transfer all of your rights under this EULA, provided you retain no copies, you transfer all of the SOFTWARE PRODUCT (including all component parts, the media and printed materials, any upgrades, this EULA, and, if applicable, the Certificate of Authenticity), **and** the recipient agrees to the terms of this EULA.

- **Termination.** Without prejudice to any other rights, Microsoft may terminate this EULA if you fail to comply with the terms and conditions of this EULA. In such event, you must destroy all copies of the SOFTWARE PRODUCT and all of its component parts.

3. **COPYRIGHT.** All title and copyrights in and to the SOFTWARE PRODUCT (including but not limited to any images, photographs, animations, video, audio, music, text, SAMPLE CODE, REDISTRIBUTABLES, and "applets" incorporated into the SOFTWARE PRODUCT) and any copies of the SOFTWARE PRODUCT are owned by Microsoft or its suppliers. The SOFTWARE PRODUCT is protected by copyright laws and international treaty provisions. Therefore, you must treat the SOFTWARE PRODUCT like any other copyrighted material **except** that you may install the SOFTWARE PRODUCT on a single computer provided you keep the original solely for backup or archival purposes. You may not copy the printed materials accompanying the SOFTWARE PRODUCT.

4. **U.S. GOVERNMENT RESTRICTED RIGHTS.** The SOFTWARE PRODUCT and documentation are provided with RESTRICTED RIGHTS. Use, duplication, or disclosure by the Government is subject to restrictions as set forth in subparagraph (c)(1)(ii) of the Rights in Technical Data and Computer Software clause at DFARS 252.227-7013 or subparagraphs (c)(1) and (2) of the Commercial Computer Software—Restricted Rights at 48 CFR 52.227-19, as applicable. Manufacturer is Microsoft Corporation/One Microsoft Way/Redmond, WA 98052-6399.

5. **EXPORT RESTRICTIONS.** You agree that you will not export or re-export the SOFTWARE PRODUCT, any part thereof, or any process or service that is the direct product of the SOFTWARE PRODUCT (the foregoing collectively referred to as the "Restricted Components"), to any country, person, entity, or end user subject to U.S. export restrictions. You specifically agree not to export or re-export any of the Restricted Components (i) to any country to which the U.S. has embargoed or restricted the export of goods or services, which currently include, but are not necessarily limited to, Cuba, Iran, Iraq, Libya, North Korea, Sudan, and Syria, or to any national of any such country, wherever located, who intends to transmit or transport the Restricted Components back to such country; (ii) to any end user who you know or have reason to know will utilize the Restricted Components in the design, development, or production of nuclear, chemical, or biological weapons; or (iii) to any end user who has been prohibited from participating in U.S. export transactions by any federal agency of the U.S. government. You warrant and represent that neither the BXA nor any other U.S. federal agency has suspended, revoked, or denied your export privileges.

DISCLAIMER OF WARRANTY

NO WARRANTIES OR CONDITIONS. MICROSOFT EXPRESSLY DISCLAIMS ANY WARRANTY OR CONDITION FOR THE SOFTWARE PRODUCT. THE SOFTWARE PRODUCT AND ANY RELATED DOCUMENTATION ARE PROVIDED "AS IS" WITHOUT WARRANTY OR CONDITION OF ANY KIND, EITHER EXPRESS OR IMPLIED, INCLUDING, WITHOUT LIMITATION, THE IMPLIED WARRANTIES OF MERCHANTABILITY, FITNESS FOR A PARTICULAR PURPOSE, OR NONINFRINGEMENT. THE ENTIRE RISK ARISING OUT OF USE OR PERFORMANCE OF THE SOFTWARE PRODUCT REMAINS WITH YOU.

LIMITATION OF LIABILITY. TO THE MAXIMUM EXTENT PERMITTED BY APPLICABLE LAW, IN NO EVENT SHALL MICROSOFT OR ITS SUPPLIERS BE LIABLE FOR ANY SPECIAL, INCIDENTAL, INDIRECT, OR CONSEQUENTIAL DAMAGES WHATSOEVER (INCLUDING, WITHOUT LIMITATION, DAMAGES FOR LOSS OF BUSINESS PROFITS, BUSINESS INTERRUPTION, LOSS OF BUSINESS INFORMATION, OR ANY OTHER PECUNIARY LOSS) ARISING OUT OF THE USE OF OR INABILITY TO USE THE SOFTWARE PRODUCT OR THE PROVISION OF OR FAILURE TO PROVIDE SUPPORT SERVICES, EVEN IF MICROSOFT HAS BEEN ADVISED OF THE POSSIBILITY OF SUCH DAMAGES. IN ANY CASE, MICROSOFT'S ENTIRE LIABILITY UNDER ANY PROVISION OF THIS EULA SHALL BE LIMITED TO THE GREATER OF THE AMOUNT ACTUALLY PAID BY YOU FOR THE SOFTWARE PRODUCT OR US$5.00; PROVIDED, HOWEVER, IF YOU HAVE ENTERED INTO A MICROSOFT SUPPORT SERVICES AGREEMENT, MICROSOFT'S ENTIRE LIABILITY REGARDING SUPPORT SERVICES SHALL BE GOVERNED BY THE TERMS OF THAT AGREEMENT. BECAUSE SOME STATES AND JURISDICTIONS DO NOT ALLOW THE EXCLUSION OR LIMITATION OF LIABILITY, THE ABOVE LIMITATION MAY NOT APPLY TO YOU.

MISCELLANEOUS

This EULA is governed by the laws of the State of Washington USA, except and only to the extent that applicable law mandates governing law of a different jurisdiction.

Should you have any questions concerning this EULA, or if you desire to contact Microsoft for any reason, please contact the Microsoft subsidiary serving your country, or write: Microsoft Sales Information Center/One Microsoft Way/Redmond, WA 98052-6399.

Register Today!

Return this
Programming Microsoft® Internet Explorer 5
registration card today

Microsoft®Press
mspress.microsoft.com

OWNER REGISTRATION CARD   **0-7356-0781-8**

Programming Microsoft® Internet Explorer 5

_____   _____   _____
FIRST NAME   MIDDLE INITIAL   LAST NAME

_____
INSTITUTION OR COMPANY NAME

_____
ADDRESS

_____   _____   _____
CITY   STATE   ZIP

_____   ( )_____
E-MAIL ADDRESS   PHONE NUMBER

U.S. and Canada addresses only. Fill in information above and mail postage-free.
Please mail only the bottom half of this page.

For information about Microsoft Press®
products, visit our Web site at
mspress.microsoft.com